WE LIVE IN
THE ARCTIC

Epicenter Press

6524 NE 181st St., Suite 2, Kenmore, WA 98028

Epicenter Press is a regional press publishing nonfiction books about the arts, history, environment, and diverse cultures and lifestyles of Alaska and the Pacific Northwest.
For more information, visit www.EpicenterPress.com

Text © 2021 Constance Helmericks

Drawings by Harmon Helmericks

Photographs by Constance & Harmon Helmericks
Provided and corrected by Jean Aspen

Cover photos by Constance & Harmon Helmericks

Cover and interior design: Scott Book & Melisssa Vail Coffman

All rights reserved. No part of this publication may be reproduced, stored in a retrieval system, or transmitted in any form by any means, electronic, mechanical, photocopying, recording, or otherwise, without the prior written permission of the publisher. Permission is given for brief excerpts to be published with book reviews in newspaper, magazines, newsletters, catalogs, and online publications.

ISBN: 978-1-941890-14-1 (Trade Paperback)

ISBN: 978-1-941890-31-8 (Ebook)

Library of Congress Control Number: 2020934475

*Dedicated to our mothers and
To the mothers of explorers:
We are sorry, Mother, that you worried.*

Books by Constance Helmericks

We Live in Alaska, 1944, Epicenter Press 2019
We Live in the Arctic, 1947, Epicenter Press 2021
Our Summer with the Eskimos, 1948, Epicenter Press 2021
Our Alaskan Winter, 1949, Epicenter Press 2021
Flight of the Arctic Tern, 1952, Epicenter Press 2018
Down the Wild River North, 1969, Epicenter Press 2017
Hunting in North America, 1956
Australian Adventure, 1972

Books by Jean Aspen

Arctic Daughter: a Wilderness Journey, 1988, 2015
Arctic Son: Fulfilling the Dream, 1995, 2014
A Child of Air (a novel), 2008
Trusting the River, Epicenter Press 2017

Documentaries by Jean Aspen and Tom Irons

Arctic Son: Fulfilling the Dream, 2013
Arctic Daughter: A Lifetime of Wilderness, 2018
Rewilding Kernwood, 2019

We Live in the Arctic

Constance Helmericks
& Harmon Helmericks

Epicenter Press

Kenmore

Contents

Preface ix
PART ONE *The Yukon River* 1
PART TWO *The Koyukuk River* 47
PART THREE *The Alatna River* 105
PART FOUR *Fall Hunting* 161
PART FIVE *Winter Hunting* 219
PART SIX *Spring Hunting* 285
Acknowledgments 359
About the Author 361

Jeanie with her mother, Connie Helmericks, canoeing the Slave River in 1964

Preface

I sit alone this April morning in my tiny log shelter beneath a vast arctic sky. Beyond my hand-hewn door, Alaska's Brooks Range lies deep in snow at fifteen below zero. I turned sixty-eight this week. Three-quarters of a century have elapsed since my young parents, Connie and Bud Helmericks, began a twenty-six month trek across the little-known top of northern Alaska, along the arctic coast, and finally into Canada. Although I was raised on my mother's stories, I had failed to read her books. Perhaps I felt I knew them, or maybe I needed my own story. Now, as I open her yellowed 1947 copy of *We Live In the Arctic*, I discover the template upon which I built my life. Without my mother's encouragement, I would never have set out on my own adventures, and without her advice I would have died my first year afoot in these remote mountains.

It is my final year in this beloved wilderness. My husband, Tom Irons, and I are taking down all that we've built over the decades, leaving only books and documentaries as our legacy. Tom, who turned seventy-two yesterday, will join me in June after the ice goes out and a chartered plane can land on the river bar. I'm here to say goodbye, to watch breakup one last season, and to explore who I will be without this great solitude. Like my mother, wilderness dreams have defined my life, and yet all dreams have a lifespan. Impermanence is the natural order. Three years ago, Tom and I began removing our whimsical log structures and replanting their footprints with sod from the roofs. We are flying out every nail and returning the land to untouched splendor. In August, when we complete our rewilding, we hope to canoe out to civilization one last time.

The world has changed since my parents were young. These living mountains are no longer inaccessible or unlimited as my mother once supposed, and as they seemed in my youth. The Arctic, I have come to understand, is as fragile as it is harsh, and the plants and animals who make it their home live always on the edge. The little grayling in our mountain stream may be thirty years old; the spruce trees (and even tiny berry bushes)—hundreds. Caribou keep traveling because this fragile land will not otherwise support them. My understanding of this is also a gift from my mother, who in later years strove to educate others on the sacredness of our wild Earth.

My parents arrived here in a very different era, when wilderness was thought to be infinite and men were assumed to be superior. Women had little power in the 1940s, and in her books Connie defers to her much larger and more athletic husband, often painting herself in comic relief. Nevertheless, both of them were new to Alaska; both endured great hardships with little fuss, drawing on stamina and grit that is at times hard to comprehend. Despite my father's fabricated tales of earlier exploits, he was an Illinois farm boy—adept, creative, and enterprising, but life-sized. It was Connie's romantic dreams that drew them north and into the wilderness, and her poetic voice which later brought them public acclaim, crafting an image of him that was perhaps hard to maintain.

Connie and Bud were twenty-three, just married and eager to explore, when they arrived in the North, June 1941, only a year before the Japanese attacked Alaska. Supplies were hard to obtain because the remote Territory was preparing for war. The following summer, my father built a canoe and the couple embarked on their first adventure—a five-month voyage down the Yukon and Kuskokwim Rivers. They arrived at the Bering Sea during freeze up. Connie's first book, *We Live in Alaska*, begins a string of five bestsellers which she would write about their travels over the coming decade. Growing fame would pull them into filming documentaries, flying small planes, and lecturing in front of thousands. Nevertheless, in achieving their dreams, it seems to me that innocence and exuberance began to fade. "Dreams," Connie once wrote, "are thin things, made of air." I might add that they also carry the seeds of their own demise. Certainly, time inexorably draws us into new territory where we must relinquish our earlier selves, and hopefully deepen. In this wonderful book, however, my young parents remain fresh with naive enthusiasm and remarkable courage.

Preface

We Live in the Arctic is an authentic adventure story, well-told and honest, the first in a trilogy that Connie would write about their epic journey across northern Alaska. In June 1944, the couple embarked in yet another homemade canoe: fourteen and a-half-feet long, and 44 inches wide, made of canvas stretched over frail spruce planks. Wiser now, they were headed for an indefinite period into Alaska's almost unknown Brooks Range—and beyond. However, they knew so little about the Arctic and were so badly provisioned that it's hard to believe they survived. I suppose the same could be said about me. You simply cannot put much into a canoe and lug it up a wild river. I had my mother's advice that an active person "eats her weight in meat every month," but my parents needed to discover this for themselves.

Connie was a gentle romantic and her voice is often poetic. Wilderness became her deepest love. In these lyrical musings I see her most clearly. She was born into an educated family and had studied classical literature and sociology. Because of this, her writing is more astute than one might expect from such a young author. Although words such as "Eskimo" are no longer considered correct, I am leaving her book essentially as written. Some of the opinions she expresses undoubtedly derive from experts of her time who espoused naïve theories such as the carrying capacity of land once predators are removed; others mirror the beliefs of her husband, a necessary accommodation. Speculation about producing wildlife for hunting and furs echo the pragmatic ideas of a man who viewed open space as opportunity. But the poetry—that is Connie. For her, wilderness was always a living presence

Although not a gifted writer, Bud was meticulous about details. He began keeping a journal that year, and some of his observations are included. Undoubtedly, the precise table of temperatures is his, as are the drawings. He was bright, talented, and admirably good at hunting, a passion which would guide his future. I was impressed with his optimism and endless stamina. One has only to read of him stumbling, nearly frozen and starving, into an old cabin and fashioning discarded cans into a working stove to get a sense of his resilience. Although his attitude towards Connie is often patronizing and even punitive, reading her book was a gift of forgiveness for me, an intimate glimpse at the young man who would one day become my critical father.

Connie's next book, *Our Summer with the Eskimos* continues this amazing story. The following summer the two found their way north over the great mountain range on an even more audacious venture: to live on the treeless arctic coast among the nomadic people who called this barren landscape home. Connie, with her generous heart and education, became the perfect witness for these vanishing families at a time of rapid change. As you read, think of her sitting cross-legged on caribou skins in a canvas tent during the dark of winter. On her lap, she is writing three books in a meticulous hand by the light of a coal-oil lantern. Outside, the open sky arches pastel above the drifting tundra, and beyond the shelter of snow blocks, the wind never ceases.

My mother spent her life exploring the natural world and sharing it through words. She would eventually publish eight books, including two on wilderness journeys taken with my young sister and me. I still hear from readers who say that Connie Helmericks inspired them to live their own wild dreams half a century ago. As I sort and digitally clean my parents' ancient photos, I am grateful that Epicenter Press is working with me to republish these classic books. I am also indebted to the University of Alaska for partnering with me in archiving my mother's (and my own) writings, photos, and films for future generations. And above all, I am grateful to these two remarkable people whose wildness and courage set a pattern for my own life.

Jean Aspen, wilderness Alaska
April 2018
www.jeanaspen.com

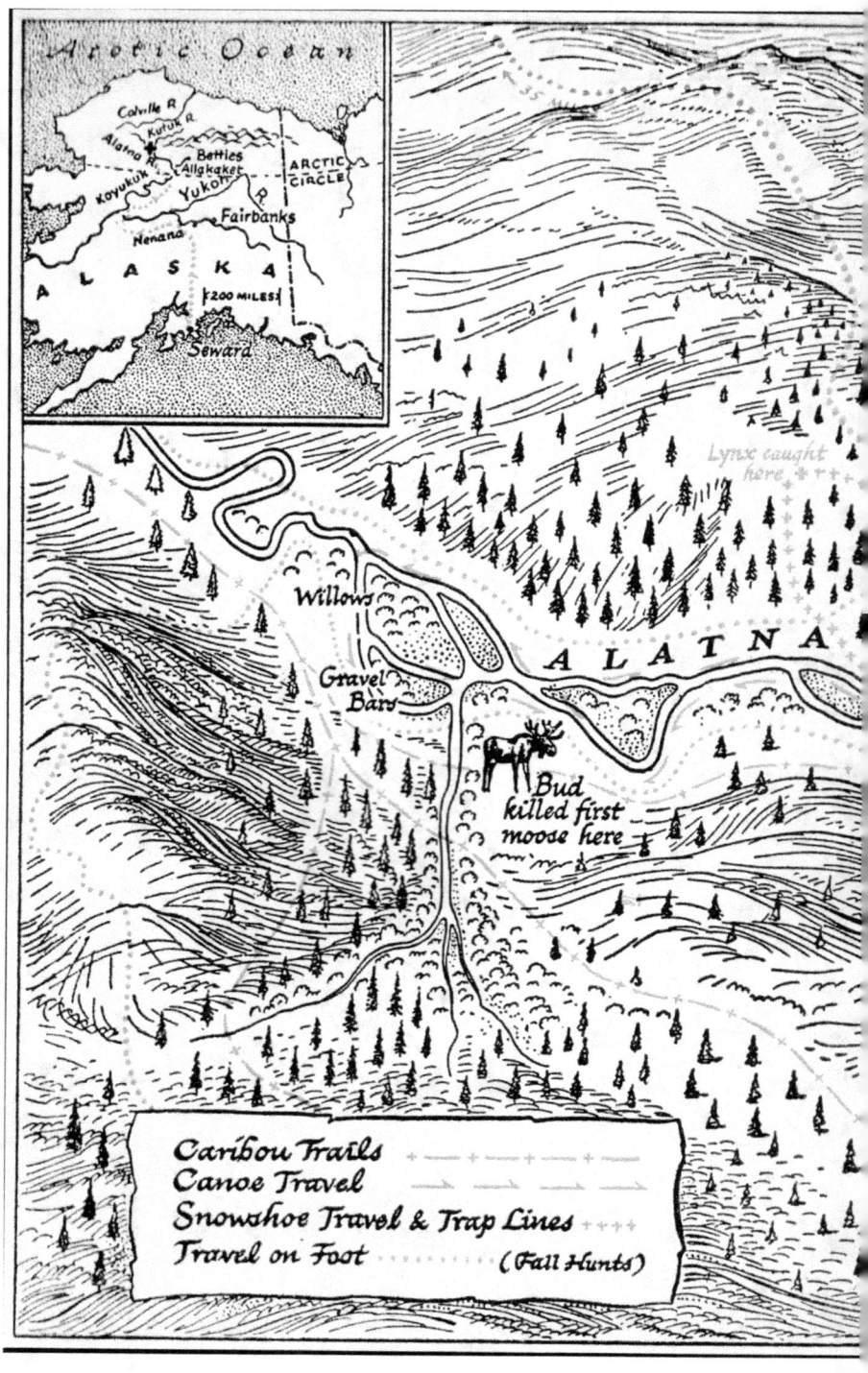

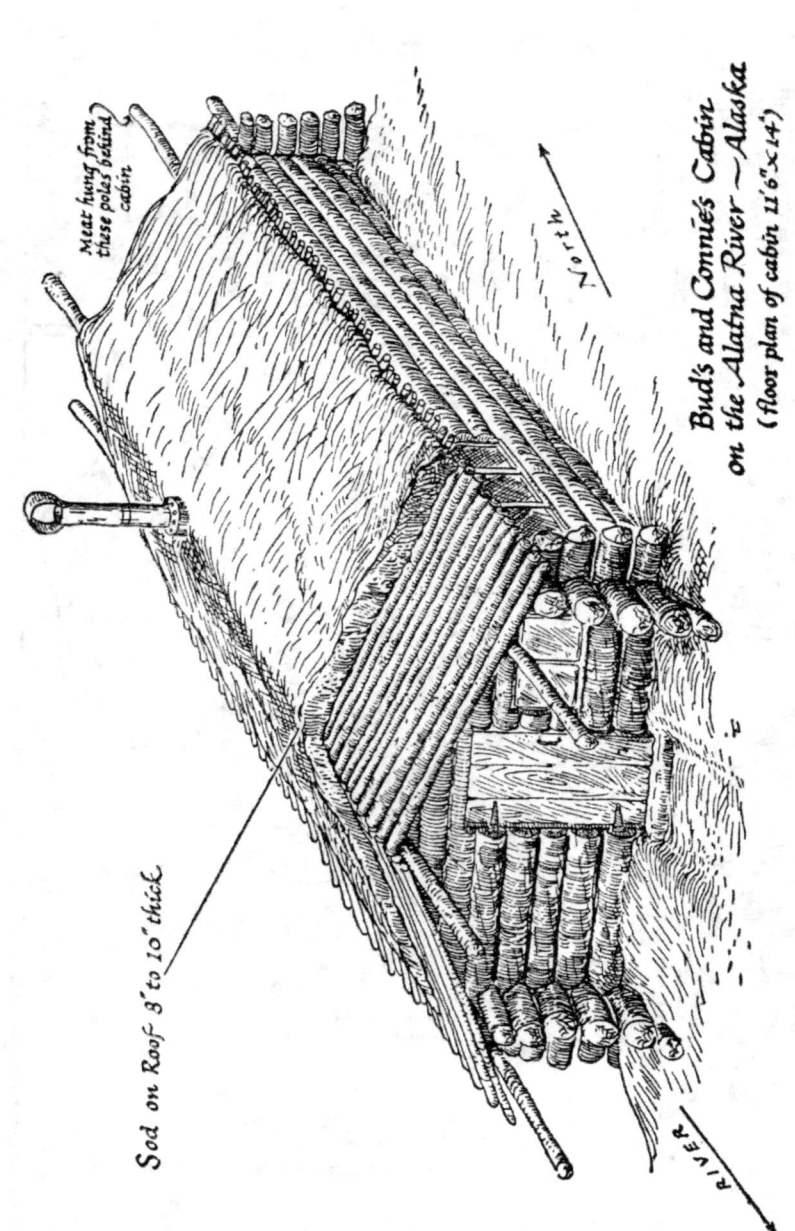

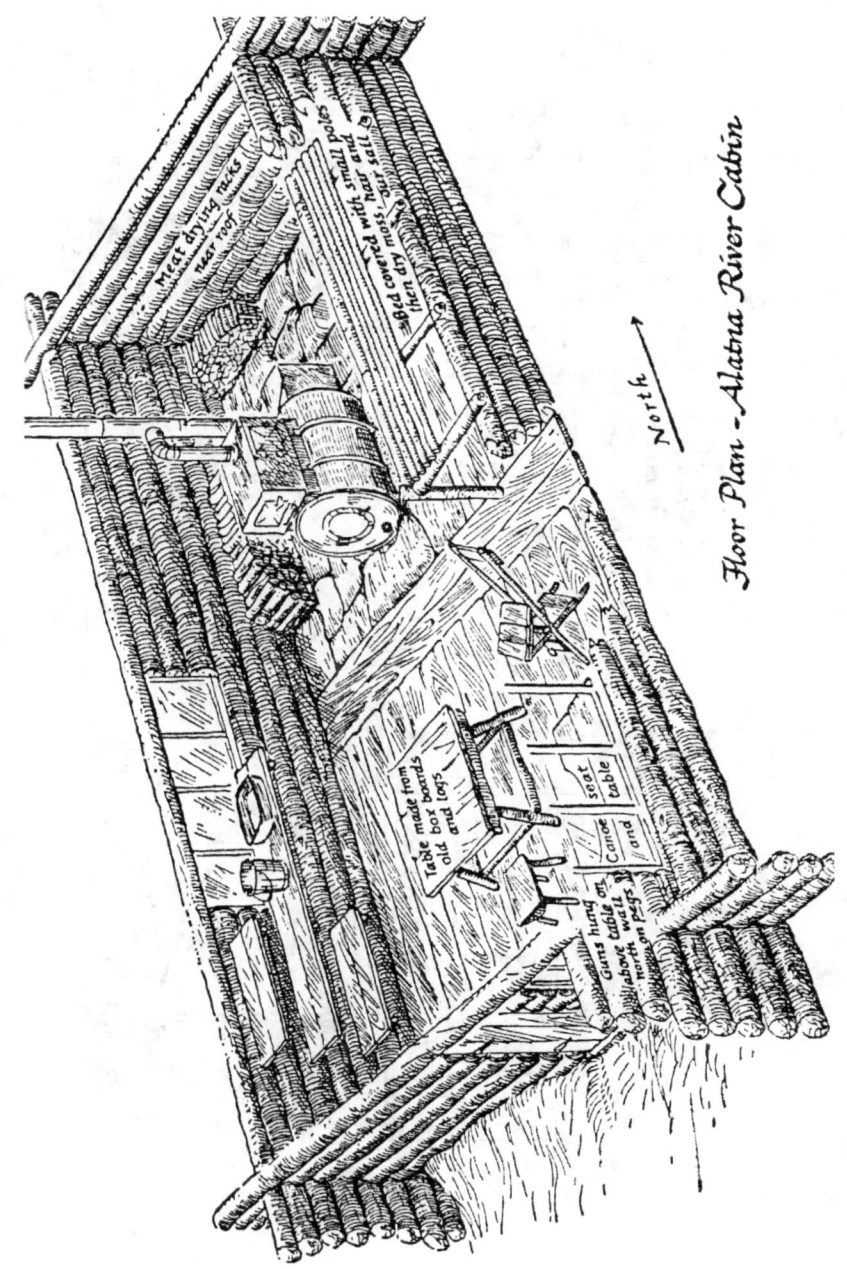

Floor Plan - Alatna River Cabin

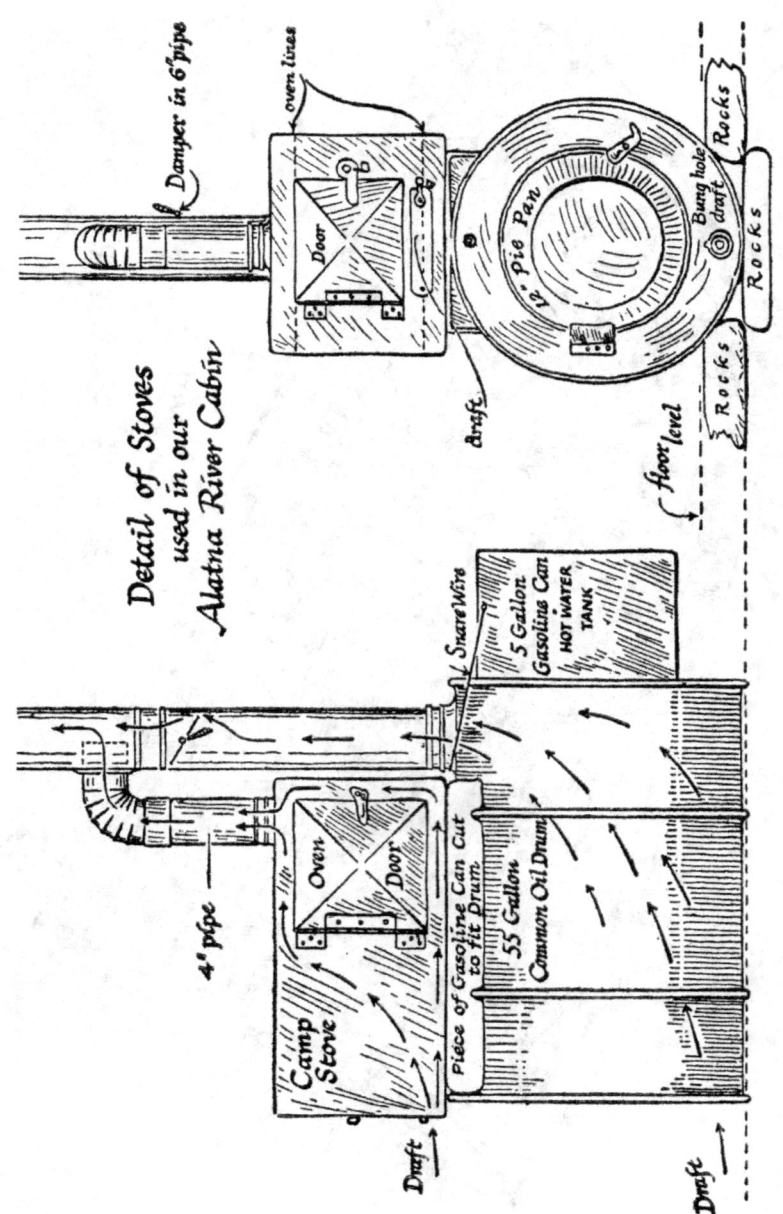

PART ONE

The Yukon River

Constance Helmericks

The steamboat arrives in Nenana

1

There is a river stretching into the north. It is a river that goes on and on. It goes to a country that is carpeted with yellow-white reindeer moss, and the moss is soft under the moccasin. It goes to a country where there are forest and prairie and mountain under the sky.

I love the summers in this land. But I also love the feel of winter winds against my cheek, when the snow squeals underfoot, and the ptarmigan, the white grouse, come whirling down from the Arrigetch Peaks once more—or any peaks in Alaska!—to talk along the valley by my house. I love the colors of the bleak wastelands where nobody goes. When the circling sun falls low, and the leaves hang and rattle in the wind, and cranberries turn to mahogany brown, and frosted blueberries taste of wine, then my cabin on the river will be snug and tight against the arctic gale. When wild grass has turned to hay, and the wild geese wing their way once more over mountain and valley to the southern land below, the canoe is put away and the snowshoe will appear. But when the arctic turns to green again and the geese return with the sun, I shall take my canoe from off the tall cache, and I shall travel on the river to see some new place.

The life of a hunter and trapper or trader is mine. We are few in all, the white people, swallowed up, lost, forgotten. We are scattered far and wide among these several hundred thousand square miles of the great subarctic and the arctic lands of the North American continent.

Usually we don't own any property here, but you might say it owns us. I am a Canadian free trader, and home to me was once in England, but burial for me will not be there. I am a missionary to the Eskimos. My brotherhood encircles the world, leading out from Timbuktu; some of us are there now. I am somebody's uncle who disappeared in Alaska half a century ago. My game is the prospecting game.

I meant to go back once. Maybe I did go back, but once was enough. I tried to make a go of it. Then that cooped-up feeling got me, the restlessness in a man's stomach when he has got used to a wider country and freer ways. They can't see even now that I'll never live south again. Whew! The climate's too doggoned hot! You see, I became a northern man.

The years just went by before I knew it. Perhaps the reason—the real reason—was that I got to watching the seasons come and go, changing from one into the other. Each has its problems of living, but each has compensations and rewards. What you can't do this year you do the next. There is always next year. That makes for a country with flavor. Perhaps, then, I just got to watching the changing of the seasons in the North, and so I forgot other things.

The river of which I speak has many names. Some men call it Yukon and others call it the Peace. The story of Alaska and northern Canada is told by the rivers which turn and squirm and go down to the polar sea.

Always, the river has been the highway of the first-comers into any land which has not yet been opened up or unlocked by civilized man. The river provided us our existence, like some life artery, and was the reason for our being here. We who know the North, or who will ever know it, are ones who have followed rivers. That is the only way, even today, that one can really know the country. There is no short cut.

To us who have followed them, all rivers in this country lead farther north. It is true they are frozen for much of the year, yet they are the highway—my signpost and my conveyance. The freighting in from the Outside of all my goods and properties is still accomplished during the three months of summer for which I wait, that next summer which calls the wanderer to change his residence. Sometimes the water is against me, but I will overcome it. Over the pass of the divide or the portage, the water flows my way again, and I travel on. Here lies

The Yukon River

the site of some great city of tomorrow, where I pitch my camp this night; here a natural railroad bed, climbing up a valley by gradual degrees. Here are copper, coal, and tar, and subterranean lakes of oil. In the reverberations of my river sings the voice of power, and I listen, thinking in the wilderness.

Here where the solitary ax rings, mankind's hope shall soar anew. Here a man looks out to distant arctic mountains that do not have a name and watching sun and shadow move knows money cannot buy them. Few have ventured into this land to live where others would not settle. And so, to them still belong these great lakes, these waterways, these game herds, of which the people in the crowded places prate, calling it America but not understanding.

The arctic frontier of the world is known to be six times larger than the American West ever was. The chances are it won't be tamed right away. How easily modern man can change it in any important respect, or even find a use for it, remains to be seen. You do not know it—oh, not you!—but there are many wild places. The person who thinks that the world has been tamed has not been off the city streets. The older ones lament the passing of the West or North they knew. But you never knew those days.

My land knows no plow. From time immemorial around the world each generation has plowed the earth and sown its bread—except here. Now the populous lands turn to the North, for they must have more food. And here in the empty miles the Eskimo hunts to live. Here no plow has cut the earth since time began and you may walk today where human beings have never walked before. Distances are incomprehensibly great. The arctic is also psychologically remote from the reach of the masses.

The airplane has barely begun to touch this land. Publicity about it is much exaggerated. There are one or two planes that fly regularly north of the Arctic Circle in Canada and perhaps four or five in Alaska at this time. We all know the pilots personally, of course; young fellows all—they always chew gum. We know the sound of each engine for a thousand miles. These airplanes of the bush pilots seldom carry more than seven hundred pounds. They are old planes and little planes, and a discussion of the insurance rates is another thing. Only little planes are practicable, for they seldom see a real landing field. There are places on this continent where an airplane has never yet been heard in the sky.

It takes certain activities on the ground to make way for airplanes, to reclaim from nature what she is constantly taking back unto herself. First there must be a motive. Secondly, there must be the men to go, for the machines of our invention do not direct themselves. There is really no magic. Although every inducement may be made to get good men, it is hard to find the right men who will be contented to work in this land. This, then, is why I am standing with an ax in northern wilderness, and why there is not yet an airplane in the sky above my cabin on the river.

How can the person on the city streets assert that there is nothing left to explore in the world—the great natural world which stretches out to the poles beyond the cities of men? Even the desire to see this natural world, greater than all cities, is considered abnormal in the face of today's fashions. "Running away from organized society" is the phrase psychologists have used to catalogue today's pioneers. Running away from "agonized" society is more nearly correct. Yet people can't be catalogued, and the world is still big.

"It's easier to face the simple primitive life than the complex civilized life," the urban dwellers tell each other from a book of psychology written by someone living in an urban house and seeing the world from behind windows. "Look what remarkable adaptations of my primitive nature I make!"

But the result is that while 130,000,000 people put up with all sorts of adaptations in the United States, only 80,000 souls live in today's Alaska, half of them aborigines, and this has been true for the 80 years of Alaska's possession by the United States. In more temperate climes, wars and depressions come and go with cyclic regularity, but in nature's eternal wilderness their passing is not heard. The ways of the world below make but hollow-sounding echoes here to the fast-sleeping arctic giant, turning just now in his slumbers.

England's millions, too, trample each other to death for standing room, and yet after hundreds of years not quite 12,000,000 human beings, mostly clustered around the southerly railroad lines, have dared to inhabit vast Canada.

Is the simple life so simple then? Not today, at least. Probably it never was. Where there is no heavy industry and but few sources of employment in an undeveloped country, life is difficult unless the colonizer has both the capital and the initiative to create his own

The Yukon River

business. It is hard to stay alive in business. Or even to stay alive. Our story of course is concerned with the latter problem.

It is a story of an ancient way of life, quite in the normal course of things and really nothing new. Our people have often left a life of ease to embark upon something new. Yes, our people, disliking those philosophies of submission and adaptation which exist wherever large crowds are herded together in order to live, will always find wilderness. We must roam over large geographical areas and eat our meat cooked Eskimo style and breakfast each day in a world really primitive. We know that we can own homes without taxation because we build our log cabins or shacks on the arctic coast of drift and moss.

Ours is a one-sided story. It tells little of cities, but much of wilderness. It is a story of survival for which neither our education nor our civilization had prepared us. When you follow northern rivers in a canoe, the main thing is to have in your heart that call which makes people leave family and friends and forget all the old ways. Perhaps our story will help to provide a glimpse of a world which you should know better than you do. We call it our Arctic America.

Geography books in school didn't know a thing about it, and our parents and teachers were all wrong. They told us about the divisions of North, South, and Central America generally, but we know now that there is an Arctic America too—not a terrible, forlorn, abominable place either, but remarkable and varied, loved by its inhabitants. This land, if you include the northern part of Alaska and Canada, becomes a playground of Cyclopean proportions—but the roamers must be hardy.

We think now of our roaming days in the present American arctic. They were great days, living by hunting and loafing in the solitudes, the prodigal existence of those who wander and are not bound. Our tale is spiced with arctic suffering—a little—but then there were also strange delights. We think of it as the story—for our generation in the mid-twentieth century—of the hunter of all ages and climes, who wanders endlessly and forever, over happy hunting grounds, always young and joyous and carefree.

Is it any wonder that we must try to justify those wayward feasts, and cast one backward glance and tear and sigh?

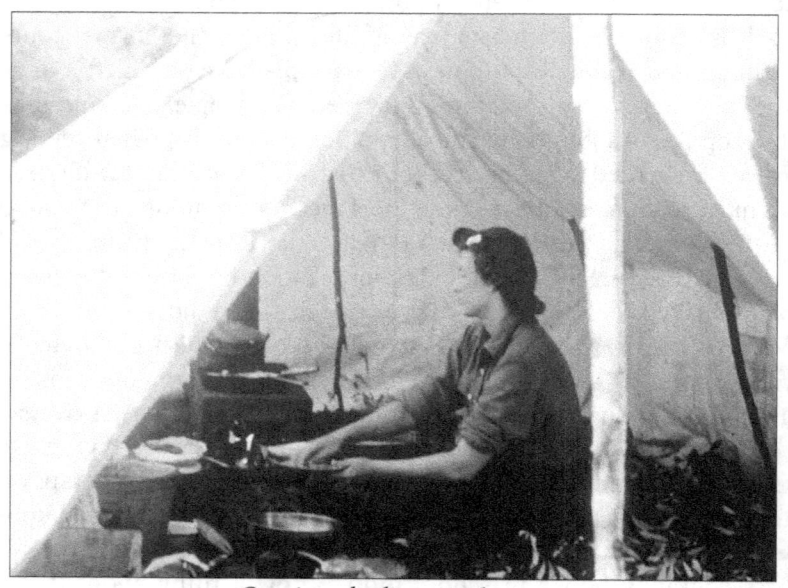

Connie cooks dinner in the tent

Native fish camp along the Yukon River

2

Bud made our canoe for us a few days after he came home from the Army. It didn't take long to construct it because we had already made a couple of them before. This one was about fourteen and a half feet long and it was made out of canvas stretched over a light spruce frame. There wasn't a slat in it heavier than what goes into an egg basket; I planed the slats myself. You couldn't buy a canoe in all Alaska and you couldn't get one shipped in from Seattle for lack of shipping space.

We planted the garden for summer for the next family who were to move into our house and live there; you couldn't let the ground go idle. We had worked on that little home in Seward for two years, and from the garden plot had removed easily three tons of broken glass from old bottles, and rocks, stone by stone—such tasks as they call "women's work" around that town. Then we painted the canoe tan and Nile green and named her the *Little Willow*. We thought that *Little Willow* was appropriate because we were heading for the land of the little willows far, far north. There, the willow is the universal characteristic sign of life. It denotes the presence of ptarmigan, moose, and rabbit, the world of creatures that feed on them and all that means to the trapper and the hunter—the human adventurers.

Bud knew privately that the color the canoe was painted didn't matter because the paint would be battered and scraped and covered with mud within the first few miles. But I had a lot of fun fixing the

Little Willow. She was to be equipped with a small outboard motor, but we would paddle or sail after the gasoline and the gas stations gave out.

Bud's concern was to keep the weight down. We had to have a craft we could take over portages. In spite of ourselves, it weighed eighty-five pounds stripped down when we had finished. It was built wide to increase the load capacity and so as to have a shallow draught, which in turn made it more stable than many canoes—really a good craft for arctic rivers and for the Arctic Ocean, we thought.

We two called ourselves amateur explorers. Amateur exploration by young married American couples seems to be increasingly popular; usually they have some special field, one of the "isms" or "ologies." Alas, we had neither. No learned society had heard of us; we had no special training, and much of the equipment we needed had been commandeered for World War II at the time we embarked, a young discharged soldier and his wife.

We are Alaskans. Bud was with the Army Engineers and then served in the Army of the Alaska Defense Command of the Western Asiatic Campaign. When he returned, we retired from the business and industrial world at the age of twenty-six, obtained a tent and a canoe, and struck out north. We were suddenly free to pursue our own interests again and to pick up the loose threads of our lives. Of course, I hadn't seen my family in the States since I had left for Alaska on my wedding day three years before, and Bud hadn't seen his parents for years; I had never met them. Why didn't we return to the United States? How our dear ones begged for at least a visit from their wandering first-born! All Alaskans have relations at home in the United States, in some cases mothers whom they have not seen for thirty years. But there was no place for us, we felt, in the States at this time. On the other hand, the arctic summer is brief; waiting would mean the delay of another year. We were going not south, but north.

The northern half of Alaska now is almost a blank on the map. Our arctic regions are less traveled today than they have been at any time for several generations. People today are packed into the cities; their edges are worn too smooth and they have too much faith that the specialists will be able to figure out everything for them. This is a very serious thing to happen to any nation. We merely were—and so remain throughout this story—a couple of youngsters bitten by the "Alaska bug."

The Yukon River

"No, I don't think the crowded part of the world needs us or will miss us down there for a while," Bud said, as we sorted and packed.

"How long will we be gone?" I asked, just once, for I didn't much care.

"Oh, two, three, or more years maybe," he replied. "We should get a pretty good hunt out of this trip anyway." We did!

We were two in our generation who did not match wits with Japanese snipers in steaming south-sea jungles or see disease and famine ravage Europe. Of our own volition we were going to canoe by the rivers into the far Arctic Ocean, and along the coast of Alaska and Canada, and so back to the United States by a roundabout way. Why couldn't an enterprising couple travel the rivers in a homemade canoe by summer and build a new home each fall when winter came? We could have the experience of living in various parts of the arctic and would really know the North when we were through. It is a goal which still remains to be accomplished, for we know now that it will take many couples and many lifetimes to do this.

As for canoeing the Arctic Ocean itself, we had our own reasons for believing that this could quite easily be done. Otherwise there is no way to see Arctic America and the Arctic Ocean except by specially owned or chartered airplane, and even then, the traveler would have to make arrangements for his fuel and the other details of his expedition at least a year ahead of time. Therefore, it is simpler for ordinary folks just to own their own canoe. There is no other transportation in this part of the world. Such a journey is, furthermore, impossible for anyone who is not an expert hunter. Usually the explorer is far from all human assistance, and the biggest problem is always to find something to eat. The threat of actual starvation is a reality to think about before plunging in. No overnight stunt this; such a tour necessitates the accumulation, step by step, of a sound basis of very real arctic knowledge. The top of the world is a big place when you measure it with a canoe paddle.

"Don't get up there and starve to death" were the last words of a friend on the station platform as our train pulled out of Seward. This is a familiar Alaskan witticism, but it means just what it says.

Four hundred and fifty miles straight north on the Alaska Railroad from the southerly coast of Alaska proper lies the little town of Nenana on the Tanana River, jumping-off point for the Yukon River in the interior.

It was June and the sky was flawless. We took our turn at the tepid drinking water tank, while the train swayed from side to side over the uneven roadbed and most of the water spilled down our necks. There were two coaches, and that was all.

"This is good," we thought, as we watched our suffering fellow Alaskans. "The temperature must be all of ninety degrees in here, with the sun coming through the windowpanes," Miss Wilkins, the teacher, soliloquized. We three smiled as most of the people closed their shades against the slanting rays, for northerners who have lived in a cool place for a few years get so that heat makes them feel ill. Our houses are kept as warm as those in any other land, but throughout most of the year we can throw open the door and let in a cool breeze whenever excessive heat becomes burdensome, or we can open up our coats and cool off. By always adjusting their temperatures, northerners soon forget how to perspire with any grace.

But Bud and I were sun worshipers, despite arctic inclinations. We had come from the Arizona desert and somehow this northern sun failed to impress us with its terrors. This unexpected heat of the great North in summer was just what we wanted. The southern coasts of Alaska with their fogs and rain and almost uniform climate the year around had held us for three years, and we wanted something new. We wanted to see some snow that was real snow, not slush. That Japan current was to blame. It was warming yet chilling with its dampness and raw winds from off a North Pacific Ocean which never freezes. Down along the Aleutian chain some wits say that precipitation can't be measured because it all comes horizontally rather than vertically, and the summer feels colder than the winter. But interior Alaska—that's another matter. You have only to go fifty miles inland to find it 50° below zero in February, and many Alaskans say they like that better than the rain. Although we had lived in Alaska for three years, like much of its population we were virtual strangers to dry snow, and we now longed to see some. And on the same mission we were going to see the sun. Unlikely as it may appear to those who are unfamiliar with our northern continental temperatures, we went north to the sun, and we took our bathing suits along!

The train ride, which took a day and a half, was slow and probably as exhausting as the canoe travel we subsequently experienced, because for all its supposed comforts, civilized locomotion seems to be

The Yukon River

a wearing affair on the human nervous system. This may be due to the ceaseless jar and jolt, or at least the vibration which comes with riding for a long time on any conveyance. Walking, with its irregular ups and downs as planned by nature, is more restful to the system.

Over mountains and past our last coastal glaciers we wound with a bad headache. The railroad tracks were yellow with thousands of full-blown dandelions, which, following the white man's plow, here raised their brave and homely heads amid the wilderness. Matanuska Valley, when we passed through it, was vermilion at this season, its fields running riot with a flower known as the Alaska shooting star. From the endless forests on either hand as the train passed on to the more advanced season farther north shone banks of wild primroses, penstemon, and gay mertensia.

The train wound down the last grade of Turnagain Arm, back to the sea, the North Pacific which comes up Cook Inlet and pours over tidal flats of gray glacial mud; the tide could be seen turning in an approaching wave—for next to the Bay of Fundy, and Mont-Saint-Michel in France, here run the highest and swiftest tides in all the world. Bald eagles sat on the trees watching the tide turn as the train went by.

Presently we found ourselves in downtown Anchorage, long familiar to us, with an hour to grab lunch and do errands before the train continued again. The settling of our last worldly affairs, making our wills and the spending of several hundred dollars, took all of our lunch hour and left us broke again. We made the train with two quarts of fresh milk, a roll of liver sausage, some oranges, and a loaf of prune bread bought at the new chain-store grocery. The food was carved and devoured with the aid of our jackknives en route, and the milk swallowed from the bouncing bottle neck, even as it curdled.

Everybody spent a stifling night at the railroad hotel at Curry farther up the track, while the train waited. I think the mosquitoes at the Curry Hotel must be accomplished housebreakers, for the smarter ones found their way into our room despite all the preventions taken by the thoughtful management. Some of them may have folded up their wings to crawl through the outside screens, but most of those that entered the hotel probably came in on the travelers themselves during the sprint from train to hotel lobby. The episode played on our consciousness; even here, no one was entirely safe from the humming wilderness outside. The following morning at eight o'clock the passengers scuttled directly from the lobby to the waiting train for the second day's ride. There was much slapping of arms and faces by those who loitered, because gloves on the hands, tucked-in trousers, and head nets pulled down over wide-brimmed hats and tucked into the collars of hard-weave jackets are the rule if one is to survive the mosquitoes out-of-doors in summer. With every mile farther north that you go, they become worse, until you reach the northern edge of the continent where they may be repelled by the sea breeze. It is said that on islands of the Arctic Ocean several hundred miles out, there are practically no mosquitoes, although a few can be expected almost every place where there is land.

The second day's travel took us past Mount McKinley, the highest peak in North America, which with its brother Mount Foraker rises from the Alaska Range in Mount McKinley National Park. Clouds obscured Mount McKinley, however, and we were unable to see it from 75 miles away on this day. As the single railroad track threaded its way through Broad Pass, we looked out the window of the train at the midget forest of spruce and birch and dwarfed cottonwoods twenty feet high and realized that unbroken wilderness lay in every direction. To the north, in a direct air line, it was about 500 miles to the Arctic Ocean from the end of the Alaska Railroad at Fairbanks; to the south, it was the same distance to the uninhabited capes and coves of the foggy North Pacific which we had left; to the west, it was some 600 miles over to the quite desolate Bering Sea, while to the east, 300 miles would take you somewhere into unexplored Canada. This hot, humming summer wilderness appeared to have little relationship to the lives of the other human beings in the train; they had walked the old red plush carpets of the railroad hotel lobby and were on their way to bustling Fairbanks at the end of the line, content to stick their noses into a Seattle newspaper. But this same summer wilderness was to hold for us a living, security, and a home wherever we might be for the next years. All of these things were here in this land for those who could take them.

"Why, do you know, when I was a little girl in New York State," I told Bud, "I always thought that if you went hunting up in Maine or New Brunswick or any of those places called the North Woods, you wouldn't dare go outside your camp without an Indian to guide you.

Those Indians have lived there all their lives, you know," I explained quite seriously, with the novice's faith in "Indians." "If you should go outside your camp there you would be lost in a minute and wander around in a circle. In fact, I don't think the Indian guides let people go out alone in the North Woods."

"Too crowded," explained Bud. "You can't let people run around that way in places where there are so many people."

"Well, now," I said, "I guess we're pretty lucky. Here we are, with one suit of clothes on our backs for the summer, just very ordinary comfortable old clothes at that, and we don't know where we'll be when winter comes, but we have a couple of maps from the Road Commission and a pocket compass, and nobody could find us in years if we became lost. Why, maybe never," I added cheerfully. "I still am skeptical of those North Woods I used to hear about in New York, but this doesn't seem dangerous."

"I guess being alive is dangerous," Bud philosophized. "But we won't get lost. It's never *you* that's lost anyway; you always know where you are perfectly well, but you just can't find the camp. I've had it happen for a day or two in Arizona but it's nothing serious. The camp always turns up eventually. Anyway, as long as we have our camping outfit with us and learn how to use it, home will be any place we stop. I can't think of a thing that's really the matter with us or a reason why we shouldn't canoe around the arctic for a few years. I've been trying, but I'll be darned if I can think of a single reason why not."

Many times, we had discussed heading farther north as soon as we got the chance. To this end, we had groomed ourselves as best we could, although there is nobody who can tell you how to become an explorer and there are no correspondence courses that you can take.

People always bring up the subject of danger, so we will dispose of it right now. A human being can travel and live on this earth any place if his essential human needs, mainly those of food and drink, clothing and shelter, elimination and sleep, are sustained. Access to areas like the arctic regions has long been termed difficult for the ordinary person unless he can bring all of his civilization along with him—which is what all modern arctic inhabitants we have met do, usually at large cost per person to the government or some large firm. But contrariwise, the primitive human being, locally adapted through centuries, meets his requirements with seeming ease. Thus, the terrors of unknown places such as the arctic, the antarctic, the jungles, the rolling deep, and even the stratosphere boil down to very simple things, involving only oneself. Technology is conquering the problems with amazing strides. But it may still be fun for a long time to come for the ordinary person to go to some of the places on the earth in his own homemade fourteen-foot canoe.

In making our plans, we knew that we must cast out all preconceived prejudices and fears. Wilderness life has wonderful opportunities for enjoyment, but only with the right frame of mind. There is no use going around afraid all the time, afraid to hunt alone, afraid to be separated from your companion for a minute, or afraid to use the tools and implements which must become a part of daily life. Out the window must go the fears, and then life becomes the freest and most enjoyable in the world.

I once sat down with pencil and paper and listed fifty terrible accidents which could happen to us: everything from freezing, drowning, and appendicitis to crunching down with a molar on BB shot eating roast duck, or choking to death on a fishbone. Then I tore the paper up and filed the notes away in memory. With later experience, we could have named fifty more terrible accidents which I hadn't thought of in the first place.

The list of them is endless, especially to the educated. But the arctic lands, as well as most other fearsome and misunderstood places, one begins to suspect, are less cruel than cruel and ignorant man himself may be as he walks over the earth. Often, he has distorted these lands in imagination, and has thereby forced them to conform to his will or defiling and maligning them has pushed them aside as worthless because he was unable to open his eyes to see what was there. The world is here, a neutral substance, but it takes man to bring it to the full fruition, at least so far as he himself is concerned. We get what we look for.

"The arctic is one of those lands that have never conformed. But that's what you have to respect about it. If we don't get out for several years," said Bud, "you know I have an idea the reason might be because we'll be having too good a time up there to go back to civilization just yet."

3

It was June 21, the longest day in the year, when we stepped off the passenger train at Nenana, a hot, dusty, dirty little trading village, not a great many miles south of the Arctic Circle and lying in what we call the subarctic. It had not a paved street in town and showed at a glance the degeneration of the surrounding Indian population from their contact for several generations with the lower classes of white men. Saloons and traders' stores and a hotel with the false front common to the old-time Western towns of legend, all of them a fire hazard, crowded along the one main street by the broad Tanana River. Their dark, sticky interiors were doing a profitable business with some newly arrived army forces who looked at once for the town's sources of entertainment. Nenana's permanent population of white people, whatever it was, kept inside their houses. We never saw any of them while we were there. They numbered perhaps thirty or forty altogether, with their families, which comprised the railroad and riverboat employees, the traders, and the C.A.A. families tending weather station for the Civil Aeronautics Authority.

Our camping outfit, along with our canoe, was unfortunately on the next train, not due for two days. The station closed ten minutes after the train let us off, the only passengers on the platform. The stationmaster was gruff; he told us in short order that there was no place there to leave our bundles and packages. We crossed the street to the hotel and learned that it was closed down because the owners had gone away on a vacation. There seemed, then, to be absolutely no place to go, and we did not want to be separated from our camping outfit.

A friendly clerk at the Northern Commercial Company allowed us to loiter. According to Alaskan custom and manners he didn't try to sell us anything, and when we did buy, we paid the bill in even dollars without benefit of price list. The clerk said he guessed he could let us have so much of this and so much of that, some of it being an obvious favor done at some personal inconvenience. Everything was of the best quality obtainable, and no questions were asked. Alaskan customers don't care what the price is but place great emphasis on quality. During the war such items as good wool clothing, butter, sugar, and shoes were never rationed in this land, as it was recognized that northerners must have them in order to exist. In normal times, too, merchants find it unprofitable to pay freight on inferior goods in order to sell more cheaply, for the customers won't buy. The N.C. Company clerk let us leave our packages in a spare corner behind the counter on the floor.

There was one restaurant in town. It served a standard short order of ham and eggs daily and a plate dinner at night, composed of a slice of roast meat, fried potatoes, an anemic canned vegetable, and very black coffee, for $1.50. The dishes were slimy and the girl who served slovenly. It was difficult to attract her attention from the soldiers long enough to get anything to eat at all. Through the ragged screen door, kicked and banged by many an uncouth foot, flew a thousand stinging mosquitoes of the Yukon watershed, so that the customer had to keep swatting with his free hand as he ate.

Bud and I like good food and comfort as well as the next person. To say that explorers take a morbid satisfaction in discomfort is all wrong. Most of the time good explorers live very comfortably. We expected to get what we considered good food in our wilderness travels much of the time, or if not, we would at least have the satisfaction of knowing we had only ourselves to blame. Here there was nothing one could do about it.

Nenana made us see why some people hesitate to leave home. We were sunburned and wanted to get out of the sun, and we wanted to get out of the rain if rain came, but we had no place to go. A couple of days spent in the open is unimportant to those who are already used to taking their chances with the elements, but in camp life you are prepared. In a town you are truly lost if you have no shelter. We merely wanted a place to sit down, and we wanted a bath, and there were no public toilets. Soon the mosquitoes had chewed us to rags and ribbons. There was no rest anywhere from them and we had no head nets. In this town the arctic mosquitoes made no demarcation between town and country. They were active twenty-four hours a day. In short, it was one of those situations which the traveler must expect to meet at the edge of the wilderness and on the brink of adventure, for such lands are made wilder, not tamer, by the presence of civilized man. Your average traveler does not get further than this; he becomes discouraged with "wilderness" too early in the game.

There was one civilizing influence in Nenana: the headquarters of Episcopalian Mission work in Alaska. We walked over to the mission the first thing, were met by mosquito spray guns at the door, chatted pleasantly in the lounge, paid our respects, and departed. Later we learned that the Bishop himself probably would have given us his own bed that night had he guessed our plight, for he is that kind of man. But at any rate we were one destitute case the mission missed reclaiming. We walked the mile back to town and still had no place to go.

Suddenly into our vision came two people whom we had once known on the Tolovana River eighty miles away. We even had some stuff for them coming on the train. We saw a tall gaunt white man with blue eyes and a long beard, a skeleton of a man in rags and beaded moccasins; and a little crippled woman four feet tall whose skin was the color of mahogany, and who was half Chinese and half Eskimo.

"By God," said Dick, greeting us with a hard-handed and hearty grip. "I waited for you folks two weeks to come by the Tolovana River, then we was all out of grub, and just about figured you wasn't coming this year, so I come on up to town. It was a bad breakup this year, river flooded over everything, mosquitoes terrible. Don't take a step without your nets. By God, it's good to see you. Oh, we haven't changed in two years. When we heard you was coming we waited on the Tolovana as long as we could, then kept a watch out for your boat in the slough all the way. Thought we could have missed you among the islands. I can see you two is just the same. Always going someplace in a hurry and all excited, eh? Oh, you're young, but hold on. You'll get over that. You can't beat this country that way. I've been trying to beat it for forty years and haven't made a dent yet. By damn, how does it seem to be back, eh?"

This wilderness couple, Dick and Mary, had taken us into their home and fed us well one time on such items as moose nose, pickled bears' paws, bear bacon, and sourdough hot cakes with blueberry jelly. At that time, we had been as green as grass. The visit with them was still our most achingly persistent memory of Yukon days and our most haunting reminder of the North which lies out there even far and beyond the Yukon.

"How's Tommy?" I asked Mary, referring to her son, now fourteen years old.

"Oh, he's fine," she replied. "You wouldn't know him. He's camped at the Cut-Off with the dogs. You'll see him there. You must turn off to our place and make yourself at home in the cabin, even if we aren't there."

"Well, you two look just the same," I said. "I'd know you any place in the world. It's a funny thing, I dream of you at night sometimes. Always I am coming back to you in a canoe."

We both laughed.

"I feel the same way, too. I wish I could see you more often. Yet we only knew each other for two days," the little woman said softly, with carefully chosen English.

"I liked the moccasins you sent," I said. "All that beadwork. No one ever gave me anything like that before. How are your eyes?"

"Pretty good now. I broke my glasses' frames, but see, Dick made me new ones," and I understood that for her catalogue lenses Dick had carved new frames out of moose horn.

"Where are you going to sleep tonight?" they asked, and we replied that we did not know.

"Well, Mary and I want to have a little fun in town tonight, see the sights you know, and by God we don't dare leave the boat. Somebody has got to watch it every minute, they'll steal you blind around this town. So now if you folks don't have a place to stay, you're just welcome to sleep right there in the bottom of our boat long as you want."

Therefore, with our sleeping bag, from which, Alaska-wise, we had not allowed ourselves to become separated, and with a bed net which was the last that could be bought in town, we spent the night in the bottom of Dick's long flat river boat, curled up on a black bear hide.

The hot sun of the next day woke us early. It was daylight twenty-four hours a day at this season here on the edge of the "land of the midnight sun" and only a few hours of sleep had been possible, exposed as we were to the brawling of passers-by at all hours. Breakfastless and long before the town was awake, we were prowling again. "I guess we could take some pictures of the trestle," suggested Bud.

Presently we were stepping along over the railroad ties seventy-five feet above the Tanana River. Up here there was a cool breeze, and we lay down on one of the little railroad platforms, watching the wide muddy Tanana sweep below. Across this trestle the railroad made a sharp turn and became hidden behind a bluff. Investigation yielded up a signboard by the bluff which said that President Harding had driven a golden spike here to complete the building of the Alaska Railroad in 1924.

"I don't feel too easy here," said I, who have always been fearful of both trains and heights. I had often in childhood fancy imagined myself, like the heroine in the melodrama, caught on the railroad track, and I now had no intention of getting into such a predicament. It took all my fortitude to walk from one airy platform to another along the openwork of railroad ties. "There's nothing to be afraid of," explained Bud with kindly seriousness. "You're too fat to fall through. Here, dear, take my hand."

As I gained courage, we walked along to the next platform in the middle of the span. Bud left me there while he climbed out on one of the bridge supports. It was then that my perceptive ear caught a sound that transfixed me. Bud had heard it too—a mile away, but presently it would come around that bend. "Bud," I yelled hoarsely. "A train! A train's coming!"

"I hear it, dear," came his call. "You'll be all right on the platform there. I want to get a picture."

The train rounded the bend with a whistle of warning which echoed across the hills. Then it came charging onto the bridge. It occurred to me even at the time that I must be a very funny sight to the engineer. I was down on my hands and knees huddled up into as small a ball as possible, on one of the one-man platforms hanging out over the mighty river. It seemed to me that the bridge was going to break down, but fortunately it must have been well built. The train was a freight, which gave forth plenty of smoke, soot, and cinders at close range.

After it passed, Bud and I climbed down the stairway into town again. I had a bouquet of wilted lady's-slippers from the bluffs (I had never lost them), and my face was black and my hands full of wood splinters.

"Do you think that helped you overcome your fear of trains?" Bud asked curiously. I didn't know, but I did know that if things ever looked bad in the arctic wilds from here on, I could always be thankful I wasn't on a trestle with a train coming.

Having returned to the waterfront, we sat on the bank the second day in Nenana and bathed our hot feet. Slowly a river boat with its bright red stern-wheel paddle moved back and forth under the trestle, loading from the warehouses, its freight bound for the Yukon. Figures in khaki wrestled with oil drums. Indian women swayed drunkenly here and there after a night's debauch. One very fat Indian woman with a shawl over her head came up to us and giggled. "Have you had a drink? We're all having fun."

Our canoe had come in on the freight train. The second and last night of our stay in Nenana we slept inside our own *Little Willow* on the docks surrounded by crates full of our belongings. The dock foreman, an old-timer, broke open a sealed railroad car for us that night so we might the sooner get our things; he and Bud scrambled into the car and handed them out into my waiting arms.

It was funny, I thought, but lunacy and discomfort had somehow succeeded in making me feel suddenly more alive than I had felt in a long time.

4

There are many rivers that stretch into the North. Sometimes there is one for each person; then quite as often there are rivers where no one lives. It seemed unbelievable that we could have a whole river, including its tributaries, for our very own any time we wanted to bother to look one up, but when we left Nenana we were already looking for it. On our river we would build our own log cabin and winter as far north as the timber went, for it would take a year to get into the vicinity of the Arctic Divide of the continent. From there we might get over and down to the arctic coast itself the second year if our luck held good. Our river was a thousand miles from Nenana as rivers flow. We recognized it, of course, when we found it, because a person always knows his river right away.

Now the Tanana River lay before us as we canoed northwest towards the Yukon. All was still. A few gulls fluttered, settled down upon the surface of the muddy Tanana and took a ride along with us sometimes. They were waiting for the first salmon to be on their way from the Bering Sea. The boom of a bank caving in came to the ear; the swirling water was eating into the banks and rotting them away. We were familiar with the sound. It commences at breakup each spring and continues until the freeze-up again each fall and is characteristic of northern rivers. Occasionally, we were lucky enough to see the banks crash before our eyes, but we steered a course clear of them. When they fell or had recently fallen, the line of eternally frozen subsoil was clearly defined one foot below the earth's surface. The Russians were said to be having a certain success in growing wheat over similar ice; we believed some of the Russian arctic doings to be probably somewhat exaggerated. But of course, we couldn't really know. Here, overhanging walls dripped their slimy residue, tinkling as we glided past.

Often the layer of frost which had grown on the bank had toppled into the water. Some trees, partly submerged, were standing in a block beneath the water, just as they were; others, still attached to the shore by their roots, lay tangled horizontally and might reach out twenty feet into the current to catch the canoeist. These are called "sweepers."

Bud was running the motor, a secondhand three-horsepower outboard, and he had his old lunch bucket filled with tools beside him. Running a canvas canoe with a motor takes care, but it can be done. We were overloaded to the bursting point. Everybody going down to the Yukon from the railroad should carry a full load, for any old rags or bones you possess and don't want will be needed there; somebody will use them. Once you leave the railroad on that downstream journey away from civilization and into the interior of Alaska, every smallest need of life from the Outside must be brought in by the seasonal river boat or the very occasional airplane. Into our fourteen-foot canoe boat, with its forty-four-inch beam, square stern, and streamlined canvas wave splitter held erect by a bent willow, had gone so many things that there was scarcely room for human occupants. The load came to well over a thousand pounds, counting all the gasoline we could haul, and ourselves. We even had a canteen of fresh drinking water, for while we were to travel in an area where a third of the surface of the earth is covered with water as seen in summer from the air, our river was so heavy with silt as to be undrinkable for several hundred miles at the outset. A sack of overripe bananas intended for a couple of Indian Service teachers of our acquaintance on downstream certainly completed the load.

The motor we had was a lament from start to finish. It was the only thing obtainable, and we were extremely fortunate to get it at all. "It may be all right for running downstream," as Bud put it skeptically, "but how we're going to go upstream when we try to go north of the Yukon, I'm wondering. Maybe we can make a deal with somebody for a different motor." That was a false hope. We never did.

The *Little Willow* proved to be a sound canoe, our solace, our darling. She had cost about $45 to build; in the States normally, she would have cost less than $15 in materials. Our ammunition we had hoarded since before the war, about the time some people began hoarding sugar, so that we had several years' supply. So much for the main items. Alaskans had never known for some years just when they would have to take to the brush. Rifles and eight-power Bausch and Lomb binoculars were of equal importance; binoculars are almost as necessary as guns in making a living in wild country. Traps, tools, winter underwear, dozens of pairs of heavy woolen socks, innumerable changes of footwear; skis, snowshoes, winter parkas and mittens; then raincoats, mosquito nets and repellents, and rubber hip boots for wading in summer—these things do not come for nothing. You can live in the arctic almost without money, when you get far enough into it, but there are few places on earth where the cost of living is so expensive. The average American traveler would find the arctic too expensive for him to travel in at all. But we knew that Indians and Eskimos and some white old-timers do live there, and let it never be said to our shame that we who were so much richer than most of them by all the standards of this ancient world could not afford to go to the arctic!

Take the frying pan, for instance. A few years ago, our own courtship had revolved around that frying pan and a carful of guns in the West; the canteen came along with us, too, from the Arizona desert, so it didn't cost us anything now. As for cash, our dwindling supply of that became a mere $17 before we had started the first winter, but by that time we had arrived at a place where there was no way to spend it. Our outfit, as we proceeded into the country north of the Yukon, was worth approximately $3000 according to the standards of that country, and it was a comfortable feeling to know that we grew richer, not poorer, with every mile farther north that we traveled.

One of the first questions usually asked is what kind of gun one should take. A gun is necessary because there are absolutely no meat markets away from the railroad and the coastal towns, which get their meat by steamboats through the Inside Passage from Seattle, 3000 miles away. In Alaskan town life, of course, we regularly patronized the meat market just as people in any town in the United States do. Meat was ordered by telephone, came on the delivery truck, and was contained in the house in a large white enameled refrigerator of the most recent design. We speared salmon for sport in a neighboring stream during the "run," which helped out on the meat bills, and put a hundred pounds or so down in brine. The previous year we had eaten about 350 pounds of black bear and white mountain goat that I canned.

Bud had always taken game wherever he was, even if it was only pigeons when he visited Chicago at the age of seven. He had done it ever since he could remember. He says the rest of his family aren't that way in particular; it may be that some people are just born hunters. He taught me to like the taste of game, although I was hunting before he knew me anyway. I went deer hunting every year with regularity when I lived in Arizona. I had found and killed a deer once in my fifteenth year, but the truth of it was that I was untrained, and most of the time hiked the mountains with a perennially empty game bag. Also, the finer part of my nature could never justify killing beautiful animals for mere sport. In such a soft environment, where the idea of actually needing the animal for food was just a pretense, I was a poor hunter. People who tell tales about pathetic deer looking them in the eye remind me of my experience. Once I shot an owl and I can still remember those eyes looking at me as it blinked up from the ground quite alive, so that I had to close my eyes to squeeze the trigger of my 12-gauge shotgun, to put the owl, as I thought, out of its misery. Then I took it home and boiled it up in a pot and my mother threw the pot out and my whole family thought I was crazy.

Still, I adored hunting because I lived in imagination. Most hunters, no matter how tame the environment in which they hunt, doubtless do the same. They imagine they are explorers, hunting to keep alive, which must be the reason why the "Keep Out" signs are often shattered with shot and probably why the necessary game laws are too often broken. However, there is a reason for hunting, and a way to hunt—almost anywhere—which makes it very real and justifiable.

When I met Bud in Arizona, we were both twenty-one years old. Sometimes we would drive 300 miles a day on the long desert highways or winding ranchers' roads shooting quail or jackrabbits which we cooked out-of-doors; they were extremely tough, but we ate them. Now I could see the sense to that, and its interest! Frequently we took along little else to eat. We were actually supplying our own food! Bud had a number of the farm boy's skills, not only in finding more birds and animals and lizards than one had ever dreamed were on the desert, but just in the way he opened the doors to freedom and adventure. Living on twenty dollars a month at that time and often less, while going to college with the rest of us, he yet somehow took more trips than anyone else I ever heard of and he could always afford to go hunting. He could drive all the way across the American West 3000 miles and not once see the main highway—and when you can do that, you're an explorer. He always managed to have some sort of house with an icebox at his disposal, along with a ten-dollar interest in a motorcycle or car of some description, and to his table came regular processions of blackbirds, elk, venison, peccary, and even bobcat made up in pies. I had never imagined anything like it. An ability of his which I particularly admired, I recall, was his fast method of whirling the insides out of dead rabbits by giving them a shake around his head. I never mastered this.

Bud had taken a hundred or more big game animals in his wanderings throughout the United States, Cuba, and Mexico by the time he was twenty-one, but he imposed this penalty on himself—he ate every one or saw that it was eaten!

In Alaska I settled down to the business of becoming a real hunter at last with a clear conscience. Not only were its purposes justified to me, but clearly, in becoming a hunter, I could heave a sigh of relief as the bars were let down on a remarkable world.

At first, we had started hunting Alaska big game, during the all-too-brief vacations from the workaday job, with .30-'06 and .405 Winchester rifles respectively. The .30-'06 is probably the most popular rifle with sportsmen in Alaska, where the big game grows really big. Many hunters even insist on its use for the tough little Virginia white-tailed deer in the States. Bud at one time owned a custom-built .30-'06 rifle in Alaska with an expensive telescope sight, but the sight got fogged up or out of line so often that he tired of fooling with it, and I discarded my .405, a good rhinoceros gun, for one that I could carry. What we needed for the Barren Grounds up north, if we ever got there, were two identical guns using the same ammunition. Bud said they should have a high velocity and flat trajectory and tried to get us a couple of Winchester .270's, but found nothing of that sort obtainable. Most people don't know how hard it is to get anything in Alaska. You can't just walk down and buy it. You place your order and perhaps wait a year.

So, we picked up a couple of Winchester .30-30 carbines, the old cowboy's favorite, attached buckskin thongs for back-packing them, and let it go at that. This little carbine, the saddle gun of the West, is also the favorite of the Eskimos. The sportsman in Alaska uses guns of high caliber, such as the .30-'06, but 35,000 natives don't know what one is. The common little .30-30 carbine, which has journeyed around the world because it is cheap and does the job where jobs are being done, kills more animals in Alaska today than all other guns together. Hundreds of tons of moose, caribou, walrus, polar bears, seals, big grizzly bears, and so on are shot yearly by the brown man with this little gun, in the northern part of the world.

Of course, the civilized sportsman is horrified. The sportsmanlike and correct attitude is that one should not risk letting his animal get away by using too small a gun. Certainly, too, the sportsman considers his own neck when hunting dangerous game. But .30-30 ammunition for rifles, along with ammunition for that most American of all guns, the .22 rifle, is what the traders sell. If you are going to journey far afield there is something in having a gun which fits the ammunition which the traders are most likely to have on hand.

The person who knows anything about guns may raise his eyebrows to hear that we proposed to make our way across the northern part of the continent with a weapon he may despise. We were fortunate in almost never losing a big game animal we had hit, and in averaging at first, until we became more careless of ammunition generally, around 200 pounds of meat for each shot.

Many old-timers will declare in long arguments that the .30-30 cannot shoot through a bear's skull bones or a moose from side to side. The way to prove it is to try it, or to look up the statistics in the gun books. The .30-30, the .22, and all other guns of American make are different from those the old-timers were familiar with even ten years ago. Charging their ammunition with improved powders has changed their velocities, range, and killing power. The .30-30's were handy for us on a rough trip where you probably wouldn't want to take a good gun, and where the weight of each article must be considered. Arrangements had to be made on short notice. The shattering blow of the more powerful rifle is an insurance for getting your animal when you do not hit him in exactly the right place, and should likewise be considered under different circumstances, where crippled animals cannot as easily be trailed as in the snow of the North or where people are not as good trackers as Bud proved to be in times of need.

In the world of hunters and sportsmen, no two can be found who will agree on all the particulars of the ideal gun. This is because there is no ideal gun, any more than there exists an ideal automobile, an ideal boat, an ideal airplane, or an ideal camera suitable for all purposes. Each model is made for a particular purpose and must sacrifice in other respects. Man has invented a gun for every animal that lives on earth, and then some. But you can't carry them all at once.

Our guns which we secured now were nothing new; the .30-30's, Model 1894. The same gun, or its forebear the repeating rifle (the .44-40), was in existence during the time of the Civil War and was used by the more progressive meat and hide hunters of the old West, while the war itself was fought by armies using muzzle-loaders, flintlocks, and the old-style single-shot rifles.

Bud has had many different kinds of guns, but while always eager for another one and with the American man's love of the feel of any smooth new mechanism in his hand, he expresses one prejudice—the prejudice against the automatic rifle or the automatic shotgun in use against wildlife. For ourselves, the automatic was not to be considered for isolated arctic regions; there is too much which can go wrong with one, and it's no gun for cold weather, at least under primitive conditions. But in use by the public, automatics are on the whole too viciously dangerous, and they are not sportsmanlike in method or appearance. When Bud saw a man with an automatic of latest design and still higher power actually going into the woods and hunting with the thing, he had only a feeling of distaste, as though for a gangster. One by one the States are outlawing the automatic as, fortunately, the trend seems to be away from the mechanization when it comes to enjoyment of the out-of-doors.

Actually, automatics do not get more game in practice; they get people. It is the man behind the gun that counts. His judgment seems to be the deciding factor, his skill in stalking, and his knowledge of the habits and anatomy of the animal he intends to get. Furthermore, limits on game are strictly controlled in most places nowadays. One shot to the animal should be the goal of the good hunter; a clean kill is the only sport we can see. The notion of giving a big game animal a "sporting chance" by shooting at great distances is not sporting for the animals. Each year many hundreds of them escape with crippling wounds to die a lingering death while the average sportsman has no cognizance of the fact that he has made a hit at all. In hunting for food, we get as close to the animal as we can before we shoot—sometimes we are almost on him. No big game animal should be shot by any rifle, no matter how expensive, with open sights at much over a maximum of 200 yards, for man himself is not equipped to do it; his eyesight and his nerves aren't that good yet, despite the occasional remarkable instances to the contrary.

And there is too much discussion altogether given to the caliber of guns, for when it comes to hunting, nine tenths of that sport is just what it says—hunting and not shooting. The shooting is only a part of it and it scarcely matters what gun you use if you know the gun and are yourself a hunter. "Don't blame your gun," Bud would say a thousand times to me. "It isn't the gun." And so, I stress this point.

It is always the member of the party without a gun who sees the game when game is needed. We each had our own rifle, therefore, and took in addition, considering our indefinite stay, a .22 rifle, a 12-gauge long-barreled pump shotgun (incidentally a meat hunting gun of which we are not particularly proud, as it is scorned in sporting circles), and a .22 automatic Woodsman pistol to be worn sometimes on the belt.

Very important, according to the journals of arctic explorers, is the kind of tent taken along when you go north. But we didn't have much choice. Ours was just an ordinary 8' x 10' tent, but it never leaked or caused us trouble. We would be in it only in summer, for a more stanch home would have to be built or borrowed for winter months. Bud made our stove for us. The kind of stove you need money can't buy. Its surface was 12" x 22", and it had a fine little oven for baking, with a baking pan that came with it. The lengths of its 4-inch stovepipe fitted into the firebox when it was packed into the canoe. This is the kind of stove the natives use. It burns wood or roots and grass, and is very tiny, intended to heat only a small and perfectly insulated arctic dwelling, where economy of fuel is essential. In warm weather during the summer we could set the stove up on any beach or riverbank and cook outdoors; in cooler weather inside the tent.

At first, I had tried to get some specially condensed foods of extraordinary potency to take along; they couldn't be had. "Pemmican. We must have pemmican," I said, planning to locate some company which outfits explorers. I had read about pemmican, although I had never seen any and scarcely knew what it was. Traders and the people who live in this North Country don't know what it is either. Derived originally from an American Indian word for dried meat carried on the trail, pemmican today probably means any trail ration with meat and fat in it, with raisins, or anything else you want to throw in—your old boots if you think they may have caloric value. The thing is, you can make it yourself. There are few lands richer in pemmican materials than the arctic.

Therefore, as we drifted and motored down the Tanana River to the Yukon, bound for still more remote wilderness beyond, we had scarcely any of the paraphernalia which convention ordains for such undertakings. What, then, about the magical "equipment" one must have to go north? The answer is that there is no magic which need be outside the attainment of any person. These supplies are all very ordinary things which one can see any day being used by American people. The arctic itself is a part of our country, and in its own way an ordinary place which can be accessible to all. Sheepherders in Montana and Wyoming use much the same gear we had, aside from the canoe.

There may have been fancier boats on the market than ours, but we couldn't afford them. There may have been fancier guns, but we didn't want them. There may have been explorers' tents, but we couldn't get them. Possibly there were special alcohol lamps, canned heat, and gasoline stoves, but we counted on willows and driftwood. Our hip boots were old, and they leaked, which was too bad because we got our feet wet, but we never caught a cold from it that I know of. Our motor wouldn't run half the time, so when it stopped, we pulled.

The Reverend and Mrs. Files and little Willie were old friends

Leaving the town of Tanana we set off on the Yukon River

5

The river lay before us and the motor had stopped. Bud had said it was time I learned how to run it, whereupon I took over and it stopped just after we entered Hot Springs Slough on the Tanana River. "I'm not surprised. As long as man exists alongside an old two-cycle outboard motor there will be trouble," yawned Bud, opening up the old lunch bucket of tools, a thing he was to do many times. "One hundred and eighty-five dollars for this thing, secondhand," he groaned.

As we were no longer drifting, having turned off into a realm of still water, we each took up a paddle and pushed up the slough toward the town of Manley Hot Springs nestling in the shadow of one Bean Ridge seven miles off the main river. Hot Springs has several acres of land under cultivation over an area of earth where there is no freezing, even in wintertime, because of subterranean hot springs. Among other vegetables exotic to this climate, the place grows corn and watermelons.

It is a quiet spot. One would never guess that a town lay hidden back here, for there is no sign of man to tell which slough to take. Young ducks slept in undisturbed tranquility upon the water.

I sighed. It seemed as though we had paddled with those heavy oars for hours.

"Maybe you just aren't as good as you thought you were."

"But these mosquitoes are eating me."

"Pull your net down then."

We Live in the Arctic

"All right. Down nets. Now. I can't see. It's getting dark, isn't it? I wonder what time it is."

"Say, look there. This is the slough all right. There are the floats holding up the old man's fish net. A good pike would taste fine. Let's see if he's got any fish."

Reaching over the side of a canoe in the dark to feel of slimy fish nets is not new to me since I married Bud and learned the joys of living off the country. The fine old fellow just spoken of caught the fish for fox feed—had been catching them here for a quarter of a century.

The fish net was empty at the time and we paddled on. The mosquitoes, scenting us from the woods as soon as the motor stopped, began to arrive in droves. "Here, do you want a shot of this? This ought to give them a headache for a few minutes." Between us the spray gun was passed and pumped vigorously, with the result that in the twilight gloom several hundred mosquitoes which had been probing with their bills around our hat brims and on our jackets flew up with a roar, while others fell on their backs, heels up. Truly, if anyone should ask which is the best gun to have in the North or which kills the most game, the answer should be the mosquito spray gun. In our agony, it was not long before every article and garment we owned was saturated with the oily insect spray which had not been designed for use on clothing; fabrics became unwashable, but one "poof" of the gun accomplished wonders. The only accident was the time I tipped the gun upside down on Bud's socks when crawling into bed one night. When he wore the socks the next day they practically took his feet off. "Oh, well," I told him heartlessly, "it's good to hear you bawl out sometimes."

The dark Alaskan summer night along the Arctic Circle retains the merest blush of color, not visible to the camera, but visible to humans. The quality of a dream was on the world at this hour for us, and yet the reality of life struck us just as forcibly as it had when we had first stepped off the passenger train in Nenana. One of the worst vices of river travel is that you never have the sense to stop and make camp. You are under the illusion always that the best camping place is just around the next bend. It never is.

You go on and on, hour after hour, in a day that never ends because it has no real ending, eventually to realize that it is past midnight again, or even far into the next day. You can barely stand from fatigue, your eyes are like burned holes in a blanket, and there is no suitable camping place for miles. You rub your face, through your head net, with a gloved hand, and know dimly where you are, but your judgment of distances and depths has become distorted. The organlike notes of birds singing all night long resound from the deep forest, lulling you to sleep.

Our progress was at the rate of a mile an hour through the clear still water of the deep slough. Waves from our paddles washed against moving grasses, shattering the magic looking glass. The green water merged with an indeterminate shore, so that it was impossible to tell one from the other until we grounded. Wisps of smoking vapor arose from witches' caldrons below us and throughout the marsh. The stars hid their fires; the color of the sky itself was pale orange. Our world was a study in orange and green, with each overhanging bough lacy against the sky, silent and perfect in symmetry. Two canoes pushed forward, one above, the real one with people in it, and the one below that was its reflection in bottomless depths.

Our arms were stiff, and our backs cramped. We shivered slightly. The thermometer we carried registered 59°. From out of the lush, overly verdant forest came a night smell, giving the impression of some quality almost dangerous. Small wonder that the ancients feared the bogs at night! Those wild spruce trees, dwarfed and tortured, like rows of impaled human beings with arms akimbo! And the unremitting drone of countless millions of mosquito wings coming night and day, until the freeze-up bound this world once again in its icy grasp!

"Listen to them! They get you, so you don't know whether you're coming or going," said Bud.

"Look, don't you think it's a little lighter?" It was. The night had passed. Stretching our cramped limbs, we saw that the green banks were white with dew. "Now, where's the town?"

"Two more bends, I think."

"That's what you said before. You know, I think we were fooling ourselves when we thought we would get in here in time for supper last night. But we should make it for breakfast. Well, we've got all the time in the world, I guess. I'm through hurrying for anybody. It was worth while staying up just to see the night, wasn't it?"

There was a spring on the side of a hill, plunging straight off into deep water, but no suitable place for pitching a tent. This often happens in the camper's life. Either the land is all composed of 45-degree angles or, worse still in a world of water, there may not be any land at all for you. We had not tried out our new tent, and did not use it, in fact, for some time; we had an alternative arrangement in traveling. Our canoe itself became converted into a house and bed. "All we ask of you mosquitoes," I told them aloud, "is just about six and a half feet of space three feet wide to lie down in for a few hours' repose. We won't be here long. You can have all the rest of the outdoors. Certainly, you wouldn't begrudge a person that, would you?"

"Like heck they wouldn't. It's slick here, so watch your step or you'll step in above your neck. Hand me out the stuff and snap into it. They're at me."

Tottering on legs that would barely stand from stiffness, I handed out our skis and ski poles, the stove, oars, the grub box filled with its pots and pans, and finally the bottom layer of 75-pound gasoline cases. No rain would hurt them. With these encumbrances stacked on shore there was room to make up a bed in the bottom of the boat. A light inner frame of slats gave added strength to the canoe's thin frailty. Then an important feature of the *Little Willow* not previously mentioned came into its full use. We had learned that canoes in the commercial catalogues, while possibly satisfactory for short trips of a few days, lack one essential element for extended travel. They make no provision for shelter from the elements for your outfit, the food and bedding and tools you must carry with you. Of course, there is the calendar picture of the hunter crouched on his blanket beneath his overturned canoe on the stream bank while the storm blows over, but that never did look very comfortable to me; I have no idea whether anybody actually does it. But if all one's worldly possessions are to be encompassed in a canoe or small boat for an indefinite time, and there is no place of succor or rescue around the corner, they must be protected from the elements even before the human being thinks of himself. Everything will fall to pieces with rot and mildew in no time otherwise.

In building our craft Bud contrived a semi-permanent canvas cover for it stretched over a bent spruce frame of slats in the shape of a covered wagon and secured together with string and tacks. It looked tacky, but, painted with a fresh coating of linseed oil now and then, it was rain-tight and covered our duffles in the middle of the boat and sometimes ourselves in emergency. The covered wagon extended between the two seats. Long projecting flaps of canvas could be wrapped around our laps as we rode, so that in rain hats and slickers we could continue traveling during a shower. At night the flaps of canvas were drawn over both ends of the boat and tacked down to make all tight against the storms, while inside we slept safely, floating in some snug harbor, not even knowing, perhaps, whether it rained in the night or not. Such a method of camping is handy at times.

The method is fine in mosquito land, where dressing and undressing, cooking, eating, bathing, and just breathing may be difficult, and where the ordinary tent provides but small security. On land not an inch of one's body can be exposed during the early part of the season. But with the right arrangement sleep can be accomplished, and that's the main thing. No mere covering of canvas could be expected to keep the mosquitoes out, for they find a way in through little cracks, so you use your bed net inside. First comes the spray gun, to dust those hitchhikers which have been hidden inside the canoe all day. Next, the bedding is unrolled, and the bed net set up by the person who is inside, on his hands and knees. Now you make a dive for it, and this part of the program is really snappy. You never escape without a few bites, but a few are part of the game.

Day is ushered out at bedtime and ushered in again at the next awakening by the slow burning of incense in a little tin tray, always within reach of the sleeper from his net. The new invention, DDT, will probably not be accepted by the greater population living out-of-doors in the North because it needs a mosquito-proof habitation to work effectively: it kills miraculously, but how about those new mosquitoes always drifting in? Incense, or the more dramatic, action of the spray gun—it depends upon your mood—still awakens the northern camper. The gun is quicker, but the slowly burning incense is more thorough because it reaches every crevice. Bottles of lotion make the pockets of your clothing heavy with bulges, but the lotion is not taken too seriously in real mosquito land. This ritual takes place each day before you dare crawl out of the bed net to dress under the canvas roof. Often the outside of the bed net is black with crawling mosquitoes in the morning.

"Oh, my poor dear Nile green canoe," I wailed after a week. "It's just covered with bodies." Yes, the carcasses of the slain piled up, while we lived with and rolled upon them.

It was necessary to stay over a day at Hot Springs to take the motor apart. When Bud got all the pieces spread out upon the ground at the landing, he lost one of them. A very simple piece, a ball bearing—we searched everywhere for it, but it was not to be found. Neither could another one be had. There were several motors in town which could not be run until after the war for lack of such small parts. Bud even tried to match up parts with some of these, but it was no go. It was the water-cooling system which was defective on ours because of an old worn-out spring. The spring could only push a tiny stream of water to keep the motor cool no matter what we did to it, except occasionally, after running for a while, when it got into a good mood. In this case we would keep it running without pause, refueling through a funnel en route and not daring to shut it off. But most of the time we could run only by throttling down to half speed in order to keep it cool. At Hot Springs Bud turned the spring upside down in a forlorn hope of giving it more power; for the missing ball bearing he extemporized with a Number O buckshot from one of our 12-gauge shotgun shells.

That evening, for a first and last celebration, we splurged on Sunday night dinner at the roadhouse. Gathered here together were fifteen or twenty white people, the total population, whose special entertainment was this weekly dinner together followed by a night of playing poker. We ate family style at a long table covered with white linen and ornamented with freshly cut blue iris in vases. The dinner was all you could eat for $1.50, complete from roast meat and potatoes and salad and rolls to homemade ice cream and cake. It well illustrated the contrast between the old-time Alaska with its generous fare and open-handed hospitality and the railroad towns with their Outside influences coming unfortunately to the fore. Such items as butter, for instance, have never been rationed to the diner at the old-time roadhouses in the wilds, so long as butter is obtainable at all; the half-pound blocks are usually placed at convenient intervals along the table and everybody takes what he likes. Of course, you pay for it. But a person is expected to eat what he likes without some of the major battles which must take place over these details in other lands.

This typical Alaska frontier meal was particularly enjoyable to us because from now on such meals would be few and far between. It had been difficult to get enough to eat so far in camping because of the mosquitoes. We drifted through the scene like ghosts, talking absently, hardly seeing people. Already, we were persons set apart.

The day of perspiration and the convivial eating of ice cream at sheltered Hot Springs were followed directly the next day by cold, rough, windy weather down among Squaw Flats, which forced us into the alpaca-lined parka jackets with hoods which were never at any time far from our reach. It is characteristic of northern river travel that one day you think you are in the tropics and the next you are caught in some wintry blast of the kind which causes even the big steamboats to tie up along the Yukon.

Squaw Flats widens out to about three miles wide, and here the Tanana River, broader and seemingly larger than the Yukon itself at this point, enters the Yukon by three different mouths. It seemed like a different world, careening along Squaw Flats through brown swirling foam and wind-swept purple skies. Here, among barely submerged sand bars and vast timbered islands, we climbed up mountains of water and down again, smacking each unruly comber a resounding whack and leveling it off with the greatest of glee. It was a good test for the canoe, and the next day might be worse if we delayed. In this life you travel when you can.

I think I was the first to see the old Yukon. We had been watching for it for seventy-five miles. "There she is," I cried, and Bud added confirmation with a nod.

"I hate to do this to a motor," was all he said, running it nearly wide open. The wind tore at us; birds were blown sidewise in their course across the sky. I knew as well as Bud that the motor must not fail us where the two currents met. Exciting moments, anxious moments—and yet I can recall none more pleasurable in their general impression than those of the *Little Willow* leveling off waves on big rivers, water flying off the bow, everything tacked down tight in front, and Bud saying, "Here, take her while I gas up," at a time when bleached gray snags menaced on every side. Fortunately, we plowed forward without power failure. She was loaded too heavily for us to have put up much of a fight with oars.

We entered the Yukon and commenced to cross with trepidation that mile-wide expanse of the third largest river on the continent. On the opposite shore could be seen the Episcopalian Mission of Our Saviour, lying above the town of Tanana. Here we knew we would find our old friends the Reverend and Mrs. Files and little Willie living in their modest missionary home. "Won't they be surprised when they see us blow in!" I anticipated, counting the minutes.

Bud said only: "I'll have to shut her off in a moment or she'll bust wide open. Get ready to paddle." Black smoke against purple sky was visible behind us.

When the motor was cut we dug in with the paddles to best the river. When we finally landed on the north side of the Yukon by the side of a beached fish wheel, the mission was almost out of sight. Bud put the lead rope around his shoulders then and staggering along the bank of the Yukon through boulders and brambles was able to pull us up to the mission within forty minutes' time. My job was to rudder with an oar from the stern to hold our craft off the shore. In this way we had our first taste of a process that is known as "lining" or "tracking" a boat, a process still in use by the bulk of humanity who are following wilderness rivers today. Poling also is in wide vogue.

The anticipated goal was reached: warmth, shelter, friends, and hot, steaming food. Walking up and down in our stocking feet in the Fileses' shabbily homelike front room, and following Mrs. Files into the kitchen, we were soon hearing all the news. The Fileses related the events of their furlough; they had been Outside all the previous year and had not been back long. We were made to feel that our arrival was a special event and a cause for celebration. Talk was then of the king salmon; they had reached Nulato lower down, where the fish wheels were picking them up by the hundreds daily; they were expected here within the week. The salmon are life itself to the Indians, who depend on them as a main means of support, and the arrival of the first "run" of the summer is glad tidings each year to natives and whites alike. Perhaps Yukoners have a special language, but we had this in common with them, that all of our interests lay here in the coming North, with the rest of the world not ahead of us, but behind, at least in some ways.

A family prayer was held after breakfast the next day before we departed, during which everyone got down on his knees and a plea was invoked for our protection on our journey into the arctic. Bud and I arose stiffly from this with a feeling of singular gratitude. We were given warm and honest handclasps which bade us a Yukon *bon voyage*.

6

The prevailing climate on the lower Yukon, the last 800 miles of it, below the entrance of the Tanana River, is rainy in summer. Mud, drizzle, mosquitoes, and cold too—these predominated as we progressed several hundred miles westerly, borne by the current and the idling motor, towards the Bering Sea. At the town of Tanana Bud had bought a spring from an air rifle for twenty-five cents and put it into the water pump on the motor to replace the worn-out spring. A day spent in fishing for grayling on a clear side stream brought us to Kokrines in weather similar to that in which we had approached the Fileses'. We took a string of thirty or forty grayling for the Indian Service teachers whom we knew to be located there. The teachers, we knew, scarcely ever got any fresh meat, even fish, other than what they could buy from their Indians.

These Yukon towns, straggling along the curving bank of the river, present a special, plausible appearance from a distance. But this appearance is a deception. They are really composed of but one boardwalk or muddy path containing the trader's frame residence, possibly a government schoolhouse for the Indians, and the log cabins of the Athabascan Indian people. The trader, along with the Indian Service teacher and his wife and, increasingly, a C.A.A. or U.S. Weather Bureau family in residence, are the only white inhabitants living behind those place names you see on the map of that vastly greater Alaska which lies away from the southerly coasts and off the railroad line.

Kokrines we knew to be a lonely post—no radio, no communications, no landing field. Our assumption that the new teachers, while strange to us, would be glad to have company was not wrong. A Mr. and Mrs. Reed, they invited us in to have dinner with them and their fourteen-year-old son, who was taking his high school work by correspondence. I was one of three white women Mrs. Reed had seen in a year.

Perhaps because of curtailments caused by the war no inspector from the Indian Service headquarters had been by here to visit the teachers, since the new couple had taken their station, directly from the States, a year ago. They were left completely on their own resources as to what day to open school, what day to close it, this depending on the activities of each particular village, and what extracurricular activities or reforms to inaugurate. They were pretty well cut off from the world. It had taken Mr. Reed seventy days to receive an answer to his telegram to Juneau, Alaska's capital, a thousand air miles away, since all wireless was tied up by military needs. The army had cornered all the mosquito repellent, which meant that everybody was, in plain words, going crazy; repellent didn't mean DDT either, for civilians hadn't even heard of that yet. But the teachers were well endowed by temperament and by their sturdy character to handle their burden. Distressed and uncertain as they felt themselves to be at times, it was notable that it was not of themselves they spoke but of the welfare of the people they had been elected to watch over. It was discouraging because there was no other white person in the country to talk problems over with, and none to care where whites existed. Indian Service is a kind of one-man battle against the world.

We were happy to reach Koyukuk, our last stop on the Yukon. Up till now we had not considered that our explorations had begun.

Continuous coughing and spitting of the Indians greeted us at this last Yukon town as we landed our boat. We made our way between probably a hundred dogs chained in the riverbank, careful to keep at chain's length. It was evening and feeding time. We saw little boys, barefooted among the human and dog excrement of the waterfront, slipping and struggling under buckets of slop too heavy for their strength, while the savage dogs, one of which had an eye knocked out, screamed and dashed again and again at the lengths of their chains. It is no exaggeration that these dogs kill several Indian children each year. It is no exaggeration either to say that you can't blame the dogs; they are maltreated by their pitifully ignorant owners until what should be perfectly good ordinary decent pooches are turned often enough into frenzied beasts. These are the so-called wild Malemutes and Huskies of the North of which you have heard—just dogs which have had a bad break.

At such towns one holds one's nose, pulls the head net down, and runs for it. Up the slimy path to the trader's house we went. Swarms of mosquito-bitten children with long ragged hair hanging down in their eyes peeped from behind their mothers' skirts or made little rushes towards us to gain attention. The mothers moved off slowly, turning their broad backs upon the white people.

Actually, it seems to us that Alaska Indian conditions along the doorsteps of civilization are no worse than conditions among some of the Indian, Negro, and Mexican groups, to name a few, which are disposed about our doorsteps in the United States. If this fact seems a rude jolt, it is nonetheless true. You see, the condition of much of the population of the earth is terrible; in this sense the world is wilderness, no doubt about it.

In Alaska, native conditions are the result of a very complex set of factors which we are not equipped to analyze here except very generally, but which mainly seem to be nobody's fault. Some people have blamed the traders. But the traders have merely come to fill an economic need; if the Indians want bourbon and canned gingerbread, well—they are citizens, and under the system of our society there will be someone inevitably to buy their furs and bring them the goods they want. In Alaska the natives are not on reservations but are treated by the government as free citizens, almost as anyone else, except that they have greater privileges. Their progress is generally esteemed greater than that of Indians on reservations in the United States.

Some people, with the modern viewpoint of disillusionment towards religious missions, whose problems seem to multiply rather than diminish with the years, even blame the missionaries for the natives' troubles. These people point out that where originally native people did not know what it was to steal, may not, in fact, have had a word for "stealing" in their own language until the Bible taught them, now it may be necessary in some cases to lock the doors and place mission property under key to prevent it from being taken away by the converts. Yet sensible people cannot blame the missionaries, who live, more often than not, in what many of us would call poverty, and who suffer much through long years.

Are our schools and educational system to blame for the maladjustment of our native people then? Perhaps partly—they need revising.

It seems impossible that anyone would question the necessity of education for an Indian or an Eskimo, yet many do; we have sat in the warm, cozy living rooms of our houses and heard these questions raised, and there are always those who say: "What need have *they* for education and going to school?" It was only twenty years ago that many people were asking this question about education for Negroes—and this question is still hotly contended today by those who have been the greatest oppressors of the Negro race.

Yes, what need have they for education in a school? "The Indians were a lot happier in their own environment when the white man just left them alone," Alaskan old-timers frequently point out. Modern freethinkers, too, frequently express the doubt as to whether it is worth all the trouble for everybody concerned to try to make the American native over to be like us in all ways. The Indian and the Eskimo were not ignorant in their world to which they were adapted, these nature lovers claim, nor were they necessarily diseased or filthy or unhappy when we found them. In fact, they were doing all right for their age. Why not let them just stay in that age in peace?

These people handled their own social problems without either the dole or the police, and as to primitive life being fraught with arduous labors—well, did you ever see a native working? They certainly have more time on their hands than we. It was we who taught them to work. We put them to work for us at low wages all over the world. We taught them to work and we taught them the blessed art of worry.

Yet this is very fallacious reasoning. The point is that the very nature of this complex age demands that all living people must change and conform to it if they are going to survive.

What this argument against education overlooks is that education is the only means to power in the modern world. Without it, any group is helpless and completely in the power of others. Ignorance is slavery. Knowledge of finance, mechanization, politics—this is the key which unlocks the treasure.

One cannot blame the trader, the missionary, or the school then, or even the "white race" as some have done, in a blind groping effort to clarify confusing affairs. Even simple savages had their own corrupt politics and their graft and their lecherous aristocracy; they had their jealousies and their own wars before we came along, just as the modern nations do today—let us not delude ourselves about that. Granted that the evils we perpetuated were on a bigger scale. Our sailing vessels carried our diseases and our systems of slavery to the South Sea Islanders, the American Indians, and even the Eskimos, it is true. But the diffusion of the human race around the globe is inevitable. It can't be helped. There are even the airplanes now to accelerate the process. It's the "times"—times beyond anyone's control. Meanwhile Indian Service considers that the Indians should be schooled, not according to practical "arts and crafts" altogether, but that they should be made literate just as anyone else so that they can hope eventually to meet the world of today on its own terms.

It seems probable that if left to themselves without medical aid the native peoples might in time build up a resistance to disease which would enable them to survive as we did—if we are to philosophize on such things. But by that time, they will not be "native" any more. It is interesting to observe that many of the present survivors are of mixed white blood. These are just now beginning to evidence a natural immunity like our own.

But to await the operation of nature's slow, inexorable laws in all things is hardly the modern or the humanitarian viewpoint. Rather we must forget our concepts of "native" and "white," open our clinics to all, as we are doing throughout the United States, and treat tuberculosis in Alaska as the communicable disease that it is. Tuberculosis in Alaska has become a public health problem of magnitude; infected natives must be removed from their families—forcibly if necessary—and a preventive campaign inaugurated for children who are now growing up. The system of the hospital airplane might be used successfully to reach people in the North where there are no roads or railroads and where the river boats don't run on schedule. This is not just to help the "native." The pure native anywhere in the world is even now a myth, a fast-disappearing rarity!

Disease, then, together with poverty and the psychological barriers unconsciously erected by the American rulers, have set a scene of hopeless misery for the Alaskan native. A nomad people in transition to agriculture, their lands are hunted out and their agriculture is rudimentary, and between these sterile worlds they wander bewildered....

Bud, with the trader, trundled supplies between storeroom, cellar, and cache—the trader who could not read or write, or even add up the account. Bud added up the account himself for us.

It was time for us to go beyond the Yukon, to go farther north. Wading out in hip boots, we climbed into the *Little Willow* to follow the next river beyond.

PART TWO

The Koyukuk River

Lunch on the lower Koyukuk River, July 1944

We stop to repair our outboard on the upper Koyukuk River

1

Far down on the serpentine lower Yukon there is a big river that comes in from the north. Its name is the Koyukuk. We knew that the Koyukuk River led into that country which we had never seen.

The place names on the map of such a country as the Koyukuk are good to see. Here there are Eskimo names that you despair of ever being able to pronounce. Then, here's "Meat Mountain." Now that's a name you can understand. But you wonder suddenly if the men who named that one might not have been hungry at least half of the time. When you see names like this you know that you haven't got America licked yet. You had better worry about the names—Poorman and Coldfoot and Help-me-Jack Creek.

In the north the sun was setting. If the sun normally sets in the west, this is not true on the Koyukuk River for most of the year. In short, they taught you wrong in school. People who think the sun always sets in the west, for instance, are just egocentric; they see it just from their angle.

Far behind the spruce trees to the north the sun sank, winking at us with a prolonged weird glow. It was midnight and we were traveling. Day and night did not make much difference. We traveled a twenty-four-hour stretch with little food and no sleep at times, and we did not feel especially tired now that we were getting used to a new way of living.

This goes for habits in eating and, I might add as a housewife, in washing dishes as well. Along the Yukon we ate out of cans. We were due to learn a lot. We had meals consisting of several articles or courses, and when I washed dishes I was bogged down in mud to the knees at the water's edge so that Bud frequently had to come to the rescue and haul me out. "No wonder not many women like this life," I sputtered. "To think I took up exploration to get out of housework. It's all right for you, you're a man. But for a woman this outdoors is just housework made harder than ever."

Then Bud hit the nail on the head with his typically masculine reply. "I've never seen," he said, "why women are so foolish as to worry so much about little things all the time. Throw the dishes into the river if they bother you. We'll get rid of them."

"Do you really mean it?" I snapped. "I'll take you up on that."

The trouble with people like us, we concluded, is that we try to bring our civilized methods of eating into the out-of-doors and it just doesn't work. It makes you miserable and uncomfortable. If we're going to travel across Arctic America together and come out at the end with nervous systems still intact, maybe we had better settle some things right in the beginning. Maybe we had better just forget a lot of notions and devise a new code of wilderness etiquette for ourselves. We are going to pit our small strength against big things in this country. Maybe we had better learn to do the little things the simplest way. Let's keep it simple. Let's not make it complicated.

I did, more or less, take Bud up on his suggestion, and it worked admirably for domestic tranquility. The dishes were not thrown into the river, but we never saw most of them until winter came. You eat out of your side of the skillet and I'll eat out of mine, or, better still, just pass me a forked stick and a lump of rain-dampened salt, and I'll get out my pocketknife. The dictionary even has a special word for it— *accubation*, which simply means reclining on a mossy bank or a couch of hides while you stuff, a whole roast bird taken in the left hand, so, or perhaps a five-pound dripping joint. Yes, we've done it for years, and it solves everything; we can heartily endorse it for all.

The town of Koyukuk lay behind us, still wide awake even at this hour, for northern towns never go to sleep in the summertime. Even the lives of the most conventional become very irregular in spite of themselves. Behind us lay the choppy Yukon, ruffling under a night wind. Up the current and against the chop we plowed, loaded heavily and without much freeboard. The motor was doing well with a richer mixture for going upstream. You should never change the standard mixture of oil in the gasoline which the motor company gives, but what you do change is the opening of the air valve which mixes air with gasoline. By opening up the valve to admit more air, even an outboard motor can be made to idle in the hands of a clever pilot; the ability to make your motor idle without clogging and stalling from the accumulation of carbon is a handy, in fact a necessary, one for running down swift, rapid-filled streams. For going up the river instead, you close down the air valve to run with full power. You also burn a great deal more gas, Bud explained to me.

The little motor took us at once to the mouth of the new river with an ease that was heartening. Behind us the pear-shaped moon hung over Yukon cliffs that had turned to black velvet. Now on the north side of the Yukon we entered a stream of water which was black and clear, and commenced to follow it up. The little motor breathed easily, as though to say: "Free of mud, at last."

When we had studied the Koyukuk River on the map, considering this country, we had seen that its source lies in a tremendous mountain chain, stretching from east to west across northern Alaska. We were looking for a way to cross those mountains. We expected to spend a year in them, a winter living right on top of the Arctic Divide. From all the inquiries we made from the southerly Alaskan people, not a thing could we get on Brooks Range, lying there all by itself these many centuries, white paper on our present maps. "There probably isn't anything there," somebody offered.

Bud and I just had to let our jaws hang open at that, while our neck fur, so to speak, slowly rose. "You know I'd kind of like to spend a year there," I had said, "just to see what it's like." Bud whistled softly. "Wouldn't we all?" he said. "But how to get there?"

"I know," I said, making my familiar rush for the map. "The Koyukuk River." So, it was that the Koyukuk River now was our highway into the Brooks Range.

Lying entirely above the Arctic Circle, the Brooks Range really includes a number of mountain groups which are not as yet all clearly delineated in the minds of the geographers. As generally listed on maps, these groups read: the Sadlerochit Mountains, the Shublik

Mountains, the Franklin Mountains, the Romanzoff Mountains, the Lisburne Hills, the Igichuk Hills, the Mulgrave Hills, the Melville Mountains, the Schwatka Mountains, the Endicott Mountains, the Baird Mountains, and the De Long Mountains, or about a dozen recognized distinct groups in the Range. In all of those groups it is certain that there are places which no man, civilized or primitive, has seen, and some entire groups have not been visited at all but were viewed from large rivers or from passing ships on the arctic coast when named. Although the Brooks Range does not exceed 10,000 feet in altitude, it is nonetheless one of the six major mountain ranges of our continent. Like an unconquered arctic Rockies, yet a distinct system from the Rockies, the Range bars from the railway, the highway, and the pedestrian a land over which not even airplanes fly as yet: the arctic slope of North America.

Of course, other known parts of Alaska are so scenic that to most people there is no justification for a man taking his wife north of the Arctic Circle and into the Brooks Range so that she can look at the scenery. But then, look for yourself—the U.S. Geological Survey suggests all kinds of easy passes through the Brooks Range. Now it says here, "By way of the John to the Anaktuvuk River and across a pass that stands at an elevation of about 2200 feet; by way of the Alatna River and its tributary Unakserak River to the Killik, across a pass of 3800 feet; by way of the side streams of the Noatak to streams tributary to the Colville, across passes that, at the heads of the Aniuk, Nimiuktuk and Kugururok, to the Utukok across a pass at about—" and so on.

Wait a minute! Did you read the word "easy" there anywhere? Still, we pored over those great remote interior mountains on the map and asked ourselves from all we knew thus far about Alaska: Could a person really spend a winter there? Would there be timber? What could we make a cabin out of? What animals might be found living there in those latitudes and in those altitudes?

If people had listed all that information somewhere before now, we couldn't find it. Actually, we know now that there were expeditions during the years 1924, 1925, and 1926, but they were geological in interest and were principally in connection with oil investigations relative to the boundaries of the mere 30,000 square miles held by the Naval Petroleum Reserve. In 1924 Bud and I were just with the kindergarten crowd. What would *we* find there in the Brooks Range this year if we were to just go there ourselves?

We could tell briefly one thing before we started. Removed from the modifying influence of the sea, any interior mountains of the North are sure to be cold in winter. Even the frozen Arctic Ocean, they tell us, warms its islands and its adjacent coastal lands, comparatively speaking, in winter, but this remote interior would cool off in the fall of the year. Colder than the arctic coast by measurement of actual temperature drop, colder at times than the Arctic Ocean ever gets, that was cold, we could imagine! Probably nobody lived there. But we would find out about that.

The Koyukuk River drew us irresistibly to this quarter, rather than selecting another river highway for our route. In the Brooks Range, adjacent to the head of the Koyukuk, lies an equally great river, the Colville, with which we had to make connections someway. One of the world's larger arctic rivers flowing down a thousand miles to reach the polar basin, this river always caused a peculiar mistiness and tenderness in our thoughts. I suppose this strange sentiment derived from its utter inaccessibility. One of our purposes in following the Koyukuk into this quarter of the Brooks Range was to find the headwaters of the Colville River. The head of some river always seems to be the "go" signal to people who have a tendency to be explorers.

How many times, then, had we gazed on the general map—for there were no sectional maps in existence on this country—and observed that it seemed to be only a little way between where the many plotted streams pour down the interior or continental side of the Brooks Range into such rivers as the Porcupine or the Koyukuk, draining the Yukon watershed, and where the fewer streams, because not charted, pour down into the timberless, thousand-mile-long Colville River of the arctic.

The Koyukuk River, across some pass to the Colville, was to be our route to the Arctic Ocean in time, if we could find the Colville in the Brooks Range and not find ourselves floating out to the Bering Sea on some other big river like the Noatak or the Kobuk instead.

But the Colville is the kind of project that takes planning. Meanwhile this year spent in getting into its tributaries, down which a canoe ride would be, in all events, a one-way ticket, was one of preparation. Meanwhile there was the lovely Koyukuk River emerging onto green lowlands from the Brooks Range 700 river miles above, which would be white and cold and still, we imagined, waiting there somewhere for us to get out our skis this coming winter and take a slide.

"We won't see anybody for the first 250 miles," Bud calculated as we pushed up the mouth of the Koyukuk, craning our necks from bank to bank of the new river. "Farther up there are some old gold camps. We must try at all times from now on to run the motor so as to get the most mileage out of it. We've got about 400 pounds of gas here. That's 60 gallons at 75 cents a gallon. How far it takes us will depend on how swift we find the current. We must learn to read the water so as to ride up the eddies easily and miss the fast water when we can. Every mile farther our load gets lighter to push, too."

"But with every mile farther on the current gets swifter," I said.

We knew there were traders on up the Koyukuk, even missionaries. But there were no more Indian Service schools; the ancient rights of these other institutions only served to make an Alaska that was much as it always had been, unchanged by the passage of time. Although the first powered boat went up the 500-yard-wide river as far back as around 1911, there was no sign now that human beings had ever been on it.

"We'd better watch out now about taking short cuts between the river islands and about taking side channels," Bud cautioned. "Going upstream a person could take some branch of the river that wouldn't come back to it. If we got lost from the main river we could travel for days and lose a lot of gas before we realized our mistake."

"Watch out for the Kuthel River coming in from the left hand about ninety miles from here," we memorized. "That's the only place where a person could take the wrong turn. Keep to the right or straight ahead there, then keep to the left after that to avoid Dubli Slough. You can tell by the way the willows point backwards there that the floods have backed up into the slough and not mistake it for the main river. We won't be going straight north. The Koyukuk has to fool around backtracking east a long ways, it seems."

"When shall we see the Arctic Circle?"

"Well, we were as close to it when we started at Nenana as we are now. We've been adjacent to it all along, but we may not cross it for a while yet. I'd hate to say. It all depends on how the motor behaves," said Bud. "The distance going upriver is not the same as down. Let's see, with a 2-mile-an-hour current, you have to run over 500 miles of water to get 250 miles, or something like that. It's hard to estimate it in miles or in days until you've made it. Every day counts from now on because we have to make the little creeks farther up while the water is still high in them."

"Well, let's make camp and sleep first."

We tied up to stakes driven down into the soft bottom in a little cove in this new Koyukuk River, and slept twelve hours before continuing further. The sky was limpid in the red midnight and only a horned owl hooted, the mosquitoes whined, or a fish jumped occasionally to break silver circles in the solitude.

Connie makes a pie with our last can of pumpkin

2

"The first black bear we see," Bud said, "you can kill with your new .30-30. We'll eat what we can, sun-dry the rest, and take it along."

Of course, Bud meant the first male bear we saw. Naturally we wouldn't try to kill a mother bear with her cubs. The foolish person who tries that is not only asking for trouble; he's got it. It is said to be a terrible experience, if we can believe those who have participated, something like murdering a family of wailing human beings, and it is certainly not one for the sportsman's book unless there is a real reason. It is almost invariable that black bears, at least, will bellow while they are being killed anyway. Almost all other American big game doesn't say a word.

When we turned up the Koyukuk River north of the Yukon the situation became different from merely killing a bear out of idleness. Of course, we were allowed ten common black bears between us yearly any place north of the Yukon and at any time if we wanted them; this was true north of the Alaska Range, in fact, or as of our starting point, right from Nenana. The law recognized here the use of bears for meat. We both knew I ought to shoot a bear myself at the first opportunity, for practice and to develop self-confidence.

"You needn't hesitate about it," Bud admonished. "You're not in the city any longer, and any person who doesn't know how to make a living hunting or off the earth by raising his food had better not get far from the city streets—and I'm not sure he's safe there.

"You never know, especially in our life, when you might need that skill. Some men get so excited when they see game they can't shoot. I've seen a man stand there and pump all his shells out on the ground and never fire a shot. I wouldn't live in a state where they won't allow a man to have a gun, myself.

"Now game is different from targets, no matter what they say. You've had lots of targets—oh, not a lot, but I think you'll do all right. Where we're going you may have to do the fall hunting while I build our house. I can't be two places at once, and often you won't be with me, and you may see game. Besides, one of us might get sick or something sometime, and the other one would have to keep things going until he got all right again. It's a big country up there ahead. I've tried to make you a hunter, and you've done fairly well so far, but both of us have a lot to learn about hunting before we're through with this.

"It's perfectly legal for you to get us a bear and we can use the meat. Don't think a thing about it, because the fact is that very likely any of these men on the traders' barges running back and forth from Wiseman and Bettles may just shoot any bear they see on the bank and let it lay. On the Yukon you and I know they do that all the time."

This was true. I knew black bears are in ill favor in the North. They are regarded as always, a potential menace in uninhabited country because of their habit of breaking into a man's cabin or cache or boat, eating and destroying everything with the sweep of a paw, leaving a man stranded miles from help. Commonly, the old sourdoughs felt they could not permit "pets" around camp in the form of bears; the black bear was accordingly shot on sight. There may have been some justification for this in some cases, but it always remained a shame in our eyes that nobody ate the bears or made use of them, at least. Useless slaughter of wild things! Have bears no rights? We knew too from an experience the fall before that there is actually no better meat for "pork loin" with applesauce, or for "beef T-bones" with French fries, than the right kind of black bear along with all the trimmings that city life can provide. We served it to our friends for both pork and beef. Experiments using two hundred pounds of bear meat in this way proved to us conclusively that nobody knows what he's eating anyway. There are a few fair-minded men of wide outdoors experience who will tell you truthfully the facts: that a good bear is probably first in line of candidates for the most versatile and best all-around food animal of the wilderness.

It was about four in the afternoon three days after we struck the Koyukuk that we saw my bear. Bud sighted him first about four miles away, gamboling on a green lawn of the riverbank ahead, and checked his observations with the binoculars. It was a black bear, all right; black bears are one of the most conspicuous animals to see against the green of summer foliage. Bud's restless eyes were always scanning the country ahead. He didn't expect to jump big game at his feet the way you do rabbits. He knew he would see his animal at a distance, most likely, and imagined the kind of setting in which he would find it. For some reason Bud materializes animals in this way, and he is not surprised. This is how the Indian or the cowboy or the guide sees so far: long experience enables him to make a good guess.

"Shall we stop soon and sneak along the bank to him? Or shall we keep going towards him with the motor running?" I asked.

Bud shrugged his shoulders. "I don't think he'll pay any attention to the motor. Let's get as close as we can. I hate to shut her off."

We went on steadily. We watched the bow of the canoe cut along through the reddish water—red because of the algae of draining lowland sloughs—but presently both of us looked and the bear was gone. He was not alarmed but merely went into the forest in the course of his natural ambling. We came to a landing on the scene. The green lawn turned out to be the merest fringe of young horsetails growing out of soft, deep, sticky mud almost comparable to quicksand. Bud, like the bear on his broad silent pads, scampered across and threw down a pile of brush for me to walk on, but it disappeared under me. "For heaven's sake," groaned Bud. "A person would think you were as big as an ox. Can't you walk?"

"No, I'm stuck," I whispered angrily.

"Well, I can't get you out. I'll see if I can find him. He was right here a minute ago."

"Wait!" I hissed, but Bud had vanished at the fringe of the forest, and although I knew he was somewhere nearby, I knew also that he was somewhat like a hunting dog unleashed, and it was plain that he didn't want anything more to do with women, notably me, at the time. A profound anger welled up in me for the ridiculousness of my situation. But that is the trouble with being a hunter: there you are, ridiculous, and there is nothing much that you can do about it. Never in my life had I ever been in the grip of such subterranean forces as now had me.

Bud had pulled me out once too often. Meanwhile the bear was getting away. I struggled violently with a will to get out. My hip boots pulled off in my struggles until I was stepping on the part that was the knee of the boot, and still they stretched. Mosquitoes whirled in clouds, sweat poured down my face and neck. I was so angry that I saw the green landscape in terms of red. Bud had gone off with both the guns, plus mosquito dope, and here was I, the mighty hunter!

For minutes I was entirely helpless, but eventually I extricated myself by stepping out of my boots in my stocking feet and onto a branch. Then followed a mighty tug of war to get the boots. Putting them on again and hitching up my pants, I made it to firmer ground. "Here, you give me my gun," I demanded of Bud, who was waiting impatiently while I learned my first lesson.

"Oh, no you don't," said he, holding it back. "What do you think a gun is? Go and wash your hands."

My hands were covered with mud where I had lost my balance and literally rolled in it. My face was mud-streaked where I had scratched. I felt it unwise to attempt to go to the river brink again, inasmuch as I had just come from there, but since Bud wouldn't give me my gun, and the bear was still getting away, I gave in against my better judgment and made the gallant attempt. By this attempt I think even Bud realized that I was somehow not inherently capable of skipping over mud, even though I weighed around fifty pounds less than he. As it was in truth quite impossible for Bud to get me out I again rescued myself, and we compromised by my wiping my hands on leaves. Applying some mosquito repellent to my muddy face and with my head net pushed back on my hat brim for clear vision and action, I followed Bud obediently and quietly along the beach at the fringe of the forest, looking for the bear.

It was then that an afterthought occurred to me, something which Bud had taught me before now. I turned my head, slowly and deliberately, and looked behind us from where we had come. There by our canoe was the bear!

He had circled us completely. What if I had still been there, stuck in the mud, minus gun? The bear could have come up and licked the salt from my face, for I recalled that bears like salt. I had to smile, but the thoughts that rule the hunter's mind now ruled supreme. Here was our game.

"Bud," I said sweetly, with the confidence born of a secret knowledge. "Look, dear, what do you see fifteen feet from our canoe?"

More quickly than it takes to tell we raced together silently for our boat and the bear. The shelter of the forest protected us; the wind, if any, was right. It was perfect, but then, *flop!* my foot stuck and I was into the mud, ninety yards from the goal. I held my rifle up as I fell. It was plain that I could go no farther in any case.

"If you bog down once more." I heard Bud making vague and terrible threats. "Now take your time, and don't hit the boat."

Bud left me with six shells in the magazine of my .30-30 and he himself slipped down the boggy fringe of the forest with the shotgun loaded with buckshot in case I should merely cripple the bear and he might attempt retreat in the other direction. Bud had succumbed to buying another new "scope" which he had mounted on the side of his own .30-30 carbine just before leaving town, but now, characteristically, I guess he thought it was too good to use around the mud, so he just took the shotgun.

Certainly, no man could have had a wife more calm and deadly with anger than did Bud when he left me with my first bear. Waiting a moment to get my wind, for it is foolish to shoot when one is winded, if it can be avoided, I peeked out through the willows from a prone position which lacked all dignity. By now Bud should have taken his stand. Sticking the rifle barrel over a convenient stump for a rest, I pulled the hammer back on one of the heavier grain shells with which Bud had loaded my rifle for bear and let her go.

The bear was sitting down with his back towards me in an attitude of meditation or reflection, his head turned around in my direction facing me. His sharp ears had detected a slight noise, but he didn't know what it was. Later I learned that in shooting any big game animal it is wise to wait, if it is possible to do so, until he turns to face in the direction you want him to run if he runs. Usually you hope a deer will run your way, but conceivably you wouldn't want a bear to if it was a big bear.

I shot as quickly as I got a good sight on him and didn't lose any time. Several times in our experience we had seen a bear up on a mountainside and climbed rapidly to the place only to find that, grazing along at the rate of two to three miles an hour, the bear was by that time on the mountain beyond. Now, seeing that this bear was in line with the boat, on the other side of it, I shot about ten feet over the boat to kill him. At such times the report of the rifle is merely a distant tiny pop in one's ears, and there is absolutely no consciousness of recoil, no matter how heavy the gun may be. The gun shrinks in size until it becomes the size of a pencil. I shot five times, remembering to count the shots, with a pause of several seconds after each shot.

The first shot is always the most important. It was this one which killed the bear. But as I knew that after each shot, having rolled down the mud bank into the edge of the river, he might again attempt a recovery, I kept shooting. This is a common story with bears, as they seem to be so compactly built as to have a nervous system almost impervious to shock at times.

It was not until all was still for several minutes and Bud sounded the all-clear signal that I came out of my hiding place, for I never had had any intention of having that bear see me while he was alive. Even now, as we came up, our guns were in readiness; I had put in more heavy-grained bullets from my pocket. Never, incidentally, run up to a bear that falls with his feet doubled under him; wait until you see his heels in the air for sure.

I gazed in wonderment at what I had got. Bud was very pleased. "He's a pretty good bear, dear," he said. "You did all right. Of course, he's kind of poor—see his ribs here? And he hasn't got as much hair on his belly as I have—but you did very well."

"He isn't as big as I thought," said I. "Are you sure we got the right bear?"

"Yes, it's the same one all right. He does seem to have shrunk considerably. About 150 pounds. Your first bear. You'll always remember this."

Yes, my first bear, and I'll always remember it! He was a walking wreck and his hide was mangy; in fact, he was practically naked. The condition of an animal's fur is a good indication of its general bodily health and hence of the flavor of the meat. The meat of this animal was unfit to eat, other than the liver, and you can eat the liver of almost anything. We carried the meat with us in a clean, empty, five-gallon gasoline can, but after a couple of days of trying to get it down, sports that we were, we gave up. This may have been an indication that this bear had been living in part on fish. But more likely it was merely that he was a summer bear and summer bears are not all that they could be by any means.

Before putting a line around his shoulders and floating the carcass down the beach where a piece of hard ground offered opportunity to butcher, Bud took my picture with my bear. It is a lovely picture. It is not the kind of which sportsmen dream. The naked dead bear lies in the mud with gore running down its mouth and from the holes in its side. Hordes of mosquitoes have settled on its nose, and around the corners of its eyes it is well chewed. I clutch my gun with its stock covered with mud, while mud and perspiration vie for attention on my face and one hip boot drags behind. In this picture, it seems to me, I look slightly larger than the bear.

We stop to study the map

3

I now felt as though I could turn around any day and kill a bear whenever necessary, and this is a good way to feel. It is not to be supposed that Bud's treatment of me was rough or cruel in any way. It was the kindest sort of treatment one could give a person who intends to hunt bears. We were both in our element as wilderness experimenters and were enjoying life immensely. The wilderness offers something new every day, an endless variation. Bud succeeded in making a pretty good hunter of me eventually, if a love of nature means anything.

Now as we proceeded along the Koyukuk River we looked in vain for some evidence that we were in the vicinity of the Arctic Zone. Long as we had lived in Alaska, like the majority of its people we knew nothing at all about the arctic. The arctic of legend, the arctic of which we had had rare glimpses in the movies, was flat, barren, snow-covered, and eternally beset by howling blizzards. The very word "arctic" meant an utter desolation of ice and snow. I had never in my wildest dreams imagined myself going to *that* land. Fortunately, there seemed to be nothing like that around here, and as we knew that we were getting close to the arctic now, it seemed improbable that the character of the country could suddenly change from this green, hot summertime. We weren't too surprised that the country wasn't yet living up to the popular expectations. After all, we had our own theories about it or we wouldn't be here. Yet it is interesting that despite the logic of our minds and the evidence of our eyes, our childhood emotions failed to be dispelled for some time. "I think the trees are getting smaller now, don't you?" I remember Bud would remark for each dozen miles of our progress, and I would reply: "Yes, it seems as though they were becoming more stunted."

Or, "Look," Bud would point out, "stands of good timber for building a cabin are getting rarer."

The evidence that timber was getting either rarer or more stunted was purely in our own minds and was the result of imagination! The upper Koyukuk hundreds of miles north of the Yukon has finer timber than we saw in the south traveling on the Alaska Railroad. It is true that many open fields appeared as the river meandered the lowlands beset by marshes and swamps, but these were only the result of local conditions, not latitude. Fine stands of fourteen-inch and twenty-inch spruce would appear directly around the corner. Some of this spruce was standing dead, killed by borers or bark beetles perhaps; some trees were hollow, rotted out at the base. The vegetable and animal kingdoms in the arctic, as well as in the warmer zones of the earth, have their parasites, adapted to arctic conditions. None of them are harmful to man so that man has imagined them to be nonexistent in these regions, but they are there. Man has probably not existed in the arctic long enough to develop parasites of his own to any extent, for infections are known to be extremely rare and wounds heal with rapidity. The fact that the soil has never been plowed and is incapable of incubating diseases such as tetanus makes the arctic, from this standpoint, the most healthy place on earth in which man might live.

As for the trees, some of the living spruce is very old. It gave us an odd feeling to make a cabin out of it, as though we were doing something wrong, because we knew that it could not easily be replaced. Certainly, reforesting the arctic would never be practical in one man's lifetime because the trees grow so slowly. The author Bob Marshall, who spent a couple of years in the Koyukuk district and described it to the world, made an interesting little experiment with trees. After he published his book *Arctic Village* he kept returning to the Koyukuk by chartered airplane on numerous vacations up to the time of his death in the late 1930's. He issued for his Koyukuk friends at his own expense a couple of small volumes which describe adventures unknown to the general public. One adventure was the setting out of seedlings north of the timber line on a hike over the divide to see if the seedlings would live. They didn't. But it is hard to say whether the experiment proved that all seedlings wouldn't. Bob's original attempt to extend the Alaskan timber line northward over the Koyukuk is the only experiment of its kind we have heard of thus far. Very little experimentation has been done yet in our arctic America, an untouched field.

It was only some months after we had entered the arctic, with more experience to judge from, that in conversation about the diffusion of timber we happened to recall that we had read somewhere about trappers living among the heavy forests of the Mackenzie River Delta of Canada within a few miles of the Arctic Ocean itself. It must be, then, that to find this completely barren arctic one would have to go to lands north of the North American Continent.

Everyone knows that Nome, Alaska, on the Bering Sea, is treeless, and it is usually considered that the reason it is treeless is that it is far north. Not so! We were as far north as Nome when we started on this trip at Nenana, and we were following the timber far, far north of Nome right now. Shelter from the harsh winds, drainage, perhaps merely seed dispersal, might be the answer; we learned that there is no definite "timber line" based on latitude, but that timber creeps far up the continental side of the Brooks Range, the trees not getting progressively smaller, but as large and straight as ever where they do exist, nestling in the pockets of the hills. We could go this year as far as the timber went!

When we think of the rivers of the North as we have known them in a canoe in summertime we think of an arctic which is swarming with life. For here are the summer nesting grounds of half the birds of the Western Hemisphere. The birds of the world go north to nest, and here their voices have curious songs and notes which are probably not heard in just the same way any place else on earth. To the northern wilderness alone is the rare secret song revealed.

One of the most wonderful of these birds is the wild goose. Few persons have ever been lucky enough to know all eleven kinds in the wild; the nest of one has never been found at all, so that the land of its origin remains a complete mystery.

Another bird is the great sandhill crane, a visitor from Mexico. Making long flights at high altitudes, he seldom pauses as he crosses the United States on his journey here each year, so that he is said to be vanishing. He is vanishing indeed from settled areas. Cultivation in the Midwest has entirely destroyed his old nesting grounds.

How often when camping on the river bar the flocks of geese and cranes make our days and nights joyful with movement and sound! Twenty-four hours a day the sun circles, the mosquitoes roar, and to our ears there comes from the far-flung heavens the hoarse triumphant cry of the geese. Some old memory in our being clicks into focus as we listen. Far away, muted by distance, the call comes to the ear like music on the winds. We look to the sky and search, straining our eyes. Finally, high up in the blue, mere specks, towards us comes the great V wedging its way through the air, a moving formation. Other smaller V's trail in the distance, long lines of birds. The long necks are outstretched, the cries are trumpeting louder; back and forth down the long line they ring! Pass far on, friends, to build your six-foot platform nests in the summer arctic where no man goes!

Or often we have seen the cranes in small groups of six or eight standing on the river bars, silhouetted at evening against water and sky. For a moment the loud cries redouble; the birds are drawn up to attention, standing straight and tall. Then slowly the long periscope necks relax, the watchful eyes search for goose grass, and all is still as the great birds graze. With long quick strides they file along the bar, looking ever this way and that. Let us make one move and they will be gone.

They see us here all right. It's hard to fool those wise old birds. If we should disappear into cover they would know at once that something was up. But if one of us remains in their vision to attract their attention...

It is seldom that we have ever been able to get within a hundred yards of the cranes. Unfortunately, one hundred yards offers a good shot for a native with a rifle, even though it is not satisfactory for photography with ordinary equipment. The pictures we secured in the North, we must say now, were secured entirely without telephoto lenses and under many disadvantages and handicaps.

Although sandhill cranes are protected under the Migratory Bird Act, which imposes a penalty for killing or possessing one of these birds, in the districts where they appear in abundance they are still called "Alaskan turkey" and are highly prized for eating. Game wardens don't get this far as a rule, and the Indians and even some of the white people where the birds live have never heard of the law. We could take a crane into the next village on the Koyukuk at any time with complete social approbation; nobody would think a thing about it.

Fortunately for the birds, they are wary. Bud hands me the camera. I go chasing sandhill cranes once more while Bud sits there getting ready for the makings of tea in the little old teapot and builds a small twig fire on the bank of some new river.

Through tall leafy willows and rose brambles and high cranberry bushes I crawl, while the small red tree squirrels and the little droves of chickadees pursue me, chattering and scolding, marking the progress of the enemy for all the world to know. My carbine is on my back at all times, even when I go for firewood. It is always loaded. We haven't kept a gun that isn't loaded in—how many years is it now?

All nature sings. There is never any loneliness or silence here. When you come to understand this world, you learn that it is actually bustling about its busy ways, just like any city thoroughfare. I creep through the bushes to watch the cavorting of the cranes, for these are the courtship days and they are putting on their dances. They run a distance with their necks stretched out along the ground and then leap high into the air and down again, sometimes grabbing up sticks or gravel in their bills to toss them on high—gay giddy birds!

But how often I have come to the beach where they were, to find only the three-toed tracks of an enormous bird's foot in the sand to tell me that they have been here and gone!

I limp into camp, scratched and bedraggled, with only the comment that those birds certainly can hike. Sandhill cranes will lead a person on for miles. But if anyone asks me why I go to the arctic, and insists upon a logical answer, I know of no better reply than to say quite truthfully (if one only could say that to people!): "I go where the sandhill cranes are dancing."

Surely the arctic of which we had been forewarned is not here. Butterflies and small frogs and bumblebees and wasps go their way, basking in the warm sun. The waters of the river are clearing to crystal green depths. We catch great northern pike on light tackle, using the little frogs, or the fin of the first fish, for bait. They help out on food. We eat canned gingerbread for dessert—interesting menus one gets here! I well remember our first lunch on the Koyukuk. It consisted of canned tomato juice, bread and butter, and cold roast surf scoter taken in hand.

Abominable bird, the surf scoter: along with the eiders he is the largest of the ducks, and like them is a northern sea bird which lives mainly on crustacea. We shot two of these on the Yukon from a large flock which were sound asleep on the water, it being our universal rule to take only those birds which have flocked up and which are therefore not nesting this year. These were big black ducks with unusually heavy bright orange and red bills and lovely orange feet with black webs between the toes. Their coats of waterproof down next to the skin made them almost impossible to pluck. The meat was rubbery and orange in color, pretty fair, although we had eaten better for flavor. The rich oils which ran down our wrists as we bit into the tough old sea ducks spoke of probably more Vitamin A and Vitamin D than most people get in an ordinary meal. They were a change at least, we agreed, from those last diminishing cans of indigestible army stew.

Now we are becoming less encumbered by cans and are almost glad to be rid of them, precious as they are. One by one the trappings are to be stripped from us and our ideas of what is necessary are to change. As we become each day more adapted to a life of wandering, life holds increasing enchantment. There are clouds, but the sun comes through again and the river is like glass, with every lush green willow and birch and cottonwood reflected in it from an azure sky. Two wild whistling swans float high upon the water in the distance, their plumage snowy white.

The water level is dropping fast. It leaves sculptured and spotless sand dunes of wavy designs where we can have a wash day for our clothes. The little rusted camp stove sends up its column of smoke on some beach and there is a frying of pancakes taking place today. Pancakes, that inevitable food of the camper—yes, you come to it. The mosquitoes are diminishing in their power. They hide in the shade beneath small twigs and leaves close to the earth in the woods, leaving the river and the ever-widening sand beaches to us. We are becoming very tanned and we go swimming every day.

The northern sun falls with long shadows over a vast empty land which dreams in blissful solitude. A human voice, hushed, breaks the stillness as we gaze out over it. Bud says: "This is such a perfect country, I can't understand why it isn't inhabited."

4

Why isn't this country inhabited? There must be some reason. Surely, considering the volumes which are being written about crowded social conditions, it couldn't have lain here all these years without anybody knowing of its existence! Or could it? Yes, we think that it could. When I was a young lady going to the university nobody told me about it. The average person in his tight home town has little conception of the spaces existing in the world, let alone in his own America in the mid-twentieth century, and it is remarkably hard to convince him of them. Even if he were convinced that the freedom of space exists and that it might be to his welfare to leave the crowd and have more elbowroom as his forebears did, he might not know how to do it, for he has lost the ability. That Alaskans know they have a good thing themselves in these spaces is shown by their hostility towards even the thought of legislation to open up Alaska to groups of Outsiders. Secretary of the Interior Harold L. Ickes became probably the most unpopular man to have wounded the Alaskan imagination in years for his suggestion that Alaska would be a good spot to dump 50,000 or so Jewish refugees from Europe. He has never been forgiven in Alaska. Uninhabited country often looks much like what we knew at home. With every mile you expect to see a farmhouse or a fence; sometimes you find yourself looking for telephone poles with their wires strung ahead across the sky, and then you must pinch yourself.

The reason for our landscape's being uninhabited by any of the countless populations of the earth who would give anything at this moment to be here lay, we supposed, in the realm of economic rather than physical obstacles. We could expect the land to be somewhat hostile to us, of course, because we were conscious of not having the modern means to meet it. Any land is hostile to a poorly equipped stranger. The United States as an unsettled land was not friendly at all times to the original intruders.

We traveled onward hopefully, enjoying rare glimpses of Alaska's brief tropical aspects. The climate seemed soft and beguiling as the United States must have been to the first canoeists. But days of precious swimming and sun-bathing could not last for long. They were brief and even somewhat unreal. Perhaps they were the sweeter for that. Soon the elements would unleash their fury and we should see the real character of this land.

Lush, still, tropical weather with mosquitoes sticking like hot pin points gave way to more mosquitoes and cold rain pouring down, down. Now the wind blew; the leaves of the birches and cottonwoods shook and rattled and showed their white undersides. Heavy cloud banks rolled up, and there was a suggestion of winter in the wind and in the creaking trees. This in July! On a day like this we noted that the young flapper geese were getting well grown so that they could practically take care of themselves. It was then that a sense of hurry, almost of desperation, would impel us.

These cold snaps come to be recognized in time as false alarms, but while they last, they convince you that winter is about to descend upon your head. Winter, after all, is the more natural season here. Garden crops of arctic residents, while successfully grown in sheltered spots on the continental side of the Brooks Range, are subject to a heavy frost at any time during the summer; however, winter itself comes on with many halts and delays and plenty of warning in good time—though we didn't know this then.

We had been making perhaps 25 miles a day going upstream and had progressed some 100 miles along our way with 150 miles more to go to the village of Cut-Off, when the motor began to act up seriously during a cold snap. We were tired from travel, but I think the worst of it was the sense of hurry that had begun to prompt us and the fact that we mentally did the work ourselves for every turn of the propeller of the failing motor.

It had become impossible to buck the current without burning the motor up. The experts who had sold it to us, guaranteeing that it had just been overhauled, had not even looked at it. Bud had, of course, cleaned out the parts himself, but the lack of the one small part on the water pump, which could have been so easily replaced in any machine shop at the cost of a few cents, caused serious trouble. All day Bud tinkered. Up till now the going had been smooth. But now at the end of each day nothing was accomplished— three miles, five miles maybe. We sat on the bank.

It was one of those cold days. Bud was standing there in his leaky hip boots, humped over the motor, with the cloud banks rolled up behind the somber spruce trees and turned-back leaves of cottonwood. Yellow patches from the sky dimpled on the water and on Bud's rumpled yellow hair as he said: "Don't be in such a hurry. We'll get there yet. We'll get there the year after if not this year. Even if we have to pole and line all the way up this river. That's been done before, too, plenty of times. You've got to remember this country takes time. It's not licked in a day."

"We'll *both* have long beards before we get out at this rate," I growled. "I'd like to know what to do. I can't see us dragging this boat 500 miles up this river, and the current's so slow at that, that it would take the rest of the summer to float back from here to the Yukon, and then what would we do anyway? Oh, why won't that motor run?"

"There's no use standing there wailing 'Why won't it run?' " Bud admonished. "We'll get there. Stop worrying. I can pole it if I have to and so can you."

Bud was not untruthful about this. For myself, I sometimes think I detest exercise. Any half-dozen of my college girlfriends could best me on the tennis court or on a hike any day. But unfortunately for me, I always had a weakness for looking at scenery, and of late years this had put me into some awful situations. I looked at Bud quizzically. He was not a well man by any means and he was pulling more than his share in every way.

"This is what I found today," he told me, as I waded disconsolately out from the bank to have a look. "See this part here? This is the drive shaft. It turns the propeller. But look at these grooves here. The thing is so worn down that one of these days soon the engine is going to start as usual, but these grooves are going to slip, and that will leave the propeller disengaged and helpless."

"That's serious, isn't it?"

"If I could get into a shop for a minute! But there's nothing we can do about it out here. Maybe I can figure out something for the water-cooling system, but we won't be able to fix the other. It's just worn-out. Whew, so am I."

"It looks hopeless, doesn't it?" I mused. "Even if we get up the Koyukuk there are other rivers ahead. I had always imagined we would ride up and down them."

"It will just take more time to get where we're going," said Bud. "We'll have to line and pole."

"What!" I ejaculated seriously, for the first time. "You mean actually *drag* this boat?"

"No, I'm not fooling you, dear," he explained easily. "You won't mind it after you're used to it."

I just sat down and clasped my head.

"This is no time for fooling," Bud elaborated. "It's only a few miles' difference one way or another. I tried all the way along the Yukon to trade for another motor, anything we could get, but you can't get anything. You know that."

Slowly I began to realize now that there had been signs all along of this eventuality. Bud had fussed with spark plugs whose pin points weren't adjusted to fire, and one day when the gas line had suddenly broken off for no reason at all, he had done something with pincers and pliers and we had gone on with a slightly shortened gas line. The motor was merely an unqualified wreck.

"Oh, I don't know why we had to get into such a mess," said I, getting morbid, and looking up the hateful river which was thwarting our hopes. "It's so beautiful—but I don't think I can do it. They all say it's no country for a white man, so what is it for a white woman? I think I'll go back to the States where I belong and just stay there"—familiar words, long grown meaningless.

"You old sourdough," Bud put in, "you're here because you like it, at least most of the time. And I'll tell you something. I think you've become a very good hunter. I mean it. You said you didn't like being an ordinary housewife, and you're as shiftless as they come, and you go feminine when it suits your purposes—but you have the temperament of a hunter and explorer. You want to see the world. I'll try to show it to you. Considering the state the world is in, I guess we can conquer our little problems here. Dragging a boat a few hundred miles isn't much."

Still, the tears sprang to my eyes as I began to understand for the first time the enormity of the task of conquering a continental divide.

Bud asked, "Do you really want to turn back now?"

"Yes." How many times in the future would I have cause to cry with misery if I didn't turn back now, right at the beginning?

Suddenly, as Bud jerked the starter rope, the motor behaved and away we went. I held my breath to see which way Bud was going to go. He turned the nose of the *Little Willow* downstream. Down the current we began to glide, swiftly and easily. Our last camp on the Koyukuk began to be hidden by the bend. Was it all over? Had I just ended my career of arctic exploration? Were both of us to just say good-by to it all like this?

The strings of my heart seemed to be attached to something which lay in the Northland the other way. I began to cry.

"Poor little wife," said Bud, "it looks as if you were meant to develop great big muscles. But you'll see the Arctic Ocean yet, darned if you won't. You'll pull the boat and maybe the sled, too, I know you will." As he patted me sympathetically on the back, self-pity suffused me.

Bud must have known that I really didn't mean in my heart a bit of what I said about turning back, for when I next looked up we were headed the right way again, limping laboriously and knowing there was trouble ahead, but still the right way, north to the arctic, where the summer's setting sun was beckoning.

We eat ducks and berries along the Alatna River, August 1944

Connie pulls the canoe up the Alatna River

5

The motor was about shot, but we kept plugging away at our mileage as best we could. Explorers are optimists by nature or I suppose we would leave the business. Everything would be all right. We knew that eventually, at the end of the summer and at the end of the river, some inner voice would tell us where and how to build our first winter's home in the arctic. We would furthermore make enough money during the winter in furs trapped or handiwork to get from a trader the precious gasoline and perhaps even a new motor, and the other things necessary to travel onward the next year. Indians did it, why shouldn't we? Then too, in this kind of life the very next day might bring some total change of circumstances for good fortune.

There were said to be two or three freighters expected along the Koyukuk River during the summer, and we had thought to hitch a ride with one of these. We had left word on the Yukon to have the first one along pick us up, and to this end we always camped conspicuously. At two o'clock one morning in the early daylight when we were sleeping inside the canoe staked out at the edge of the river, a freighter came by indeed. When Bud peered out he didn't know for a moment what time of day it was or where on earth he was. A human voice had awakened us, coming into our dreams. It repeated several times, "Hello there. Say, are you all right?"

Then as Bud shouted back that we were, the man said, "We thought maybe the bears had got your boat."

"No, we're O.K. Thanks. Hey, how far is it to Cut-Off?"

"Ten miles," was the remarkable answer.

"There's another freighter six hours behind me, and he's going straight through to Alatna," the man called across the water.

"That's just what we need," Bud shouted back jubilantly, thanking the stranger. As we heard the motors start up again, pushing the forty-foot barge ahead, Bud turned to me and said, "Did you hear that, honey? We've got ourselves a passage straight through."

The wonderful news sent us into such excitement that there was no thought of sleep after that. Fearing that the freighter might possibly even be ahead of time, we got up, bolted breakfast, and started for Cut-Off at once.

Arriving at a new trading post or river village you haven't seen is always a thrill and we had been looking forward to this for 250 miles—all of it upstream. As we rounded a bend our first impression was of some unusually attractive young Indian girls with blooming cheeks and dark hair down their backs who were gathering salmon from their nets. Trundled up the banks of the village from the boats by a community wheelbarrow, fish, fish were piled everywhere. Our progress had been so slow that the salmon had beaten us in arrival.

There was, as we expected, only one white man at Cut-Off, a village of less than thirty people. Jack Sackett, the man who had just passed us six hours before in his freighting boat, met us at his combined home and store. He and his half-Indian wife, Lucy, were Alaskans typical, hospitable, and homey. Jack Sackett is a man who knows more about the natives than probably any other man in the Koyukuk region and is the only one who can understand the northern Eskimo languages when he hears them.

When Jack first settled down here fifteen years ago after a life of prospecting, Cut-Off had a reputation of being one of the most dangerous spots left in Alaska. Killings were not infrequent. A traveler could never be altogether sure he was safe on the Koyukuk River. The Indians could not speak or understand English. Today, in coming up the bank from his boat to Jack's store, the traveler who did not know this past history of Cut-Off would never guess it. The people did not turn their backs or regard you with a blank stare. If a person ever thinks that the natural facial expression of the Indian is the stoical mask or the blank stare, he should think again; he obviously has never seen a normal friendly Indian village at its work and play but has been only in a village where there is much resentment.

A happy Indian village we found to be a noisy place. We were overcome with pleasant amazement to be greeted at Cut-Off by groups of sociable smiling people, all of whom wanted to shake hands from the first to the last, including the toddlers. Of course, strangers were an event here, but all certainly made us feel much at home. Some of these people had never been so far south in their lives as to see the Yukon, especially the girls and women, and rarely had one ever seen the inside of a school; this phenomenon soon became common to us. This lack of schooling and sophistication was combined with a completely unselfconscious charm. They acted as though they expected to be treated as equals as a matter of course, not as inferiors. This was because as a group they had never come into much contact with any white persons who would cause them to feel inferior. About the only white person any of them had known intimately was the old trader who had married in with the Indians himself, and they loved this man.

We tramped into the store and half the village followed. Old Jack sat down and lit his pipe with the utmost composure. An ancient potbellied, cast-iron stove of antique design sat, fireless at this season, in the middle of the floor. The glass case of the counter, with its few candies, combs and ribbons, and the bolts of print calico and the canned goods stacked behind on their dusty shelves, rested on a downhill grade. The counter was propped up on a packing box bolstered with some planks which were not quite thick enough to balance the other end and make the thing level. Three feet up the wall of the room from the floor was the muddy high-water mark of this spring's breakup a few weeks gone by.

From an inner door came Jack's strong, handsome young wife, Lucy. She had her month-old baby, born out in a tent, in a basket covered with mosquito netting. Lucy had attended one of the mission schools on the Yukon at one time. Now she kept store for Jack, did the bookkeeping, wrapped packages; the store was almost entirely in her care. Like most of these women she was good with an ax and would as soon be outdoors cutting firewood as inside doing housework; she and I could agree on that theoretically—at least I didn't like the housework. During succeeding winters, she always won the women's prize for driving the fastest dog team. Daily she fed her dogs and daily now went to her fish nets with her "kicker"—for she was handy with a motor, too—to gather her salmon, pike, and whitefish, which she cleaned, split, and hung on a rack in back of the house to dry for winter dog feed. In summer fresh fish were served on the table and in winter she snared white snowshoe rabbits and ptarmigan. Jack seemed to take a sort of paternal interest in all these things, seldom interfering, always kindly, keeping himself in the background.

"I couldn't live in such disorder and confusion myself," you might think, glancing around at this old-Alaska scene. For his home is *their* home, if you know what that means in an Indian village. But the truth of it is that you can't say exactly how you would live in this country until you start living in it. Sometimes the best way to get along with one's environment is not to create too much resistance. On the other hand, as with some of the other old men we have met in the North, knowing this man was an education in being a gentleman. A man who had lived practically all his life with Indians and Eskimos until he had become like one of them in a way, he was their self-appointed guardian and teacher; he had taught these people to speak English, and many of them to read and write. "First when they came to me and wanted to learn," he said, "I made them learn their alphabet, both forwards and backwards. They always want to write a letter to a friend right away. But I tell them they must first study. So, they start to study, and once they make up their minds to it, they learn quick, too. But they have to see the reason for it first and be able to apply it in their own lives, you know, or they don't want it. We write a lot of letters around here. Now they teach each other."

A prospector in his younger days, Jack had lived the life of a hunter and this was of main interest to us at the time. He told us he had lived for years near and among what he called the Arctic People beyond the timber. We listened at the store, like persons in a trance, to all he could tell us. The Arctic People, he said, had no permanent home; their homes were skin tents stretched over little willows. Where the herds went they went, and always they carried these little willow sticks on their sleds. That's all they needed, with snow, to make a home anywhere. For fuel they burned roots and the like and got by. "They were hunters, those men," Jack said. "The people here have forgotten how to hunt, but over the Koyukuk those others were hunters."

"Where are they now, these arctic hunters? Are there any of them left? Do they still live like that, and how many are there?"

"A couple of hundred—women, children, and all—not more," was his estimate. "There never have been many Eskimos, you know. They are a small group of people in the world. The Arctic People used to be up around Wiseman a few years ago. About every two or three years they would appear to beg a little coffee and tea. But they never trapped anything and never had much money. They were hunters and they wouldn't work."

Jack seemed to have large admiration for the abilities of these hunters to be able to live as they did, "where a white man would starve."

"They can get by," he told us, "with just a few old sticks and skins— oh, they have tents and rifles now, of course—and their dogs—fine, fat dogs—and they're at home and warm, too. They have learned nearly perfect insulation in a cold country, you see. They can lie down and roll in snow at 50° below zero and never feel it, wrapped in the skins of the caribou. You never saw an Eskimo with cold feet. They know how to dress for this climate better than the white man has ever learned, and everything he invents, even now, is just a poor imitation of caribou skin. If they don't eat for a week it doesn't hurt them. We could do the same thing, of course, so don't let it worry you. Indian, Eskimo, and white are much alike. That civilized covering we have is very thin, if our food is taken away from us. The secret in traveling where they did, though, doesn't lie in strength so much—it's knowing how."

We were bound for the Arctic Ocean via the Colville River next summer, we told Jack Sackett, in bursting excitement, and what did he think of the idea? He had never seen the Colville, he admitted, but it sounded like a nice trip if you learned to live in the country. He surmised that we'd find a fairly settled population of Eskimos scattered along the arctic coast once we got there, and a trader every couple of hundred miles or so; a friend of his had gone over to trade about twenty years ago, and we could say hello.

"Do you really think we'll get there?" we asked him.

He nodded his head. "You'll get there if you keep at it long enough. I've often thought I'd like to go over to the other side myself."

So, it was that we received from the old-timer at Cut-Off our first real encouragement. We had come all these hundreds of miles by rail and river just on a guess, until we found the man who could give us that specific local information which is better than all maps, who could speak our language, and who could tell us how to pronounce the funny names of those rivers we had considered our highways.

"We had thought to build our home this coming winter over Gull Pass at the head of the Noatak River, maybe," said Bud, getting specific. "Then early next spring we could cross by Howard Pass at the head of the Noatak and then float down the Etivlick so as to get into the Colville." Getting out our sectional map covering the Koyukuk and the Noatak districts, we pored with Jack over all the old familiar places he knew, converting the impersonal chart of marks and lines into a real land which now took shape before our mind's eye.

Jack had crossed Gull Pass and seen all the Noatak country back in 1918. He and a partner, taking a two years' outfit, had gone up the Alatna River to Gull Pass from the Koyukuk, and there crossed to the Noatak, but they left all their grub on this side in the end, because of the transportation problem. It was necessary to go on foot with only rifles and packs to prospect, and the two had merely remained the summer after all, living on nothing but sheep meat.

"I got thin but tough as a board that time," we recall him recounting, with a gleam in his eye. He almost seemed to regret that that day had passed.

"What food did you miss most when you had nothing to eat but meat?" we asked him curiously. "Bread," he said. That's usually what arctic men say.

"You cut out quite a piece of country for yourselves for one year," Jack commented kindly, as we waited for his judgment. "What do you want to go over to the Noatak towards the Bering Sea side for?"

Bud told him we had just looked at the map and had set our hearts on building our cabin this year on the head of the Noatak River. Jack informed us there was no timber there of which to make cabins. "It's just the same as it was in 1918," he told us reasonably. "No timber is likely to have growed since then because it never was timbered country.

"There's timber all the way up the Alatna on the continental side of the range," he continued, "but only one tree at Gull Pass. The Eskimos have thought the world of that tree for generations, so don't cut that one down. You could get into the Noatak River all right over the pass, but there's nothing there when you get there. The Arctic People used to hunt in that vicinity, but I heard they moved out of there, so you see if you should get into any difficulty over there at the present time there wouldn't be anybody to help you. It's 800 miles down to the town of

Noatak at the mouth of the river, you know, and no timber until you get there." That was about 200 miles due north of Nome.

Bud and I considered this. By the very calmness and deliberation of Jack's manner we could see he wasn't one to exaggerate. We wouldn't cross the Brooks Range that way, then.

"You want to get to the Arctic Ocean, you say?" he elaborated. "Meanwhile you will want to settle on some little Koyukuk tributary for this coming winter and I think you might like the Alatna River."

Jack explained to us that the Alatna River, coming into the Koyukuk about 250 miles farther on up above Cut-Off, was a clear stream, well timbered, and, what was daily becoming more important to us, accessible this season before summer gave out. The Alatna River is the dividing mark between the land of the Indians and the land of the Eskimos. On the river's southerly bank lay all we had known; on its northerly side you were in Kobuk land and could go on to the arctic coast—the little-known land where the caribou hunters live.

If we trapped any creek coming into the Alatna we would probably have a pretty good winter, Jack supposed. Of course, we would have a pretty good grubstake. Hunting parties of Kobuks might come by and sort of keep an eye on us to see that we were getting along all right.

It turned out that Jack guessed wrong about this last part. But at Cut-Off we had found our river. Its name was the Alatna, and its course lay entirely above the Arctic Circle, coming from the Endicott Mountains of the unexplored Brooks Range.

6

From Cut-Off we rode three days on a barge up the Koyukuk River to Hughes. The barge was pushed by two boats lashed together side by side—the outfit of Les James, trader at Hughes. When we first met Les at Cut-Off he was rather noncommittal because he hadn't slept for some forty-four hours on the upriver trip with a full load from the Yukon, and what remained of his waking mind was absorbed with the intricacies of the channel. The river was dropping six inches every twenty-four hours and Les had two more round trips on his itinerary for this season. Piloting on a river where there are no buoys or markers is always a nerve-racking occupation for the owner of a several-thousand-dollar freighting enterprise. On his mind is the danger of losing the whole outfit quite suddenly at any time. Five Indian men from Hughes were the crew, fine fellows all, and expert local pilots.

Our canoe, the *Little Willow*, was of course stowed on top of the barge with us. As it rained, I spent my time under cover inside our canoe lying down reading. The members of the crew were on different shifts, standing their watch and taking the eternal soundings with their long river poles. They had their meals in the cabin at different times, and we cooked our own separately on the boat's wood-burning stove when they weren't using it; plenty of hot water was supplied from a barrel rigged up with the motor, and you could wash, too.

At last, towards the end of the voyage, seclusion commenced to weigh on me and I was forced to emerge from my reading nest. Bud had long since become acquainted with his surroundings and made himself agreeable. There had been one tie-up a few hours because of winds, and the fish nets were set out to augment the food supply. I was privately thankful I wasn't asked to cook on board the boat for so many strange men. There had been motor trouble once, a mosquito clogging the carburetor. Mosquitoes in the gasoline are a nuisance as they sometimes get poured into the tank through the funnel or the gas pump, despite straining.

Now I followed Bud hesitantly along the catwalk of the moving barge into the warm, cozy engine room. Here we lingered many hours with friendly Les James, who had circles under his eyes from lack of sleep while we were surfeited with it. As the voyage proceeded there came to us a gradual unfoldment of Les, our neighbor and close friend while we were in the Koyukuk and Alatna River section of Alaska a year.

Les had been in Alaska ten years at that time. He always moved on to a new place just ahead of his relatives, he said. He described to us a childhood spent in North Dakota where the pioneer family survived drought by summer and raging blizzards by winter. Many a time, he told us, he had seen his mother grind up the grain of the cattle so that the family would have something to eat for supper. Nothing he had ever experienced in Alaska could compare with the privations and hardships he had endured in early North Dakota. Les seemed well endowed for the hazardous career of a trader in northern Alaska, which he began at the age of fifty-one. His former life as dragline operator and construction contractor had faded into the past. His life had always been hard; he had always had to work for everything he got. Life as an Alaskan trader was the most satisfying life he had ever found anywhere. He smiled as he said, "I wouldn't go back a year if I could."

We had heard already that Les James had a white wife north of the Yukon. Mr. James talked freely about her on the boat. "At first," he said, "when I sent for her to come to Alaska, I didn't know how she was going to take it. She was crazy to come here, but I realized she hadn't been out of the city in years. Here she wouldn't have any of the things she was used to—no place to go for entertainment, no white women for companionship most likely. Well, she stepped right off the airplane and we went to work together in a mining camp. She was waitress. We worked a year. Then we bought up this place. She flies over to Fairbanks a couple of times a year now to visit or do business, but she can hardly wait to get home again in a week. Lately she hasn't wanted to visit town at all. I have never seen such a change in a person. You wouldn't believe how a city woman could take to this life. Why, she runs the whole thing. She's responsible for everything that's done around Hughes. We have the swellest little layout you could expect to find anyplace, if I do say so."

Through the clear green waters of the rushing upper Koyukuk our two throbbing gasoline river boats pushed the flat barge ahead. A flock of around a hundred molting white-fronted geese were caught in one place between two high banks of the river as we crept up upon them. They were moving almost as fast as we to get away; the great flock melted as though by magic and we passed through, while baby geese tottered up the banks. Les reported that he and the boys had counted twenty-seven black bears along the river on this trip. As he himself was definitely not a hunter and did not like to see things killed, no Indian on his boat was allowed to shoot a gun as a rule. Jack Sackett had said Cut-Off often saw cranes and black bears on the sand bar directly across the river in front of his village, but they were not usually molested. This was possible because the people had their fish and lived in one of the richest trapping districts of all North America. However, below on the Yukon, it is doubtful if anything alive is safe from gunfire.

Hour after hour went by as we followed the beautiful winding river. As we neared "home" Les James knew every turn by heart, and we ourselves perked up to attention. What kind of place was this town of Hughes hidden away here, of which Mr. and Mrs. James were the only white members? What kind of woman was Mrs. James?

Les James was not wrong in having some pride about Hughes, a spot out of which he had doubtless made a good deal in recent years but which in turn he had caused to prosper, thus tying up a good deal of what he had. In business of this sort a person may be grossing many thousands a year, but what the gay crowd can't understand is that it is possible nonetheless for that person to be living in dirty work clothes and not be able to dig up as much as $200 in cash suddenly when he wants it. Things in Alaska are often done in terms of long-range credit. If you dream of becoming a millionaire in Alaska, where the skilled laborer traditionally has always made more money than bankers, university presidents, and Senators in the United States, see yourself first not driving in your limousine along a paved street in a top hat, but at work paving the street yourself, with millionaires who probably wear old clothes all of their lives.

Hughes was one couple's little model town. In contrast to the trader of yore who married in with the Indians or Eskimos in their more primitive state, Les James had a civilized white wife from the United States who worked with him. Former beauty operator and city girl, Mrs. James was a keen businesswoman and a natural born trader. Everything around Hughes was in shipshape order. Things were arranged for comfort and convenience. As soon as we arrived from the boat, fresh towels and hot water were supplied us; we sipped some sweet fig wine of Mrs. James's own brewing while the others took a Scotch and soda; then a roasted chicken and three newly baked cherry pies appeared from the oven and were set upon a ready-laid table.

It was the first time in our own wanderings over a period of months of extended canoe travel that we had ever been served any "store" meat in interior Alaska off the railroad. The chicken was explained by the fact that Mrs. James had fresh meat flown in from Fairbanks by arrangement with a town butcher shop. The fact that it cost a dollar a pound explains with no further comment why Indian Service teachers and missionaries don't have it. As for the old-time traders, they have gone without store meat for so long that they are past caring, and meat would be the last thing they would pay to haul in.

But eating in the North is a person's main recreation, so why not set a good table if you can? Fifty to a hundred pounds of those cuts of meat which the Jameses enjoyed was consequently kept fresh frozen at all times in an oil-burning refrigerator. A new electric refrigerator served for daily table use. A gasoline-propelled electric plant, with another identical generator in reserve, supplied house and store, and Mrs. James enjoyed the usual gadgets from toasters to beaters which satisfy the female heart. Alaskan women, in fact, probably have more power gadgets than the average.

The Jameses had built their house and store with their own hands, including plumbing for the kitchen sink, and had furnished their living quarters with rugs and furniture freighted in by river. I washed our clothes in the electric washing machine. They had no bathtub but used a tub of the folding "camp" variety for the Saturday night plunge.

The majority of white resident Alaskans, some 40,000 in all, get along without bathtubs. All bathtubs must first reach the Alaskan coast by laborious steamship route through the islands of the Alexander Archipelago, as must all ware, and it usually takes an extra year or even two years to get them into the interior by river boat after that. Somehow the bathtub always comes last because there are other things of greater importance. You get used to its absence.

While Les James rested from his upriver journey with his cargo, we were guests for four days at Hughes. Bud gave Les's boat motors an overhaul and I found myself official cook, because in addition to handling the store and keeping books—the only place we had found, incidentally, where each native is given a receipt for each article he buys, and his account is kept under a modern filing system—Mrs. James worked for the U.S. Weather Bureau as a side venture. She had five radio schedules daily, starting at 6:20 A.M., to report meteorological data, and she kept this up during every day in the year without exception.

Besides the apparent enjoyment of having a white woman to talk to, Mrs. James was taking amusement in "fattening us up" for what she considered to be a lean winter to come. The couple had a generous garden, and while it was too early for strawberries, far northern gardens not bearing harvest at all until almost fall, it yielded up fresh spinach and lettuce planted around the doorstep against the south wall of the house in order to take most advantage of the sun. A glass hothouse was maintained to supply their own fresh tomatoes, cucumbers, and squash, which would come later. Ice cream was popular with them, and their ice house was stocked with blocks of river ice cut each winter to supply the freezer the year around. I had a good time of it myself those four days in the kitchen; I recall a series of desserts with canned whipped cream on top. The Jameses liked a snack in the evening just before going to bed, and Bud and I took readily to this custom; we could eat all the time and never stop.

One evening at the Jameses' residence, because we had all been eating a good deal, I was just mixing four cans of vegetables together for a little salad and completing a layer cake to go with a gallon of ice cream when Mrs. James exclaimed: "What, no meat?" and that was the night we had two-inch T-bone steaks and a mountain of French fries as an afterthought.

The Jameses had put in a landing field and an airplane came twice monthly with mail or anything needed from Fairbanks. They had contact by radio telephone. If the Jameses liked to eat, they earned their country appetite, as did we all, by being great workers. Hughes represented ten years of work and still Les James spoke of the improvements he hoped to make next year. It is always "next year" with Alaskans.

The town's population consisted merely of a few Indian families, but the traders had the trade of some 175 Indians from the vicinity of Alatna above. "We don't want any more than we have here," Mrs. James told me. "Their health is much better when they live separated in small groups." At Hughes the Indian log cabins had tin roofs and none of them leaked, according to Mrs. James. Above all, here was no filthy waterfront draining into the river. Mrs. James made each family build its own toilet, a revolutionary reform in native life. How was it that the Jameses were able to accomplish in one right-handed stroke that remote goal of which missionaries and Indian Service teachers despair throughout the length and breadth of Alaska?

It was Mrs. James who laid down the law about sanitation and the common rules of health. She ordered hot water bottles and made each family buy one from the store, along with other standard household articles. A rigid quarantine was enforced with colds. In cases of occasional infection, Mrs. James used common table salt in the wound, a practice now approved in modern medical circles; the salt eats up toxic bacteria and leaves an insignificant scar. Mrs. James always made a great ritual over small cuts to impress the importance of general health habits on the person injured, as a teacher would do with a child. Les said, "You never saw such a bunch of babyish Indians as we got around here now." All rules were rigidly adhered to with a straight face. Almost every day Mrs. James held clinic at the store to treat children who came to be painted with ointment for impetigo, or perhaps a grownup arrived with an arm in a sling. Down through the years she had squeezed oranges flown from Fairbanks and made hot soups for invalids in time of need, taken temperatures and administered cathartics with gusto.

That the Indians at Hughes seemed to have confidence in their guardians was shown by the fact that when the traders left their house, store, and warehouse to take a trip, nothing at Hughes had ever been locked. "Something might catch fire, and we like to have the people come in once in a while to see that everything is all right."

The natives considered the store as their bank, and it was

unthinkable that any person would touch anything that did not belong to him, but which affected the community interests. A thief would have had a hard time of it there to get away with the smallest thing, with the sharp eyes of an entire town watching.

When we first stepped off the boat at Hughes Mrs. James thought to herself, "My God, missionaries!" She made no comment, but it was with explosive relief that she found out that we weren't looking for a mission site. Both the Jameses enjoyed a warm prejudice against anything even bordering on the clerical or religious. Their feeling was deeply rooted in childhood experiences. Hughes wanted a government school, but according to Mrs. James, the Indians begged her to intercede and not let anyone put in a mission school here of any religious denomination, which she promised to do for so long as she might live.

"You are really quite a missionary yourself," I told her, while she huffed. "There are a lot of missionaries who would like to know just how you keep Hughes so sanitary and clean."

"Oh," she replied, "you have to build a village yourself as you want it. The first thing is proper housing. There were just two or three filthy old shacks when we came here. We furnished materials and made the natives buy them on credit from the store and build according to our specifications."

"But how could you make them do that? What did you do for people to make them want to live in the town?"

"That's easy," she said. "We have more candidates to live here all the time than we can use. We don't go to the Indians, they come to us."

Now I saw how a trader has every advantage over the missionary and the government educator. A trader may keep the natives in poverty and debt, working for this one man, and neither education nor salvation can alter the fact of a trader's power. But a good trader, on the other hand, may create both work and prosperity in his little kingdom, and do incalculable good.

When a missionary comes, or a schoolhouse is erected it is at a village already permanently established for generations. Missionaries and teachers pursue the native to his haunts. They must wheedle and coax to hold their clientele. But a trader can come in, pick his spot, and settle anywhere in fur country, and the natives come to him. Many of Alaska's traders are in their seventies and even older, and these usually have no modern ideas of hygiene or social reform. But a modern, foresighted trader can make changes if he has a mind to. "We just cut off their credit at the store," said this pert, saucy white woman, "until they build a toilet."

Of course, traders located in an isolated place where there is no competition have an immense advantage in engaging in reform if they wish. The Jameses had the power to enforce certain standards because there was nobody else nearby from whom the Indians could get the things they needed. The town of Koyukuk below on the Yukon did not have this advantage. Had the trader attempted reforms there it is probable that the Indians would have moved to the location of another Yukon trader more congenial to them. Koyukuk had few permanent residents anyway but was just a bad meeting place for people camping in tents who perhaps never had any real home at all. Contagion and sanitation clearly could not be controlled there, among a people who do not even have a roof overhead. It was said that the Koyukuk trader himself, in his own wretched house, had gone bankrupt three different times trying to hold on. This was largely because of the undependability of the river. The Yukon may rise forty feet within three days' time, following an ice jam in spring. Cut-Off likewise, on the Koyukuk River, comes each year within an ace of being washed off the earth because it is built on low ground. But at Hughes there was good ground of sufficient elevation, not apt to be flooded.

One of the greatest difficulties the Public Health Department and Indian Service face in their work in Alaska, we considered in observing orderly Hughes, is that the river-eaten ground upon which the ancient villages are standing is oftentimes a bad foundation, where the old ways of doing things are taking generations to change. Modern government buildings touch only slightly the lives of the people, who within sight of these buildings carry on their old ways of life without sanitary facilities.

"Some of those villages ought to be burned to the ground to start with," said Mrs. James, "and then rebuilt on some new good high ground on the river."

"You see," I told Bud emphatically, "where a white woman goes, civilization follows."

Yes, Alaska needs white women.

7

Mr. and Mrs. James of Hughes were the last human beings we were to see for a year. Our four-day interlude with them was to be long remembered and dwelled upon. It was Mrs. James who put up our grubstake for us.

Prices at Hughes were fair at 75 cents a gallon for gasoline, $1.00 a dozen for fresh eggs or $2.00 a pound for canned dried eggs, and 50 cents for a can of No. 2½ size regardless of contents generally, except that the canned fruits such as pears or pineapple ran to 75 cents a can. Our simple fare included a half-dozen cans because the cans could be used as containers at the cabin. An experienced woodsman does not load his canoe with cumbersome cans from this point on. All of the food you carry with you into the North, if your living quarters are uncertain, must be of the dried and condensed variety. You will learn to live without fresh vegetables and fresh eggs. Even the dried eggs at $2.00 a pound are after all quite a luxury, like eating pure gold dust. Likewise, evaporated vegetables; we didn't take any but spent our last money for common dried fruit instead.

Incidentally, World War II will always be given credit in the public mind for the invention of the condensed foods, but this is not correct. Dried meats, parched corn, and dried peas are a very part of American pioneer tradition, going back at least three hundred years. Almost every standard vegetable, along with powdered and condensed milk and dried eggs, has played a large part in Alaska for years. Almost every imaginable dehydrated or condensed food that has proved practical has been used in some form before now by the pioneers of most habitable lands. These products were homemade before they were put up by large commercial firms.

Rice was chosen rather than evaporated potatoes because of its wearing qualities. It is both a dessert and a breakfast cereal, besides a main course with meat and fish dishes. Dried potatoes are about five times as expensive as rice. We had good reason to know that potatoes could be the common daily food of only a very agrarian and highly civilized country.

Including tools, traps, and such items as a kerosene lantern, matches, and so on, our bill came to around $150 for a year's outfit; this included also a $25 fee for transportation. Only a part of the total was actual food, as shown on page 95 by the copy of our bill.

Our mainstay of food was only 100 pounds of flour, 100 pounds of sugar, and less than 75 pounds of other assorted foods. This was an extremely small supply of food for a year. Usually 2000 pounds of food for two persons going out for a year is considered a reasonable margin of safety, but we were inexperienced in spite of our previous general camping adventures on short terms, and we had little comprehension as to how short our grub list actually was. No matter what a person proposes to do in Alaska, it is difficult to elicit any surprise from anybody, so no particular surprise was evidenced here. We had but $17 left, and privately decided that we did not want to extend our grub list so as to have to live and try trapping under the shadow of debt.

But the main consideration of all was that we realized our little canoe just couldn't haul any more. A larger boat, on the other hand, couldn't have got up into the Endicott Mountains at all, so there were no regrets about the *Little Willow* being too small; anyone would have had to travel light to get in there. That's just the way it was. It was cut the margin, or not go at all. No doubts about going even occurred in our minds. It was our intention to make a serious attempt to find a pass to the Colville River over the divide by one of the tributaries of the Alatna, in order to get farther up to the great river's headwaters than people had ever been. If we could find such a pass we intended to return the following summer with a new grubstake and cross over that way. But we never did. We saw this country only once.

Date			194		
M	Bud Helmericks				
No.					
Reg. No.	Clerk	Acct. Forwarded			
1	Pancake flour			1	75
2	Flour 100#			13	00
3	Corn meal			1	50
4	Sugar 100#			15	00
5	Rice 25#			4	50
6	Salt 6 sacks			1	50
7	Klim 4-5#			23	00
8	Eggs 5#			10	00
9	Apples 6#			3	00
10	Prunes 10#			3	75
11	Paper				25
12	Yeast 12 pkg.			1	00
13	Butter 4#			3	00
14	Shovel			3	25
15	Lantern			2	50
				87	00

Date			194		
M	Bud Helmericks				
No.					
Reg. No.	Clerk	Acct. Forwarded		87	00
1	Coal Oil 10 gal.			8	00
2	Gas 25 gal.			20	00
3	Oil Sac 30 1 gal.			2	00
4	Soda				25
5	Baking Powder				25
6	Naptha soap 12			2	00
7	Linen thread 4			1	00
8	Beans 21#			3	00
9	Hack saw blade				50
10	10 glasses (windows)			2	50
11	Nails, 6 penny 4#			1	00
12	Shot gun shells 12 ga.			15	00
13	Matches				25
14	Tea 1#			1	50
15	Molasses			1	00
				145	25

Date			194		
M	Bud Helmericks				
No.					
Reg. No.	Clerk	Acct. Forwarded		145	25
1	Bacon 7 ¾			5	50
2	Syrup			1	00
3	Auger			1	50
4	Chisel			2	00
5	Pumpkin 4			2	00
6	Tomatoes 2			1	00
7	Bit				75
8	Seeds				50
9	Traps No. 2			9	00
10	Drum			3	50
11	Stove pipe			4	50
12	Baby Ruth			2	00
13				178	50
14	Rifle 40.00				
15	Liquor 12.05				
	52.05			126	45

Date	July		194		
M	Bud Helmericks				
No.					
Reg. No.	Clerk	Acct. Forwarded		126	45
1	Transportation			25	00
2				151	45
3					
4					
5					
6	PAID IN				
7					
8	FULL				
9					
10					
11					
12					
13					
14					
15					

"If the motor holds, we'll be there in a week or so," said Bud jubilantly. "We'll be building our cabin. We'll take garden seeds and plant them on the river bars by the house right away." In the long hours of arctic sunlight, it would be possible to plant even as late as August and yet have some semblance of a crop to harvest by fall—lettuce and turnip greens anyway. It would all help out. Then there were always fish and berries. And game. The game laws, which make no distinction for a person having crossed over into the Arctic Zone proper, are nonetheless very free. We could take between us, on two resident hunting and trapping licenses, ten black bears, four grizzly bears, two moose, six caribou, twenty wild geese, twenty beavers, and almost unlimited numbers of ducks, grouse, rabbits, and muskrats if we could get them. Surely, if we could just get our two moose alone, we would have enough food on hand to keep us eating all year. This is what an inexperienced person imagines.

The problem of food in the arctic actually concerned us less than did the problem of clothing. What we would have liked to have was real Eskimo fur clothing such as we had read of in narratives of exploration and such as Jack Sackett described. This clothing has almost disappeared, unfortunately. The Indians at Hughes and Cut-Off dress in short jackets of cloth weave the year around; a person always near his warm house, and not facing the blizzards on the long trails that were once a part of life here, has no need of the old-style wear perhaps. But we're inclined to believe none of the population is well-dressed. Native seamstresses today are of no account: they are forgetting how to make the skin clothing of twenty-five years ago because substitute clothing, dreamed up in New York, is supplied by the store. All of these Indian men, the hunters, had what were called "parkas," to be sure, but these were mainly fancy jackets worn fur out and of little more than waist length, being worn for style. Since man has not changed this climate yet, tragedies are sure to occur when a population continues to run about ill-clothed, in disregard of its laws. The old ways of making and wearing a parka should be preserved by the people living in such a country, where it can be made from their own materials; all other equipment thus far invented by the white man has proved exorbitantly expensive and furthermore is not available yet to the common person. It can't be obtained, yet some sort of special arctic clothing is necessary for anyone who wants to see anything of the North outside of the interior of his own house or the interior of his airplane far away in the sky. Besides, houses and airplanes in the arctic hold in them an inherent element of danger, as long as the arctic climate exists; still, one must have the right clothing.

For the Brooks Range we didn't even have these dressy fur parkas, which are so popular with Alaskans in city life. We didn't even have the long fur-lined "Siwash" outer mittens which are generally considered a "must" for the trapper's hands, for fur clothing is some of the most expensive in the world itself, and in fact in the southern parts of Alaska is obtained only by long standing order if you know the sources. It was only a generation ago with us that these same long hide mittens, along with buffalo robes, were extensively used in our own prairie states by our frontiersmen, who lived largely out-of-doors. But if you possess a pair now you have practically a museum piece. I don't think I ever played in the snow as a child in the Eastern United States without getting cold hands and cold feet. People considered it inevitable. After living in the arctic of course I know now that being cold is merely a result of poor and foolish dress, resulting largely from style.

In the arctic we couldn't afford to suffer from cold because we had no one but ourselves to rely on for safety. Yet this year to start with we had only rubber shoepacs, which are something like arctics, for our feet, and which by northerners are considered warm weather clothing, not to be used for anything much below zero. Well, we would get by somehow.

Yes, a person can get by even in the arctic if he has to or if he wants to badly enough. This shows the arctic to be a very livable place. Many an old prospector has never owned any kind of parka made out of fur and yet has managed to lead all his life in the North; he sticks close around his shelter and must depend upon that. He may not mind this, for it is all that he knows, as it is all that most of us know. In real Eskimo clothing, however, one can be almost independent of shelter.

The day we were to leave, pushing the barge to Alatna seventy-five miles above, was an exciting day indeed. Mrs. James decided she would go along with us to cook and feed the "boys," and thus a kind of picnic was made of the event. Many pies and loaves of bread were baked ahead for the two-day voyage, and Mrs. James, diving deeply for olives, pickles, and jams, emerged with tubs of hot beans and five chickens cooked up with noodles: things to fill men up. Some of the

Indian families of Hughes were ready to leave for their trap line already, and with their dogs and various gear piled onto the barge they huddled beneath the shade of a canvas to get out of the sun. It was a moving, noisy, colorful panorama. Dogs were excitable and hard to manage. Their shrill screams rent the air as all together in a great chorus they threw back their heads, closed their slanted eyes, and howled. It seemed to be impossible for one man to hold his team in check, he was dragged skidding along the beach as his leashed team ran to greet their friends. Plumed tails in the air, waving—then the sudden flash of white teeth, and a dogfight was on.

When the fight was quelled we had time to observe that all manner of craft were being tied on at the sides and behind; we were a flotilla. Of course, the Indians had to take their boats with them.

The sun beat down and everybody panted; it must have seemed to everyone that we never would get started that day. One of the most patient and unruffled of our crowd was old Bill, the prospector. There is always a prospector on the scene somewhere, you may be sure of that. We never knew his full name; his counterpart must run into many hundreds. He was old and failing and had heart trouble. Having wandered into Hughes some months before, he had set up housekeeping in a vacant cabin Mrs. James arranged for him, and now the Jameses were apparently grubstaking him to get him started again. He was a sweet old fellow. He used to come to visit evenings in the Jameses' living room but had been shy of the "company" since our arrival. The gentlest and most unassuming person in the world, he didn't like to impose on anybody. Mrs. James would have him at the clinic to have his tooth treated with oil of cloves, "mostly because he likes the attention," she confided. Old Bill hadn't been Outside for forty years, and on this hot day in midsummer it was noticeable that beneath his plaid woolen shirt, open at the neck, the old Alaskan still had on his cleanly washed long-handled underwear of winter; apparently, he never took it off. He sought the shady side of the deck with alacrity.

If there was one sunny day in the year, the Alaskans were so afraid of it that they sat in the shade! The Indians, also heavily dressed, were merely enduring the summer until winter should come once more. Since they were afraid to expose an inch of skin to the ultraviolet ray, only their faces and their hands to the wrist had ever known the light of day. Here they were darkly tanned from some unavoidable exposure, but the skin on the upper arm or on their bodies beneath the clothing was remarkably fair—certainly as light as the skin of southern Europeans.

Old Bill was to be let off on the bank of the Koyukuk River along our way, close to the end of our destination, at the junction of the Old Man River. Here he planned to build a cabin and settle. Just how he would do this alone I did not dare guess myself, but this was what the old fellow wanted. He was completely wrapped up in his plans for prospecting, and it was believed that he could get his cabin up before winter somehow. Nobody thought that he could live too long, but all felt that he at least had the right to do what he wanted and die happy. There is an institution for such old men in Alaska, the Pioneers' Home at Sitka, but many pioneers prefer to spend their last days in some little cabin of their own along a river, living the life they have always loved.

During his stay at Hughes, Bill had taken a fancy to a young female cat about the place and Mrs. James had given her to Bill. Bill and "Little Miss Muffet" seemed to hit it off at once; they had a sort of understanding of their own. Along on the barge with us all came Miss Muffet in a crate, from which the prospector could scarcely bear to be separated, even for meals. We saw him stealthily leave a little breast of chicken at the edge of his plate and take it in his hand after dinner to his cat.

Bill wasn't alone in such surreptitious and shady dealing. I had my eye on a dog, the most melancholy I have ever seen. She had whelped, and with a single offspring was being taken to Alatna as the property of one of the Hughes Indians to be sold to another Indian for ten dollars. So starved and thin that her body was just a ribbed shadow on rangy legs, her eyes staring from her long skull like great limpid pools, she was said to be a "good breeder." After dinner I had collected a small bucket of scraps to take to her, feeling meanwhile that I was intruding on Indian business which was none of mine and that I might also be bitten for my pains, and I remember what Bill said to me, for my ears alone. He said only, "That was an act of God to feed that dog."

When we let Bill off the following day at the spot where he was to stay and build, the first thing he did was to let the cat out of the box so that she might refresh herself from the tiring trip. The last we saw of Bill as we pulled out, he was looking into the brush, calling, "Miss Muffet. Here, kitty. Miss Muffet."

"That cat will be a lot of company for him," said Mrs. James briskly. There was something thought-provoking about the scene which made the rest of us unable to say anything. Only children and old people can attain that strange affinity with the simple source of their beginnings from which the rest of us are for a while shut out.

When we reached our destination, the town of Alatna, also known as Allakaket (meaning the mouth of the Alatna River discovered in the last century by a Lieutenant Allan), it was late in the afternoon of the second day's ride. There were other larger towns far above on the Koyukuk River—the arctic gold camps of yore—but this was our getting-off place. Mr. James never went farther above because this was the extent of his business zone, and from here on the river becomes very swift so that boats and barges must be assisted by cable in places.

The town of Alatna, we learned, was split into two parts—the Alatna or Eskimo side of the river, and the Allakaket side where the newer cabins of both Athabascan Indians and the Kobuk Eskimos were clustering around the tiny Episcopalian Mission of St.-John's-in-the-Wilderness. Both sides of the river were generally called Alatna from old habit. The post office maintained by the mission, however, was routed as Allakaket.

The only white persons residing at this mixed village where the Indians and the Eskimos meet were two unmarried missionary women of middle age, one the schoolteacher and one the trained nurse. Airplanes landing twice monthly on the river bar in summer when the bar was not submerged, and on the river ice in winter with skis, were the main communications; airplanes are just barely beginning to get into the Koyukuk for general use. Another communication the two mission women could utilize in case of emergency was the radio telephone possessed by a half-breed trader at the other end of the village; he could notify Mrs. James of anything needed and, down at Hughes, she in turn could relay the message out to Fairbanks. A yearly visit of inspection by the Bishop was the greatest social event looked forward to by the missionaries, to whom the Bishop was a personage of immense importance. He was said to make an extremely rapid trip from Nenana in his speedy streamlined river boat.

A funeral was just about to be held when we arrived. The mission ladies had on their best dresses and were standing on the muddy bank surrounded by Indians. Their pale, delicate faces—pale from being much indoors—provided a false vision of missionaries as one might imagine them, standing always on the muddy banks of the world. Their backs were as straight as ramrods. Their greeting, a little formal, set us on edge by making our crowd feel like the roughnecks that we were. Then suddenly, in meeting those honest handclasps, we saw humorous eyes, lips that trembled slightly. We heard a catch in the voices and heard our own catch uncertainly. They were glad to see us! Why, of course they were! They were true adventurers, good comrades.

After the funeral the Alatna natives poured onto the deck of the barge and began unloading the wares. Mrs. James in green slacks, with a cigarette hanging from one corner of her mouth, was in the middle of them, giving directions, filling new orders with her pad and pencil, and asking personally about their children in the river jargon in which she was completely at home. While to Mrs. James business was a game to be played lightheartedly and with finesse, the missionaries did not have this point of view. They hated it, and moreover, in the name of the church, it was impossible for them to transact the least business in co-operation with traders which might give even the appearance of trading. For this viewpoint the mission was considered impractical and unrealistic, since the Alatna natives were hard-pressed for wares. On the other hand, one of the mission women at least had seen three different sets of traders come and go at Hughes during her time here alone, and the mission being much older even than this, it regarded all traders as questionable, or as mere vulgar upstarts. Despised for their small salaries, their pettiness, their small way of doing things, the missionaries nonetheless had something in their point of view which no money could buy.

The missionaries retired and awaited the traders at dinner in the house (the traders were bringing some large steaks) until the necessary work was completed. Mrs. James was, for the moment, in her element as complete kingpin. The friendly rivals soon met, forks busy, over the table, and the clicking and scraping of peaceful dining might have been heard.

Unloading our canoe from the barge and repacking it consumed precious hours that were all too soon gone for us. Time was getting short. It was the last week in July and we believed that our very lives might well depend on reaching before long the location at which we would build our cabin for winter. We had only about a month now before the first blizzards might be expected.

It was unbelievable how much stuff we had to put into that overloaded canoe. Although we were invited to dinner by our new friends, we regretfully turned down our last civilized meal, because our problems were too pressing to leave. The usual 400 pounds of gas, plus traps and ammunition, plus our own weight, was enough to sink us alone. Window glass and stovepipe were necessary for the house we were going to build: the list seemed endless. The crowning item on the very top of our load in front was an empty 55-gallon oil drum for cabin heater; secured for $3.50 at cost, it did in time prove to be an inestimable blessing after we got the thing up the river. We weren't going to be cold in the arctic, not us!

At any rate, when we waved good-by to the Jameses and to our kindhearted and anxious missionary friends, whom we were to know better only at a later time, and headed the *Little Willow* into the swift Alatna mouth, we were saying good-by to more than any of us knew then. We were certainly going to have a chance to make our own discoveries, whatever they might be, without interference. Without assistance, might be another way to put it. We saw no one for a year and never so much as heard the hum of a distant airplane. It is doubtful if anyone could have found us.

The experience of spending a year alone in the arctic wilds, to find out just what it is like, was worthwhile in itself to us, we can say right now. Our friends and neighbors on the Koyukuk River, sitting beside their stoves on winter evenings, must have thought of us. They were quite safe in their several-thousand-dollar establishments, which of course they did not leave for an entire year, not even to visit each other.

They must have thought now and then of the young couple who disappeared completely from sight and could not be expected to be heard of from the Brooks Range until the following year. They must have thought of us when Thanksgiving came. Did we have anything good to eat? What did we eat and how did we pass our time, and what were we doing on Christmas and when the New Year came?

We thought of them, too, perhaps as often as of our families, who, knowing nothing whatsoever of this kind of life at which they looked askance, were far, far away as though they belonged to a dream of another land. Did our neighbors on the Koyukuk look forward to seeing us again next summer that we might all exchange the news? What would be the news concerning the world?

Our journey was to take us far up the Alatna River, whose sources are in the unsurveyed Endicotts, lying, it is known, between meridians 145° and 154°. Our river, it was. It led into our country which still lies there now alone, beyond the end of the white man's telegraph and even beyond the sound of the white man's wars.

This country had been prospected before our day, so that a fair chart existed showing the valley itself, with the place names of the tributaries from which we could recognize where we were in the valley at any time. But beyond the valley on either side stretched white paper—probably pretty rough mountains there, and apparently no neighbors.

Our neighbors in the arctic for this year we had already met. They were the mission ladies at Alatna, at about 240 river miles, the Jameses at Hughes, 315 river miles, and Jack Sackett down at Cut-Off, about 500 river miles away.

PART THREE

The Alatna River

Connie drinks from the Alatna River

1

The river of our dreams is of clear water and has about it an air of eternal morning. It is summertime. In the sky the cumulus clouds of fair weather rise in white puffballs on far horizons. The sun lays a warm hand on cheek and body, an old familiar touch. Yet there is a little lazy breeze on even the hottest day to rustle the leaves just enough to show that leaves and grass are real. The clouds should move, too, a little, changing their conformations like herds of woolly sheep, and the birds should chirp.

Yellow spatterdock water lilies stretch and unfold themselves in deep green pools; dragonflies with turquoise eyes zip about their business and settle upon the water, scintillating beneath the sun. Wrapped in amorous embrace, other dragonflies with vibrating wings sail off in curves together at incredible speeds through sun-warmed space. The morose, sulking spider warms itself upon a hot rock; the jar of a footstep will put speed into him! Large black ants are at work in the rotten log. A bear coming along rolls the log over with one effortless sweep of a paw, the downhill way. Ants swarm about his feet; he licks with a long stained tongue. In the peat swamps many mushrooms have provided suitable incubation for the larvae of the flies that have pierced them. Here the beautiful skunk cabbage flower has waned like a waxen calla lily—for she is a lily!—beneath the last moon.

In the distance the climbing purple hills are seen, and the river flows swiftly. Mud bars give way to sparkling sand and gravel filled with small red garnets, and the glint of gold. Presently the river rushes over solid white granite and is bordered by troops of Iceland poppies, all nodding on their slender stems. Elusive arctic grayling, most aristocratic of all the trout, dart in alarm before the splashing intruder.

The waters of voluptuous summer are tinkling in the ear; the elements do not rage, at least not now. Look, and you will see— along the banks of an arctic mountain river in summer the moss is green and studded with orchid stars! From the crevices of rocks spring forget-me-nots in such arrangement as man has never seen. Then there are those hanging blossoms like Jacob's-ladder growing out of vertical mountain slopes, and you tug and pull—if you think of transplanting the thing—only to find in your hand at last an infinitesimal wilted droop of a wild flower, at the other end of which is a root seven feet long!

Here, in the country of the white reindeer moss, where everything must be brought in with you, there is no metal. An empty oil drum will be your stove and a single discarded gasoline can is treasure. Here your socks will become patch over patches held together by pieces of thread unbraided from old canvas. You won't mind living in poverty and rags, because the explorer is rich, and it is others who are poor. The wolves are his watchdogs and a drifted-over track is his highway, but he is glad.

The dream river is the more mystical and the more precious because it is so impermanent. It is like the smoke wreaths from the pipe of a dreamer which can be blown away in a puff, because here and now, in Alaska, winter is but one month away.

The same piece of country up here never looks the same again. In another season you would not know it. Another summer the bends of the river will never be as they are now. You can never know for sure that you have been there. You can only remember.

On every side the bare and rugged mountains of the arctic commence to rise. One by one they arch their backs above the girdling forest. One by one they fall away before the path of the river. Yet some of them hang in one place for days as you toil onward. Giving up their place with reluctance, they move backward like large jewels through the rarefied atmosphere, guarding their mystery.

This is the beginning, just the beginning of the greater North.

Nobody knows how many hundreds of great all-white, curly-horned, long-haired Dall sheep graze these pastures which are their natural habitat. There are tens of thousands of caribou and thousands of wolves, foxes, owls, ravens, wolverines, coyotes, lynx cats. These creatures are permanent, year-around residents, and live here because they like it and these waste lands of the world are their home. They know nothing else, nor were they pushed here, as some might think. They have always been here. They have never heard of the dwellings of men in their domain, where the largest city in America, if dropped here out of sight, might cause the authorities considerable embarrassment to find it again.

The tops of the mountains roll away, always to the north, some of them connected together in great chains, where a man can walk on top for fifty miles without coming down. Some give way to precipices above the river floor, flaunting sheer drop-offs along which the sheep trails go at their narrowest, connecting with the plateaus and far-flung lawns above.

There are blueberries and cranberries and bushes bejeweled with red currants, where Siksik-puk the fat hoary marmot sits beside his hole by a big rock and becomes sunburned across the front of his blue pelt from facing into the sun. High above, among the clouds, he watches over all and whistles his clear joyous call all day long across those steep airy meadows of his highland retreat. Below him rushes the river, forested by green spruce, filled with boulders, frothing, inaccessible. Below him gleam the lakes in which the giant salmon trout is swimming. Around him swings the ferocious golden eagle across the sun, a screaming huntress of northern lands.

When we went up the river we had two ideas in mind—first to winter in the Brooks Range and learn about the mountainous phase of the American arctic, and secondly, to find a pass to one of the headstreams of the Colville River through the Endicotts, over the Arctic Divide, if we could. That the first was accomplished we think the ensuing narrative will disclose. In it we shared a part of the unpublished experiences of many hundreds of human beings gone before our time, and we do not claim to be unique. But we believe that we can make some points about the arctic of today, the arctic which has leaves and grass all in their season just like any place else, the arctic where the passing of the primitive Eskimo way of life is having a greater effect on America's future than any of us can yet guess.

On the voyage between Hughes and Alatna we had crossed over the Arctic Circle and were now into the Arctic Zone. This imaginary line drawn around the earth designates the latitude where on December 21, the shortest day of the year, the sun does not rise above the horizon if the land is perfectly flat at sea level. As you go north from here toward the North Pole there are correspondingly more days of no sun during midwinter and more days of midnight sun during the summer. It was too late for us to catch the midnight sun this season, but midnight daylight we did have for a while yet, as we had had it from the beginning.

The Arctic Zone has more hours of daylight than all the other zones of the earth except the Antarctic. The main difference is in the angle that the sun strikes and in the way that sunlight is distributed. Here, it is distributed all at once in one season. This is true also in the Temperate Zone to an extent; it is seen by the long days of summer as contrasted with the short days of winter when darkness may fall as early as four o'clock in the afternoon in some areas of the United States. It follows, therefore, that as you go northward this seasonal contrast in daylight hours becomes increasingly magnified, even while cold predominates in climate. The seasonal contrast in climate is found to be greatest of all in any area comparable to an inland plateau far from the oceans, and so it was, in a way, with the Brooks Range.

The sun, striking on a slant, seldom reached into the canyons of the Brooks Range, but bathing the slopes of the mountains far above, it made some of them positively hot in summer. Here, then, there were no glaciers and no eternal snows! The snow melted from sight in summer on all the tops of the mountains in the range that we saw in the interior area above the Arctic Circle. We had never seen this before in the formidable coastal Alaska a thousand miles to the south.

It is possible for a person to get badly sunburned in the summer in the high latitudes, but the season is so brief, and the phenomenon generally so localized, that the main question which raises itself is how human beings in the far North can be expected to get along with so little exposure to sunlight. It would be interesting to analyze the sunlight in these regions for its health-giving properties, inasmuch as none of it is received by people, animals, or plants directly, but always on a slant. If this sunlight is defective in the growth-generating qualities it should have, there is no real evidence of this, despite people's suspicions and fears. One noticeable quality which did impress itself on us is its bleaching power. The far northern sun can turn a red shotgun shell almost white within a few days, and fabric clothing of brightly dyed colors bleaches out in no time north of a latitude of 70°.

The main change in your attitude toward the sun in the North, we had already learned, is that you become used to its absence from your direct vision during certain periods. You realize that it is always somewhere nearby, and the long hours of twilight make its absence scarcely noticeable so long as there is light. South in the coastal regions from which we had come, from December to February the sun never gets down into the bottoms of deep valleys where most Alaskan towns lie, and often because of local weather conditions we had gone weeks, if not months, without seeing it.

This winter we would have our first real experience with the Arctic Night. Although we had a bottle of vitamin capsules along with us, little faith was put in them by themselves, but we trusted that the arctic could supply our needs if given a chance.

The problems of human existence were the same for us as they have always been for our predecessors, and we were to meet them with much the same means.

Our food consisted of exactly the same basic items carried by the American people of old: bacon, beans, flour, sugar, yellow corn meal (or pea meal or oatmeal), rice, dried fruits, tea—and we had powdered milk. These are the items the wilderness traveler still takes, for nothing better has been invented for his purposes—at least these are what he is still using in practical reality. Thousands of Indians and other northerners live on these.

But what about vitamins? I don't want anyone to imagine that I was ever, from the very beginning, one of those housewives who ignore the place of the important and much advertised vitamin in the family diet; we had them every day. As a matter of fact, when we were first married, my husband was plotted in curves on a daily nutritional chart. I counted all the units of vitamins and minerals which we ate at each meal for a while and added them up in calories. Originally, we were both brought up, of course, to believe in a daily health quota, which, if I remember correctly, goes something like this:

1 serving lean meat or fish daily
2 cooked vegetables, leafy green or yellow, and potatoes
1 or more raw vegetables
1 fresh fruit
1 egg
1 pat butter
1 quart milk for children, 1 pint for adults
1 serving whole-grain cereal or 1 slice wholewheat bread
1 8-ounce glass fresh citrus fruit juice or a citrus fruit
10 glasses water

Children are still doubtless being taught this little refrain in the schools, as are the mothers of families who attend nutrition classes, and with good reason. These items are supposed to meet the minimum nutritional requirements, plus whatever sweets and starches you want to add. But if these minimum requirements must be filled in the manner listed, how did all the population of the earth get along these thousands of years until now? We can surmise that human beings the world over have always had the same fundamental nutritional needs which our experts have worked out for us in terms of our standard of living for today. But the different civilizations of the earth have met their nutritional needs in different ways! For instance, in the United States, a lot of us get our Vitamin A from properties associated with carotin in the "yellow" of butter, cream, cheese, oranges, and egg yolks, to take a few examples. (New York City is an exception. It proves its independence of Vitamin A by being the world's great fashion center in pale-yolked eggs.) But butter, eggs, and oranges are expensive Vitamin A in most of the world. People in the South American countries, Mexico, and India may be doing all right in Vitamin A by eating quantities of yellow sweet potatoes, melons and yams, for all we know; these cost a great deal less. Alaskan Indians may be doing all right on Vitamin A by eating salmon, when they never saw either a fresh egg, a sweet potato, or an orange in their lives, except conceivably as a novelty. At least we know that all these diverse people must be getting some Vitamin A from somewhere. In this way one could run through the alphabet of vitamins and all the known minerals and show how, or make a good guess how, in different parts of the world the human being is more or less meeting his nutritional requirements just by accident and without even knowing it.

Bud and I never started out in life to become nutritionists, but our trail was to take us into the field of nutrition. Here there were actually none of the prescribed items for food, and what we ate depended on what we could get. We were informed enough to know, for instance, that scurvy is the inevitable result of living on a dried-foods diet such as we had chosen. The men who formerly died of scurvy in northern regions and elsewhere lived on such a diet. Since we had not one item in our outfit possessing any antiscorbutic value, what should we do?

Scurvy was the traditional plague of the gold seekers, and almost no arctic expedition was without it. Yet now in the same land we have never seen a case of scurvy nor would we expect to unless we were physicians associated with a large hospital. Otherwise well-informed educators in modern-day Alaska don't know what you are talking about if you say "scurvy" to them. Have we forgotten so soon?

From the time of the Civil War it became recognized that scurvy came in when fresh fruits and vegetables gave out. All people venturing into those areas where fresh fruits and vegetables were not available in sufficient quantity were apt to come down with scurvy, sometimes within four or five weeks' time, depending on the individual constitution of the person. Scurvy was peculiar in that it was a white man's disease, however; it belonged to the white way of life. Natives living in the difficult regions never had scurvy themselves! In the old days this was attributed by uninformed people to the "primitive" constitution's somehow being different from the white man's and having different needs. Oddly enough, there are still people who believe this.

There were many supposed cures. In the days of Jack London in Alaska, the eating of raw potatoes or raw onions was strongly advocated: this idea arose probably because these vegetables were the most likely to be in camp. You can talk with old fellows all over the North today who will give you their own cure, such as the eating of spruce needles or drinking of rain water from the base of a spruce tree—only a mild poison if taken in small doses!

Prevention lay in maintaining a certain amount of fresh things in the diet, but importation of them to every remote creek and gold camp in the North Country was never possible. For a long time, scurvy was a barricade against penetration into the whole great North, for there were only a few edible wild plants there during much of the year; some of the missions have lists of these plants, used today.

At last, with the isolation of Vitamin C or ascorbic acid, scurvy generally disappeared. It disappeared in the North because of the new availability of the little tin cans of juices and whatnot on the traders' shelves. Today's Alaskans who live out of the tin cans, while sophisticated in many ways, still have no idea of what scurvy is or was about, and it seems likely that if it were not for airplane service and the traders' ability to supply foods other than the dried variety, north Alaska's population would be beset by scurvy again.

But the explorer will find it useful to know something about scurvy. He knows that if he gets far away from fresh foods in an unsettled country, he must depend upon the country to provide. In 1881, Lieutenant P. Henry Ray, 8th Infantry Commander of the International Polar Expedition to Point Barrow, wrote: "Fresh meat is the great safeguard against scurvy in this region. I never saw a trace of it among the natives, and meat is their only food. The immunity of my party from all disease or sickness of any kind I deemed was owing to the fact that through our own exertions and with some assistance from the natives, we were seldom without it."

It now seems to the broad-minded modern person almost incredible that so many like Vitus Bering, the Russian explorer who died of scurvy and was buried on a rocky island of the Bering Sea, could have lived for years with the antiscorbutic element on every hand in the presence of the wild game seen daily and not have discovered for themselves the benefits which fresh meat contains. Human food prejudices and notions on diet remain deeply ingrained and are difficult to change.

We ourselves expected to eat berries, fish, or meat every day from the outset, because even if we had all the dried foods and ready-prepared foods on earth crammed into our canoe, their quantity would be small safeguard for health over a prolonged period of isolation. Far from being squeamish or afraid to eat any new meat, we were wise enough to realize that the human constitution cannot store Vitamin C or the antiscorbutic element for any length of time against the future but should have daily replenishment of it.

The arctic is the land of great meat feasts. It produces nothing else right now. Why not enjoy it then for what it has? Even the game laws make provision for this, taking into consideration that in Alaska persons in isolated places are naturally expected to use the fresh meat they need.

Our experiences in meat eating were to go far beyond the casual experimentation we anticipated. But we have often thought that maybe it is better that it turned out that way, if it will help others toward a better understanding of the northern world.

Anyway, it's a certainty, that we had vitamins to throw away during our northern hunting existence, and we didn't have to give scurvy a second thought. The fact must be known now to most people who read, or should be: the antiscorbutic element exists in the fresh qualities of any food, no matter what the food is. When you can't get salads garnished with orange blossoms, any fish or animal you can get hold of which wiggles or crawls, and which you can kill, becomes oranges and grapefruit to your body. Modern man is a lucky fellow, even given only a canoe. He can meet his adversaries and turn them aside because he is armed with knowledge.

Connie picks up every spilled bean

2

As soon as we got onto the Alatna River we saw at once that our motor was almost useless. The Alatna River was 100 yards across, widening out to 300 yards in places, but it liked to split up into channels and islands. When it did this, of course there was not enough water left to go through any one channel with a motor. It was a mountain river and a swift one. A strong motor might have gone through many places in the deeper swift channels, but ours lacked power. In some seasons with high water, people had found the Alatna navigable for long stretches. But it had many turns, and while it was navigable at times along the straight stretches, at each turn we found ourselves brought up against shallow riffles rushing over naked bedrock. Not only was tracking or lining going to be necessary, but we would have to climb our way and swim our way up it.

Our friends on the Koyukuk guessed nothing of this. The Alatna River was known to them merely by hearsay; except for Jack Sackett back in 1918 none of them had been up to it, and it was imagined when we started out that we would be at our location and erecting our cabin soon. But this was not to be so easily attained. Setting our goal at ten miles a day, we began to fight up the river, probably pulling ourselves as much as we used the motor. The method was continued as long as summer held out. Our necessity was to keep the boat moving, and we did. If we didn't always make our ten miles, at least we gave it a try. There were a lot of miles and a lot of turns on that river.

In case no one has happened to hear before of people conquering the arctic in bathing suits, this is what we did on the Alatna River. One unusual factor especially made this possible: we had discovered by accident perhaps the only place in Alaska or in any arctic regions where there were almost no mosquitoes. The steep mountainsides of the great arctic range were well drained and did not incubate them. Here in this winding valley of the mountains, sheltered from winds, blessed by the golden sun pouring down its heat for eighteen hours each August day, in a climate high, dry, and exhilarating, we could indeed use the bathing suits brought along for a lark!

However, lest any of you commence to equip yourselves solely with bathing suits to come North, let us say quickly that we had never before used them in Alaska until this summer, and that we lived in bathing suits or abbreviated attire on this occasion largely because we had got ourselves into a spot.

In my clumsy hip boots, which leaked anyway, I was wet to begin with as I thrashed up the shallow stream bed dragging the canoe by a stick thrust through a noose in the lead rope. Then my trousers got soaking wet when I got into the canoe and sat down again with the boots on, because they flooded backwards over me. This got the boat full of water. Most important, while wading in the water with such weights on each foot I was unable to be of any real use because of the great water resistance. Legs bare to the thigh, though, can slice right through swift water when pulling heavy loads.

"I won five silver cups once when I was a kid, for water sports," I boasted to Bud with clenched teeth, "and *this* comes off right now. To pull this boat, I'm going to undress!"

After the first day I lived in a bathing suit or a long-tailed shirt and a pair of old light shoes without socks, to fight the river. That was my job. Bud's job as mechanic and chief navigator was a little different. On his long legs he waded in hip boots, with his .22 pistol now on his belt at all times. But I became a water nymph in earnest, forgetting that I had lost the extreme agility of childhood. The water was cold, but I could thaw out around hot spruce fires built on the riverbank on the more chilly days. Although sometimes I felt nearer fish than human, I seemed to thrive remarkably well during the 240 miles of this travel.

Bud had put what is known as a "skak" on the motor. This had been advised by his Indian friends at Hughes. This was a piece of strap iron which projected down into the water two inches below the whirling propeller blade to give us warning of the depth and prevent breakage of the precious propeller or the "break pins" on the rocks of the river bottom. When we felt the skak hit bottom, Bud had to cut the motor instantly. He kept sounding all the while with a willow, the lower part of which he had peeled with his knife to denote the safety depth, so that when he saw the white wood of his stick appear above water he could tell almost exactly when we were due to stop the motor and walk. With one hand guiding the motor he punched all day into the water with the other. The water was so clear that its depths were deceptive. Riding along slowly, while the motor strove to keep its pace against the current, we would gaze down glassily at the round symmetrical inlaid pebbles, gleaming up at us in yellow, rust, and blue black. When the *Little Willow* nosed her way from side to side of the river in her endeavor to find a channel, Bud would deduce abruptly: "She shallows all the way across. Get ready to go overboard." This meant that I had to get out of my alpaca-lined jacket quick or go overboard with it on—my winter coat! As soon as the skak hit bottom and Bud cut the power off, then out I would leap in a flash into the ice water, grab her by the lead rope close to the nose, and lay into it for dear life. Bud would join me in the water as soon as he could get overboard. Working his way to the canoe's bow he most frequently would take the lead rope from me while I would drop back to take a death grip on the stern handles and push, taking advantage of the boat's wake, where it was easier to stand. In this way, pushing and pulling, up around the steep turn we would march, inch by inch.

To lose your outfit might be almost synonymous with losing your life. In dragging the canoe Bud knew that should he lose his footing in a bad spot the canoe would swing sidewise so quickly we wouldn't know what happened. Then no power on earth could hold her. Whenever this happened I just let her swing clear around with the current and held her there by the stern handles, nose downstream, until Bud got there. Once or twice I was pulled downstream in this way on my feet, dragged with the boat. In such water if a person lost his footing seriously he might never gain it again, even though the water was shallow. But whatever happened, one of us must stay with the canoe so as not to lose it.

Often on the bad turns Bud would be almost horizontal as he

bodily lifted the 2000-pound load up such a hill of water. At such times the heavily loaded boat might be two thirds under water as it plowed its way, canvas tacked down tight, drum stove on top of the load in front, making a resistance nearly insurmountable. Clinging to keep my own footing at such times, using the bulwark of the boat as a means of support while I trudged, I doubt seriously if I was the powerhouse of strength to Bud that he seemed to think I was. Mine was not an iota of the strength needed. Very probably just the knowledge that I was there gave Bud the will to do what he did. He always said that it would have been quite impossible for one person to have got the canoe up the river without a partner.

    Not all the marches we made were difficult or dangerous. On the easier marches I would sometimes lead the boat alone many miles, not seeing Bud until teatime, while he scouted the country ahead, for it was necessary for him to support us meantime. Many of these days that I pulled the boat along the edge, footsore from the rocks rolling underfoot but otherwise feeling very fine, I began to be filled with some of the most solid contentment I had ever known. While it was the kind of back-breaking labor that puts a person to bed at the end of each day thinking he will never rise again, he nonetheless invariably rises and finds it the kind of life which makes him eager to see what each new day will bring.

    The short distances the motor was able to take us made us retain it for what service it could still give. Dragging the motor and its load of gasoline became pleasure of a sort because there was always the hope of a future chance to ride a few yards.

    A person can't keep up work like this and not get very slender, however, in short order. There was exhausting work which seemingly never ended. Just the camp work alone at first was enough to keep two persons worn-out all the time, merely attending to their own needs. Now the tent had to be pitched each night and rolled again next morning. Our tent poles looked like corkscrews. Erecting the stove in the tent without regard for wind direction caused the stove to work in reverse. If a rainstorm came we found, we had camped in the run-off. The canoe had to be staked out with ropes at each end and usually a third stake ashore for good measure, since beavers or porcupines have a way of gnawing through ropes occasionally when a camper is asleep, just for the fun of cutting a canoe adrift.

Possible floating driftwood and the depredations of bears were boat hazards which were always on our minds. Wading back and forth to unload sleeping bag and grub box, to get a bucket of water, to cut firewood, to lay spruce boughs for bedding after the day's traveling was done, we packed loads up steep banks and through briar patches before it was possible to eat or sleep. Once in making camp I lost the stove from my grip and in dismay watched it go banging down over the embankment, but it was a strong little stove. "Fish the stove out of the creek," I yelled through the subsiding din. We got it. This often happens in rough country.

On the big rivers we had been in the habit of doing our odd jobs, such as cleaning guns, sewing on a button, or picking birds, as we motored along. Now all these chores were added to camping time. Birds are pinfeathery in summer and we almost gave up on them. Natives have a trick of roasting summer grouse or ducks in coals or hot rocks with the feathers left on, but we never have tried this. We skinned our summer birds and always had them boiled with rice or with baking-powder dumplings in the Dutch oven.

At our reach at all times as we traveled had to be paddles, gasoline, and oil; the tool kit; rifle, shotgun, and the .22, with ammunition for each; knife and matches always carried by us both; cameras and attachments and available extra film; raincoats or heavy coats for cold weather; work gloves; binoculars; the diaries and usually the personal kit, including toothbrushes, soap, sewing paraphernalia, and so on. Usually all these items were used each day. There was a lot to think about in all.

One of the things I thought about at first was being murdered. I bring this up because one of the questions people ask is about the North's general safety from a standpoint of law and order.

"One never knows," I would think of an evening just before falling asleep. Since we were really off the beaten track it would be downright easy for one of the Koyukuk River natives to have followed us without our even guessing it. Knowing the country, any person who so wished could leave his boat on one of the turns of the river behind and taking some short cut overland could ambush a newcomer at his camp on one of the turns above. We knew that many a person has been ambushed and shot for his outfit, and ours was of the kind which would be a strong temptation to natives. Later the missionaries told us that there are indeed natives in any village who can remember having taken part in some past killings. "They know more than they're telling." However, northern Indians and Eskimos are peaceful people on the whole, and they furthermore attribute almost supernatural abilities to the power of the government, which has rarely if ever failed to track down the culprit and gain its revenge. When you stop to think how easily a body could disappear and never be found in such vastness, it is remarkable how extremely rare crime is. Natives and whites alike here are most kindly people. They are much more likely to risk their own lives in helping you in this part of the world than to wish you any sort of ill luck. Yet in the more settled United States, a person is being murdered every few minutes throughout the twenty-four-hour day. It would seem in all that life is more dangerous throughout the more settled and populated countries.

We had nothing to fear from human beings then—which was more than the rest of the world could say—and we had nothing to fear from animals because we had good guns. Soon we were far from all possible human enemies.

As for animals, the friendly Hughes Indians had told Bud that they had not always lived without fear. The old men could remember the time before guns, when food was much harder to get, and the animals, according to their stories, were at the same time bolder and more disposed to attacks upon men than today. At least they thought so.

The shortage of our food was our only possible concern. All our staple provisions were packed in such a way that we couldn't easily get at them while traveling—and besides, we hesitated to break into our winter's grub supply so early. One time when the *Little Willow* got cut by rocks, we got a good meal when we had to unpack everything to turn her over and sew her up. Bud had brought along some empty five-gallon gasoline cans; we built a fire and, being careful not to melt off the soldering, boiled out the fumes, wiped the black soot off the bottom of the cans with grass, and the rest of the day spooned and poured our 100 pounds of sugar and our 100 pounds of flour into these cans and screwed on the small caps, making them airtight. "We were lump-heads not to think of this in the first place and darned lucky we saved our stuff," Bud kicked himself.

An important hope of subsistence during the summer as we traveled was fish. One of the things we had looked forward to were

The Alatna River

marvelous days of fly fishing. But occasional attempts had only proved that grayling were not to be caught in the main river; they would have to be got in the swift little brooks or side streams which would be numerous later on, but which did not appear on the map for the first hundred miles.

It is said that no one can starve to death wherever there are fish, and it is popularly considered that anyone can catch fish anywhere in Alaska. That a person does starve every once in a while, however, the Alaskan always has in mind.

Included in their emergency food rations and emergency camping gear, along with rifle, ax, and sleeping bag, the Alaskan airplane pilots during a part of the year, at least, commonly carry fishline and hooks with the idea that a party that is forced down can always await rescue or possibly make its way on foot to the nearest settlement, meanwhile living on fish. Don't be too sure of this. Don't be sure you can always catch fish on hooks, or enough fish. From mature consideration of this subject we can now advise would-be fish eaters to take along a good fish net and a knowledge of its use. A person can stand on the bank and starve to death waiting for a fish to bite or starve to death just pulling them up one by one—a discovery on our part!

Lacking a fish net as food insurance we were soon to realize that we were dependent at all times on the sportsman's entertaining but most uncertain game of luring fish singly on hook and line. Fishing by hook and line, furthermore, took valuable time, when traveling was imperative before winter should catch us. We had to eat: we were caught either way.

If we had had a net it could have been set each night to work for us while we slept. Being sportsmen, we had not thought of this. We had not considered that exploring in truly wild, uninhabited country was anything more than a kind of vacation, and that the circumstances the explorer meets are different from those of a civilized land with civilization's customs as we were trained to them.

Bud had made an attempt to get a net as a last-minute thought, but as all the nets the village possessed were then in use, nobody could spare one. These were gill nets of salmon size.

We saw several jaded-looking dog salmon coming up the Alatna and one monster king salmon, which, weighing probably sixty pounds, rolled out of the water on one occasion under our eyes like a red and purple whale while our stomachs rolled over in time, but as a whole there wasn't much of a run for salmon in this river so far back in the mountains from the sea. Those fish that arrived were almost fallen to pieces with rot; the sea gulls, well-gorged on the early summer's birds' eggs, awaiting them even here. We knew we could probably never catch these salmon on lures. Another fish which inhabited our river, and which does not bite, was the delicious far northern whitefish. Many principal food fish never bite at all!

We turned to looking for spruce hens, which are small northern grouse. In the summer these are scattered widely throughout the forests, so that it may take a good deal of tramping to find one. In the fall, as every inhabitant of the wooded parts of the Northland knows, they may appear by the hundreds if not by the thousands along the beaches and open places to peck gravel, where they will stand their ground and ruffle their feathers when approached. In the fall they are most commonly shot with the .22 rifle, either on the ground or as they sit on the branch of a spruce, from which it is difficult to get them to flush. For this behavior they have also been named "fool hens." Their foolishness derives from their instinct for camouflage, at which they are well-nigh perfect.

The limit for "chickens" at the present time comes to 1200 birds a person for one season when you figure it up. Nobody takes that many that we can imagine, but the traveler, trapper, and prospector customarily take them as needed. In the North the spruce hen has not yet been given the status of an important game bird. Large bags of the grouse may be prepared all at once within a few days of winter, since after the snow once falls and they turn from berries to a diet of straight spruce needles, the meat is popularly agreed to lose much of its delicious flavor and to become rather bitter. It is doubtful if anyone hunts them up to January 1, as the law permits.

As for the larger game in our domain, an illustration may suffice. On one beach where we camped were tracks of beaver, otter, black bear, grizzly bear, a wolf, and what looked like trampling herds of moose, all within a few yards of where we pitched our tent. Some of these tracks were two months old, having been imprinted in early spring, but it showed that the animals were there, which was what we wanted to know.

It was doubtful if we would want to take any large game yet, unless in very dire extremity. Game laws, although there was no game warden to be seen, should be kept if possible. The inhabitant of wilderness regions should let the game pretty much alone to rear its young in the summertime. A large animal would have been of no use to us aside from a meal or two, for we could not have taken it along.

As Bud looked over the game signs he was confident that he could feed us and keep well within the spirit of the game laws.

Because big game animals range over a large area, it might be a question of some time before we saw any. Big game, while plentiful generally, may be absent from any locality, say an area of fifty miles, at any time. The important point was that the tracks told us that big game was there, that it traveled back and forth through this valley, and that it would come again. Of this fact Bud took pains to assure himself in deciding our chances for the future as we went on.

Bud enjoys lingonberries and blueberries

Bud begins construction while Connie packs supplies

3

We had just got started riding in the boat when the motor stalled. "Jump!" Bud told me, but I hesitated one moment too long; as Bud went into action with the stalled motor we were borne backwards instantly into deep water and down the stream at a great rate. I couldn't jump out, Bud couldn't start the motor; shallow riffles, replete with plenty of teeth, gurgled below in the bend.

"Get your paddle then!" Bud yelled at me, making a grab for his own, but it was useless to try to paddle in that water. Then we were, bearing down sidewise on a snag which looked as if it would take the bottom right out of the boat. Up reared the snag beneath us. At the same instant Bud shouted: "The sleeping bag: It will roll overboard!" Belatedly I noted the sleeping bag, carelessly packed that morning in a precarious position atop the load. I made a mental note: "This is how accidents happen."

But everything was all right: we broke the snag that time. The weight of thousands of pounds of water carried us along with the snag until the water shallowed and we could get our footing again and get untangled.

"There's nothing marked on the map for this place," said Bud, as we worked up around the spot the next time. "Look, a river comes in here. I wonder what its name is."

It was a slow river with red water, really what we call a tundra slough; they are countless and nameless. "Maybe we can catch some fish," we thought, so while Bud began to take a few tries with the fly rod, I made a pot of cocoa. The cocoa, in a pint-sized can brought from the Yukon, was unfortunately our last. We should have had more of it, but we didn't.

"There should be something in here," Bud said aloud, knowing that fish can't hear conversation.

"Anyway, the grayling are sure to bite by the hundreds later on," I encouraged him.

"Yes, everyone says that. They run up the little creeks to spawn and the creeks should be jammed full of them. Don't worry, we'll make out. We'll build our cabin right at the junction of one of those spawning creeks. We can dam up the creek then, if we have to, and the fish will wait right there at the mouth when they try to go back into the big river again. Or maybe we can make fish traps as the Eskimos do in some places. I've even thought of making an artificial pool we might keep fish alive in all winter. We'll have fish galore." This was a thought which made our mouths water. But it was never to be realized, for by the time we got to our location to settle that year, the grayling had escaped from all the small creeks where they might have been caught or trapped and had disappeared into the main river for the winter.

Bud did not hope for grayling here in the Red River, but he did hope for pike. "Of course, they might have a fishy taste because they eat fish," he called sarcastically, but I said I wouldn't mind that. We were always making sarcastic comments referring to the food prejudices of people we had known.

"Come get your cocoa," I called.

"Don't you have a little something left over to go with it?"

"Those cold pancakes?" I hinted. "I was saving them."

"What for, your old age? Let's eat them," said Bud. "It takes food to get food. We might as well have a little butter and corn syrup on them, too. Nothing but the best. And why not?"

"Why not?" I said in glee and served up the repast.

We felt better after we had eaten.

Exploration of Red River for a short way was fruitless. What kind of small game could we eat? Perhaps it was not winter, as the storybooks tell, but summer which is the hungry season in the arctic!

Taking the shotgun, Bud left me on the bank to complete the

survey. "I thought I saw a little creek coming in over there," he said. "Probably it isn't anything. I'll see you down below."

When I saw him again presently he said, grinning, "Do you think you can stand a shock? There's a creek over here with grayling." He pointed.

Yes, Bud had found a grayling creek, where none could have been expected, to meet our extremity. It was a shallow icy brook whose banks were crawling with otter tracks. In small crystal pools and along the riffles the grayling were packed nose to tail, and they were so wild with hunger, or possibly with an excess of high spirits, that they frequently caught the fisherman's fly in the air before it struck the water. Flying fish!

After making a quick camp, we fished all night. We have memories of countless typical camps like this, when, pausing at the entrance of some new creek or river, we went fishing to get our lunch or provisions ahead. Then with Bud leading the way with his pistol on his belt and one of us with the rifle slung on his back, up some creek bed we would splash, making a pilgrimage which lasted the night, fishing through the small hours when the grayling bite best.

Sometimes you may see a marten, the animal commercially termed sable, hunting in the trees for birds and squirrels—swift-climbing shadows. Frequently you hear a wolf howl beneath the pale and lovely midnight sky. Once Bud caught me a pair of juvenile horned owls which had moon eyes and clacking beaks and curved talons like knives; just bundles of fluff and hisses they were. Their mother was teaching them to fly. On the creek of the Red River I was fishing a pool quietly when a figure came streaking downstream underwater and popped up on the surface before me. I heard a low call and at the end of my fishing pole sixteen heads stuck out from under the water as though on uncoiled springs: it was a mother fish duck (American merganser) and her obedient brood of ducklings who had been awaiting her there. Like me, they were night fishermen. There we remained together throughout the silent hours, while the babies fed on spawn.

All night long the colors of the sky were reflected in varying hues. I took to fishing with fish eyes for bait; the grayling weren't seeing the flies anymore and they wanted something white. Bud had showed me how to carefully peel the eye out of a dead fish and slip it onto the tiny hook. When the grayling hit this bait, the slippery eye would run up the line, and, unharmed, could be used over and over again until it was worn-out—a mean trick to play on the fish, but a good food-getter. Laying my carbine beside my accumulating pile of fish on the bank not six steps away, I kept a lookout over my shoulder for bears, which do not sleep much, if at all, during the summer season up North. Nearby beavers splashed *ker-plunk* the whole night through.

"How did you make out?" Bud greeted me in the dawn, coming down from above.

"How about a lift?" was all I said.

Since there is no possibility of fishing such a stream out, so long as it remains connected to the main river and the general system is itself unharmed, we had taken this occasion to augment our ten pounds of cornmeal and the ten pounds of pancake mix on which we were living these weeks by all the grayling we could conveniently catch at this creek; when we staggered to bed and sleep at last, our consciences gave us no pang. Except for footsteps on the beaches soon to be washed away, no mark was left to tell that we had been here.

"I see the beavers have eaten the cork handle off your fishing pole," Bud accused me when we next awoke. "You left it out all night. They've even cut one of the tent ropes while we slept."

At Red River Bud continued fishing the second day. Busy at drying fish, I stayed at home in the tent. I was supposed to remove the spine and ribs from the baked fish, then spread the meat out to dry in a shallow pan in the oven. It was a slow business, so I hauled buckets of water up the bank and washed my hair. This kept me chopping wood pretty constantly.

"I needed a day of rest like this," I told myself contentedly. "A woman needs a beauty treatment once in a while. You shouldn't just let yourself go."

Wilderness life did not change the meaning of these feminine morale uplift exercises; it only modified the method. I curled my hair on a pencil and was quite as satisfied after a bout with the cold-cream jar when I gazed into the cracked chip of a mirror which I carried in my pocket as I ever was when gazing into the larger mirrors of town life under a more critical eye.

"Look," said Bud, one fine day—"moose tracks. The moose are still with us anyway."

I was on my nose with the color camera. Bud carried the camera with the black-and-white. All I had seen was flowers until Bud came up.

Some of these flowers defied the photographer. This one which was annoying me was a plant four or five feet tall growing along the water's edge. From the middle sprang several spiral stems on the end of which hung a single dark red or rust-colored rag of a flower which Bud termed "shotgun cleaners." Each time a group of the shotgun cleaners was sighted I ran excitedly from one plant to another. But all summer long I never succeeded in squeezing the release of the camera on one of them, for every time I approached within close range, the spiral stems spread apart, and gazing into the heart of the plant revealed nothing but leaves and no flower at all.

"Well, where are the moose tracks?"

"All around here, not light on their feet either. I'm surprised you didn't see them. Jack Sackett knew, all right."

As a matter of fact, most people would not expect to find moose in the Brooks Range so far north. But these assumptions have been based merely on lack of evidence. Jack Sackett down at Cut-Off had assured us we would locate moose, and he had said, furthermore, that in recent years moose have appeared clear to the arctic coast. They have been seen from airplanes even in the vicinity of treeless Point Barrow. Formerly it has always been generally understood that moose inhabit the northern coniferous forests only, and do not go beyond the timber. But now Eskimos who have never before seen a moose are killing them.

Moose, known as "elk" when we read of them in European tales, formerly abounded throughout north Germany, Norway, Sweden, and Denmark; our Alaskan moose is of this same type, now pushed by encroaching civilization almost to extinction in Europe. It seems possible that this continent was populated with moose coming from Europe through Siberia, where they still live. The smaller New Brunswick or easterly Canadian moose most commonly known to our own country's sportsmen is a slightly different animal.

The moose population could be increased in the far North, if conditions were favorable. It goes without saying that such an increase would be rare fortune for Alaska. From our own limited observations, moose extended the length of the Alatna Valley into the Endicotts during the time we were there and seemed to be distributed as thickly there as anywhere, although not numerous. For a time, we thought they were limited to the valley somewhat as palm trees are limited to an oasis in a desert; later we learned that they went everywhere, even climbing the mountainsides to the highest and most barren peaks. As it happened, none of the animals we were able to observe carefully presented any of the immense racks of antlers of the famed Kenai moose near Seward, farther south; their horns weren't much.

During the summer weeks only the great cowlike tracks gave evidence of their presence. Everything was in deep foliage, making a protective screen for the breeding and nesting activities of all wildlife. But soon, when the deciduous trees were bare of their leaves and the ground was sere, the moose would make themselves conspicuous when the right time came, we trusted. Becoming fat and bold with the approach of the rutting season, the bulls would travel great distances, prance along banks, swim rivers, and even in some cases threaten to charge the hunter.

Because we had lived in the city, it was only the year before that I had seen my first real live moose outside a zoo. This was in the Kenai, surrounding Seward; it is probably the greatest moose country in the world. There were almost no moose there before the turn of this century, but they arrived from other parts, and many of them established themselves in a 2,000,000-acre reserve.

Neither of us was acquainted familiarly with moose at the time, but we were able to get away from town for a week to hunt bear before the legal moose season opened. I was anxious to make the most of my vacation; I walked myself to death. Then, on the fourth morning, as I was about to plunge across a field within sight of the cabin in which we were camping, I stopped short. "Why does Bud have all the luck?" I asked myself for the thousandth time. (He had secured his bear the second day and we were living on it.) "Why don't I ever see anything when I try so hard?" Bud had schooled me in the fundamentals, but the time had come when, if I was ever to become much of a naturalist, I would have to learn to find game by myself; to this end Bud had given me every advantage. Now he had sent me packing off at dawn with directions to follow a game trail he had found. Right then I changed my tactics. Before plunging across the field, I stood at its border and decided I had better learn to use my eyes before going farther. Obviously, there was nothing in the way of game in that little field before me, but I let my imagination play on its lights and shadows. Presently I unsnapped my binoculars from their case and taking a rest across a limb focused them on an opaque spot in the underbrush. A cow moose was standing there motionless, broadside, with ears pricked forward, watching me. I suspected, rightly, that if I took an hour to cross the 500-yard field, putting one foot ahead of the other very slowly, I would not be recognized as a moving object, provided I made no noise. Many wild animals have eyesight which is inferior to mankind's; they depend greatly on their hearing and sense of smell for information. I did the right thing: when there is no cover for a stalk and the animal already sees you, approach directly and openly with no creeping or sneaking attitudes in posture, and if you go slowly you may have remarkable luck. I went directly up to the moose in such a way that she did not seem to mind, odd as this may sound. At closer range I saw what I had not seen before, that the cow had with her a great bull calf about a third as large as herself which had at first been hidden behind her body. Still moving slowly, I walked steadily up to the pair, rifle in hand, and spoke good-day to them. The cow advanced towards me a few steps until she was but a few feet away, with no obstruction between us. Yet killing a moose correctly in season, when killing is to be done, is far from being as simple as killing a cow in a pasture, according to the phrase for it. Another side note: don't try this with a cow moose in spring when the calf is small; this was fall. A cow moose with a small calf is not fooling.

Presently, as my friends the cow moose and her bull child trotted off, I looked around with the glasses and learned that I was in a field together with eight other moose which were placidly standing on all sides of me. Three of these were bulls with sizable racks of antlers, and all of them were nearly within good rifle range, as I know now. This was not on the reserve but in the hunting country where the season was due to open within three weeks. Of course, after the first shot was fired by hunters, the tameness of the animals might be a different story. But the point which was recorded in my mind by this experience was the illuminating fact that an inexperienced city hunter can walk right through a field with tons of animals on either side of him, in an area trampled down and chewed up by game, and never see a single animal if he doesn't know how!

My education in moose came fast upon that one day, when the bull moose were just beginning to "run." Finding the game trail Bud had described to me, I progressed slowly, with a frequent use of the binoculars, expecting moose to pop out of the landscape on all sides, which they did. The game trail wound for miles over a mountain pass. It was three feet broad in places and hewn through the dense underbrush of alders on a side hill as though by an ax, except that no human ax had cut the naked roots away from the earth and one had to watch his ankles in stepping over them. I sat down on my slicker in the rolling mists, took out the glasses again, and was far away in thought, watching a 1200-pound bull moose shoulder his way through the alders on the opposite hillside, when a nearby grunt awoke me. At first, I didn't recognize it as a sound; it was repeated several times, and I came to with a snap. Then you may be sure that I sprang into the air. The fighting call of a bull moose was what I heard! Another bull moose had walked up upon me while I was gazing into the glasses, and he meant to crowd me off the trail! When I looked up it was to see this new bull moose standing at the bend of the trail just over my shoulder and above me, cracking the branches with heavy tossing antlers.

As for me, I am no tree climber, and there were no trees handy for me anyway. My palpitating heart made no argument. Dropping my hat and leaving the slicker where I was seated, and even the precious glasses, I ran. Into the tangle of brush on the uphill side of the trail I fought my way with difficulty. I pumped a shell into the chamber of my rifle as wet sleet commenced to fall. The bull wanted to pass; I had cleared the way, and I hoped he would soon make up his mind about it. When he passed me broadside where I was crushed back into the brambles as far as I could get, he was but fifteen feet away. When just opposite me, he paused, turned his big head leisurely, and fixing me with a piercing eye reached forward sniffing into the brambles at me with a velvet Roman nose!

In this I believe I was about as close to a wild bull moose in the forest as anyone has been who has not shot it. As I was conscientious about the legal moose hunting season, that thought principally preoccupied me. I had looked the moose over, and they had looked me over, too.

The Alatna River

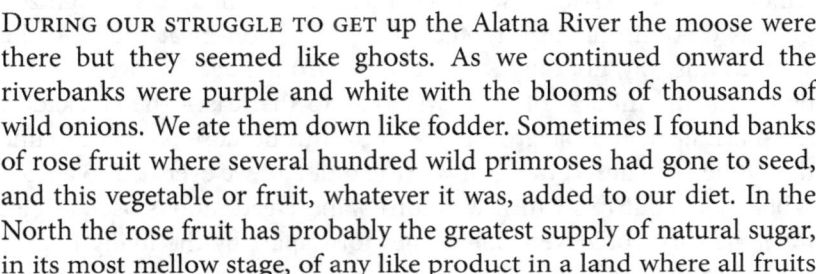

DURING OUR STRUGGLE TO GET up the Alatna River the moose were there but they seemed like ghosts. As we continued onward the riverbanks were purple and white with the blooms of thousands of wild onions. We ate them down like fodder. Sometimes I found banks of rose fruit where several hundred wild primroses had gone to seed, and this vegetable or fruit, whatever it was, added to our diet. In the North the rose fruit has probably the greatest supply of natural sugar, in its most mellow stage, of any like product in a land where all fruits are proverbially sour.

We had brought no shortening with us for our baking but needed a bear for this. Tracks of grizzly and black bears along the valley showed they too were hungry, waiting for the berries on the sides of the mountains to ripen. The bears would have to get the shortening on their sides first before we could bake. Still we waited.

The Indians had told us always to try to make camp in an open place this time of year because of the big bears. They said sometimes during the hungry season the bears will watch a person's camp with an intent of making a meal on him. "Bears are hungry before the berries get ripe," they repeated. Knowing that, according to the best naturalists, no animal will intentionally kill man for food, aside from a few freaks like the man-eating tiger of India, and one case in Alaska where a man is believed to have been actually killed by wolves, we had attributed this to native superstition. But further explanation seemed to give the belief a possible verity. The Indians explained that the big brown bear will kill a human being, whose odor he dislikes, with the intention of allowing the meat to become carrion before he will eat it. The Indians said the bear would wait there in that vicinity until this happened, were other food not sufficiently available.

It is true, our experience proceeded to testify, that, mercifully enough, in the animal world most animals do not seem to recognize a dead companion or a dead thing for what it may be. To them it is usually food, and nothing is wasted. They have no moral scruples, as have human beings, against eating their father. Sled dogs are fed wolf meat and wolves in turn will eat dogs eagerly. Dogs will eat dogs. We have seen Eskimo sled pups gnawing on the decapitated head of a sled dog lying in the village at Point Barrow, and so it goes. Add to this now the love of all animals for carrion. Any meat, a human being included, which becomes carrion loses its characteristic scent and is recognized only as carrion; this in turn may draw even non-meat-eaters to the spot. In this way, not only will bears feed from a decomposed human body, but the mildest of birds will rally to the feast—the chickadee, the ptarmigan, and the grouse. We know this because on the trap line they stole our bait. Rotten fish was the best bait we ever had to attract rabbits and squirrels which we didn't want. Dead rabbits used as bait for large carnivores were sometimes torn apart by the living rabbits who came to play and who, according to the reconstructed story, apparently tossed a decapitated rabbit's hind leg about among each other like a football.

Our relation to the animal world becomes at once very clear to a hunter of his own food in the North. The Indians and Eskimos, in fact most people about the world other than the Americans and the British, still think of animals first of all as a means of food. A lot of us have got so far away from this viewpoint by living in civilization's exact centers that we can buy our meat at the butcher's and gloss over our animal movies with the sweet syrup of a child's world of fantasy.

The world which the Indians understand but which, among white people, only the farmer or the trained naturalist fully realizes, is the world where an animal is always busy trying to eat some smaller animal and then is in turn eaten up by a larger animal than he. The Indians observed this carefully and they had their own philosophical ideas about it—not profound, but perhaps instinctive. The Indians and the Eskimos have superstitions, yes, but the white man's superstitions about his arctic and about its animals are the worst.

4

Our hearts were light because we had got above the Canyon. It had been a tough assignment, well done. There had been no place to line, and all the water rushing through that steep narrow bend made the river deep so that we could neither wade nor push as we had been doing. Bud climbed up on a ledge which dropped sheer into abysmal depths, got the canoe out on the end of the line, and crawled along on his knees while I came very near to pulling him off the cliff with my ruddering.

We awoke relaxed and Bud looked leisurely at the motor with no especial misgivings. It had slipped its drive shaft on the Koyukuk as forecast, not once but a dozen times. Bud had fixed it before with tin snips and a piece from an oilcan, and he would surely do it again.

But this time he dove down and emerged with a connecting rod warped all out of shape. I remember it was a warm sunny morning, the leaves turning golden up above the Canyon, and the airy mountain cliffs ahead all smoky. We thought it might be a forest fire. It was Indian summer.

"It's odd," Bud explained, "but you know when cast aluminum decides to bend one way, it will generally not bend back the other way again. I'm going to give it a try anyway. You go out and see if you can find us something to eat."

I couldn't find anything to eat, so I shot a raven that morning. It must have been a young bird and inexperienced, for its behavior seemed to me unusual. It glided silently out of a tree toward me, and around and around my head it flew, circling low, for three circles, when I finally shot it with the shotgun. When I picked it up, entangled in the bushes to which the crash of the fall and the dying wingbeats had guided me, a single stream of red blood trickled from the pickax bill, and I thought, "The Indians never kill a raven because they fear bad luck from the watchful spirit."

It is the only raven I have ever killed. Solitary bird of the northern wilderness, his musical cry on the early morning wind was a sound we learned to love among those sounds familiar to the ear far from human habitation. Most people do not know that even the raven has a liquid song sometimes, almost like dripping water, and different from his "caw." Sometimes the raven truly sings!

As I approached Bud, carrying the raven by the heels, I heard the news from him that bad luck had struck and that the motor was not going to run again. Perhaps this is why I recall that particular raven so well. The connecting rod, it seems, had broken in two as neatly as you please with Bud's first gentle taps to bend it back into shape.

The remaining cylinder had not enough power to move the boat along—we tried that, too. Again, in memory I can hear it cough and die for the last time.

"Oh, well," said Bud, "we'll only go about sixty miles further." He brightened. "Now we won't have to worry about the motor at all any more. I was getting tired of putting up with it. By lining we can still get to where we're going, I think."

The motor was put away permanently inside the boat with acceptance of the situation and a certain feeling of gratitude for what it had done. It had helped us quite a lot.

I picked the raven of its feathers and dressed it, intending to eat it. All it had in its craw was three blueberries. It was hungry when it saw me. So, this must have been why it looked me over! But raven was one meat we never attempted. In the end, after carrying it with us all day as we traveled we finally threw the tough, feathery old carcass as far as we could throw it. Bird of ill omen!

Bud hunted the woods for food until worn-out. We were living mostly on a ten-pound sack of corn meal at this time and were trying to stretch it out, for we did not want to break into our precious winter supplies. I had been on short rations myself for weeks, leaving Bud to eat two thirds of all that was eaten, whatever that was, for he was doing tremendous work. He was responsible for us both. The welfare of us both depended on fuel being thrown into him in ever greater quantities. We were neither one getting enough. Every waking thought seemed to be devoted entirely to food. Nothing could fill us up. Fifteen to thirty grayling, averaging a pound each, had gone down our throats every two days. Fish are mostly water, and the only way we could begin to consume enough fish to supply the energies we expended was to eat a dozen dried fish, in the condensed form, along with the corn meal.

I pulled the boat all day on the day of the motor failure with the vision floating above my head of the small bowl of rice which would be my reward at its end. Nothing on earth, it seemed to me, would be so heavenly as the moment I could get at that rice. I didn't dream of nonexistent foods which were more fancy; I concentrated on the reality that was. Bud returned from the woods at night with a single squirrel of chipmunk size and a handful of mushrooms to go with it. He was praised as though he had provided us with a moose. Whatever was eaten was almost totally fish or small game. Whatever we ate—and we always ate somehow—we were equally glad to get it.

The kind of country we had for lining seemed utterly impossible. The dangerous rocks and riffles gave way to mud bars stretching beneath the surface of the water invisibly all along the river. Leading the boat, one followed the curving edge of a bar, looking for a way to get the boat across or around it, and it would take you out to mid-river almost to the opposite shore. As the mud or sand sank beneath your weight, you were soon up to your armpits, but the canoe still could not float. Following the edge of the bar back in, you would seem to make progress upstream, when you would find yourself brought up against another invisible bar which curved out in an arc downstream, over which but two inches of water flowed. Lining from shore with a rope was not possible because of the softness of the exposed ground; you could not walk on it.

In desperation Bud took to lining along the cut bank whenever there was one, and I put on my clothes and, shivering after my immersion, rode in the boat. The cut bank is the side of the river which is sheer, the outside of each turn. A heavy growth must often be chopped away with the ax before proceeding, although an expert with ropes may learn to flip the rope around bushes and trees in such a manner that he can pull the boat past them and remain untangled. Continual paddling from side to side of the river was necessary to stay by the cut banks, during which crossings we tended to lose a little ground, flail the water as we might.

Many were the camps on that river. There were camps where you had to climb a bank three hundred feet high to pitch your tent, such as Five Channel Camp, or like Camp Tundra where there was trouble with tundra fires which started beneath the stove—peat and the beginnings of coal, containing some ingredient which drove you out of the tent with smarting eyes. We had been setting the stove up off the ground on lengths of stovepipe, but even at that, fire smoldered all night beneath, until when we arose next morning to start breakfast we had to take a stick and dig out its various channels in the ground. There were camps where strings of fish hung at the end of the ridgepole and camps where you woke up to hear rain pattering on the roof of the tent and just lay in bed half the day listening to it and that cozy sound of beans simmering away on the camp stove.

There was one camp where we stayed over a day to go on a blueberry expedition and followed up the mountain a small creek running orange from iron rust. Bud climbed three thousand feet to the rimrock above the river. It was a stunning disappointment to us to learn as a finality there what we had begun to suspect—that it was a poor blueberry year. Along the riverbanks we had found many blueberry bushes, but they were going to bear no fruit. Now we found this condition to hold in the higher altitudes on slopes where there should be millions of blueberries. We got only about two quarts. Bud said the cause of the shortage must have been late spring frosts which nipped the budding flowers.

One day that remains notable for me was the day I found the largest compound beaver dam I have ever seen. We had made camp late and both had gone hunting for our supper in opposite directions. I had shot a cock grouse as it looked at me from the branch of a spruce tree with a red spot over its eye and its tail spreading into a fan. Picking it quickly while it was still warm, I had hung it by the neck between the forks of a birch to cool and await me on my return. Then with rifle in hand and a folded sack intended for berries in my pocket I fairly sprang up to the top of the hill to see what could be seen. The hill was covered with reindeer moss. I threw myself down among crisp cranberries and began raking them into my mouth with bits of leaves and grass and they were wonderful; the sourness tasted good. Eventually some of the berries got into the sack to take home.

Exploring over the rim of the hill among golden birch trees I saw half a dozen blue lakes shining up to the sky. As I came down to the lakes I saw that they were on different terraces and that silver water poured serenely over a dam at the lower edge of each lake. Canals, often choked with grass, which were a part of the old stream bed, connected the imprisoned lakes with each other and ran out to outlying parts of the swamp. These were the "locks" where logs were floated here and there about the area. There were overland trails, too, including several steep muddy shoots straight down the side of the hill from which I had come. It was apparent at a glance that several generations of beavers must have engineered out their lives here.

So long had the beavers inhabited this basin which was spanned by their dams that they had eaten up most of the available food over several acres. The food of the beavers is birchbark, although they apparently digest and assimilate a considerable cordage in wood; but they like tender young shoots best. These they store under the pond for their winter's food. Cottonwood is also acceptable to them. But these beavers were so hard pressed that they had been girdling and even felling spruce trees for materials. It was quite a climb now for a beaver up to the top of the hill where the good birches and cottonwoods were.

Imprisoned grayling splashed in the largest pool, leaping for mosquitoes and invisible water gnats. The beavers were no menace to them. Only an otter, finding the lakes, would play havoc with all in the beaver paradise. Around the lakes ran a game trail used by the more or less compatible moose and black bears in the summertime. These trails followed the line where the swamp land met the hillside. Any hunting animal coming along would follow this contour, and I followed it now.

"Beaver lakes must be a headache for geographers," I thought. They are subject to change and it must be difficult to classify them because they are artificial lakes. These lakes, along with many others but two or three miles around, were not indicated on our map. Thousands of arctic puddles—how can there ever be room on any map for them all?

The day was becoming overcast and heavy as evening came on. I walked over and back, fifty feet across the brink of the largest dam, which held my weight. These were bank beavers. They tunneled out their lodges from underneath the water up into the banks; no beaver houses were to be seen. There was no evidence of beaver habitation here aside from the piles of trash which composed their dams, and the white wood chips similar to those left by a chopping block, scattered everywhere.

As I sat down to untangle a coil of fishing line, an immense old beaver appeared, swimming around in circles in the middle of the lake. There was a report and water flew ten feet into the air as with his broad flat tail he gave the surface a wallop, and almost instantly the entire lake was filled with beavers. They had waked up and come out for the evening's work. Across the lake one of them emerged to work up on land. He sat broadside to me, chewing loudly. Right at hand, almost within touch of my fingertips, a mother beaver came swimming by with three silver-gray half-grown muffets in her wake. Her heavy head turned this way and that, moving stiff brown whiskers. Slowly the old beaver hoisted herself out on top of the dam. She had fingers like human hands on her front feet, but the tremendous heavy webbed hind paddles had only four toes on them. One by one the obedient youngsters followed; then they slipped over the other side and were in water again, swimming down the canal. I could hear them talking to each other as they passed. They did not talk loud, for the beaver language is the merest whisper.

I thought of the gun in my hand and quite unemotionally considered food. But we weren't so badly off as to eat summer beavers yet. The first instinct of all too many people with a gun in their hand is to shoot whatever they see.

Around Alaskan beaver ponds today lie bloated bodies, polluting the water, turning paradise to horror. These are the ponds accessible by rail and automobile road and foot trail to the larger Alaskan towns. Five years ago, many of the beavers were personal pets of the residents. With the new country being opened up and newcomers arriving, no wise beaver can afford any longer to be tame. Beavers are about the most easily shot out and trapped out of all the fur bearers. It was largely because of the new accessibility of the beaver areas to town dwellers that the beaver trapping season had to be changed from the open waters of spring to the dismal month of February in coldest midwinter, adding greatly to the wretchedness of the professional trapper who now traps and drowns beavers altogether under ice.

As I sat beside the beaver dam I heard a splash and the clack of a hoof striking rock. I shivered with alarm at first, then calmed; this meant that a moose was coming along. As I sat motionless, another long step on the part of the visitor brought it around the bend within easy toss of a pebble.

Yes, it was a cow moose. The first I saw of her she was head down drinking water as she came clattering up the creek bed. As I was within plain sight of her with no cover, I didn't bat an eyelash. She looked up absent-mindedly. Her ears shot forward like sound-amplifiers and her face registered what I suppose was wonder. But she could not make out what I was. Having strained her eyes as hard as she could, she gave it up, heaved a long sigh, and stood there to drain off her bladder.

This cow moose had no calf with her. Many calves are lost each year in the crossing of rivers and swift creeks. Some of them are drowned, but mostly the mother loses them, according to what experienced guides maintain from observations of their areas year by year. If the mother becomes separated from the calf in such a crossing, she quickly forgets all about it and goes off, leaving it to die. Another likelihood of losing her calf occurs when the mother stations it in some hiding place and leaves it for an hour or so to browse. Bears and wolves are waiting, and even the magpie in more southerly parts are waiting for a chance to peck the gelatin out from the soft hoofs of the young calf. As the calf will follow anything he sees moving, he may also lose himself. People who find an orphaned moose or deer youngster, or allow themselves to be followed by it, are most often not finding an actual orphan at all but a pretender. Whatever the various reasons, only a small proportion of moose calves grow to maturity, for most of the cows you can see by late summer have no calves with them.

When I returned from my intimate associations with the beavers and the moose, I found about fifty pounds of fish hanging by the door of the tent and Bud was busy, making the scales fly.

The sun these days was like an electric light bulb in a cold room. You might take off your shirt and warm the side of you on which the sun beat, but the other side would be cold. Fish or meat would spoil and was "blown" by flies if you did not hang it in a tree in a gunnysack so that air could circulate about it. Yet that the sun was losing its power was shown by the fact that in an otherwise cloudless sky a single wisp of a cloud on the horizon, always standing to veil the sun in gauze from any quarter, was a definite interference with its heat-giving properties.

Giant rock fortresses rising sheer from the spruce forests ahead gave way to Takahula Lake, a landmark Jack Sackett had said was two hundred miles up the Alatna River. There was an old tumble-down cabin standing by, its windows long ago broken out. Some long grizzly-bear hairs hung on the edge of its yawning doorway. The river was before the cabin; the deep sunken mountain lake lay like a set jewel a few steps over the rise behind. The lake had been a part of the old stream bed in ages gone by.

I commenced taking my turn pulling the boat and wading again in ice water as above Takahula Lake the Alatna abruptly became fast and dangerous with brawling gravel riffles once more, where we crawled inch by inch. Ruddering itself was no simple job for the person sitting in the boat when we lined. You had to learn the exact pressure which would steer the craft out and around obstructions in midstream and back again to hug the shore, yet not be drawn in against obstacles there. All summer, so to speak, Bud had had me on the end of a seventy-five-foot rope, and it was a good thing that he was strong and that I knew my ruddering well by now. Often my whole weight was thrown against the rudder to hold her nose out until I thought the oar might break in my hands. Bud and I would be fighting each other's strength, it sometimes seemed, as he plowed along the bank and a great wave rolled out before the boat, sucking the swift channel dry.

We were out of meat again, camping opposite a waterfall pouring down the cliffs into the river from four hundred feet on high; the dark green spruce forest in which we camped below seemed only as high as moss by comparison. There was one grouse for supper and Bud had it with rice while I just had rice. Next morning, we went hunting again before breakfast for our breakfast. I shot four grouse with the 12-gauge shotgun but two of them were shot at too close range and had to be thrown away. Bud got three grouse and sixteen squirrels, all shot in the head with the .22 pistol.

These Alaska squirrels are red in color but are not the large red squirrel of our Eastern United States. They are only the size of a chipmunk. A shirt or jacket made of their pelts is considered the last word in attire, and since they overran the valley we had begun a collection with a view to using the fur in some way. The meat is good, but it takes so many to make a meal that we were really hard-pressed if we used them for food.

5

Taking my .30-30 rifle with open sights, Bud had gone inland up the Nahtuk (or Big Muddy) River which comes into the Alatna right here. Bud was gone many hours. It was about dark, and I was beginning to be a little lonely at camp when I looked up at a slight sound to find him returned at last. Rolled up on his shoulders and tied with the four-foot piece of leather thong he always somehow had along with him in an odd pocket, was a large black bear robe which he threw down with a sigh.

"You know that thing's heavy," were his first words. "Just try to lift it."

My astonished rapture knew no bounds, as I sprang to my feet at the vision. "I was beginning to worry about you," I said. "But where's the food? Did you only bring home that hide?" I still couldn't believe what I saw.

"Open the package and see."

As excited as a child at Christmas, I untied the thongs, spread out the hide to the fullest, hair down, and there inside were the fresh heart and liver. These are the parts usually eaten first from the kill for several reasons. In hot countries and even in a cool country these are the most perishable parts, hence they are at their very best when eaten immediately after being taken out of the animal. They are the easiest to carry to camp if the hunter is tired or in a hurry to provide supper. Steaks and roasts should not be cut from the carcass, properly speaking, until a few hours have passed, in order to allow the muscles to set, and give opportunity for a good job of butchering—that is, if you want a professional job rather than a haggled one.

There are many prejudices held by our people about what meats are fit to eat. We forget that it is only very recently in the total history of the world that agriculture has come to take a large part in the human being's economy of life. We also have the notion that meat in general can be eaten only in limited amount for good health. In the United States we eat two meats: beef and pork. Aside from chicken on Sunday, these are really the only meats we know. A smaller proportion of the population will eat mutton, or "lamb" as it is pretentiously called at the butcher's, but it ranks far down the list in America, a lagging third in popularity with the great masses, as a survey of Army menus or the menus of large public banquets will show. People won't eat it; you are safe in serving only beef, pork, or chicken at a large affair. Many people won't eat any kind of fish or seafood; some will eat them only if they are served in a certain way and are expensive. Liver, tongue, brains, heart, and the other variety parts of even familiar animals are palatable to possibly one person out of five. This is why people in other parts of the world probably could not conjure up much of a feeling of sympathy over the sufferings of people in the United States due to "meat shortage" during the war.

Let's cast out the window right here, before going further, a few superstitions. Here is one: that climate determines how much meat a person can eat. Meat is commonly thought of as "heavy"! Too much of it is thought unsuitable in a hot climate. Too much of it is thought unsuitable for children. I can remember being put to bed on porridge eaten alone in the nursery while the grownups at dinner parties had meat, and I've always resented it. Why do children have to eat gruel anyway? Nobody else eats it, I've noticed since, and meat contains everything that cereal does besides the fact that you can chew it. That meat is "heavy" is pure nonsense. It is one of the bulkiest of foods, meaning that it has so much water in it and is such a mild diet that by contrast a meat eater in the North would suddenly have a good deal of digestive disturbance if confronted unexpectedly with the "light" mixed salad and banana split which the New York secretary's stomach has become accustomed to in her efforts to keep cool of a hot summer's day.

We hold that we can eat as much meat as we want to anyplace, in any climate, and our only worry about it would be whether we could afford it.

It was only a generation ago that grandfather had to eat meat three times a day in the United States, or he considered that he wasn't well fed. People can get by with less meat than grandfather ate because they are not having the physical exercise he did. They can get by, too, because they have to know that the world is getting short of it in relation to the terrific populations to be fed. Customs change. Cheap substitutes are found—chemical compounds, synthetic vitamins, soy beans. You can raise a lot of soy beans on the pasture it takes for one steer. In southern Arizona at the present time the government stipulates not more than one steer to every forty-eight acres, and much of America's best grazing land has long been plowed under. All of this is perhaps well enough. If people seem to do as well on one small serving of meat a day and are satisfied, that's all that matters. But for goodness' sake, don't be *afraid* of meat! Animal proteins are the world's original best food!

If a person is hungry, any animal (barring those afflicted with parasitic disease) is edible. Banana splits for the New York secretary and seal blubber for the Eskimo are one and the same thing nutritionally, with the Eskimo probably a little ahead on the Vitamin D side. These foods can be interchanged successfully by the same human system, and the tongue would be the only organ to know the difference. Your stomach and your body don't know the difference; grub is grub to them. It all goes through the mill.

Sportsmen who themselves adore hunting are strangely enough often the most prejudiced and the least informed about how to use their foods. An animal that is classed as carnivorous or predatory in its food habits is considered not good to eat. But this rule does not hold when we really learn to know the habits of animals, for, like us, they do not always eat just one set thing which is ascribed to them in our categories. Their diet is variable, and they eat what they can get.

The reason why many sportsmen will not eat their bears is that the bear is known to be partly carnivorous. But the hog, a reputable animal and our great current source of riboflavin, on which armies are said to march, is just like a bear in this respect if allowed to forage for himself. In the United States, during the 1940's, while more and more hogs were being raised on scientifically balanced rations, more than half were doubtless fattened on city garbage, while the old-style filthy pigsty is still in wide vogue, as anyone may see. Naturalists know that left to himself, the hog, whose proclivities to lie in cool mud of a hot summer's day have made people think he likes filth, would probably be as clean as a bear.

Hogs are by nature quite as carnivorous as bears. In some places hogs are fish-fed. This gives the meat a bad taste. More common in our own country is the fattening of hogs on old horse meat. Bud has seen hogs run after and kill both sheep and chickens. Every year several small children are eaten by United States hogs.

That delicate bird the chicken, so loved on the Sunday table, is also carnivorous. She is a great scavenger. The sight of a chicken pecking maggots off a dead rat in the barnyard is not an uncommon sight. Hens rush in at the chopping block to drink the blood of their sisters or will mob any other chicken which has received a wound drawing blood and will soon peck it to death. Once hens get the taste of blood it may become a vicious habit. To avoid this, farmers may outfit all their hens with red glasses obtainable from the mail-order houses to prevent them from pecking their kind.

These observations only show that the pet notions of people about the animal world and about animals as food for human beings may not always be established on facts at all but rest largely on custom. Although certain animals have thrived best under domestication, there are other animals just as good to eat as those we are used to. Some of them might be raised for food purposes at any time that it ever seemed commercially feasible to try it.

Now there are likewise countless superstitions held by our people about the care of "wild" meats, often very amusing. The main principle Bud followed was to deal with them in all ways just as one does on the farm and forget that "wild" theory. For, allowing for minor differences in structure, all animals are the same. There is no such thing as a wild flavor, which will be made clear in time.

For Bud, who at the age of twelve took charge of practically all the butchering done at home on his parents' farm, butchering wild meat in the field was a simple matter if less convenient. It never failed to amaze us that friends of ours in the out-of-doors, some of them registered big game guides for years, had never learned the simple arts of butchering to make meats tender and palatable. Not only that, but their methods might be positively unhygienic; after some hunters get through with an animal, a self-respecting dog wouldn't eat it. Intestinal fluid, blood, feathers, and hair, also sand in the meat—it is small wonder all of us do not care for game. Actually, such foolishness is unnecessary, as a skilled woodsman can show you.

We know of more than one guide friend of twenty-five years' experience who haggles meat out *with* the grain rather than across the grain, in cutting steaks which should by rights be sirloins in the $2.00 classification. Apparently, his clients must live indefinitely on this too-well-done, leathery fried meat, along with fried onions and fried potatoes, plus very black coffee. Perhaps this is what they pay for, or perhaps they have stomachs of cast iron.

People not knowing what kind of meat they are eating reminds us of the joke a prominent Arizonian played on a group of his friends a few years ago. He had gone deer-hunting, and his trusting wife had prematurely invited everybody to a venison dinner. But he didn't get his buck that year! "Bud," he said, "for heaven's sake, I've got twenty people coming to a venison dinner tonight. Go down to the Chink market and get us some veal."

Bud knew what to get and he got it. The dinner was prepared in due time. As the dinner was served, Bud said some of the guests, who had never tasted venison before, looked timid. Others, according to the venturesomeness of their temperaments, declared it was the most delicious meat they had ever tasted in their lives; one could really tell this was something special! The conversation turned to a comparison of the flavors in meats, as often happens at a game dinner.

"Yes, you can tell the difference," one lady agreed. "It is a little coarser-grained than beef."

Another said, "It's a dryer meat, not so fat. One can tell that it is very rich, though."

A six-year-old boy said, "Daddy, I can't tell any difference."

Everybody listened respectfully while the man pointed out to the little boy the differences between venison and beef. But the honest child was difficult to convince. Of all that assembly, the child could tell no difference. The years have passed, and we have never been able to tell any particular difference ourselves.

An Alaskan housewife I knew held a notion about bear meat which we consider extremely curious and which since then we have had occasion to hear repeated. This lady said, "You know, I could never eat bear meat, because, if you will notice, a bear looks just like a human being the way it is constructed, the paws and all. I roasted a young cub once and we had to throw it out because it looked just like a cooked baby."

We had to admit we had never seen a cooked baby, but one can agree that it might be possible for anything to look like a baby if the animal was cooked *whole*. Apparently, the wife had not cut it into the appropriate pieces, which accordingly gave it this peculiar appearance to her imagination. Animals and even fish have a basic skeletal and other systemic development not far removed from the human being. Bud has heard grown men refuse to taste bear meat from an animal of their own killing because they maintained that a skinned bear looks like a human body to them.

The superstitions held about the care and preparation of wild meats are too numerous to mention. Almost everyone must be familiar with a few. It is probably a rare reader of these lines who has not already said to himself, "Why, that's me!" Good cooks who know how to prepare anything else often have elaborate special preparations for game to make it edible; the average cook will not even attempt it. Why this setting apart of game?

It would be a hobby to travel around the United States getting local ideas about the preparation and the edibility of game today. The superstitions of aborigines aren't so ludicrous, for we are supposed to be enlightened people.

"Of course," as Bud put it reflectively, when he began to tell me the story of his bear, "this bear had all four feet on the ground and we may not like the flavor because he did not have one foot in the air."

Bud had climbed up the mountain by the Nahtuk River, and here he had found what we had dreamed about—acres and acres of blueberries as big as grapes.

"I dreamed we might find something like that," I sighed in envy of Bud's day spent there. "Just one sidehill where the spring frost didn't hit!"

It was a sunny day and Bud followed the ideal procedure of the bear hunter who takes off but one day to get a bear. With the binoculars strapped to his side he just lay down among the blueberries in the sun and ate steadily for several hours. Of course, he selected a high and particularly advantageous location for this pastime, where he could see for miles over the great arctic range in every direction. Actually, he hoped to see a big grizzly bear because he believed that the black bears might have been largely driven out of this high country by the grizzlies.

Bud raised his head with a mouthful of blueberries. Into the long shadows of the late afternoon sun came a bear over the rim of the hill. The bear was a thousand yards away when he first saw it, a tiny figure lost in immensity. Every time the bear put its head down for a moment Bud would sprint forward a few yards. Every time the bear raised its head, Bud crouched motionless until it resumed its feeding again.

In this way the hunter approached within one hundred yards of the animal on the bare mountain. Now he could see the rapid sweeps of the paws as leaves, sticks, and trash—everything within sight—was raked into that greedy maw; there is no busier sight than that of a bear among the blueberries. Gobbling, sniffing, pivoting, the black bear ate on, unconscious of danger. He was so active that at moments it was impossible to tell which end of the bear was which. As soon as he was facing in the direction Bud wanted him to be, Bud shot, and heard the bullet say "plunk." This sound, when a large thick animal meets a bullet, is one of the surest ways for the hunter to tell if he has made a hit. We would always listen for this sound and watch closely the behavior of the animal for that slight flinch which may indicate several things of greatest importance.

This bear never flinched visibly or gave sign of being hit but jumped up and ran straight ahead for two hundred yards and over an embankment, with (as was later ascertained) the heart shot in two. During this flight Bud placed one other running shot which went through the stomach and out the other side, leaving a trail of blueberries behind the bear. It is the sportsman's rule never to cease firing on a fleeing animal upon which you have once opened fire until the animal goes down or is lost from sight. Otherwise we don't shoot at the posterior of an animal.

"When I opened him up," Bud said, speaking of the blueberry episode, "he smelled just like a soda fountain inside."

As Bud had only a penknife with him it took some time to skin out the 350-pound bear, and this accounted for his tardiness in getting home. Many were the times after Bud's first bear in the arctic that I was to see him come staggering in with a heavy load at nightfall, and, after that, the later he was the gladder I might be because the heavier would be the load he must have.

This bear meant the difference between poverty and riches. If you have only a little sugar, flour, corn meal, and rice you are on starvation rations. But if, added to these things, you have a bear or moose or other big game down you have immediate security, all the comforts of home, and all that one could ever want or hope for.

The following day Bud got out my heavy laced high-top boots, plus the socks I had worn all summer, and, taking pack board, ropes, hatchet, skillet, and some large sugar sacks for the gathering of berries, he carried me on his back across the Nahtuk River shallows, and we climbed the mountain to the bear carcass, intending to labor there all day and have our noon lunch there. The bear would provide our lunch counter.

On the mountain 1500 feet above, however, we were met by overhanging clouds and snow flurries, with everything wet. It was a world of stones, purple and gray. The trail upward ran along the brink of a chasm. Stepping over the gray skeleton of a fallen tree, up and up we went to pastures white with snow. Eight white ewes and their lambs disappeared before us into the misty land of the mountaintops. But it was not the place today that Bud had described. Where were my blueberries?

Far above timber line, Bud uncovered the bear carcass from beneath a pile of blueberry brush and reindeer moss and chopped out the meat into the appropriate sides under conditions resembling those of a meat icebox. The carcass was a sight for famished eyes. It was covered all over by an inch layer of fat as sweet-looking as dairy cream.

"Let's eat first," I said, "and then pick berries." I could see the berries above the two-inch covering of wet snow, drooping on their stalks.

"Do you want to taste some fat?" asked Bud and cut me a small cube. I had noticed that he was chewing it as he worked. I had never tasted raw fat before nor thought of eating it, but we were very hungry as we started our cooking fire, and it seemed as though we couldn't wait to eat.

"Why," I said surprised, "this is good!"

Civilized people look on the eating of raw fat with utter abhorrence, and I felt a sneaking qualm. But I noticed it tasted quite different from the greasy burned fat of fried meats which was all I had formerly known and never liked; as a child I wouldn't eat bacon. This was mild as beeswax. Nobody could find anything about it to dislike, for it had no definite taste. We had to smile at ourselves that day as we stumbled upon a technique which we were to utilize quite often in the North from then on—the eating of raw animal fat for a "pick-up." We were certainly getting to be like savages!

What we didn't realize then is that raw animal fat is the most easily available and easily assimilated food from which the starving hunter can gain quick energy if he has nothing else. This precious substance is, moreover, something no wild animal can have too much of for the hunter's needs. It is known that native peoples living by hunting eat first of all the fat and the fattest parts of the animal, and this holds true from Alaska to Africa, where hippopotamus fat is loved by the black hunters in the same way certain fats are prized by the wild foragers of the arctic. No one could have told us this before, but we were learning it: that there is absolutely no difference between the "primitive" stomach and the "civilized" stomach, but merely different attitudes and customs, and above all, differences in circumstances.

Sitting beside a fire of roaring spruce knots on a rocky ridge and devouring pounds of rare dripping steaks, completely raw in the middle, from off forked sticks, and finishing up with bowls of blueberries picked at our feet, we forgot the falling snow on our backs and agreed that never in our lives could we ask more of comfort or delight. So hard had we sweated climbing the mountain that now the hot fire felt good, drying our sticky hair. It was certainly good to be alive!

But I wept with freezing hands when we tried to pick enough of the miserable berries to carry back. Although a bear might still make a good living here among the blueberries, no human hands could pick them because they mashed at a touch. Enchanting berries that tasted of wine and could not be gathered! I wailed, and Bud allowed me to thrust my hands up into his warm armpits. So, it was that we were forced to descend to the lower altitudes, knowing that we had arrived one day too late ever to eat a blueberry pie. They were the last blueberries we saw.

Bud carried 175 pounds of meat and I took what was 50 pounds or the odd hind leg. By cutting out some of the bones we got the best part of the whole bear out in the one trip. We had a feeling that we had got him none too soon.

Snowballs from the sky buffeted us on the head briefly as we struck the tent the next day and moved onward, the bear carcass somehow finding room inside the canoe. Bud remarked he thought the mountains might smooth out and become more rolling, with broader passes for migrating game and better chances for trapping just ahead. Only about twelve miles by air distance was a side valley entering our valley where we thought we might settle. We had seen it from the mountaintop.

6

After Black Bear Camp the river split into islands and we had some close calls as we tried to get through one channel after another. There was not much of a river left any more. We could not be very far from Gull Pass itself.

The water was extremely cold and turquoise, with white foam and the red leaves of tall highbush cranberry bushes showing along the banks. One particularly alarming experience occurred when Bud was lining along the cut bank through dense brush while I ruddered out in the millrace. Bud wanted the ax from the boat. He tied the canoe by the lead rope forty feet ahead and walked back while I ruddered in to shore to hand the ax to him. Then, "Crack!" went the snag to which Bud had tied me, as, with the accompanying bushes, it started to tear loose from the bank. Bud raced to the snag just in time to catch me as I swung out in midstream unavoidably. He pulled at the tangle on shore but was unable to budge the canoe. Then I discovered that our longer rope, seventy-five feet in length, was trailing from the stern and was entangled somewhere on the bottom. By the time I managed to reel it in while attempting to rudder so as to hold the canoe's nose into the current, Bud's waning strength was almost gone. The whole bow of the canoe seemed to go under water momentarily as he pulled us out of it. He later said I went white as a sheet. But I could say that he was purple.

The next side valley coming in was called Pingaluk Creek, which we shall always remember as a part of our own home locality, for we were getting close to home now. It was August 25, which we designated as the beginning of our arctic fall. Bud climbed one mountain and I climbed another and we communicated from our different peaks by showing ourselves occasionally on points. Bud presently joined me by coming down an adjacent ridge. Of course I could never hope to keep up with him. The mountains we chose for me as a rule were cut down to my size. Bud would always be able to run circles around me—we had faced that fact from the outset—and I had no right to slow him down to my pace. Husbands and wives who hike or hunt together must consider these differences in strength.

Nothing in particular occurred that day at Pingaluk but it was one of the most memorable days in the wild I ever spent for contentment. My mountain turned out to be an unexpectedly grueling test of skill. I was caught for hours, it seemed to me, in jungles of slide alders growing ten feet tall, their limbs all pointing downwards. Then there were the cliffs, and moments when I had to lay the rifle in a niche, praying not to see it go clattering down to destruction. I had got used to mountain heights gradually. Mountains seldom fall straight down, really, and then there are always little bushes of some kind to hang onto. Even grass has very strong roots. I inched myself up and up, refusing to be relegated to the obscurity of the slide alders below. I topped out amid the early snows of winter, now lying on the north sides of all the peaks.

On the south side of the mountain blueberry bushes were to be found, but too late. Offal of the grizzlies showed them to be living entirely on field mice, marmots, and roots they dug from the ground. Sheep trails were many but the sheep themselves absent. Bud said perhaps we had seen our last sheep because they go high in the wintertime to be where the winds blow their grass free from snow. Sheep are grazers; moose are browsers, or bud and bark eaters. The sheep, which we had never had a chance to investigate, other than seeing their tracks occasionally on river bars below, might leave the vicinity with the turn of the season, their grazing grounds being too far removed to be of any practical purpose to us.

Both animals, the sheep and the grizzly bears, seemed to live in distant areas from our river valley, which was for the most part separated by cliffs from the grazing grounds above. The character of the Brooks Range is described as an ancient and weathered plateau, according to geographers; the river we were on was one of the weathering agents which cut down the plateau.

On the southerly or "Indian" side of the Alatna Valley the jagged Arrigetch Peaks, of an estimated 7000 feet, had risen slowly as we climbed. They looked like the teeth of some monster, black and forbidding. "Even the sheep must shun them," we agreed. Slanting out in weird angles, they appeared to be a howling hell of winds and rock. Somewhere on the opposite side of those hundred or so square miles of rock we knew lay Walker Lake, the source of the Kobuk River, draining the arctic westward. It was said to be a serpentine lake about twenty miles long, winding among cliffs. It had an evil reputation with Indians who claimed that a great fish living in the lake will swallow any man in a canoe venturing upon it. This fish was called *Karlukpuk*. Bud and I would have liked to see him ourselves, for he is doubtless a remarkable lake trout attaining great size.

To get a good view over the country in which we proposed to winter, we had gone up around and in back of the cliffs which face sheer on Pingaluk Creek and climbed up from behind. Now there was a thousand-foot cliff far below us. We were so high that even the cliff of Pingaluk was lost in the vastness of our land. We wandered through a sweet-smelling, scattered spruce forest swept clean as a park for many miles, and as we wandered gazed at the incoming valley entering the Alatna just ahead.

The name of the next river coming in was the Kutuk River. We thought it looked good. Here, temporarily, the country was more rolling, more grassy, smoother, fairer. Twin mountains, conical in shape, rose four thousand feet from behind our house—if we built there. One of these mountains especially was a perfect cone from the face of it; when seen from above it stretched into a vast plateau behind. It was timberless and covered only with a fringe of blueberry brush which had been turned red by the frost. We named it Red Mountain.

Smiling like a friend from far away, Red Mountain veiled the faces of the glowering rocky Arrigetches just behind and gave a more hospitable expression to the landscape. There was a little stand of good spruce running along the base of Red Mountain in the valley, but the rest of the country was open. We had gone about as far as the timber goes. The glowing slopes of Red Mountain and this openness were attractive because they offered perfect opportunity to see migrating game of all sorts where game existed. When we heard the fall wind whisper, this looked like home to us.

A two days' journey from Pingaluk Creek brought us to the place. I arrived behind Bud, wading, pulling the boat the last mile through the shallows. I was bare-legged and blue to the gills with cold. My shoes had popped at the seams and had given out. They were ready to be thrown away. They had served their purpose and I had other ones for winter. Bud would probably make a knife sheath out of them or something, as he usually did.

Bud had sickened a bit the last two days. He would walk a few yards and then sit down.

Actually, it took us two months to learn why we were sick with diarrhea, a condition which continued at intervals all fall, much to our weakening and disability. Now we are just about sure that the cause of this illness was soapy dishes. We had heard certain old sourdoughs in Alaska swear before now that using soap on dishes will kill a person. Naturally, we hadn't taken this belief of the old northerners too seriously but had put it down as eccentricity. Yet there may actually be some truth to the belief, in the case of the person who is living on a meat diet, because the grease of meat in cooking pots which are used three times a day and then washed each time with soapy water may make a base to which the lye in soap adheres and cannot successfully be removed, under primitive conditions. The trouble may go away, but then it will come back again. Scour the cooking pots as we would in an effort toward extreme cleanliness, we yet continued to have periodic spells of severe illness which became at last an actual hazard to life and work, until finally, out of sheer desperation, we gave up washing dishes with soap. After this we used only boiling water and a dishcloth on the end of a stick for a swab for our cooking pots and dishes for as long as we remained in the arctic. The cooking paraphernalia remained greasy and unsanitary but at least not poisoned, and we thrived. Later we found that this method of caring for dishes is entirely typical with people who are living on meat in the arctic.

It was high time to call a halt to the summer's travel. Summer holds great enchantment for me. We give it equal importance with winter in our narrative despite its brevity in the arctic because it is so little known to those who have doubtless heard overlong of arctic cold and snow.

Because we must have come easily 40 miles above Takahula Lake, which was said to lie 200 miles up the Alatna River from its mouth, we had come 240 miles all together on this river to make our home. The very first day, we had started pulling the boat with our own strength alternately with the motor. That was five weeks ago. The last 60 miles we had packed the motor away useless and had not even seen it since then. We must have pulled the boat ourselves 60 miles plus half of the remaining 180, which would be 150 miles of the total journey altogether.

"Do you remember what a sorry spectacle we were the day we arrived at our new home?" Bud would recall later. By looking at the spot then one would have wondered how anyone could ever make a home out of it. The winds were raw as we sat by an open fire on the beach and looked around us at the unnavigable, yellowish water of the Kutuk flowing over veined quartz into the clear water of the Alatna. We drank a kettle of scalding bear soup into which we were too weary to stir any salt. You had only to stand shaking on that spot to realize you would never get to the Colville River by way of the Kutuk as a pass for summer travel.

Opposite the Kutuk River mouth, high on the bank in the good timber, with a far view looking over our valley down to the thousand-foot cliff of Pingaluk, we made our last camp. This spot, our home, not exactly located at that time, we called roughly 68° 28' N. Lat. 154° 12' W. Long. "A good enough address for us," said Bud. So, it was that we settled in the beautiful remote valley of the Alatna, our arctic river, where two might live for one year—but only two.

PART FOUR

Fall Hunting

Bud notches logs of the growing cabin walls

At last the ridge pole is up, September 1944

1

Bud locked the blade into his new Swede saw and spat on the whetstone in his hand, preparing to give his axes a razor edge. The day after our arrival our house for the winter was going up in the little stand of spruce in the hill. This spruce had stood here since before the American Revolution waiting for adventurers to come along to the base of fair Red Mountain. The binoculars used inverted were a handy aid in counting the rings of the larger trees which were felled on our property; some of them were over four hundred years old.

"You can unload the boat," Bud directed. All day long I packed loads up the hill a hundred feet above the Alatna River and placed them in neat rows beside our tent, which looked out to where the waters of the Alatna and the Kutuk meet. Bud burned brush, leveled off the foundation, and felled timber in swaths. By nightfall of the first day he had three tiers of logs laid, notched, and locked into place. It took him only two and a half weeks in all to build our home. The inside dimensions of it were 12' x 14'. You want a small house because you will have to cut the wood to heat it. We intended to be warm during our stay and we were.

To make this size cabin necessitated the felling of around 70 trees, remarkable as this large number may seem to be, and, Bud thought, 100,000 strokes with the ax. No nails or spikes were used in construction, but holes were bored with the auger through the logs, and large wooden pegs, chopped out with the ax, were driven into the holes. Such a structure will last in a northern country for a man's lifetime.

It used to be thought nothing for two experienced men to throw up a livable log cabin in a short time. But men who can do this in our generation, especially alone and with no instruction, are certain to have a hard time of it at best. We have never found any correspondence courses in log cabin building.

For I was not much help. Although the stroke of an ax may be likened to the stroke of a golf club, this was a skill my parents neglected to teach me in my childhood and it was not one which I could pick up quickly now. How Bud learned his axmanship I have never been entirely sure, except that Bud could do any kind of job, no matter what, that had to be done. An old man ninety-one years old had once tried to teach me to split stove wood in Alaska. Old "Dunc" was the best axman at Cooper's Landing. His age and his fragility seemed inconsistent with the fact that you could see him quite effortlessly raise the ax and let it fall to split stove wood all day long. Old Dunc was patient with me when he took the ax from my hands to show me how again, but although I was eager I never acquired his art. The way I swung an ax was not only ungraceful; it was so mightily dangerous to anybody in the vicinity that it seemed best to desist. I chewed the ax handle near the head and the wood I chopped flew high in the air to come down, most likely, on top of my own head, while at sawmanship I threatened to break Bud's saw blade in two and he couldn't risk it. Bud decided the only thing to do was simply to build the cabin himself and let me hold the tools—certainly one skill at which I was more adept than he.

A person in the wilds must avoid any injury or sprain or strain when he is far from outside help. We succeeded well in guarding against accidents. I don't believe one of us so much as cut a finger during that year. What would have become of us from this point on, had Bud, for instance, sprained his back in the early stages of building our cabin before winter? We thought of this and together tried to spare his strength for the tasks which lay ahead. We had arrived very late. There was no harvest. We depended on Bud as the principal hunter for the large supply of winter's meat which each passing day told us we must soon secure if we were going to have food to eat. There are ways to lift loads fairly safely, and Bud conjured his brains for time-saving methods and the tricks he knew with ropes—the loops of the cowboys and the Spanish windlass. Bud got many of the logs out of the woods by himself; we hitched ourselves to others and dragged and floundered like two good dray horses. Our cabin was built of both green and dead standing logs, the green ones being much the heaviest.

One of the most difficult jobs, after we got the walls up, was to raise the great heavy rafters twelve feet off the ground on the down hill side, for the support of the roof. The eighteen-foot ridgepole in the middle of the roof we rolled up by degrees until it fell into its place.

The unloading of the canoe had disgorged an amazing amount of junk, it seemed to me, but had given up an alarmingly small supply of what was actually edible food. During the building of the cabin we were extremely fortunate to have a bear ahead, but our food worries were not to be over for long. Eating it three times a day caused the bear to shrink rapidly before our eyes until suddenly it was borne home to us that the whole bear would be gone at this present rate within three weeks.

"Don't worry," Bud said, "as soon as I get a free minute I'll make a real sashay around these parts and see what we can make of it. It looks like fine country to me. Keep your eyes peeled all the time. The chances are we should see game right from the cabin any day or night. Anything that passes through the Alatna or Kutuk Valley is bound to pass right under our eyes. That was one hunch made me decide we had better build here."

My principal job now was to scout the surrounding countryside for cranberries, which we deemed almost as important for winter's happiness as meat. In this way I happened to be the first to explore our new homeland.

I can see again those first wondering pilgrimages of mine along the old familiar mounds and up the face of Red Mountain, which took me hours from home. I have always loved picking berries. But cranberry patches were the hardest to find of any I ever searched for. Likewise, the absolute lack of blueberries brought up a strange apprehension in my mind which unaccountably grew upon me. "Do you suppose," I asked Bud, "that the lack of blueberries this year could have made all the bears leave the country?"

"Where could they go?" Bud shrugged noncommittally. "Haven't you seen any sign yet at all?"

I shook my head. "One old bear wallow going through the pass behind Old Rip Mound. Maybe we could set one of the big traps there?"

"Nope, we'd just lose the trap. You could sit there all day and watch the pass if we had the time."

That was it—we didn't have the time! We knew that last year our trapper friends Dick and Mary had put up six bears for winter—mostly shot at close range with the .22 rifle, by the way—and Bud had said: "We ought to average a bear a week from now on until hibernation time the way Dick does." But it began to look doubtful whether we would. It seemed as though one by one the animals and the growing things upon which we had counted were being eliminated.

These were freezing nights and golden days. Everything was dry; down timber crackled under the feet of the hunter. All of the fireweeds stood tall with scarlet leaves and were blooming with white fuzz. The yellow candles of the dwarfed cottonwoods glowed as though lighted by some celestial fire from within. I walked over a glowing land. The cranberries nestling in the yellow-white reindeer moss only made me think of big bears and I wondered if, like the *Toklat* grizzly of the Alaska Range where McKinley stands, some of the bears in this country might not be yellow to match their background. There might be bears in these mountains, for that matter, of perfectly unknown colors.

How large and unconquerable a land it was, giant mountain and meadow rearing up to the sky, and, peeking through fringes of willows from behind at intervals, the black Arrigetch Peaks, seven thousand feet of rock!

As the weather grew wintry and rainy by turns and Red Mountain turned to brown, picking cranberries and housebuilding were cold business. The winds rose and left the fireweeds forlorn and naked of their fuzz in one day. I climbed three quarters of the way up Red Mountain on the eternal quest; the wind sweeping down from those summits was repelling. The land was cooling off; somehow, I knew then that to climb the mountain again this winter would not be possible for me. The elemental forces ruling there supreme on those slopes gave no indications of themselves to people below in the valley.

Three miles up the Kutuk River from our place was another cabin. This old cabin was found after we had started building ours, but even if we had known of its existence we would not have wanted to move in there. These old cabins were usually abominable holes, the dens of former gold seekers. There was no recent sign of man in the Upper Alatna beyond the junction of the Iniakuk River, which was a hundred or more miles from our house, but San Francisco newspapers, dated 1905, with pictures of ostrich plumes on women's hats and an advertisement of the "White Gasoline Machine" had been stuffed into the casings of door and window of the Old Kutuk Cabin to show the date at which the former adventurers had tried their fortunes there.

The Kutuk Cabin was a spacious, well-built place, in a remarkably fine state of preservation considering the time which had passed, and it showed some fancy ax work which made poor Bud's enfeebled solitary strokes look downright amateur. But what a dismal place to live! The floor had never been anything but the bare earth. The roof, constructed too high and now sagging, deposited its seasonal burden of snow into one corner. Glancing at the height of the room, even the novice could profit; the foolish prospectors could never expect to maintain room warmth in this climate thus. The miserable bunks, built close to the earth from "store" planks brought in hundreds of miles, looked like pretty cold beds, even in their heyday. Apparently, the inhabitants of the Kutuk Cabin had only one small cooking stove to heat the whole place. A person soon becomes a detective in reconstructing a scene from the bits of evidence where there are no human lips to tell: we thought they must have almost perished if they stayed there during the winter, and the presence of old doghouses indicated that they did. The bottom and sides of the little stove were completely burned out. It told its story. It was cheering to think of our own prospects for an arctic winter that would at least be warm, by comparison.

Our own cabin we never attempted to make pretentious. The doorway had a high sill to step over and the top of the door was kept low. The best cabin which the far northern pioneer can make for warmth is the one where, standing outside, you can reach out your hand from your shoulder and touch the roof.

Interior decoration is a matter of taste. We used an old Scandinavian trick of setting the bed high up off the floor and climbed up near the roof to sleep. There was accommodation under the bed for everything to be stored out of the way. Half a cord of wood at a time could be stored in the back of the room behind the stoves, while our containers allowed us twenty-five gallons of water, plus a hot water tank on the back of the heater. Of course, everybody thinks his house on his river is best, but with our commanding position over our valley we often felt comfortably that we could withstand a siege if necessary.

Our house was not a dark, gloomy place, but sat where the first sun of spring would find its first awakening, and where the last sun of fall would linger in golden glow. Its ten small windowpanes were set to the north, south, and east, as was the door, to make the most of existent daylight at all seasons. To prevent breakage, the windowpanes did not go in till the last; with his pocketknife Bud whittled out the window frames from willow sticks and sealed the glasses between them in slits, securing them with tacks. Although the window casements were not as tight a fit as could be asked, the ice which formed on the inside of the panes in winter from condensation of moisture on a cold surface successfully sealed them. In our case, with our roaring monster which digested three-foot logs in his belly—our big 55-gallon drum stove—we were more often on the verge of roasting than freezing during our first arctic year.

One of the most ludicrous sights in the movies is the picture of the northern wilderness dwelling as modern movie audiences imagine one to be. We see the hero, usually a Mountie, dressed in whipcord breeches and tight leather boots, looking out the window of his cabin upon a snow-covered landscape. But in life one finds that when the weather is cold the Mountie or anyone else cannot see through the window because it is frosted; people living in cold countries use double or even quadruple windowpanes if they expect visibility. The sliding window is unknown. Windows which open inward on hinges may be used for ventilation, but more likely even the town house may have fixed windows which do not open at all. Instead there is a ventilator in the roof. Another of the details the makers of movies overlook is that these primitive cabins do not have board floors in real life. Where would one get the lumber? One may be a thousand miles from the nearest sawmill. Neither does such a cabin afford an open fireplace, for the fireplace is merely the device of the hunting lodge as sportsmen like to imagine it, and now no one takes one seriously for warmth.

All of the time all winter it would be a freezing temperature on our floor made of ax-hewn planks. A housewife could not mop such a floor if she had a mop because water would merely freeze there, trickling down beneath the cracks into the earth. One imagines mopping to be a rather recent invention. Neither could it be swept if you had no broom, but that was fine: occasionally we raked it. A part of our flooring was composed of flat rocks picked up from the river bottom, for the safe erection of the stoves. Because everything we owned was under one roof we felt we should be unusually careful about fires. Fires are perhaps the greatest of all hazards here. Bud built a tiny smokehouse out in back which never was used for smoking meat, but we did take the precaution of keeping out there a sealed can of matches and ammunition. Since, when we left the house, one of us always had a .30-30 along, and since the ax was always left out at the chopping block behind, we calculated that we could probably get by somehow even if the house should ever burn down. We would keep some separate meat caches, too.

It was a happy moment when I came home from a day afield and found Bud had moved us from the tent into the cabin. We had got the roof on, sixty poles to each side, cut and trimmed by Bud as fast as I could haul them. I had chinked every crack between the log walls with arctic moss. Within three days the place was nearly dried out by the roaring drum heater. Now Bud made racks for our guns, and pegs to hold the skillets on the wall, started up his watch again at an arbitrary hour, and hung up the calendar. Our library on its rack above the window consisted of a good bird book, a photography manual, a dictionary, a heavy volume of polar literature, a pocket Bible, and two copies of the *National Geographic Magazine*.

It was some time before we got a door on our cabin. A canvas hung over the low doorway. We had no idea what to do for hinges until Bud made a tour to the old Kutuk Cabin and got its door and attached hinges for us. As it weighed a hundred pounds before it was cut down, Bud had an awkward time getting home through the brush with the door on his back.

It might be asked at this point why we did not have a radio set with us in these remote travels; now certainly, as we set up housekeeping, a radio was going to be missed! It must be plain, after our discussions of the limitations of a fourteen-foot canoe, that we would not have been able to haul it, even if we had had one. Many people living on their rivers have battery sets and some of them are in working condition at times, but seldom up a river like ours. Usually these radios are for musical entertainment only because it takes special apparatus to send as well as to receive. I'm sure I don't know what kind of rescue expedition could have reached us had we called for rescue, and now that we were here it seemed probable that a radio would have been greatly handicapped by the tall magnetized mountain peaks of the area.

One of our windows turned up cracked, as was our wall mirror. Looking into the mirror at ourselves for the first time was a revelation. We both looked pretty wild. Our hair was long and our cheeks were red. Our faces surprised us by their thinness and the delicate blue shadings around enormous, serious eyes. Somehow in our eyes seemed to be the story of all the places we had seen this past summer and what we had gone through. Bud, who had not shaved all summer, was an Airedale whose bristling muzzle hid the mild pink angel beneath. His body was so wasted of any possible fat that he seemed composed merely of muscle. I had lost probably twenty pounds myself.

Our muscular strength had become terrific. I don't think we had any conception of how strong we were. Several times daily we were taken with cramps in the legs which would catch us unexpectedly and cause one or the other to look very ridiculous. These were the cramps of the overdeveloped athlete, I had no doubt. Bud and his brother had always been troubled with them at various times. The cramps seemed to grow worse as we grew leaner.

But we are getting ahead of our story. While the cabin was going up it was only occasionally that Bud could take a day off to hunt. I was filled with daily alarms and forebodings. Should he hunt or should he build? Food, or shelter, which came first? Never having tried such a venture before, one hardly knew what to expect next. All may work out well in theory about getting plenty to eat, but until one has put it to the test, there is always that element of the strange which makes one wonder. What about that unexpected factor?

When presently Bud took one day off from homemaking and climbed in full winter raiment to the snows of Red Mountain's top, a few days after my attempt at it, he reported no sign of bear to be seen any place on his twenty-five-mile circuit. Nor was there visible food for bears.

Later an Indian told us that others, too, who were likewise dependent on bears were disappointed throughout much of the Koyukuk. "Last winter," he told us reflectively, "many bears starve to death, I think."

This may or may not have been true. It is not known how many bears inhabit the Brooks Range.

2

The first snow caught us on September 8 while we were still living in the tent. We had been settled for just a week when it came. We awoke that morning to gaze unexpectedly upon a world of white and upon the specter of our incomplete cabin, the roof not even on, no floor, unchinked. Chinking of a cabin with chunks of arctic moss gathered in a gunnysack must be done before the snows come unless you want to dig the moss out from under the snow—which we did. Many shovelfuls of sod should be thrown over the poles on the roof to make it tight after the roof is completed. How can this be done if the ground has frozen?

It was Bud who rolled out first that morning. He touched a match to birchbark and wadded it into the little camp stove with dead spruce sticks. Then, noticing that the roof of the tent was sagging inward upon us and that all was rather dark inside, he gave it a bump. The load slithered off and the tent sprang up. Banging with his palms all the way around the tent roof, he roused me with the words: "Wake up and see the snow!"

I sat up in the down sleeping bag as the tent warmed and peeked out of the door, swallowing a gasp of alarm. I had expected snow in the arctic—eventually. But so soon!

As we ate our breakfast of corn pone and tried-out bear cracklings, we sought to readjust our point of view. Outside the open tent door, while the hot stove roared within, the snow sifted down silently. It was a magical world, silent and hushed. Who can describe the mystery of the first soft snow that comes in the night? "I'm just a kid at heart," I admitted unexpectedly, with a sudden surge of joy. "I can hardly wait to get out in it. And we might as well laugh as cry."

This was foolish but true. The berry picking was ruined, our house was unbuilt, but we were glad because we were comfortable for the moment, and because we had decided upon a day's vacation.

"We'll use this snow for our advantage," Bud said rapidly. "This is just what we've been waiting for. Now we can go hunting and have better chances than ever. Tracking animals in the snow is a whole world in itself; you'll love it. The snow makes everything an open book. We can tell what animals are in our country now for sure. We'll drop everything this morning and see if one of us can get onto a fresh bear or moose trail."

"Now we needn't go far," cautioned Bud. "We want to get our moose, if we can, right on the river or near the house so we can get him out. You have to think of that. Moose are probably passing right by our cabin, below on the flats, at any time, so don't think you have to go a hundred miles to find one. Don't wear yourself out. I'll see you, then, in about four hours. If I hear you shoot I'll come right away, for you won't be shooting at anything else. Don't try to skin it out alone and don't leave it or you might not find it again. Build a fire in that case and stay there until I come."

As we walked down the hill on our path now buried beneath snow and crossed in our empty canoe to the opposite side of the Alatna to search the flats spread out before our house, the snow continued to fall silently from a leaden sky. Bud left me on the south side of the junction of the Kutuk River. The flats, covered partially with brush and scattered spruce forest, might shelter many animals passing day and night along the valley floor by our house without our happening to see them at the right time. Hunting takes persistence and patience. We could even stand some kind of vigil yet if we had to in order to get something, but the numerous signs of game in summer throughout the valley did not indicate that our plight need come to this.

The snow was a foot deep on the ground and it seemed unlikely that we would see the ground again before next spring. Surely any bears in the country would be driven to early hibernation. We knew now moose was our main hope. If one of us could come upon a moose trail today, assisted by the snow, he could probably find the moose standing nearby; such a trail would undoubtedly be fresh. Moose will not stir about on such a day. Visibility was but a few yards through the snowstorm and the snow muffled all sound, so that if moose were present the hunter who was clever might walk right up on them.

Slow and cautious procedure is the prerequisite. Of course, we were wringing wet after the first hour of plowing through wet snow, but this is not uncomfortable on such a day if one keeps moving. I moved methodically at a pace calculated to keep warm, and what with the lure of striking a moose trail at any instant, the hours passed for me like nothing. Occasionally I paused to eat mouthfuls of snow off the branches of trees, or hearing snow fall to the ground with a nearby thud would be recalled enough to wonder just where Bud was in this silent world with me.

I had killed my moose the year before on a day like this, but an even wetter day, were that possible. The snow instead of being one-foot deep was five feet deep in the moose country near Seward, far down in the Temperate Zone, and we got snowed in. The hunter, looking over a moose trail in five-foot snow, could hear an earth-shaking rumble from the nearby mountains: snow slides coming down.

We had been staying out at that same unchinked Forest Service cabin where Bud had got his bear and I had seen my first moose and had decided that the snow was getting so deep that we had better get out. It was eleven miles to the highway; we had no snowshoes, but they would have been useless anyway. One day was spent in making half this distance, while snow continued to fall. With us we had on our backs the down sleeping bag, two frozen sandwiches and our little pup tent four feet high. When too worn-out and disgusted to flounder further, we cut spruce boughs and pitched our little tent on the pile. As we crawled into our bag inside the miniature tent to get warm, we hardly cared then if we ever saw a moose again in our lives or not. Inside our sleeping bag—not the first time the northern hunter has resorted to bed to get warm—we waited some eighteen hours for the weather to improve.

Although our thoughts were entirely directed toward the goal of hot food and shelter, as we followed the return trail on the second day's travel, you may be sure that little in the wild escaped Bud's attention nonetheless: we weren't out yet, and he was as always the eternally vigilant woodsman. On our trail perhaps four miles from the road, Bud saw three moose. Snow covered their backs; huddled among snow-covered Christmas trees they were barely visible in the storm. They saw us and walked slowly down a hollow and up the other side. I was going to plug on and let the moose go their way, but Bud said, "Hold it! I think I see horns on one."

All of the moose seemed bunched together between the trees so that I could make out little but a blur through the snow, which stung my eyes. But presently two of the three, the cows, slipped off ahead, leaving the bull to trail behind. At least Bud said he was a bull. He appeared gliding out from between branches and paused broadside one moment before going on. I took Bud's word for it. I raised my rifle and fired for the thick part of that broad shoulder just behind the shoulder blade.

I thought I was aiming for a heart shot on the moose. Had I hit exactly where I aimed it would have taken him high up in the lungs. What most people don't know is that the heart of all the deer family, but perhaps especially moose, lies low down, not far from the belly line. It seems very fortunate to me now that I killed him with one shot at 100 yards which broke the spine behind the shoulder—my first moose! It was a small bull moose, weighing not more than 600 or 700 pounds and having small horns, but some old-timers subsequently told me that this was exactly the kind of moose they all envied me for eating. This statement about the young herbivore being more palatable than the old is dubious, but I was pleased.

We returned to the village with the heart and liver of the moose to find the country store filled with city hunters and their guides. They had been sitting around the stove telling yarns, all with plaid shirts and an amazing variety of calibers of guns. Some of these hunters that day happened to be from Wisconsin, and they were wishing they were deer hunting in Wisconsin because the weather was keeping them inside, here. When we limped in we were two proud hunters. Bud gave them all some liver as they had no fresh meat, but I always suspected that they never believed that a woman killed that moose.

My first moose, I thought now, as I wandered familiarly through the forests again with a wet hide and the .30-30 on my back bound with tape at the muzzle, didn't have a bit of fat on it. Nobody's moose is fat these days. Nobody's deer is fat, in Pennsylvania, Arizona, Carolina, or

California. Seward moose used to be fat at hunting time before the war. The haunch of venison which hung by the Pilgrims' door, according to tales we know, was fat, not lean.

Today in the United States we know there has come a change in the status of animals according to the values they have for society. If we eat lean stringy game today it is because the majority of the hunters prize an animal for sport and not for food. In practically every state, and now in civilized Alaska, the game commissions have been obliged to postpone the legal hunting season far into the winter. By three weeks after rutting has commenced, the male animals which we shoot have run off every ounce of fat they have accumulated. They are at their very worst for food of any time during the whole year! The horns have lost all their velvet and are right at this season for mounting the heads. Furthermore, if the legal hunting season is late, the bucks will have more or less finished their rutting so as to insure the future of the next generation. Game wardens who decide upon our hunting seasons know that rutting animals are so visible and so easy to kill just before and during the early part of the season when they "run" that masses of hunters cannot be allowed out in the woods if the game is to be saved. Game management, then, today, is really "public management."

Here in the arctic, however, we wondered if the moose were already rutting, and presumed they were. There had been almost no fall; summer had changed immediately into winter. Our case was serious. We had brought a six-pound slab of bacon and four pounds of butter here with us, and that's all the fat we had. It was urgent that we kill not merely moose, but fat moose, at once. Getting fat to cook with or use generally was going to be a problem. In these mountains it was our greatest nutritional lack which we had not counted on at all, when we had thought only of vitamins on our budget! Now where was a fat moose to be found?

Bud cuts poles for the roof while Connie carries them

Chinking our cabin with moss

3

As I progressed slowly, looking for a moose trail and occasionally pausing to wipe off my gun with my sleeve and ascertain, as Bud had taught me to do, that the action was not becoming frozen up in the sleet, I reflected on our new arctic life. I was contented. This was really all familiar to me and I was already at home in the Endicott Mountains of the arctic Brooks Range. Five hours later when I found Bud by the beached canoe, he had built a fire and was standing by it, busy singeing in the flames some grouse which he had shot with his .22 pistol along the way. The fire was liquid orange, the water of the Alatna was dead black between its banks by contrast with the new-fallen snow. Bud was turning the hairy grouse over and over as he held them by head and feet in the flames. His rifle waited against a branch with its tape unpierced and his pistol was on his belt.

Bud's pistol alone was destined to keep us fed for the next weeks, for big game was not to be found soon. The pistol was destined to kill more game animals, if not game as measured in meat poundage, than all our other guns put together that year. Bud wore it on his belt during all his waking hours and was able to get with it small things that jumped up, even fish, while he labored hunting big game. Bud happened to be an expert with this little target pistol which the average person imagines to be a kind of plaything. He used it as most people use a rifle, not firing offhand but always leaning it against the side of a tree or some solid support, or, if this was not possible, resting it over one arm to fire or holding it with both hands. Incidentally, in our hunting I doubt if we have ever fired more than a half-dozen shots at the larger game without some such support or a "rest." Offhand shooting as one sees it so splendidly done in the cowboy movies simply doesn't rate.

No moose or bear trails had been found by either of us in the snow near our house. "Never mind," said Bud, "sooner or later their luck will run out." This was not the only day in the year. There might easily be a fresh trail near our house on the morrow, and, as Bud said, finding a fresh trail in the snow was just the same as getting that animal.

The tale of our fall, winter, and spring hunting in these arctic mountains is one of experiment, invention, and much endeavor. The truth of it is that there are many possible sources of food in the North, and in nature generally. When one source fails, another, sometimes totally unexpected, may see you through. Very rarely do all sources fail at once. Eskimos sometimes come near starving because of their improvident ways, but not often does the final ultimatum actually overtake them. It is amazing how even the more provident civilized person can fall into this carefree point of view following wide wilderness experience. He is in no worse position as a rule than the city dweller whose organization has gone on strike for a while. He may have to extemporize, but eventually everything will be all right, and his life and work will go on somehow.

Now came the saga of the rabbits. It was an odd thing, but Bud and I had shot exactly one in our lives in Alaska before this time. This was partly because we had come to Alaska during the "low" years in the rabbit cycle. Their increase and decrease is a mystery. Periodically they become so overabundant in some areas that they are underfoot everywhere; then, contracting a fever or disease, they seem to disappear entirely off the face of the earth. No tularemia, the disease dangerous to man and attacking rabbits, grouse, and some other wildlife, is known to occur in Alaska, as far as we know. But our entire residence in the North had coincided with an absolute lack of rabbits where we were. The snowshoe rabbit was as much a stranger to us as to any southerner who reads of him in northern books.

Coming up the Alatna River in the summertime, we saw no rabbits and gave them no thought. Then, a week before our trip came to an end, I saw one.

"Bud," I said, "I almost shot a rabbit today. But just as I slipped the safety catch off he got away." He was brown and looked just like any other rabbit to me. We thought no more of it.

Now, amazingly, the fresh snow around us was all at once alive with rabbit tracks. If it wasn't a good year for bears it was for rabbits. Bud lost no time in putting his initiative to work at this turn of good luck. As they seemed to be almost altogether nocturnal in their activities, they would have to be trapped. Giving me a dozen of the smallest No. 1 and No. 1½ traps to start with, Bud took me to the flats and laid out for me my first trap line among the willows. Some people use snares, but we never became proficient with them and used small traps altogether. "These traps won't hurt you," Bud showed me, "if you set them as I say and keep your fingers out of the way. I started setting these traps when I was six years old. I used to set one at home in Illinois by using a two-by-four wedged under the kitchen stove to force the spring down, then carry the set trap a mile out to the spot where I wanted to leave it. If I sprung the trap I would have to walk back home and set it all over again."

"Did you ever catch anything?"

"Sure. Lots of farm kids do. Muskrats, possums, skunks. When I was about nine I finally got a mink one day. You never know what you'll catch. It's always a thrill to look at your traps each morning."

Trapping for a season is one way of becoming familiar with all manner of animals which a person could live with in a locality season after season and never even see otherwise. Hunting and trapping are both realistic means of coming to know the North, especially in relation to the several thousand other human beings who are living in it by these methods; to understand the natives also was a part of our purpose in coming here to study the arctic. Our own small trapping experiences bordered on big ideas dealing with whole groups of people. This years' experience would put us in a position to know this part of the arctic intimately as no others in our generation did.

Trapping rabbits is a good start for the person who wants to become a trapper. They are probably the easiest of all animals to trap in the world; they are quite foolish. As they have no conception of what a trap is all about and no wariness of it, one merely lays the trap upon the ground just as it is without camouflage, and if there are enough of them around, some rabbit which has come out to dance in the moonlight will be almost sure to put one of his big feet in the trap before the night is out. The trick lies in putting it in the right place. As Bud went on to explain: "There's a lot of country where animals can put their feet."

The early snow enabled us to see the rabbit runs or trails which were thoroughfares of rabbit traffic through the undergrowth. We left traps on the most prominent of these. No bait is used because the food of the rabbits is bark and buds and shoots which exist everywhere in their world. A trick which helps the trap to spring in the desired manner is to place the trap on one side of a little windfall or erect an artificial windfall, a small branch laid across the rabbit trail so that the rabbit will bound over it and onto the pan of the trap.

We marked the place each trap was set by a small white first-aid bandage tied to a branch. Every trapper has his own methods. We have not met one who would divulge his methods, so that it is possible ours might be unique. Even now I sometimes come upon an old recipe in our bankbook, where Bud jotted it down one time for lack of other paper. It offers no explanation to the banker, but says only:

1 gallon rotten fish oil
4 ounces grated cheese
4 ounces glycerine
¼ tonquin musk
4 ounces beaver castors
MIX WELL

I found personally that there is nothing quite like trapping to sharpen your eyes and that it takes some experience before the trapper will not lose traps. Blaze marks may be made high up on trees with an ax in routing out the invisible trail of the trap line, but one should not mar trees deeply and there is some question as to how easily the more crafty fur bearers (except in settled country where they are used to people) might be alarmed out of the district by untold disturbances of the natural scenery. The trapper alone knows his trap line by heart as well as all of his secret traps by personality and number. He may move the traps around from time to time.

Each trap we bought came with a short chain and a ring, which I understood it is common for the trapper in the United States to slip over the end of a stake which is driven into the ground to secure the trap in one place and hold the animal. Sometimes special steel stakes or toggles are included when you get your trap. But these are not used in arctic trapping. The ground is frozen to such iron during the trapping season that driving stakes, unless in open water, would be utterly impossible. Here we used a northern Indian trick and found it very satisfactory for securing the trap. The trapper cuts a forked willow branch about five or six feet long for rabbits and leaving it quite untrimmed slips the ring of the trap chain over the cut end and up to the fork, where he makes a loop with the trap chain, drawing the trap through the loop, thus securing the trap to the branch. Then the trapper merely throws this weak little branch onto the ground with the set trap and leaves it. The first thing a trapped animal does is make a leap, and the attached branch or toggle, as we call it, goes with him. Into the thickest possible brush, the animal tears like mad, instinctively thinking to find protection in it from the thing flopping behind him. There is not an animal born, from rabbits to wolves, who will not drag the toggle into the nearest thicket and wind himself up like a package for parcel post. The fight with bushes and trees, which are torn up all around in the case of the larger animals, as though a cyclone had passed through, soon exhausts the prey. For wolves, of course, our toggle was more a log than a branch; it weighed many pounds. The skimpy ring and chain of the trap as dreamed up by furniture store dealers could not have held a wolf in any trap invented for him if he once turned his strength on it, so we fix him with the trap ring attached to the toggle by bent spikes so that the trap is free to swing in every direction—the swivel principle. The wolf then goes in circles. The trapper in the snow may follow the trail of the large animal half a mile or a mile to discover it wound up with the toggle and trap. The larger animals could not be successfully trapped at all were it not for this principle of the mobile toggle.

My little rabbits with their toggles of untrimmed limber willows were never more than a step off the trail before they were wound up. Bud advised me to visit my line the first thing each day, because the nocturnal animal, even the rabbit, becomes restless with the coming of daylight and if not caught tightly may be able to twist his toes off and make a getaway. We do not believe it common, according to our observations, for a trapped creature to chew off a foot or a toe. The toe concerned in these stories is twisted off at the joint as the animal circles around the trap in agitation. Traps are so constructed that they never turn loose or slip. The longer the muscle of a limb is pulled in an effort to get out, the tighter clench the jaws of the trap, which cuts off circulation. (Toothed traps are used only for wolf and bear.) It seems probable therefore that the trapped limb is numb within a short time. This would the more easily enable an "amputation" to take place, but we have never had this happen. The more intelligent the animal, in fact, the less he will abuse himself in the trap.

In arctic trapping, large numbers of the animals caught are found frozen solid; at fifty below zero the trapped animal instantly begins to freeze, and his troubles are soon over.

"Oh, he holds the lantern while his mother chops the wood, he holds the lantern like any good boy should," sang Bud.

Bud was happy working himself to death on the cabin. He was happy because he was leading the life he loved. Bud saw reasons for optimism everywhere—in an early snow, in a late snow; it was all one to him.

Turquoise sky without a cloud, white dazzling snow patches, silhouettes of dark green spruce against a background of wild mountain peaks standing out like jewels in the rarefied atmosphere. If we labored mightily all day long—which we did—at least we labored in a paradise.

Each day I rose early while Bud still slept and slipping down the path to our landing would paddle across the river as quickly as could be to make the daily tour of my rabbit trap line on the flats. I became a trapper of rabbits, convinced that our lives depended on it.

I was proud of that trap line. There in No. 5 would be waiting for me a big hoppy bunny. I saw the rabbits daily while they were turning from brown to white. No. 5 always was a lucky trap. One time it even caught a grouse. On my back I always carried my carbine as I was constantly on the lookout for the bigger game we had to have soon. Bud's pet .22

pistol on my belt was handy for shooting the trapped rabbits, and we had a good supply of .22 ammunition. To kill any animal instantly, no matter if it is the biggest animal in the world, it is merely necessary to put a .22 bullet in the brain. To find the right spot, mentally draw an X where two lines drawn between ears and eyes would cross. Since an animal which is shot in the brain will bleed and become messy when carried, however, the veteran trapper learns how to rap small fur bearers on the head with a stick. Bud usually picked up his rabbit gently with the left hand and, holding it by its long "snowshoe" hind feet, gave it one clip on the back of the skull with the edge of his right hand. The rabbit went limp and that was all there was to it. But you had to know how to do it. This is the method commonly used in killing domestically raised rabbits for market.

My trap line surveyed, up the trail I would swing with my load of dead rabbits from the landing and home again for breakfast. Between his labors at the sawhorse and chopping block Bud would have breakfast on the table, the stove crackling cheerily. Breakfast consisted in large part of rabbits secured the preceding day. Sometimes we had a couple of pancakes with cranberry sauce. One pancake to one rabbit was about the ratio. For a treat we would save up all the hearts and livers for a couple of days and have these all at once. They were really the most wonderful fried rabbits I have ever eaten, and we never had any complaints. We ate sixty-four of them in succession.

Coming up the trail to home and breakfast with Bud, I swung my rabbits jauntily, but one morning when I looked in trap No. 5 there were only the feet of my rabbit left; something had eaten him! Dead mutilated rabbits were likewise found further along the trap line at Nos. 8 and 9. Bud came to the flats to look for himself. Cutting a forked stick and sharpening the ends, he anchored the remains of each rabbit to the ground, so it could not be dragged away, and carefully covered each trap with fall leaves. Thus, he showed me how a "set" is made for marauders. The next morning when I came along the trap line to No. 5 and heard, at my step, the exciting rattle of the trap chain in the bushes ahead, a very small creature was held there. Its body, long and sinewy, was arched in the middle like a cobra coiled to strike, as it reared back. With a high-pitched tiny voice and open red little jaws, it squeaked angrily, only awaiting an opportunity to attack. "Easy Weasel," I breathed and dropped on my knee.

Bud and I had had a pet weasel named Easy for a while coming up the Alatna River. It had come darting around my feet at the chopping block one morning, attracted by the odor of marmot meat hanging on the tree in the gunnysack. Bud came out of the tent and shot the little killer of the woods with the pistol because I had never had a chance to see one close up before. He aimed for the head, one shot twenty feet away. He hit it through the neck instead. The weasel fell over; Bud ran up and the weasel shrieked out in rage and defiance. Bud knew instantly what had happened: the animal was only "clipped," as we say. One of those freak shots, the .22 bullet had passed right through the neck without touching bone or jugular, making no wound more serious than a stiff neck for a few days. Bud took a small swivel from an old fishing lure and some snare wire and made a collar with a short leash, then staked him out in front of the tent for a watchdog. When we pulled up stakes to move on, we pulled up the weasel's stake, too, and took him along with us for some days in the canoe, riding in rage through the rapids atop the load.

Easy was quite a personality. He was very active, alert and vicious. Perhaps his was not a forgiving nature. That little heart-shaped face with its rounded ears and mild inquiring look was deceptive. Every once in a while, he would go into such fits of hysterical temper as to become an absolute maniac. Shrieking to the sky if forcibly picked up with the glove, he would give off a fragrant odor from his musk gland. It was especially interesting to watch him eat. Far from refusing food as many wild things will in captivity, he was at all times a voracious eater, consuming his own weight in meat each day. Nor did he express gratefulness. He attacked the outstretched hand in flying leaps the length of his three-foot chain. Everything we fed him disappeared down his throat. One noon we gave him a small bird to eat. Eying us with red eyes, he did his war dance around and around it. Then he placed all four feet upon the bird and, while we watched, rapidly ate the inside out from the feathers. The feet, the bill and head and wings—all disappeared. Bones were ground to powder under his teeth. The thoroughness of his technique was so appalling that we began to doubt whether we wished to continue feeding this ravenous beast.

The end of it was that one day he leaped upon Bud's thumb with grinding jaws. Choked to unconsciousness to make him let go, he came to and instantly repeated the performance on Bud's other

Fall Hunting

thumb. "Be careful of Easy!" I cried, but Bud slapped the weasel on the head then; blood spurted from its nose as well as from Bud's two thumbs. Easy grew limp, his eyes glazed, and we solemnly laid our tiny pet on the grass. After Bud had bound up his thumbs with iodine he decided maybe Easy could be brought back to life; the weasel did not appear to be breathing but pressing on the slender ribs Bud said the heart was fluttering. A little artificial respiration and a sprinkle of water on his nose, and magically, Easy was as good as new again—and ready right now for a fight! But we had had enough fights. Wild animals take a great deal of time and patience to train or tame, and we had never intended to keep this one long anyway, only enough to photograph him, as we never liked the idea of keeping an animal in a cage. We let him go.

After that experience we saw Easy Weasel many times in the North, but we never tried to cage or change him.

"Easy Weasel," I said now to that little heart-shaped face and tiny weasel voice barking at me from the trap. And, tempting him to bite a stick, I rapped him on the head with another little stick about the size of a pencil. Then I reset the trap for rabbits and carried my pretty trophy along with care. At trap No. 8 the second weasel of this pair of hunting males was secured in the same way, and you couldn't have told them apart. It is one of the countless wonders of the wild how a weasel which weighs scarcely half a pound can track down and slay not only many great rabbits held in traps, but free rabbits, too. The weasel is a hunter and a fighter to his last breath. We would never have secured another rabbit on that trap line had not severe action been taken. The marauding male weasels would have returned again and again, systematically destroying the rabbit in each trap.

One of the first things we did when we moved into the cabin was to set nine or ten small traps around the floor. Something had begun noisy nocturnal attacks upon the drying hides of our rabbits and the summer's marmots which were stretched on boards by the walls. There were traps all over the place. We had to be careful where we stepped. Our night prowlings were few after the traps were set; we stayed safe up in our high bed.

I awoke one night in the blackness to caution Bud, and we both lay silently listening. Whatever it was, it moved like lightning about the cabin, investigating every corner. Now it climbed up the wall to our bed—I was sure of it! Light-footedly it brushed over the ends of my hair on the pillow, and there was silence. I had a feeling it was glaring at me two feet from my face. A waft of perfume trailed behind as it bounded to the floor; I was sure then what it was. We had not long to wait, when *bang!* in the corner four traps went off almost simultaneously. Cautiously, Bud climbed down with the flashlight. The struggle in the corner and the rattle of trap chains brought me in my nightgown to the scene, where we retrieved an enormous silver-gray weasel which Bud said was almost as large as a mink. Some of the weasels on the Alatna actually measured eighteen inches by the tape. This one was caught by all four feet at once in different traps and by the nose, so he couldn't even squeak. The second prowler of the pair was caught fifteen minutes later when we had once again retired. We have never seen a female weasel. They must be confined with many litters each year underground in the nest. Three of these little animals, the smallest of the fur bearers, are, as ermine, worth to the trapper the equivalent of a hundred pounds of sugar on the usual world market if he could get it up the Alatna. An ermine pelt pays around $1.00.

The snow rotted in the rains and my trap line was running out of rabbits. The traps needed to be moved to new runs, but no new runs could be discovered until it snowed again. After this, as it happened it scarcely snowed at all until near Christmas. I went back to picking cranberries, many of which were mere shells, having been rotted out inside by the freezing and thawing action of the inconstant weather. I carried my carbine on my back at all times, but I could find nothing. Eventually I accumulated for winter supplies a sack of berries weighing possibly seventy-five pounds.

As the days passed we found ourselves listening for sounds from the outside world, a distant airplane perhaps. But no sounds from the outside world came to our waiting ears. Presently we stopped listening.

4

The small wild things about the doorstep of the wilderness dweller are a never-ending three-ring circus. One of the first things to be added to the completed cabin was a bird-feeding tray outside the window. Here our faces as we ate breakfast upon our Nile green canoe seat (now become breakfast table) were but inches from those of the birds which came to dine. These birds were the Canada jays or camp robbers, as most Alaskans call them. No sooner had we beached our canoe and announced out loud that we were going to build our home here than the first camp robber fluttered silently down from a spruce tree beside us. No sooner had the first tent stake been driven than the second camp robber came to rest on top of it. With their bright eyes they inspected us, hopping tamely along the ground just out of the camper's reach, and with their strong bills they pecked at everything. They had sampled the bear meat before it was sacked and hung in the tree. They already knew intuitively where the garbage pile would be. Before the week passed Bud had them taking scraps of meat from his hand. We knew that the greedy camp robbers drove away song sparrows and warblers we should like to become acquainted with, but then they were permanent residents and would remain with us throughout the arctic night.

The quarrels of the camp robbers and the grouse they teased, their disagreements with the squirrels who rocketed madly up a tree trunk and shouted back, the quarrels of the squirrels with each other and with the grouse, continued as intermittent feuding the year around. As with the differences of human beings, there was much to be said on both sides. The grouse were unassuming, minding their own business, but it was true that they were also crotchety, breathless, and fluttering, and once upset would cackle like the old hens they were for the rest of the day. The squirrels and the camp robbers had plenty of food for all in our leavings put out for them, but not knowing, of course, how long this good fortune could last, they were possessed of a passion to make hundreds of different caches of it in the stumps and trees. Day after day they labored, packing off the booty. And several times each day all pandemonium would break loose when Chupper, our pet squirrel, would dash at full speed up a tree with an old grouse wing from the garbage pile in his mouth and two camp robbers close behind him. He had waited until the camp robbers turned their backs and then robbed one of their caches! Back and forth they would have it all through the mellow fall days, robbing each other in turn.

We never killed or trapped anything near the house. Chupper the squirrel was our alarm clock. He woke us every morning. When we heard him go off we knew it was time to get up. One day Chupper, chasing another squirrel, or the strange squirrel chasing him—we don't know which—came at a gallop down a tree trunk. Up another tree the pair went, leaped from on high, caught a neighboring limb, and down to the ground they came once more. Bud, standing there, had no conception of the part he was to play in the show. Bounding over the ground the pursued squirrel saw Bud's figure and must have mistaken him for a tree. Up each leg came a squirrel; they met in the middle and, in alarm, leaped to the ground. Bud watched them disappear over the hill, still going up trees and down, through the forest.

But this was not the carefree scene that we would think in all cases. It is quite often a matter of survival when we see squirrels leaping high in the trees. They are males carrying on serious warfare in gangs, and when examined it is seen that they may frequently be scarred from head to foot. The squirrels that chatter and scold, the squirrels that the camper sees, are males; females are rarely abroad.

The end of Chupper we were never sure about except that we had only known him two months when we believe he met his end in some way. A very possible cause of his disappearance could have been one of the falcons which hurtled down the mountain over our house now and then. None of us could know when a falcon was coming because it came so swiftly, swishing down to earth and making a grab, just as Chupper got under a root. "I wish Chupper would be a little more careful," I would say to Bud, but we had no idea how to suggest it to him. He seemed to have no real comprehension of the dangers forever lurking but would forget all caution as soon as the deadly wings passed on.

One day I was sitting on a log by the house preparing grouse or ducks or something when out of the hole in the root behind me emerged a weasel. This weasel was pure white, the first ermine of winter. I never knew he was there. It is hard to tell how long he had been making feints and mock passes at the back of my jacket, which swung in the breeze, when Bud came up and informed me that an ermine was coveting my birds. As soon as I turned around and faced him, the ermine gave ground, slipped into the hole under the root, and sulkily would not be lured out again. That was Chupper's hole! "I wish Chupper would be a little more careful," I mentioned again, as Chupper was seen skipping unconcernedly in and out of that hole the following day. We never saw him again. For a while even the camp robbers seemed a little lonely because they had nobody to fight with.

It might be wondered at this point how the person who likes animals and has pets about the place can at the same time be a hunter and trapper in the other part of his life on the other side of the river. Yet many northern trappers are in this situation, which is not at all uncommon, and the course is not so inconsistent as it would seem. Such persons hunt only for food and do not kill except to supply their own needs or eliminate some harmful predators.

We both admit that the average American man likes to own a gun and go hunting or wishes he could. Almost all men would do more hunting than they do now if they had the chance. On the other hand, the American woman you meet, either at a bridge tea or over the clothesline, is touchy on this subject. Hunting on the part of the males in her household has been an abomination in her life. She herself has no desire to kill any wild thing and does not understand how any civilized person could do it or enjoy it. Where does the truth about the proper attitude toward our American wildlife lie, between the gun lover's and the nature lover's point of view?

State game associations, ranchers' organizations, hunting clubs, game protective societies—in other words, largely the hunters themselves—are the ones who have proved the friend of wildlife. But for their efforts in feeding methods, extermination of parasitic diseases and predators, game would have long since disappeared from many areas. Today many states have more game of certain kinds than they ever had originally. Furthermore, foreign species, such as the ring-necked pheasant, have been imported to our land. This shows what can be done with modern game management. The idea behind game management that is progressive now is not to hold the hunter down to a small limit eternally into the future, but to find ways of increasing the game which can find a living in a certain area, and to make that area rich and safe so that game can increase. In the open lands yet left in the United States there is almost no limit to the increase of wild game under controlled conditions; game management around the world has just begun! If millions of people want to find enjoyment in hunting in the wilds each year, that should be no occasion for worry about decreases in wildlife. By using the right methods there can be hundreds of pounds of wild game available for each hunter and the country would never know of their losses from the multitudes.

Bud expressed his attitude about taking game in two ways: first, he had noticed that animals themselves prey upon each other so that a life of hunting and being hunted is not new to them, but one to which they were born whether man interferes for his own uses or not. Secondly, he likened the taking of a mature, full-grown animal in proper season to the picking of a ripened fruit which is otherwise due to fall to the ground, burst, and be dissolved by the elements. Wild animals never die of old age. Wild animals are felled by others or by the laws of nature generally before they have much passed their prime; in lean years thousands may die of starvation in those areas of the world where they yet roam without interference by civilized man. Or upon great increase they succumb to parasitic disease; such is their fate and we might as well face that fact. The armchair naturalists often seem to have the idea that all was paradise in the wildlife world before cruel man interfered. Far from it! Certainly, Bud and I could see by the wasteful, painful results of nature's laws throughout the vast untended arctic—a genuine "virgin wilderness"—that the contrary is the truth.

Controlled hunting is very desirable for a country inasmuch as hunting is the motive which inspires us to further the increase of great numbers of animals to grace our landscapes and make otherwise worthless areas productive. But the main thing is that hunting helps the people who are to be the hunters by making out of them a strong, skillful people who can go primitive when they have to. Even in modern warfare the training of the hunter ranks as important as it ever was. Much has been said in recent years of the importance of hunting and outdoor sports for public recreation to build up the health of a nerve-weary and crowded population, but especially to supply the physical and psychic needs of its young manhood.

I myself would go a step further, because I love hunting, and say that women too ought to investigate and see what hunting is all about. It should be a more common event than it is for a man to take his wife and children along to camp in a tent for a few weeks each year, for the whole family should benefit from a good hunting and fishing trip. Women and even children are quite capable of going on "serious" hunting trips by themselves. The wives and children of the primitive family go, and accidents are rare with them because they are used to the life. There is a wonderful world in wilderness, and the object of "hunting" may give some purpose which it otherwise does not have. Only the very old are content to observe life placidly. The bulk of us must act if we are to remain well and sane. There is nothing quite like a happy hunting trip to put us in par, revitalize us, and make us all young again. Why should men only have the monopoly on this good commodity?

Hunting and fishing, more than the poolroom or the baseball park, have been a strain on the national marriage, one could say. We are not advised on the strains other sports afield impose on marriage, but we can say that hunting and fishing frequently become so fascinating that they become more than a mere sport. They are a mania; they are a way of life. In them the man who is depressed by domestic burden or business strife finds increasing escape and the chance for the self-assertion usually denied him. The jealous wife finds here that she may have a rival to her affections conceivably more deadly than another woman. For here is a rival of which the lover will not tire until the day he dies. It is one that is constant and comforting. Those fields and streams forever call him. The North and the West are full of men like these, but the cities have even more of those yearning secretly to escape.

Men, anyway, will have to go hunting a bit, and we shall be wise if we learn to understand the fundamental reasons back of this and its justification. Women in Europe would find it hard to understand, as would our own grandmothers, how we could fail to be glad when the husband brings home game from the field and the forest. To them it would seem incredible that a day would come when a woman would refuse to dress a bird or to do those fundamental things which are necessary for eating and human existence. That we could raise a generation that doesn't care to learn seems very strange when one sees what poverty can be in the world. When you think about hunting in this way, it is something which is elemental and vital to the people.

When John brings home a couple of beautiful mallard drakes and exhibits that hard-won prize to Jane, there are more intelligent ways she can greet him than with the shout, "Get those nasty things out of here!"

In our country it seems popular to say to the girls, "You know John *has* to go hunting," for which tribulation you will gain sympathy.

"Yes, men are just like children," your friend with the red-lacquered nails will agree as she sips her tea and nips at a cookie.

Yes, indeed, John is funny about his hunting as a rule. Perhaps he doesn't analyze his motives, but hunting is a sacred privilege to him: the free man's right to own a gun in a free land where there is yet wilderness. It's hard to take him seriously as a food-getter. He talks all year about his hunting trip, but first and last in terms of grains and caliber and pitch of stock, and the reverberations of the loud explosions on which he dwells.

But how about hunting and the purpose which alone makes it entirely reasonable—hunting for food?

5

In the late fall, great northern pike took the place of the vanished rabbit trap line in helping us eke out our diet. Bud's method of luring a pike on hook and line before beginning to hunt for the day was ingenious. He used a piece of our precious bacon for bait at first, and later on, a fin. There on a rock which dropped off into a deep quiet pool near our front door I could generally find him peering and slowly waggling the bait back and forth. These pike would not take artificial lures and they did not strike. They came up to the bait like slow murky submarines; then, thoughtfully taking it, they would begin to chew. After considerable meditation they swam away lazily with the line, while Bud waited, leaning over the pool. He had learned that these crocodiles with their long-toothed mouths were at heart timid souls; the least flippancy with the bait and away they would go in a cloud of dust. We never learned why it was that in the fall the far arctic pike would not take a lure in the approved sporting way; they may be a different variety. Some days Bud secured two or three of these moody, munching pike for us, until even they gave out. His largest one measured thirty-seven inches in length and cracked his trout rod when he hauled it in.

Bud started to make a fish net in the evenings when the day's work was done. Driving forty-eight nails into a board, he hung forty-eight strings from which we began tying loops of a certain size; it took four hands to make it and the loops slipped out of shape. The principle of the gill net is that fish trying to swim through the holes get caught by their curved gills, since the body is too big to pass on through and they cannot back out. Each net catches fish of a standard size. The loops must be standard and must not slip. Our net was to be twelve feet long by four feet wide when complete. We thought we could even learn to set it under the ice during the first part of the winter, as we were aware that the natives do, but we had no one to show us how to make the ties to construct the net. The net-making phase passed as another abandoned idea.

One day, over my own footprint of the day before in a squashy snow patch along my rabbit trap line, I found the unexpected imprint of a crushing, ponderous heel. I was thinking of myself as in a small game world. My heart stopped in my mouth. I looked quickly around for Bud. The waddling steps, closely spaced and broad as dinner platters, depicted the state of mind of an enormous grizzly bear ready for hibernation. This grizzly was so fat and lazy that his trail, crossing mine, wound around the ends of logs instead of stepping over them.

While the valley was still bathed in blue shadows, early in the day I was on my way, following the big grizzly trail which was less than twenty-four hours old. Bud has said he should have trailed him himself. But Bud was busy cutting vital winter fuel and was half sick from overwork and undereating. Would I like to go? Indeed, I would.

It seemed possible the grizzly might be found nearby. Bud advised me to go carefully because the tracks would in all likelihood double back upon themselves. The bear might be at any quarter of the compass, a fact I knew well from trailing moose.

"Be sure to get as close as you can," Bud warned, "but don't ever let him see you."

I started to throw a shell from the magazine into the barrel of my rifle. But something was wrong. For a moment the queerness of it came near to throwing me into a panic.

"I know what it is," said Bud, after a moment's hesitation. "The loading mechanism won't pump a shell because the magazine spring is frozen. It's well above zero. Some moisture must have been in it. I'll show you how to thaw it in case it happens again."

Reaching into a spruce tree Bud broke off a couple of armfuls of those lacy brittle twigs which are some of the best tinder in the world and touched a match to the pile. Soon the barrel of my rifle had become warmed by the swift twig fire. As for alarming the bear with the smell of smoke—had he not already passed within sight and scent of our house, showing no alarm? The lesson that the frozen-up gun pointed to was that a person could never take his gun for granted. Would it not have been embarrassing to have met the bear, thinking that I was armed with a gun, only to discover that it was but a stick? Many of my discoveries in the art of becoming a hunter must be commonplace to outdoor people who have hunted all their lives, but Bud always reminded me that a gun is not a weapon but only a pile of junk in the hand except when cared for and handled in a certain way, and I think he was a good teacher. Because they were meant as weapons we always kept our guns loaded. We treated even a child's toy pop gun as a weapon when picking one up in order to develop the correct responses, something which everyone should do who ever intends to use guns at all.

Although this was the first time I had been on a grizzly trail, Bud was not afraid to let me go alone; I had been well-trained and might do even better by myself. One person to follow a trail is plenty. Two people make not twice as much noise as one but five times as much. Three people make a hundred times as much noise as that. And bears, including the biggest grizzly that ever roamed, are more alert and shy to locate than a timid deer. A person hunting alone is almost sure to see twice as much game when it comes to stalking big game as he can with a companion, even a trained guide. For this reason, and also to cover a larger area between us, with better chances of intercepting animals when the animals were there, we hunted alone as a rule.

What I know about grizzly bear hunting would not fill a thimble and I'm afraid my tale of a grizzly cannot reward the expectations of listeners prepared for a saga of the hair-raising variety. The bear led me a long trail winding up the Alatna Valley. I remember sitting down on a log and putting on some lipstick and thinking, "Well, there's nobody around here going to beat me to the bear, anyway." It is nice to be able to take your time and quite a privilege to have a bear all to yourself.

I found trees where bears had stood on their hind legs and stretched their claws like a cat. When another bear comes along to such a tree it is said he tries to make his mark a little higher; marks on the trees twelve feet high off the ground are not unknown with these big bears. I found places where the bear had dug holes with his paws for roots of vetch, the wild pea. The vetch roots, left carelessly by the bear, were a gift to Bud. We always were bringing each other "gifts." To our surprise we found them to be excellent for human beings to eat, and for days thereafter we industriously took the shovel in the canoe and dug up vetch plants by the score along the flats by our house, but we were never able to get another single one of the special roots. The plant, Bud thought, must have been a biennial, and only certain plants possessed the tuber during a certain year; the bear had perhaps already dug up the good ones in our vicinity and eaten them. The question was, how did the bear know which plants to dig up, when we didn't?

The bear knew how to traverse the valley with the least effort to himself; if you want to get some place easily, just follow a bear's trail. He knows more about that country than you'll ever know. Of course, he didn't mind crossing right over swamps showing open water, where I bogged down. I had to make a detour around these.

For some reason bears like to stand and gaze out over water. In several spots my bear had stood and gazed over the Alatna River for some time. With growing suspicion, I came to realize what was on his mind: he was getting ready to cross the river. I learned how bears go about this. They cross by the islands.

I had thought about the probability of his losing me in this way at the outset. The bear swam with ease the deep icy channels I could not wade. "Perhaps he'll come back to my side of the river yet," I thought, and followed up the bank another mile and found the big waddling tracks once more. But I lost them for good when he plunged in and crossed to the island above. The bear thus went up the river by the islands, keeping always to the side of the river which had the flats, feeding on vetch.

I didn't get my bear; he left me five miles of brush and swamp from home. My breakfast of two flour-and-water pancakes was wearing thin. Unrolling my lunch pancake from my shirt pocket I slowly ate it, sitting on a log. I had been thinking about it for hours.

The next day there was no meat in the house; we ate rice boiled up with cranberries and chopped bacon.

THERE WAS THE INCIDENT, then, of the fish ducks. They were seen floating in the backwater just below the mouth of the Kutuk River where it comes into the Alatna as visible from our front window. Bud stalked them and shot them with the shotgun; the Alatna River in late fall was just wide enough by our house to shoot across. I pushed out into the stream in the waiting canoe and we retrieved the ducks with effort. Hanging them up one by one by the necks on a thong, we skinned them behind the house; their waterproof breasts would perhaps make mitten liners this winter. The meat we soaked hours in salt water in hopes of eating it. Many sportsmen soak all their small game in this way, believing that salt water, or even plain water, draws out the gamy taste. There are other magical solutions, too. But we have always found all small game, like any other meat, best when it is prepared and eaten immediately. Soaking destroys precious vitamins and flavor together. We have never made a habit of soaking small game, therefore, except under unusual circumstances: either when it has lain a long time in a game sack undressed or is badly shot up—which are the causes of the famous gamy flavor and what people mean, no less, by a "bad" or a "strong" taste!

Now these fish ducks! Bud was to eat three of them and I was to eat the fourth; he needed the food. When I started pulling young pike out of their gullets up to seven inches long I felt no covetousness! A kind of digestive juice from their stomachs ran out of their bills when they were carried upside down. But the main thing I noticed was that the color of their intestines was blue, just like the raven I had once intended to eat! That blue was not from eating blueberries. It was the typical intestinal coloration of the scavenger.

We roasted these four great ducks—otherwise fine-looking—in hope. The house was filled with a terrible odor. Out from under a snowdrift in back of the house I retrieved a can of meat drippings from our black bear which had been set aside for bait during easier times—not the first occasion a trapper has eaten his baits, I guessed.

But I was wrong in our case. When we portioned out the fish ducks and the fox bait—that was one night when we went to bed with absolutely nothing for supper.

"I'll tell you what we'll have to do," said Bud. "We can't go on like this. We're not getting anywhere. We're just breaking even from day to day trying to catch enough small game to eat. We'll simply have to make a big concerted drive for grouse and rabbits until we can get enough ahead so that we can live for a few days and devote our complete time to hunting big game properly. Then we'll leave the cabin and try another area. We've got our canoe here for transportation. What are we waiting for? I've been wanting to look over some of that country up ahead anyway."

Bud and I kept records of every bird and animal taken for food while we were in the arctic and a record of every important specimen observed. During the few weeks of September and early October at our cabin we know, for instance, that we lived on 64 rabbits, 4 fish ducks, 6 eating ducks, 37 grouse, 12 pike, and some 35 grayling, and still lost weight steadily. We may be doubted by those who have not had this kind of experience, but we know why the American Indian went when the buffalo went.

We know that it is possible for a human being to live splendidly on meat alone—the aborigines of this continent formerly did, and we can observe that Alaska today is supporting 35,000 native people doing practically this—but here is a nutritional law that works: the meat must be fat big game. You cannot live on small game. A person will starve on rabbits and birds, no matter how many he eats of them.

Our rabbits were built like little Shetland ponies, thick and juicy across the saddle; our grouse were rolling with yellow butter in their throats as fall progressed. They were foods for the connoisseur's table, given the proper trimmings to go with them. But what of the person who hasn't the trimmings?

The terrific energies we expended hunting, housebuilding, berry picking in the cold winds, our clothing torn and elbows hanging out, had rapidly depleted our resistance following the five weeks' swim to get up the arctic river. At the last it was the fat red bear meat of former meals which had enabled us to keep driving ourselves onward—not rabbits!

There are a few small game creatures which can supply big game energies; in our experience these are beaver and muskrat, or probably all the swimming and hunting animals which possess the red-meat attributes; the marmot; and probably the wild goose should be classified as big game where nutrition is concerned, as a person can live well on geese indefinitely if they are good. Other small game, especially the "white meat" variety which is not oily, lack what it takes for good living.

Fall Hunting

Anyone who has ever read anything on northern life has probably run into the common information at some time that Indians and Eskimos and even some white adventurers eat a great deal of blubber or fat meat. Just what is there to this blubber business? We had wondered ourselves when we read these old arctic books and had found no answer in contemporary Alaskan city life.

The simple fact is that normally we Americans in our civilization consume immense quantities of butter, cream, bacon, lard, ice cream, vegetable oils, and so many rich foods supplying fats in one way or another that few of us have any conception of how luxurious life for the civilized person now is. Even the poorest crop picker can buy all the flour he wants and all the lard for shortening that he could conceivably utilize, for a few cents a pound. The fat shortage in diet is especially noticeable today in the overpopulated countries and in those desolated by modern war, but in many lands, even in good times, fat and rich foods have never been easily obtainable. One of the finest gifts which a traveler may be offered by peasants in southern Europe is a vessel of sheep's fat.

To anyone having all the butter and ice cream he wants to eat in daily life the idea of a vessel of sheep's fat is not attractive, especially if he has not been brought up on it. But supposing the butter and ice cream are not to be had? Since large populations rarely get to taste these luxuries which Americans take for granted as common food, they use different fat commodities: olive oil, goose grease, mutton fat—these are the ice cream and the bacon of the entire Eastern Hemisphere. The Eskimo has his blubber from the northern sea animals and fries doughnuts in it today sometimes.

Each person consumes fat, then, when he can get it, according to the chemical and nutritional needs of his own body without being aware of it. The amount of fats we burn up are dependent on our exposure to cold and on the hard work we do, to name two factors which would be especially applicable to the northern pioneer. When a civilized person starts leading the Eskimo life he can soon eat very much as the Eskimos do, and in fact will almost be bound to do so, except that his habits might be cleaner. The white person, the Indian, and the Eskimo on a meat diet in the North develop remarkably identical tastes in foods. Certain meats are universally preferable; certain parts of an animal are prized on the basis of their high caloric content almost as though by some guiding instinct within us. In this case it is not the tongue but the stomach which is the guide, as one's system cries out for more nutriment to support it.

This may not be noticeable so long as some civilized food holds out. For instance, we thought rabbits (usually preferred by most white campers to bears) were fine so long as we consumed two pounds of sugar and two pounds of flour along with them daily to bolster them up—not to mention the bacon grease that we fried them in. But as soon as we tried to cut the sugar and flour ration in an effort to hoard it, within a couple of days' time it became physically impossible not to break into these supplies again. Our bodies simply lacked the fats and carbohydrates which a ton of rabbits could not supply. Therefore, we craved "heavy" foods—sugar, bacon, and flour—like fiends. Sugar, especially, acts as a substitute for fat. The fact that Americans consume such a tonnage of candy and sweets is a great reason why fat meats in general are not appreciated today among our people as they were a hundred years ago. Sugar, especially, helped to bolster the lean rabbits with us—but at the rate of two pounds a day, our hundred pounds of sugar would be gone in fifty days and we had almost a year to go on it!

We had made deep inroads into our winter's grub supply by the time we left home to hunt big game. We had eaten most of our candy bars meant for Christmas, a quarter of our winter's supply of sugar, and we had only one pound of butter left. Bud's strength was waning. He was a sick young man.

On our big rabbit drive Bud shot ten rabbits, all hit in the head with the .22 pistol, while I got four with the .22 rifle. It was an experience to observe Bud's technique in the field, while the rabbits, like long-eared white ghosts against a bleak brown landscape which had no snow, sprang from every bush. Going down the flats we kept parallel to each other in a line a few yards apart. In this way we were able to shoot the rabbits ahead without danger of shooting each other. As the rabbits were retrieved Bud carried them in bunches and hung them by the hamstrings along our route on the broken-off limbs of small trees. It was black night when we picked up each rabbit cache and threaded our way home through the river flats, yet Bud knew where every rabbit hung. Weariness and difficult straits had only made him the more methodical.

While I held each carcass by the hind legs Bud peeled it out of its furry jacket in the dark. The skins were put into one sack, the meat in another, and all was packed home that would be of use to us.

"Tomorrow," said Bud, "we'll leave to hunt big game. I know now the mistakes we made. We arrived too late; we missed the best fall hunting, which I can see now comes in this country in August; we missed most of the berries, everything. Now it's October. We tried to do too much. We'll never be able to think of exploring a pass to the Colville River this year because we'll be doing well just to keep alive. We brought too little grub up here. But we can cook up all our rabbits and take a little tea and the sleeping bag in the canoe and really find time to do our fall hunting at last. We have a home with a roof on it to come back to, and I'm not worried about that any more.

"Of course," he said, "I suppose we could try to get out of here yet. Maybe we would be wiser to load everything into the canoe and get. I'm not worried about getting big game before long, but we know we won't find any more civilized food growing on bushes around here. What do you think?"

"What?" I replied. "Go back after pulling that canoe all summer to get up here? After building our home? And are we going to limit our range in exploring just to the range of our foolish stomachs? We can't live for eating alone. We can get along without that civilized food for a while when you think that we'll have it again later all the rest of our lives. Besides—I would like to see what it's like in the winter. I—kind of like it here."

Bud had voiced the doubts because he wanted to make sure that I had my say. Two must be agreed, and then anything is possible. "Well, now," he said, "let's get down to hunting."

The Alatna River was running light ice.

It was already late in the season when Bud finally killed a moose

6

It was early in the morning when we left home, lining the empty canoe along the high dry beaches of the sunken Alatna. The sun did not get over the mountain until ten o'clock now. Bud with the lead rope around his hips, as of old, began to walk the miles off. I knew Bud would smell out game if there was anything within a hundred miles.

To travel again, even now without rest, filled us with delight. It seemed to promise hope of something. Full of rabbit meat for the time being, we felt fine. All nature, having reared its young in the summertime, waxed fat with a strength and vitality that bubbled over, to make any human heart feel glad. Grouse strutted and courted as though it were spring; their courting was one of the reasons for their being conspicuous in the fall. The camp robbers opened their raucous throats in totally unexpected glorious song.

Two months behind time in our arctic hunting, strangers in the land, we were faced with the possibility of serious consequences, yet Bud always maintained later that the presence of game in the valley, the occasional tracks and so on, never caused him to feel the slightest doubt about the outcome. For a person living on such a river as the Alatna all the year around, he said, who planted and harvested a vegetable garden, all seasons could be fruitful and leisurely, really. Here a man with an ax in two weeks' work out of the year could put up all his fuel, but how long does the civilized man have to work to pay his fuel bill? Here, meat and fish cost nothing, and even now it seemed strange to recall that there are places where people pay seventy-five cents a pound for meat. Living here, a person could provide for all his needs in a natural paradise—yes, this was the arctic Brooks Range! A person should put up a couple of thousand pounds of vegetables each fall. At Alatna village a cabbage was raised by one of the missionary women so large that it made the wheelbarrow which contained it look small beside. Cabbages, carrots, and rutabagas put out real poundage for food in the arctic continental regions; and like our neighbors in Siberia we were partial to these. They could be preserved by freezing. If dipped first in water and then frozen quickly outside the house at, say, 30° below zero in the late fall, all vegetables and even eggs will keep eternally fresh until they are thawed to use. Here one could use nature's own icebox to preserve foods for the future, one of the great natural advantages of arctic regions. With a few garden seeds then, and a cabin or cabins, rifles, traps, and the like, a person could live in the wild arctic interior indefinitely and never know an hour of real insecurity or want.

So dreams the explorer. Midafternoon that day found us pulling off the main river into some quiet sloughs through a swamp and expecting to spend the night there.

"We'll take a lesson from the natives. You know I have no special admiration for the natives in all things, but I was just asking myself what an Indian would do in our place. I'll tell you. I think he'd keep traveling each day for half a day, and then he'd make camp and patiently watch and wait and look for signs. If he didn't find signs he'd keep on the next day, until he did. It might take him a long time, but eventually he'd find it, where the white hunter would fail."

Prepared for a long siege of it if necessary, Bud and I parted on our separate ways to hunt once more. He had not been gone from my side fifteen minutes when I heard his rifle speak. There were three loud reports followed by the sharp cracks of the pistol. They were the best sounds I ever heard in my life, for I knew Bud had something down. Leaping over fallen trees, I ran for the canoe as hard as I could go and got the ax and pack board. I was shaking so my hands fumbled. I met Bud and he led me to a bull moose he had just killed, lying in a field, a three-year-old.

The moose was quite white, or yellow, over the shoulders as it lay there among the standing stalks of dead hay. It blended to the darker shades on the belly, contrary to our more southerly moose. He would never have been cold in the winter, had he lived to enjoy it, for some of his hair was five inches long.

"By golly, you know, I almost lost this fellow," Bud related, as we stood looking down on him. "The telescope sight was out of line."

Bud said that he had meant to "target his 'scope in" at the cabin, but he hadn't taken time out to do it and later had hesitated to awaken the echoes around the house that such firing means. But here was a lesson learned. Bud had emphasized to me dozens of times how important it is to test your rifle periodically, especially for travelers whose guns are subject to knocks and jars. Time and again in the past I had called off scores for Bud on improvised targets. He always maintained that even in wild, remote country it is better to sacrifice a few shells at targets than to shoot the same amount of ammunition at an animal only to cripple it and allow it to escape.

"Well," said Bud, "we might as well get to work, I guess." Together we managed to roll the thousand-pound animal over on its back. I took my place astraddle the neck and chest to hold it on balance; my feet barely touched the ground. With his long-bladed razor-edged skinning knife which I had brought from the canoe, Bud began a seemingly effortless slit up the belly. He never allowed anyone to touch that knife, for it was never used for anything but this.

While we were skinning out, Bud told me the story. He had picked up fresh tracks right away in a single patch of old snow. He followed them over bare ground, filling in the missing links with imagination. Then, there was his moose before him, three hundred yards distant in an open field; it had already heard his footsteps, but stood poised broadside, a sight in that setting to fulfill a hunter's fondest dreams. With its fifty-inch rack of horns, it made the kind of "calendar" picture, as Bud put it, that one rarely sees in real life.

Taking off his telescope cap, Bud had taken a standing "sight" and fired. He rested the rifle barrel against a tree trunk, as the willows were too high for vision had he lain down. Bud fired, and completely missed the animal. The second shot, aimed for the shoulder, hit the bull in front of the hips, the bullet going just under the spine. This second shot knocked the great creature down. Here is where Bud made a big mistake. He was so sure he had the moose and so overjoyed at the alleviation of our anxiety about food, that he ran up at a happy gallop, forgetting all caution. When Bud was only a few feet in front of the animal, it opened its eyes and saw him for the first time. Suddenly, it reared to its feet with amazing vigor. Bud had only time to thrust out his gun instinctively and fire without taking aim, as the bull moose hit him and knocked the gun from his hand. Of course, Bud had reloaded his gun from old habit, in closing in, a rule followed in any kind of hunting—and that was fortunate for us. The bullet, which was shot from a crouched position at close range, plowed underneath the jaw and out through the top of the head. The moose fell, paralyzed but still alive, and Bud killed him with the .22 pistol.

Bud could not say whether this moose actually charged him with intent to kill or was merely crazily trying to get away. But the practical result to the hunter would have been the same had he succeeded.

Eagerly we skinned out the moose with but one dominating thought: how much fat were we going to get? We simply had to have some tallow if we were going to have bread. How could we use our flour? How could we fry meat?

First, Bud skinned the whole moose of its hide, beginning on the legs. We skinned one side, then rolled it over and skinned the other side, so that in the end the animal lay on its own hide.

Breathlessly we opened it up to see what we would get inside. "That looks pretty good, doesn't it?" I would comment hopefully as Bud grunted and groped, plunged and struggled. He had thrown off his shirt and was in to the shoulders.

"I think he's pretty fair, dear," was all Bud would assure me. "We won't get anything extra. See, the old fellow has been rutting already because that one horn is cracked from fighting."

"Do you see any intestinal fat?" Bud pawed at the great stomach filled with leaf pulp and managed to cut it loose from the diaphragm muscles which grow really heavy on a moose and roll it out. Out came the big liver, and what a beauty that was! This prize was placed on top of the pile of intestines which mounted up around us. One must never lay meat on the ground or even on grass except with great care, and that's no superstition! Any camper who has dropped the bacon and tried to scrape sand off it will know that you might as well throw the bacon away.

"Hand me the ax." Bud chopped unerringly through the brisket.

Fall Hunting

"Look at the size of that heart! There's some fat on that." . . . "Won't a steak taste good for a change!" So, our conversation went, and let no one think that this was not a time of prayerful thanksgiving for us. Just to get our hands on the flesh of a real moose made our confidence rise and soar and go out anew to all this mighty land. Nothing can be a happier moment than a successful kill when you are hungry, let there be no mistake about it.

In three hours the sun had dropped, and we had the job completed, with all of the quarters hung up off the ground on the nearest tree for the night; it was a small tree and looked as though it might collapse. It was necessary to halve the shoulder quarters again before they could be lifted. Bud almost split himself while I was trying to make the hitches around the tree with the ropes.

Wiping our chilled and stained hands on grass, we took the delicacies in a sack to the boat. These were the tongue, brains, heart, liver, and the meager scraps of fat which I had peeled from the ropes of intestines. This sack full weighed about forty pounds.

"I think we'll be able to work the canoe almost up to the moose tomorrow, through the swamp," encouraged Bud.

Reaching camp, we called our labors over for the day, and a feast was in order. The night grew black, windy, and bitter, but our hearts were carefree because we now had money in the bank. No one could have been more comfortable anywhere than our own impoverished carcasses, unaccustomed to any luxury. Seated before a large log fire against a background of wild forest and river, with a thousand-pound moose to eat all ourselves, gave us a feeling of luxury and plenty that it would be difficult to duplicate anywhere. Bud had built a fire of big logs—one that really roared. We cooked ourselves first on one side and then on the other; Bud raked a small fire out of the conflagration for the meat. He sat with it between his knees, doing our dinner, while the big fire gave light to work by. From the fresh liver of dishpan size, I recall that he cut extraordinary steaks; at least that is the impression that remains in imagination. They were thick steaks fast-fried on hot iron over the coals. Bud kept cutting these liver steaks and frying them until far into the night.

No eater of restaurant liver or even home-cooked calves' liver prepared with the conventional flouring and onions has any idea of what this tasted like. I used to believe one had to "dredge" liver after it had been in scalding water and then fry it until "well done" and you had to have scalloped potatoes and lemon pie. Yes, that's good in its place, but most hunters will testify that there is nothing quite like fresh wild liver from something you have killed yourself; it needs no disguise and very little to go with it. We must have eaten nearly half of the liver, along with great gulps of hot tea, before we thought to pause.

Going hungry or having but a limited menu of very plain, unadorned foods to eat at odd intervals sounds like a terrible way to live to those who have not experienced it, but not in our case. You see, no matter how elaborate the gourmet's menu, he has the capacity to enjoy his food only so much, because, poor fellow, he is too well satisfied all the time to know what appetite is. He should have all of his spices taken away from him and be starved a while, dependent on his own prowess as a hunter to stay alive in northern wilderness, if he really wants adventures in appetite.

When people say, then, "How could you endure the terrible hardship to live on bloody old meat?" or "I would like adventure, too, if there were not so much hardship involved," they do not understand that the body makes its own compensations for circumstance: you get used to it. Who can say by measure that you do not enjoy your puritan pleasures, such as they are, as much as any king enjoys a state banquet? Kings have been known to envy the capacity for enjoyment which is God's special gift to the poor man.

The peculiar delicacy and mildness of fresh liver from a moose or deer or what-have-you derives from the fact that it is fresh. After we got home to the cabin and tried to eat the rest of this liver, it had lost much of its charm. We scarcely touched liver the rest of the winter and had to dry about sixty pounds of it in order to preserve it and eventually give it away. We think that in the case of liver some action occurs in freezing or in keeping it even for a few hours which impairs its true flavor. After having eaten fresh liver from innumerable animals of our own killings in the wilds we find ourselves hungering for it thereafter and unable to match it exactly in any meats which money can buy.

The sportsman who has never experienced it before is almost invariably ardent over this liver cooked fresh. Of course, it is full of vitamins, enough so that one meal of the primitive kind can in fact last a person a week. No civilized meal that we know of holds any comparison for sheer energy-giving power. But perhaps the main reason for our subsequent preference, during the rest of our time in the North, for meat other than liver was because our tastes were just then passing beyond the sportsman's stage and into the stage of your true aboriginal meat eater. Yes, even after a couple of months on meat, already our tongues were changing, unknown to us! These taste and preference changes were to be to us one of the most remarkable and unexpected phases of our whole adventure.

Liver, for instance, happens to be the least prized item of the animal among primitive, meat-eating Eskimos, unless, as in the arctic, it is eaten sometimes raw frozen. It is fed to the dogs and rarely eaten by people unless the larder is extremely low, simply because liver is lean, and it is fat meat these people prize when subsisting on a low-calorie diet of bulky food.

The valuable parts of the animal to people on such a diet come to be the tongue, brains, head meat, the fat brisket, and the ribs—in other words, all of the bones, but especially the lower leg bones on herbivores. These bones are never left on the field by the primitive who is living off the country, and we can say ourselves after a winter spent in the totally uninhabited and unexplored Brooks Range that white hunters who cut meat off the bones of their animals and merely pack out the meat to save themselves effort are misleading themselves in the worst way.

That "the sweetest meat lies nearest the bone" is one of old grandfather's sayings which had a reason behind it and is not wrong! People who eat meat without roasting or boiling the bones in it must have lost their sense of flavor. Today there is a growing tendency for the American family to buy boned meat—the most insipid, abominable imitation of good eating yet invented. Only at the finest hotels or at some Middle Western farms is it possible to get in our generation those flavors brewed from bone stock. Because of the popular hue and cry for boned meat to "save waste," the butchers are not selling bones; people just won't buy them any more for household use. America's cattle bones are sold to packers and made up into canned dog food and bone-meal preparations to feed laying hens so that the hens can meet their calcium quota. America meets its own calcium quota by drinking one pint of milk daily—or attempts to— and sincerely proclaims that the rest of the world in all reasonableness should go at once and do likewise.

There are 400,000,000 human beings living on the primitive plane of existence in the world today by hunting and fishing and following their semi-domesticated herds as nomadic wanderers or practicing primitive agriculture. They have never drunk a glass of milk or orange juice and they have never slept in a bed. Some of these tribes, as in Arabia, are not even conscious of the name of the nation in which they run wild. Many of these people, especially up to this century, have lived entirely on meat and meat products and found meat a complete food. Yet we don't know how or why. It's against all our rules. Our nutritional charts to date will go so far as to admit that if a human being should eat two pounds of beef daily he would apparently have everything he needs except Vitamin C and calcium. It is stated with positiveness that meat could not supply these two elements. But we among the host of primitives are here to say that it does. Dr. Ales Hrdlicka discovered that primitives in the Aleutians and along the west coast of Alaska have a veritable gold mine of Vitamin C in the raw livers and intestinal parts of the walrus and the seal. The nutritionists have only begun to analyze wild meats; nothing whatsoever is known about the qualities of game. Moreover, primitive people are bound to eat their meat differently from civilized people to maintain the health that they do.

Dr. Vilhjalmur Stefansson proved satisfactorily a decade ago that meat *does* supply Vitamin C or the antiscorbutic element in northern diet. Not only did Stefansson live for years in the very far arctic on nothing but unsalted meat and water during his polar expeditions, but he taught scores of his pupils, among them the notable Sir Hubert Wilkins, to subsist on this diet for months at a time in perfect health and even with enjoyment. The nutritionists, some of them, are still angry about all this, and still shaking their heads and mumbling into their beards, but it is so.

But there was a secret about Stefansson's meat eating which he learned from the northern Eskimos. When we put it to use naturally enough in our own situation, we were only following well-established arctic precedent. The Eskimos eat their meat cooked rare or underdone, which preserves this Vitamin C that they never heard of. They eat a lot of raw things, too; so have the more adventurous and intelligent of the explorers. This winter we contented ourselves with large quantities of rare English-style roast beef and let the vitamins go at that. As for calcium, what the analysts don't understand when they cut off a cube of meat and maul it over for its properties is that the primitive meat eater cooks his meat with the bones in it. The only meat he may eat is that next to the bone, for he eats it for the flavor of the bones, you might say; his dogs get the boned meat. These bony parts, the vertebrae of the back and the ribs of the animal, are always boiled. As they simmer away in the boiling pot the calcium comes out of the bones and goes into the meat and into the broth, which is drunk by the wilderness wanderer or, if he is so lucky as to have a tablespoon of flour, is made into gravy or soup. There is no way here for the nutritionists to measure how much calcium may be brewed out of the bones and absorbed by the human being, but we imagine that something like this takes place. We know that we chewed cartilage and gelatin off bones that were sieved with tiny holes. The soup which came from the bones and which we drank at meals by the bowlfuls three times daily solidified into gelatin if allowed to stand an hour. Whatever the qualities all of this had, it made us the strongest physical specimens in that environment which we had ever been or ever hope to be, and when we got out of the arctic two years later we had so many red blood corpuscles, according to the physicians who at once examined us, that the physicians were shocked and amazed. We seemed to have a kind of superabundance of everything in our systems, according to the analysis, which is not often found in the civilized person—far, far above all requirements.

Are there dangers inherent in eating rare meat? We know for sure that it was safe enough in the case of the northern game; of game in more tropical climes we are not sufficiently informed. We have since met persons of repute who are afraid of parasitic disease, but a great many reputable people agree that the rare meat, the raw frozen fish, and so on, are perfectly safe in Alaska. Modern-minded civil and military physicians recently with the armed forces, observing that the natives are eating rare meat with impunity, have urged its acceptance upon the white population. The only case we have heard of where any danger resulted from the eating of rare or raw meat was that of a young surveyor with the naval forces who shot a large brown bear near camp, which had been living off the garbage piles. Being an experienced outdoorsman and scout, he had some rare steaks prepared for himself from this bear and ate them; he came down with trichinosis. Articles were written in popular publications about the curious case, with the result that people were alarmed all over Alaska and warned each other about eating rare wild meats because of a fear of the trichinae which might exist in Alaskan bears. But we happened to have an opportunity to meet this young surveyor, who explained to us clearly the details of the furore. His was the only case of its kind ever to be known in Alaska and it is now believed by all the military physicians called in on the case that the bear contracted the parasite only because it was a garbage-fed bear which had eaten raw navy pork thrown out on the trash pile and incidentally infected with trichinosis. This is presumed to be the only bear in the North ever to have contracted this disease—a war casualty.

Into the canoe the following day we loaded our whole moose, and little was wasted. The horns could be carved up into something or other useful, the hide went for rawhide and its hairs would make stuffing for a pillow. The hoofs—could we make jello out of them, flavored with cranberries, perhaps? Take them along; we would try!

With freezing bare hands and our gloves laid beside us in order to grip our paddles dexterously, we plied down the swift turquoise curves of the Alatna in the midst of a snow flurry, and so floated our moose home less than thirty hours after we had left for a prolonged hunting trip.

7

The fine October weather and two days of gorging on moose meat in our cozy home sent us hunting again. Bud said, "I guess we'd better get out and get that second moose down."

"Yes, these easy times may not last," I agreed. "Winter will soon be upon us. I have wondered if all the moose might not go south or something at any time. Did you ever think of that?"

"I've never found a cast horn," admitted Bud. "There's no absolute proof they winter here. But I suppose they do."

The temperature was 26° Fahrenheit—hunting weather! Eight o'clock in the morning found us upon our way. While Bud headed down along the base of Red Mountain to the Arrigetch Creek area I crossed the Alatna in the canoe to survey for what seemed the thousandth time the flats near the Kutuk River nearer home. With some impatience I headed at a fast pace for the gullies and rock slides beyond, because I knew all these acres so well nearby.

I was no more than half a mile from home when it was my fortune to jump a solitary young bull moose in the dense timber. It was such a wonderful thing to have happen to me after endless weeks spent in searching that I was taken with a severe case of buck fever. With my lack of caution, I had roused it from its bed where it lay sleeping on the ground, but I didn't know this at the time. All I knew was that I was hiking along when suddenly a running moose appeared. The soft moss must have deadened my footfalls until I was almost upon him. With his long bell dangling to his stride he whirled and trotted from my path to get out of the way. I saw the horns and the broad brown back and then he was gone.

I had not even taken my rifle from my back! My self-confidence oozed out and left me standing there completely shaken.

It was fortunate in the end that I did not shoot fast when I had this chance, because the rear end of a disappearing moose presents a poor target. The hunter would have to shoot through several feet of moose from this angle to reach a vital spot.

It was also fortunate for me that this largest of the deer family, like all his relatives, has one weakness in flight: he will sometimes enter a thicket and then stand and look back to see what alarmed him.

Slowly I took the rifle from my back and managed to get a shell into firing position. There was a slight ridge just ahead, partially open on top. I figured my moose might pause there. If he did . . . Oh, we simply had to have him for food! This was my only chance. Buck fever must spring largely from the inexperienced hunter's fear that this is the only such chance he will ever get in his life. Because of this fear, many a hasty, rash mistake is made. But you are bound to have many chances if you keep on hunting.

Within a few steps, which changed my point of view, I looked out onto the open rise and almost succumbed. There indeed was the blurred form standing in the dense bushes, and he had begun to eat. He was tearing off bark and breaking up alders and willows sometimes as large as my wrist, eating the wood right down.

I felt that our whole future life and winter's survival depended upon that one shot. As his head peered around in my direction I raised my rifle to my shoulder. I was in bushes myself. I would have to shoot offhand. In another instant the moose might be out of sight. I cocked the hammer and saw the gun barrel describe a wide arc.

"This will never do," I told myself, lowering my gun. It would be better not to shoot at all than to make a terrible blunder. The responsibility which weighed upon me made me break out in a clammy sweat. Oh, I would certainly hit that moose all right, I knew that, but could I kill him outright? If I should merely cripple the great animal, I felt I should never be able to live with myself for the rest of my life.

I tried to lift my rifle again, but the sight would not stay on the mark, while that browsing head swung like a pendulum. I did the best

I could, accordingly: when the sight and the moose's neck both came back into line where I thought they should be, I let her go and prayed for the best. "Ker-wham!" said the gun, puncturing the stillness.

I must have closed my eyes and flinched badly, for the shot could hardly have been worse. The fact that a moose's whole bulk is a large target does not mean much; the target you have to hit is still no larger than a rabbit. The bull reacted by turning and trotting off.

I was in utter despair. But wait! Something in its manner was strange. Not forgetting to reload, I tore through the bushes after it. Luck was with me. Unaccountably the moose stopped, allowing me to get in another shot. The second shot felled the bull like a wall of loose bricks. He piled up with a ground-shaking thud just a few steps away from where he had received his first shot. I was exultant.

Remembering all of Bud's instructions, I advanced with caution from behind the animal, walking up to him in such a way that he could not see me from where he lay. All breathing seemed to have stopped. In about a minute the eyelashes stopped blinking, and then I got a stick and prodded him from all sides. Still, I wasn't going to go near those hoofs or horns which are capable of "reflex action" and can disembowel or kick the teeth out of a careless hunter. In our kind of calm hunting for food we wanted no dramatic ending.

I made no attempt to dress out the moose alone. My strength and ability were not sufficient. Neither did I dash up to cut its throat and drain the blood. Bud did not belong to the school of throat cutters. The reason for cutting an animal's jugular in controlled butchering is that the animal is hung up on a hoist or beam after being shot or clubbed on the head, and the heart, which is still beating, pumps the blood out. With game killed in the field, however, the heart has stopped by the time the jugular could be cut, and because of internal injuries the blood will all be coagulated in the abdominal and chest cavities anyway. Bud found that it makes no discernible difference in meat flavor, so long as the animal is cleaned reasonably soon and the meat put to chill. A moose, being so large, will sometimes spoil slightly in one night, even at a temperature of 30° below zero, unless the entrails are removed, and the chest cavity is left propped open with a stick in order to let out the body heat.

"I must find Bud," I thought, looking fondly at my great prize. "And I mustn't lose the moose." Now that I had shot it, I still was subject to alarms, and rightly, too. We hadn't got it home yet.

With my knife, quite dull as usual, I cut marks on the trees, barking my knuckles through my light mittens and not even feeling it. It took me hours to carve up the trees in blazing my trail home. Then I realized belatedly that I shouldn't blaze the trail home but to the nearest channel of the river so that we could get the canoe as close as possible to the moose. Bud said later it was the worst trail he ever tried to follow because I had carved up all the trees in the forest with my dull jackknife.

Far down at Arrigetch Creek Bud heard the fusillade of shells I fired into the air at home where I danced and paced, awaiting him. Looking at the sky, I expected snow to start falling at any minute to cover my moose; perhaps an arctic blizzard would begin and keep us confined to the house for days!

"What did you think I was shooting for?" I asked Bud, rushing to meet that long-striding familiar figure at last. He told me calmly that he supposed I had shot a moose. "But I killed it with two shots," I impressed upon him. "The rest of them were just to bring you."

Two hours had elapsed by the time we got back to my moose. "Not such big horns, but bigger than yours," I had prepared Bud, but when we got to it, it was really a coming two-year-old shot at close range, a paced distance of only sixty yards. We re-enacted the story from the prints. Bud showed me the moose's bed where I had roused him. He went over my own trail and picked up my bullet cases from the ground where they had been ejected from the rifle. In this way we evaluated the situation and studied it like two detectives gathering data on a case.

"You just need more practice," Bud said. "Hunting only really begins to be fun when buck fever doesn't grab you anymore. But that day will come. My, I'm proud of you. You got him all right, and that's what counts." He tapped with an investigative finger on the belly of the little bull. It sounded like a ripe watermelon.

"He's really fat," I offered.

Bud shook his head. "I'm almost afraid to open him. You better stand back."

Gingerly Bud's sheath knife slit the hide and then the flap of the belly. During the two hours which had passed, my moose had blown up like a balloon with internal gases. Now at the first puncture the "whee-ee" of escaping air came to our ears as the bull deflated to about half size.

"This job's going to take a lot of care if it's going to be fit to eat," Bud commented seriously, while I looked on with a lugubrious face. "Now we'll see where the shots went."

"I'm sure the second shot hit him in the heart," I asserted, but this did not prove to be the case. The first shot had hit the bull in the flank, entering the lower intestines and spattering intestinal fluid all through the abdominal cavity. This wound lost us pounds of meat by spoilage, for I had "gut-shot" my game. Considering that the majority of bucks shot in the United States each year are gut-shot, and are then dressed by amateurs, there is one more reason why all of our venison is not what it could be.

My second shot, which missed the heart and entered the lungs, must have caused death by systemic shock as much as anything else. We were using 170-grain boattail bullets whose striking force, against a great solid moose, is magnified in comparison to that of the same bullet against the smaller whitetail deer, oddly enough. Still, moose, for all their enormity, expire easily. Neither of my bullets had had enough penetration to go out the other side. If my moose had seen me and had been able to get to his feet and start running—what trouble! The largest of the deer family gives up the ghost easily only if he is not alarmed. Most of our animals have never known what a human being is or been aware of the killer at any time.

When the moose was dressed it was imperative to get it packed out at once. Already a camp robber had greeted us, perched atop the great carcass when we first arrived. The camp robbers, the ravens, and the gulls can eat a whole moose within three days. It is amazing how they do it, but they probably start working in through the natural body openings and through the bullet holes while the animal is still warm, and once inside they hollow it out in no time at all, until only the ragged hide is left. If the animal has any fat on him at all they and the squirrels will strip every last morsel off during the first hour that it is left unguarded.

Bud had brought a couple of the No. 114 wolf traps along. For these he needed a trap setter, a pair of wooden pincers for squeezing down the springs, but he hadn't got around to making a trap setter yet. After we had the moose packed out to the canoe, he was able to set the traps at the site of the kill with his bare hands, which most people consider a goodly feat of strength.

Four days after the killing of Bud's first moose we were sitting at our corner table by the window at home, having a supper of cold sliced tongue, rare pounded hamburger steaks, a boiled moose hock, a fifteen-pound rare roast with gravy, some roasted grouse with fat crisp skin, some cranberry sauce, and fluffy golden biscuits, when Bud saw through the window in the twilight of evening the black silhouette of a moose walking along the edge of the water, coming up the Alatna Valley to us. Bud reached for the binoculars on their rack, unsnapped them. "It's a cow," he said, scrutinizing. "Do you want to take a look?"

For forty-five minutes during supper we watched. The moose was close now, gracefully picking its way, first walking on the beach and then in the water with a white flash of dripping knees, the placid evening river mirroring the lovely silhouette. It did not see the house above on the hill.

Reaching the point of land directly below our house where the entrance of the Kutuk River into the Alatna barred the way, the animal stopped, hesitating. Then a peculiar incident occurred, when before our eyes "she" turned into a "he."

"Bud," I said, "that's no cow. I believe I see a horn on it. Take a look."

Sure enough, Bud, peering again at closer range, verified beyond doubt that our cow moose was really an eighteen-months-old bull with one tiny antler on the side of its head, almost obscured by the large ears; the other antler was a bud beneath the skin which had never grown.

There the animal stood, with no idea that a house was here or that there were loaded guns on its walls which could kill him from the front door. He did not know how long we had waited in agonies of uncertainty, suddenly to see three bull moose within a week's time. How easily he could be added to the others which were needed for meat, for he would never be missed from that vast landscape!

Yes, that would have been a prime moose, that one with the tiny antler, because the lack of horns would mean that he was not a fighting moose and therefore not a rutting moose, and therefore a moose that was probably pretty fat. "Well, I'm too full to care now," we groaned from our supper table, as we looked lazily at the lovely scene.

That's the way it goes in the wilderness. A full stomach gave us trust in the nature we loved, and we let that moose go.

PART FIVE

Winter Hunting

Connie's moose will feed us into winter

She saves every scrap of fat from the guts

1

There is no more memorable Alaskan picture than that of the little cabin beside the frozen river. Its icicles are hanging from its sod roof, smoke issues from its chimney, the evergreens beside it are sleeved with snow to the ground, and a path is shoveled neatly through the drifts to the woodpile.

Inside, socks and mittens are hanging over a line or rack behind some improvised "Yukon stove" meaning any kind of tin can stove you can get, and the skillets are on the wall, while a rabbit's foot is a duster. There are only three dishes to wash and you can sit at the table and reach everything in the room. That's the kind of house I like myself, where you can look out the window and see—what is it today?—three otters sliding like elongated and very frolicsome "sausage hounds" along the river ice below. Now I know why otter fur wears best of all and never has a hole.

Yes, inside the cabin it is warm and cozy when the snow falls silently by the pane and wilderness is just outside the door. The red eye of the old monster glares balefully as you open the bunghole draft. The sourdough bucket gives off its lovable alcoholic odor from its warm shelf as it "works" away. Hundreds of contented sourdoughs, the old men of the North, are sitting beside their rivers in their log cabins as these lines are written. Here is the spirit of old Alaska, which lives in the bottom of a sourdough bucket!

To the clan of the sourdoughs the sourness of the batter is a living institution. The term "sourdough" bespeaks a weathered individual, often a bachelor, or one living with an Indian or Eskimo wife and a batch of multicolored youngsters. In popular terminology today, he may be a perfectly respectable, hardheaded businessman in one of the larger cities, or quite as easily a woman, because all Alaskan citizens like to call themselves sourdoughs; it implies that we are experienced veterans of the North and is a matter of pride.

Fermented yeast has come to be the symbol of the man of the northern wastelands; this man scorns the use of baking powder. Only the little box of baking soda is visible on his cabin shelf or in his grub box.

A book on the American arctic must include the recipe for sourdough. To make sourdough, you take a cake of granulated yeast, and dissolving it in some warm water add flour and a tablespoon of sugar to make a soupy paste. You set this soup aside for a day or two in a generous container to allow it a chance to sour or work. As soon as the batter has soured it is ready for sourdough pancakes. Pour out as much as you want into a mixing bowl and add salt, a melted shortening, and as much water as is necessary to make it of the right consistency for pancake batter. It is ready to pour onto the griddle right now, but the taste would be sour. The batter is therefore sweetened with a pinch of baking soda. Soda is the magic wand.

A few tablespoons of the original sour batter must always be left in the bottom of your sourdough bucket as the starter of the next batch. No more yeast will ever be needed; the starter builds onto itself year after year. Its bulk may be increased any time merely by adding more flour and water; it will usually be ready if set overnight. It can make pancakes, raised breads, shortcakes, cakes, dumplings, doughnuts, and even home-brew. If the starter becomes too sour, just put it outside the door in a snowbank to freeze: it will come to life again unharmed from the coldest temperature as soon as it is thawed.

There is a legend that the more ancient a sourdough starter is, the better its flavor; ancient ones are prized by their owners like some rare jewel. There are sourdough starters in Alaska well over thirty, forty, and fifty years old. Some of them must be parents and great-great-grandparents of numberless progeny of the present generation. It would be an education in the history of Alaska to know the peculiar hazards through which the sourdough bucket has ridden victorious, on the trail and at home. The times it has been dumped overboard into the rapids of great rivers and perhaps been recovered again, the long miles jolting from ocean to ocean on a dogsled. The numbers of gold seekers it has seen dying of scurvy. The numbers of dead field mice which have been pulled out of the sourdough bucket by the tail!

For ourselves, we could afford to use only a little of the precious batter about once in every three days. What kind of foods does a person miss when he is obliged to live on a primitive meat diet? Is it not a terrible hardship?

We can honestly say that it is not. Our diaries for the rest of the year are filled with almost nothing but descriptions of what we ate. The more we ate the more we liked it and the more new flavors we discovered. I don't think we ever sat down to one of those marvelous moose joints without expressions of thankfulness and a few moans as well.

The foods a person misses vary according to temperament. One of our favorite games was, "What food would you choose if?" Sometimes one of us would harp on one item for weeks; then a few weeks later it would be something else which was all the rage. Long hours of exhaustive and penetrating discussion were lavished on the subject of ordering up imaginary menus of civilized food, the very thought of which gave a certain satisfaction. But meat itself did not grow tiresome. We found ourselves presently including exactly what we were eating in our menus of the imagination. For instance, if I could order up any menu today, I would start with this very moose joint, and then go on from there. We never tired of meat; we only wished we had something else to go with it, at times.

It is interesting that we never listed either fresh fruits or vegetables or salads in our menus, except incidentally; they were minor with us under the present circumstances. What we dreamed of instead was a plate full of spaghetti with lots of spicy meat sauce. We had always missed, too, those hot Mexican foods of the Southwest, and now on the Alatna River our imaginations were consequently torn between the lost delights of the ice cream soda fountain, the popcorn stand, and a little restaurant we once knew which served hot tamales. This in itself would seem to prove that most of our cravings were purely in our heads, not a nutritional urge.

The thing which fancy always came back to, however, perhaps

because it was more likely to be obtained, was a sourdough pancake or a piece of sourdough bread. I have yet to find any modern housewife who thinks this coarse heavy bread edible. But to us it came to taste like the lightest and rarest of angel-food cake. Bread or something akin to bread—in other words, sugars, starches, and carbohydrates—is the most coveted by hunters living on an all-meat diet. Any primitive meat eater who has never tasted anything but meat and fish finds bread acceptable to his palate before he will take any other civilized food except coffee and tea, and these last have as much ceremonial as food value, perhaps.

On an all-meat diet a person soon comes to prefer boiled meat for daily use; steaks are desired only once in a while, and you may have more of them on hand, or more lean loin, than you know what to do with. This can be understood if you try to live out of the skillet for just one week straight on a camping trip; you will be so tired of fried meat that you can hardly get it down. Steaks eaten three times a day without the rest of the menu to go with them rapidly become tasteless to the palate and are found to lack flavor compared to the juicier boiled bony parts of the animal. The average old sourdough may not agree with this statement. There is the standing joke about the old Alaskan prospector who, dining in a Seattle restaurant, ordered steak for one order and beans for a supplementary order, to the surprise of the waitress. Pushing the beans aside where he could see them while he ate his steak, he addressed them: "There, damn you, just set there and watch!" From the numbers of old Alaskans who blow fresh into Seattle or into some Territorial town wild for a steak (and steak is almost the only thing which you can order in the unimaginative sourdough restaurants of all Alaska) you would get the idea that they never had a moose steak in their lives. However, we must remember that many of these sourdoughs never have regarded "wild" meat as in the steak classification of good food; some have lived almost altogether on flapjacks, bacon, and beans, and you can ask the nutritionists to account for that one!

Yet genuine old arctic men knew it all along—the men who lived on boiled meat. They learned it from the Indians and Eskimos, those old ones. Originally the northern natives did not know that there was any other way to cook meat besides boiling, and until a few years ago none of them knew what salt was and got along without it. We find that the human being's taste, before it has been corrupted or educated, whichever you want to call it, is very sensitive to the strong bitter flavors of fried meat and is repelled by them. Likewise, there is no craving for salt on the part of the meat-eating primitive who has not yet contracted the habit; enough organic salts are apparently supplied his body in the meat diet peculiar to arctic living without additional supplies of the white man's inorganic salt. Although all of the last untouched Eskimos in Alaska have by now tasted salt, they do not have it in their camps most of the year and have to get along without it because money usually goes first for tea and tobacco.

It was amazing to us what a variety of things we could cook up with our limited supplies. One of the most successful was jello. No, we never could make jello from moose hoofs, although we boiled hoofs for days, but we did get clear gelatin from boiled leg bones and had only to add cranberries and sugar and chill it to get a jelly which we thought was more delicious than any commercial brand we had ever eaten; in our enthusiasm we ate buckets of this "jello" for much of the winter, in feasts which caused us to howl our approval.

Cranberry-apple pies with a crust using moose tallow were of course no original innovation when we could afford to make one. Mince pies, made of dried apples, cranberries, and prunes for lack of raisins, and with a generous quantity of meat and suet in them, were an exciting discovery: mince pies having real meat in them have it all over the kind with only fruit. We had heard of people spreading rendered-out moose tallow on their sourdough bread for "butter," but we don't think those people discovered the right kind. The sweetest and rarest "butter" comes from the leg bones of herbivores—in other words, it is bone marrow! A moose may carry three to five pounds of marrow inside his legs in all and you have to eat a whole moose to get it. And the problem is how to get it. We found early that the flavor of this marrow when boiled in the meat is delicious beyond words; in fact, without it, boiled meat is almost insipid. But better still is the marrow eaten frozen raw! Of the appearance and consistence of country butter, it can be obtained by cutting out the bones and chopping them up with the ax—only a corresponding sacrifice must be made in the flavor of the boiled meat. The discovery of the delicacy of bone marrow was our own that year. Since then we have been told many times that this product is and always has been the greatest luxury that man can eat. How did we happen to discover it when placed in primitive circumstances? Well, the discovery just came naturally.

Ice cream is one treat which we think everyone should have regularly after his meat course in the arctic where ice and snow are perfectly free. This is why we spent as much money getting a few cans of powdered milk as we spent on flour; we also concocted frozen custards of sorts with our milk and powdered eggs. With cranberry snow ice cream beaten up pink and fluffy to follow the main meal, any wilderness supper, combined with great natural appetite, is a delight. That winter we must have eaten several tons of snow in this way along with our meat.

Bud and I had never seen a river freeze before, and the process was a great curiosity to us. Freeze-up came on the Alatna by October 24. After freeze-up we were there to stay the winter out, come what may, for better or for worse. Two hundred and forty miles down the river bed would have been too far for reasonable people to start walking in an uninhabited land, where there was no shelter and with no dog team to carry camping equipment and provisions. It might be asked why we did not have a dog team. It must be clear now that we could not have supported a dog team, and that a canoe in this mountainous country was simpler all around.

As for walking out to civilization, we found that even in the arctic, such a river as ours, with its steeply falling riffles and its tendency to freeze to the bottom in places and then burst through and overflow periodically on top of the ice, is not a ready-made highway by any means. It was a surprise to us to observe that just below the Kutuk mouth, for instance, open water lay before our house for much of the winter, no matter how low the thermometer dropped. We hauled our water from here, which was simpler than melting snow.

One of the greatest hazards would be for a person to break through treacherous river ice in low temperatures and get his feet wet. Such dangers are doubly magnified for one not equipped with changes of clothing or with the right arctic clothing in the first place. Soft snowdrifts, pressure ridges of ice, and unseen depressions made for up-and-down walking on much of the river at best. Even a person who ultimately ran out of food would be wise to remain near his shelter and hunt, rather than try to make a break for it later on in the winter.

Of course, we had nothing to worry about as long as everything continued to go normally. We never had a sick day out here, and accidents we intended to avoid.

Lower and lower sank the mountain river in its bed until its voice had become but the smallest murmur in the ear, until its voice ceased altogether. A skin of light ice formed a shelf out over that quiet pool where Bud had once caught munching crocodile pike. Then some large pans drifted down from above and came to a rest there. The Kutuk flowed over the ice and froze from the bottom up. It poured tinkling over a little waterfall laced with icicles into the larger river.

Gradually we began walking across the Alatna above the Kutuk mouth, using skis to distribute our weight. Our canoe was dragged up onto the bank and turned upside down. Later, when the snow was deep, and the river rose from its layers of overflow, we dug her out and hauled her higher still; we tied the *Little Willow* then by ropes at each end to the trees of the forest. When the snows melted this would leave our canoe tied up in the air off the ground and safe from flood.

The sun was to leave us early and be gone for a long time because of the high surrounding mountains. For a time, we had two distinct sunrises. On a clear day we would see the sun from 10:15 to 11:30; then it would pass behind Red Mountain and reappear on the other side of that flawless cool cone at 12:00 noon, to remain with us until perhaps 1:05. It may sound queer, but we don't know exactly when the sun permanently left us.

The sun had been playing hide-and-seek with the mountain peaks for some time, and then there were some cloudy days. Sometime before November 10 the reflection of the sun no longer touched the surrounding peaks within our vision except as a rosy afterglow, and we didn't see it again for around three months. This is considered a long "arctic night" even for the polar explorer who goes into extreme northern latitudes far beyond the continent, for his terrain is so flat that even a low arctic sun will be visible to him for more days out of the year than ours was to us. But at no time during the arctic night were we restricted entirely by a lack of light. The light was sufficient to hunt and explore by, and much of the dreaded darkness proved but a myth.

As the cold of winter progressed, we had no warmer clothing, for we had already put on our warmest by fall. We were like swimmers who plunge into cold water when we ventured into the climate outside our door. The swimmer could maintain bodily warmth only if he kept exercising all the time. There was therefore no loitering along the way for us; four or five hours a day in the cold stream was all we wanted. Past that time, we found the body continually lost heat from any longer exposure.

It is possible that there was a peculiar advantage in having become used to cold by battling the river the past summer. The American Medical Association reported in one of its magazine issues that persons who feel cold in winter can cultivate local or systemic immunization to cold at will by immersing as small a part of the body as one finger in water chilled to 50° F. several times daily before the period of winter exposure sets in. Winds being almost completely absent from this great frozen interior of the Brooks Range, we often would not even have realized the degree of cold when stepping out into it from the house had it not been for the thermometer which reminded us. Whatever the reason that we did not feel the cold, throughout every day in the winter we were out-of-doors, ill clad though we were, enjoying life in a state of exuberance which caused us to thrive like creatures of the wild. This feeling doubtless accounted for our optimism in all things. Presumably we had nothing to be happy about as the world sees it. But each day was a revelation in life and nature, as we took tremendous jaunts along our trap trails. Like most of those placid old-timers, the sourdoughs, we didn't catch much or make our fortune in fur, but we came home with blooming cheeks to enormous meat feasts each eve, proving that even if we never had less in our lives, still, we could never have more as long as we live.

2

In the past, the economy of the Northland depended upon fur. And the world depended upon trappers to produce the fur. Thus, it was the trappers who really explored the new lands and laid out the trails for civilization to follow.

Civilization has followed these trails, until only in the arctic is there now room for the wilderness trapper. His cabins and caches are widely scattered throughout a vast area; his trails, hardly discernible to the uninitiated, weave a sparse web throughout a cold land of mountain and spruce, and from there north to a land of rolling arctic prairies and at last out onto the sea ice of the frozen Arctic Ocean itself, where the white fox is the only animal trapped.

Yes, the wilderness trappers are a widely scattered clan. Many people would think their lives lonely and barren, for often they see no one for months at a time. Yet their lives are wrapped up in the study of the natural world about them. They have friends most of us never heard of, and the fresh snows hold stories for them that are not written in books. The stories are brief and change with the next snow, so they never become tiresome. How much they can read depends upon the individual, for really the story is all there.

It was along with the going of the sun that the saga of the wolverines began. One morning I found what I supposed was the trail of a young cub bear wandering around by our bone pile over the bank. What a chase he led me! Through the forest, along the river, going under low brush close to the ground and crisscrossing his own trail many times, he led me eventually toward the rocky ridges behind our house. The footprints so close together seemed to tell that the little wanderer, all alone in the world for the first time, certainly must be close by. Imagine my outraged sense of humor when I saw our smokehouse through the trees and found myself led home again after four hours, right up to the bone pile from which I had started!

This is typical of wolverines, the great little walkers. When Bud saw the tracks, he admitted that he had had that same joke played on him a week before. But now he was sure the culprit was a wolverine.

Neither of us had ever seen one. The largest and most vicious of the weasel family, the wolverine is rarely seen in the wilds unless you have him in a trap. Wolverines, we knew, follow the trapper's trap line and rob the catch and spring the traps. With caches of food supplies they play havoc, for their other name is glutton. Once a wolverine has come up to your house and has stood there in the darkness looking at the light from your window at night, you might as well start shaking in your shoes. He is an evil spirit.

"We'd better do something about this quickly."

"Oh, well," said Bud placidly, "it's Sunday, and we won't do a thing today but haul logs and rest."

Most Indians and some white trappers think that wolverines are impossible to catch. The Indians make small effort to molest them and they can tell you tales of wolverines turning bullets aside. The headwaters of the Alatna River were believed by the villagers below to be the place where all the wolverines now in the world originated. Perhaps the villagers aren't far wrong! Wolverines are a mountain animal, and this was indeed their veritable stronghold.

We hope we didn't cut off the world's supply of wolverines, but we were fortunate to trap everyone in our locality and in the end secured a large bale of them. We caught more of them than of anything else in the valuable fur-bearing line. If wolverines rob your traps, one way to fool them is to set traps in your own snowshoe or ski trails where you walk daily. Wolverines, wolves, and foxes love these trails, which seem to convey little of the man scent to them, and may use them for a highway because the walking there is easier. The trap is set in the middle of the trail and is buried beneath a film of snow. To prevent the trap from freezing down, the trapper lays a piece of thin tissue paper over its pan and sprinkles snow on it and over the open trap jaws. The paper prevents the snow from melting on the steel, and it is said the snow must be sprinkled with a hatchet blade or other metal, not with your glove. No bait is used with a "blind set," purposely contrived for the animal which is a master at stealing bait or too skeptical to touch it.

The circumstances in which Bud caught his first wolverine were peculiar. It was trapped on top of an ex-prospector's bed. Bud wrote in his diary:

> There is an old cabin about a mile from here in the middle of the Arrigetch Creek forest. We lived here a long time and never found it. It's hard to tell how old it is. Only the rear part is left. In this part, under the fallen rafters, is a bunk. I have a small No. 1 trap set there for ermine. The trap is only pegged to the wall. A wolverine crawled in here and up on the bunk and got caught in this trap by one paw! He then proceeded to pull the logs from the bunk and up from the floor until he was buried under them. When I came along, a shot from the Woodsman stopped all the racket. He was 46 inches from nose to tail and weighed perhaps 25 pounds. These animals are unbelievably strong. How the little trap held him is due mostly to the fact that he couldn't get a fair pull, the way he was caught. The roars and growls of this animal were louder than a bear's . . .

The majority of the wolverines we caught were males. Some of them measured nearly six feet in length, although we must confess that the true size and weight of wild animals as merely seen and not measured is apt to be exaggerated out of all proportion. There was never a red fox born, for instance, that tipped the scales at more than some ten pounds, and five pounds is often enough the total substance of that airy vagabond which most of us imagine to be a large animal. But a big beaver may go ninety pounds and have as much edible meat on him as a whitetail deer. A wolverine looks much bigger than he is because of his ferociousness and his long erect hair.

Wolverines have no relation to wolves, despite the similarity in their names, but are considered an equally dangerous adversary when cornered. With their short powerful hocks, their square, heavy skulls, and their strange heavy square teeth with the lips curled back, as I most often saw them in the grin of death, they reminded one of a cub bear more than anything else, except that they looked more ominous. Like a bear's, their hair was coarse and black. Many had gaudy stripes of tan hair down the back like the stripe of a skunk, which in old males terminated in a small brilliant orange pattern on the front of the chest. This orange and black Halloween motif seemed appropriate considering their spooky nature and the legends about wolverines.

One night Bud had brought home two ermine from the trap line, and while I held the lantern for him, he deftly removed their skins. He had suspended two strings from the ridgepole inside our cabin to hold the animals by the hind feet while he skinned them.

"You know many trappers are superstitious about wolverines," he suddenly said. "Now you take this morning. A wolverine has followed our trap line and eaten two ermine today. He found every one of the traps and sprung them or stole all the bait from the rest. Of course, he was just lucky he was on the ermine trap line where no big traps were set. He'd better look out if he follows the other trap line, I'll tell you." Bud finished the last ermine and stretched the skins upon two boards he had split from a piece of straight-grained spruce.

If the wolverine could have heard and understood our conversation in the cabin perhaps what happened would have been avoided. I am sure that Bud would have put a much heavier drag on a certain trap if he had known. But that's the fun about trapping—you never know what will happen next.

A thick haze like the smoke of a forest fire hung low over the Alatna Valley when we awoke and looked out our window from the cabin on the hill the next morning. We could guess without looking at the thermometer that the temperature was about 50° below zero because a fog usually hung over the river ice in the low temperatures. As I begged off from following the trap line, Bud prepared to leave alone. He placed in his packsack the clamps he used to set the heavy traps; in went a short length of rope, some snare wire, and his little hand ax. I watched him take his snowshoes from in front of the house and my rifle from its peg outside the cabin. This carbine, for ordinary daily work, was never brought indoors except for a rare cleaning. It is usual to leave guns out-of-doors in the arctic, because if they are brought inside after use they become covered with frost that melts, leaving the gun as wet as though it had been soaked in water.

Bud waved and turned down the trail, the big snowshoes under his arm. I saw him putting them on down below on the river, and in a few moments his familiar form had vanished into the spruce timber out of sight of the cabin window.

It was midwinter, when the sun never rises, but there was plenty of reflected light. I busied myself about the cabin, fed the chickadees that came to the feed tray on the windowsill, and brought in some moose meat to hang on a buckskin thong in a corner and thaw for the next day. Each time I stepped out I listened for a sound in the stillness, for often I could hear Bud shoot or would see him from the cabin's elevation, far down the river.

The short arctic day quickly faded and presently only the stars lit up the scene. I glanced out the door more often. About three hours after dark I heard those familiar footsteps and Bud came in, carrying the largest wolverine I have ever seen. It was a great ferocious-looking male, dead, of course, and it had a bright orange spot on its chest.

Bud's hood over his trapper's cap was rimmed with frost, while even his eyelashes twinkled. Despite the stiffening of his cheek muscles from the intense cold, he was smiling from ear to ear. But how, in this whiteness, did he ever get such a dirty face?

It was late after dinner, while Bud removed the wolverine's skin, when he told me the story.

Near a certain trap he had found a large wolverine's trail joining ours. His stride on snowshoes quickened as he hurried on to the big hidden toothed traps lying beside the trail. Sure enough, the No. 114 trap and its six-foot log drag were gone.

The trail of the wolverine led into thick spruce, where the log drag had at first become tangled. Small brush all around was chewed and torn; small trees were cut off and broken. To the trapper's eye the story was told of the violent battle which had raged down the glades. The wolverine had managed to get the drag free and continue onward, but it continued to catch in the thickets. At last the drag on the end of the trap chain became lodged between two trees too big to chew off. What happened? The wolverine had managed to chew that drag log in two right close up to the trap ring.

This allowed him to travel easily now with the half drag following in his trail instead of catching in all the brush. The big wolverine headed straight for some great rocks about halfway up the mountain. "You know the spot?" Bud interrupted his narrative. "Right above the big lake."

"Yes, I know, but how did you manage to get him?" I asked.

"Well, the old fellow had remembered a cave up in those rocks"—and Bud went on.

He described the trail in the snow leading up between the large boulders and at last through a crack where a part of the mountain had slid down a couple of feet in prehistoric days. Here a cave opened up right into the mountain. The tracks led into this cave and Bud could hear the rattle of the trap chain coming from within.

He got down and peered into the dark recess. Menacing growls greeted him as he took the .22 automatic pistol and fired into the blackness. But no luck. The cave went down and back a few yards and then turned, and the bullet fired from the pistol could not go around the curve. At last Bud hit upon the idea of making a torch and going in after the wolverine. There was plenty of birchbark nearby, he said, and he had the snare wire with which he tied the torch to a pole.

The flames of the torch lit up the narrow sides of the cave while the smoke, following the outward draft of the mountain's vent, streamed into Bud's face. The fire stirred up another torrent of growls, snorts, and chain rattles. Bud kept the .22 pistol aimed ahead of him and crawled some twenty yards into the mountain. The cave grew smaller and smaller until at last he could only wiggle forward by inches, but the growls were very close now.

Then, there they were: two large red eyes blazing from the blackness, only a few feet ahead, just around the corner. The cave fairly rocked as the pistol went off, but worst of all, the explosion had blown the torch out. Bud panicked; he tried to turn around to get out of the cave, but it was too narrow. He tried to back out the way he had come in, but only managed nearly to break the cave down, as he put it, by banging his head against the roof. Somehow, he managed to shoot several times more at the spot where the eyes had been; he finally got his bearings and backed out of that cave.

Once outside, Bud waited a long time listening, but all was still. What to do now? Lighting a second torch, he resolved to try again, for he was determined to get that wolverine; he braved the smoke from the torch once more to reach the back of the cave, and there he found the animal dead.

By now we had finished the skinning, as Bud related his story, and we examined the wolverine to see where the bullets from the .22 pistol had hit. There was only one hole that we could find—right between the eyes. Bud imagined this to have been in all likelihood the very first shot fired before the torch went out; the beast may have struggled some moments before its dying gasp.

ON TOP OF THE RIVER ice, twinkling frost flowers shone, touched by gold and rose from the twilight sky. Nature's book lay open, its pages inscribed with the prints of snowshoe rabbits leaping six feet at a bound across the snow. The raucous, beloved voices of ptarmigan sang out, and a whirl of the white birds broke along the valley. Somewhere north of our house wolves wailed in sudden chorus, and we hoped they would fall into our traps waiting beside the moose kill. And deep in the forest of Arrigetch Creek there was a surprise package caught in one of the No. 3 traps baited for wolverine. It was an eagle, held flopping by one toenail, and quite unharmed.

Had I not been along with Bud when he visited the trap, he would have shot it at once. He knew that eagles are great enemies of the mountain sheep and believed that they might account for the complete absence of sheep here where we had expected to find them. Game wardens universally despise eagles for their widespread destructiveness.

But I was so taken with this eagle that Bud resolved to keep her for a while at least, to photograph. Even as she raged in the trap, my hands fairly itched to hold the wild beautiful prisoner.

Bud managed to hood our captive's face with my leather glove which I willingly donated and releasing her long toenail from the trap he carried her home under his arm, where she rode all the way relaxed, not making a motion to either escape or harm her captor. We put her into the smokehouse on an improvised perch, deciding not to feed her for two or three days because she was well stuffed on bait when captured. She was kept hooded. "Isn't she a dear?" I said.

How eagerly that evening in our cabin we got out the bird book to see what it would say! Ours could be a young bald eagle, which had not yet grown the white pattern of head and shoulders; this bird, the largest of the American buzzards and a fish and carrion eater, is found by the thousands along Alaska's southerly coasts and would not be much of a prize. On the other hand, this bird could be the more rare golden eagle which is a truly noble bird of prey, even if a sheep killer—fierce, intelligent, also of the buzzard family, the largest bird used for falconry besides being one of the very largest birds that fly. The golden eagle ranges even beyond the northern continental coastline to islands in the Arctic Ocean at its extreme course, we read. Like the mountain lion and the grizzly bear upon whom the cattlemen of the Rockies have waged relentless war, this eagle is becoming rare in the United States, although it is still plentiful in Mexico.

The question could not be solved at once because juveniles of the bald eagle may bear a striking resemblance to the adult golden eagle from a superficial view. The golden has feathered legs clear to the feet and a golden ochre ruff of plumage around the neck. But our eagle was ragged and, because of its floundering in wet snow, practically naked. We would have to sleep on the subject and consider.

Bud brought the eagle into the house the next day and we took a look in the morning light. We presumed it was a female because female eagles are larger than the males. I named her after my sister Janet. She rode blindfolded on Bud's glove, gripping instinctively with her feet, while Bud held a short thong to which she was tied. Now we saw that the bedraggled feathers of yesterday had a warm sheen like satin and that each feather was stenciled in its exact place. The eagle had tidied herself up meanwhile! Around the base of the neck there fanned out a spray of orange ruff against her warm brown glowing coat—the unmistakable royal sign!

How exquisite she was! Her great heavy yellow feet, almost as large as my hands, with stocky ankles the size of my wrists, were adorned with curving gray talons. It would be well to keep away from those. "God, don't ever let her get a grip on you!" Bud said warningly.

We devised chores to do at home so that we could play with her all day. Hour after hour Janet sat patiently in the house on the rung of the table over which Bud leaned, perspiring and stripped to the waist, rubbing soap into skins. Only occasionally would she shake her stenciled feathers or make a little bird chortle in her throat or raise one heavy foot slowly to scratch at her hood. To pet her was a queer delight. Placidly she accepted the stroking of folded wings and hunched shoulder blades, and you wondered if she felt it at all. "It's like petting upholstery, isn't it?" I observed, delighted.

By the second day we began to feed her. She ate about a pound of raw meat at a time. This we fed her from our fingers; the hooked yellow beak took each morsel delicately, much as a grateful pair of wire cutters might. A small amount of light came underneath the hood at the base of her bill and she could see food thus presented. Soon we let her scoop the morsels neatly up from the flat of the hand. The craw on the front of her breast would bulge out, large and firm as an indoor baseball. "I think she's full now," I would say, measuring the gauge.

Never since my sandhill cranes of the lowlands had I found any bird towards which I exhibited such partiality. Bud said he fancied more the speedier gyrfalcons of our mountain locale, but although one of these fell into a trap by accident in the same way later in the winter, the bird's leg was broken, and it was therefore shot. As things stood, certainly a bird in the house with you becomes closer than the bird in the bush, and nowhere had I ever had opportunity for such acquaintanceship with any bird. Her great size along with her dangerous disposition and the difficulty of a woman's handling her made her the most intriguing plaything I could have found. To tame that wild spirit was a challenge even to an experienced handler.

Each day I could hardly wait to get up so that I could go out to the smokehouse and get my eagle. Bud and I of course knew nothing of the art of falconry. I put on my heavy jacket and Bud bound my right arm to the shoulder in burlap whenever I handled the bird. It was an apprehensive time for all of us, the blindfolded bird trying to keep its balance on my glove, Bud looking on, and me tottering on the slippery path. There was a gap, too, between glove and cuff where the bare wrist might become exposed to the eagle's grip unless care was taken.

"Let's take her hood off!" I begged. Bud yielded. Our curiosity to look at her head was great. We wondered if she was bored.

We shall never forget the look on the eagle's face when that hood came off. She was hunched docilely on her usual perch under the table; the brooding shoulder blades were the very symbol of dejection. When the hood was removed the golden eyes met ours for the first time at home. She blinked. The thin inner membrane of the eyes flicked up, and down. Suddenly the dilated pupils turned to pin points as she turned her gaze on us. Then a fierceness swept over her expression. Quickly we tried to clap the hood back over her head, but it was too late. She broke loose.

"Look out for the windows!" Instantly we knew she would go right through them. Her six-foot wingspread was too large for those small panes, but that would not prevent her from breaking the windows out of the house. Bud grabbed the feathery bundle. As he held her, struggling, we noted that her strong heart pounded so loudly that the sound was audible. The hood was put on. Once more the eagle sat on her perch by the hour, with brooding shoulder blades.

The wild eagle was tame as long as she was kept hooded. She would sit wherever she was placed if her hood was on. She did not realize that her perch was only a foot above the floor when she could not see it. Birds have a very acute fear of falling. More than any other creatures they know what height and depth mean, for they have had reason to know since they were hatched on high in the aerie.

"Janet," we told our tame turkey, joshing her, "we're playing a joke on you. You think you're up on top of a mountain crag as soon as the hood goes on. You think you will fall below and be killed on the rocks if you make the slightest move. So—that is why you sit so still with us." People had used this principle to tame fierce birds of prey since time began, because of the hereditary docility of the birds when hooded.

One day I came home alone and ventured to get Janet from the smokehouse by myself. She stepped up upon my glove of her own accord now and looked forward to our meeting each day. I carried her hooded into the house. "I could hold you on my lap, sweet thing," I was telling her, while she listened. "You're so cuddly, but you have long nails."

Holding her out on the glove at arm's length, my arm quickly tired of the load. Unconsciously I made the mistake of bringing my bent elbow in until it rested near my side and relaxed my vigilance. I could hear Bud outdoors. He had just arrived home. The eagle, to keep her balance on my slanting arm, left the glove and began walking up my forearm, and before I knew what had happened had made her way along the packing up onto my shoulder. I stood and yelled for Bud. He came running to disentangle his wife and the eagle from each other.

I cannot say just how it happened. But when Bud got inside the house he found me standing quite petrified and even afraid to speak, while the eagle stood placidly on top of my head!

Bud was naturally frightened as well as indignant to find the eagle on this perch. If those powerful talons had closed down upon the soft flesh they certainly felt beneath them, I would have been scalped right there, and Bud might never have got the eagle off my head. I will always maintain that it was because my pet felt some affection towards me that I never received the least harm as she climbed from my exposed shoulder to my head and roosted there.

Removing the eagle was a delicate job because her instinctive reaction was to clutch the object upon which she sat for support. "Good night, you look just like a totem pole!" Bud told me, as he induced her to walk off upon the glove. Having an eagle stand on my head had been one of those dangers I had not accounted for on my list and one of which I never dreamed.

We discussed letting Janet go as soon as a clear day offered the best chance for her pictures. Our captive was grieving her heart out for freedom. There were no tears but sounds of what I thought were grief welled up in her throat often in a mournful dirge. Of course, it is possible that eagles always make that sound when roosting. That was the night we kept her inside the house all night and lay and listened to her weep.

Every time her hood was off she wildly tried to escape. "She has never tried to hurt us. She doesn't even know what it's all about," I quavered.

"Neither do I," quavered back Bud in a low voice. Taming the spirit of the eagle was going to break all our hearts in the process.

It was the next day that we tied her outdoors beside the door unhooded—a last desperate effort to orient her to her new home with us; she received her petting with unhooded face. But when left alone, the desperate bird thrashed her wings once too often; the buckskin thong slipped from her leg and she was free! I glanced out the window just in time to see her go. Catapulting from the hill on which our house stood, she lost altitude rapidly and came to rest in the top of a spruce tree in the valley not far away. Was this because she was weak and tired, or because she hesitated to leave us? In this vicinity she stayed one day, and the next day she was gone.

Our usually tranquil household was in order once more.

We lay out a trapline in the first snows

Ptarmigan are plentiful in early winter

3

I was sitting by the corner table at the window when Bud slipped up from behind the house outside and tapped cautiously on the pane. Placing his finger to his lips in a signal, he cat-footed to the door, where I let him in. "Great big grizzly bear standing right there across the river!" he gasped. "For heaven's sake, haven't you got eyes? He's been there for twenty minutes. Don't you ever look out the window? I've been expecting to hear you shoot any minute."

"I was writing in my diary," I replied. Then, "A grizzly! Oh, our only chance! But it's winter! It can't be! And I've never seen a grizzly in my life!"

"I've been running to get here," Bud panted. Later he told me how he had seen the peculiar hump on the shoulders of the great bear from some distance and knew in a flash what a prize we had visiting us. He had come on a run for home, and, when the bear turned his head the other way, had reached the door of the cabin in full sight of him but unsuspected. As I gazed excitedly from my window now I could see a square-rigged brownie of considerable thickness sitting down on his haunches near some bait across the river by the Kutuk mouth below. The distance was about 175 yards, as well as one might measure steep mountain and river.

Only the day before, Bud had targeted in his telescope sight on his rifle for this exact range. He planned to use my rifle from now on during the rest of the winter for all ordinary occasions and keep the other, with its delicate telescope instrument, on the wall over the window, for wolves or those food animals that might come wandering right by home.

In less time than it takes to tell, I grabbed my own rifle from its pegs. It was loaded. But Bud, in cleaning his rifle a few hours before for what he supposed would be its long winter's rest, had not reloaded it. Bud's stunning phrase, "Grizzly bear," had the same effect on me that a person would get by suddenly bursting into a calm assembly of people and yelling "Fire!" Expecting Bud to follow me, I flew headlong out the door. I thought this was what I was supposed to do. The bear must have heard the small squeak of the door. At any rate, he never paused to look. The next thing I knew, the immense timid creature was swinging his obese hindquarters into a lumbering gallop, six feet at a bound, for the nearby cover of the forest. I had had no intention of shooting without first giving Bud a chance to place a good shot with his telescope sight, for we must get the bear for the meat and especially for the wonderful fat he was carrying. However, when the bear became alarmed, there was nothing to do but fire upon him as fast as I could in a desperate hope of stopping him. How was I to know that Bud was under the bed trying to find ammunition?

It seems incredible that Bud could recover from his handicap in the way he did, but he had somehow stuffed two bullets into his gun and thrown himself down beside me in the snow. His first shot rolled the bear. "He's hit!" I cried. But he recovered almost instantly. Like a bouncing ball he was on his feet again. Bud's other shot went wide, as did all my four shots, and the bear vanished into the forest. I had been shooting crazily, under the notion that quantity of shots would bring him down. It was a sad sight to see that immensely fat timid bear make his escape. And now we had a wounded grizzly on our hands!

A hunting companion should never rouse his friends by exciting methods but would be wise to keep a calmness in his manner if it is possible to do so during these crises. By yelling "Grizzly bear!" at any dozen odd men in a hunting cabin, one can well imagine all hell breaking loose—the race for the guns, the wrong ammunition, the wasted motion, the crippling shots, and ninety-nine times out of a hundred the ultimate escape of the pursued animal.

If there had been a dozen persons firing on our big bear all at once, then, with all the ammunition in the world at their disposal, this would not insure that the grizzly would be killed; the grizzly might escape every bit as easily from only two excited hunters—except that in the former case he would be more likely to eat somebody up before the fray ended.

In the first place it is doubtful if any big bear or moose should be fired upon from such a range as 175 yards for sure results. Bud probably could have killed him with one or two well-placed shots using his telescope sight, since he knew by heart this tested range and just what his little .30-30 carbine would do but failing to get a good shot he fired at the bear as it fled only because we really had to have it and because snow on the ground at least offered a chance to trail it.

We were two considerably calmed-down hunters as we loaded our guns again, crossed the river, and silently took up the trail in the forest. There were big splotches of red blood, and it looked good for us. The trail led straight as an arrow for the steep mountains. The grizzly bear is a mountain animal and it was for rocks and crags that he flew. For an hour we followed the trail, hardly daring to breathe. "One certainly pays for mistakes in hunting," I thought.

At first, we thought to find him any moment. The animal blew out a fine spray of blood from his nose at every bound as he fled. But presently, as the tracks slowed to a steady, mile-eating pace, the external bleeding ceased altogether, and we could see that our pursuit was merely driving him farther from home. "No use running him anymore," Bud sighed at last. "See, he lay down here, but he heard us coming and got up and went on again. We'd better go home now and wait overnight and pray it doesn't snow."

"Do you really think we'll get him?" I asked, brokenhearted.

"Yes, I think so. As soon as we stop pursuing him, maybe he'll stop. If we can get him to lie down, maybe he'll stiffen and not be able to get up in the morning."

We went home and waited overnight, watching the weather and watching the hours tick by on the watch, while I plied Bud with much rare roast meat and morsels of raw dried tallow to hearten him for the trail ahead. Next morning, Bud took my .30-30 with open sights, preparing for a close-range encounter, and followed the trail alone. He asked me if I would like to come along, but I declined this offer. We both knew this was a job for one person, and not an inexperienced one either.

Bud's incredible luck was with him once more, only he didn't call it luck; to him it was just a way of life. He soon found a "bed" after the bear had crossed the valley and begun to climb; this bed was on a sidehill overlooking the bear's own back trail by fifteen feet. This gave Bud the idea that he would do it again. The bear had then moved on, because the pressed-down snow was frozen into ice where he had lain. Many beds and many ambushes followed. Bud knew that the old patriarch was sickened to the death and in pain. Pity welled in his heart, but he also knew that in trailing a wounded big bear to his lair the hunter has all the odds stacked against him because the bear has every chance of smelling him or hearing him coming, so that the hunter is apt to find out too late and at close quarters that he is the one who is being hunted.

As the trail led up the mountain into tangled brush, thick spruce forest, and large boulders, Bud craftily left the trail altogether as he did not think walking along it to be a healthy occupation; he came no nearer the actual trail than forty yards, but circled above it, always keeping where he could look down from a vantage above. Step by step, inch by inch—then he stopped in his tracks, carbine in hand. There was the great bear before him. He was lying down between two huge boulders, his nose resting on his paws, taking catnaps and watching out from on high. His small eyes were fastened upon his own back trail. It would have been a fatal encounter for the hunter following that trail.

Bud studied the bear one moment thoughtfully. Although he had talked with Alaskan hunters who had filled him with yarns about how a big bear's skull sometimes cannot be shot through, he believed that those hunters probably just missed the bear. The far-reaching reputation these bears have is enough to instill fear into the most confident person who has heard Alaska bear stories. Hoping for the best, and with a certain confidence born of his knowledge that other people do kill bears, Bud crept up behind the bear, from the side, and squeezing his finger on the trigger was able to cock the hammer without a betraying click; then he shot the big animal in the head just behind the ear, from a distance of thirty-five feet.

Without so much as a moan the bear rolled over, kicked slightly, and lay still. He had been killed instantly and had never at any time seen the hunter. The Atlas joint, which connects head and neck, had been the target. Bud stretched himself, breathed deeply, and it being ten degrees above zero started up a fire and sat down to wait for me.

At home I heard the shot for which I had been listening, whereupon I at once hoisted the pack board on my back with the necessary things and went to the spot.

Frequent warming of the hands was necessary during the butchering, which took the rest of the day. It was a grand bear, an old male, perhaps seven years old. Weighing about eight hundred pounds, it actually offered more meat than had my small moose. The chocolate-brown robe, about eight feet square, matched the brown of the bear's broad nose and the bottoms of its heavy cracked feet with blunt nails.

The greatest prize to us in our present position was that the bear carried about seventy-five pounds of pure fat along with the rest of him, which could be peeled off the meat in layers and rendered into lard. If it hadn't been for that one bear we would have been due for a pretty hard time of it to keep properly fed at all, because of fat shortage. The bear represented more in food value than we, in our abysmal ignorance, had brought up here for a total year's grubstake to begin with!

Our bear must have been just ready to hibernate. Grizzly bears, it seems, may not hibernate as early or as totally as black bears, but we hadn't known this. The hibernation of bears in the arctic, as elsewhere, may not depend upon the coming of cold weather at all, but entirely upon feed conditions. The bears go to sleep when there is no more grazing because the ground is covered with snow. Tropical bears in the jungle which have continuous forage and polar bears, which are carnivorous, do not hibernate at all, because their food supply is constant the year around.

Bears go into hibernation with an empty stomach; the stomach of this one was completely empty. This was fortunate for us because the crippling shot had passed clear through the animal, shattering the stomach and intestines; if they had been full of food matter, they would have pumped their contents through the animal's system as he ran. Gut-shooting and subsequently running an animal, then, is the key to the mystery of that unpleasant gamy taste. Consider how one would like domestic meat if it was treated in this way! It would taste a little gamy, too! On the farm, and in the packing companies, animals which are to be butchered are not fed for twenty-four hours directly before that event, to simplify butchering. In the wild, animals are generally killed with a full stomach.

Deer and moose are usually compared to beef cattle for general household use; the bear has food values similar to those of the hog. For one used to skinning and dressing deer and moose, the dressing of a bear is a different proposition. The hide is thick and attached like iron to the muscles of the body all the way, and the musculature is so powerfully laid onto the frame that it is evident why bears can withstand the shock of bullets from high-powered rifles as they sometimes do. It is a real job, needing a certain know-how, to disjoint a big grizzly bear properly—the small bones are so hard that hatchet and hacksaw are hard-pressed to make a dent in them. The gelatin of the tendons, so delicious with venison, can scarcely be softened by hours of boiling and generally would be considered inedible, although we ate it. The bones are almost solid, with no marrow. A person who eats a whole grizzly bear during the winter, along with his other meats, is practically certain to develop a strong set of jaws. The flavor of the inland grizzly cannot be too highly recommended.

For a week, while Bud cut firewood at home and worked himself into a lather scraping fatty tissue from the heavy grizzly hide, I packed out the meat. It was in quarters, which meant four complete trips in all. The quarters were left buried under the snow to chill, where they were safe from the predators for a doubtful time. The total distance to get them home was about two and a half miles. The quarters must have weighed about ninety pounds each, or even a hundred pounds in the case of the big shoulders, so I must have been quite strong at that time on my outdoor life and all-meat diet, or possibly I just had to be. Although I grumbled loudly, I nevertheless thought nothing in those days of walking over to the bear kill in the morning, digging out a frozen quarter from the snow, roping it to the pack board, rolling somehow to my feet, and, bowed beneath a pack so mighty that it almost obscured me from sight, trudging across that vast snowy stage to get it home by noon. The worst of it was that all of the fallen logs were covered with snow so that there was no place to sit down for a rest on the way; once down on the ground itself I might not ever get up with the pack again. Sometimes therefore I would make it all the way home without a breather.

Back-packing in the North may be easier than in a warm country, we think, because of the stimulation of cold to bodily vigor. A light pack of fifteen or twenty pounds must be carried everywhere in the timber country in a day's travel because of the great variety of equipment that the northerner needs. But as one gets used to these things his strength soon becomes prodigious.

Besides the pack, there was always my rifle to carry. I'll never forget the only day in the year I didn't lug it along. We had been living entirely on meat, not even drinking tea, for the last twenty days. I had carried the last bear shoulder part of the way home and, having left it along the trail, delayed getting it for a few days. This spot was just at the base of the mountain in the valley; the meat was buried in snow, but I knew where it was. I know now that the place I picked for hiding the meat was a game highway, where any predators loafing along the valley would be sure to find it. Find it they did. The life of a hunter is one long battle against the elements and other animals which conspire against him: you can expect a loss of easily a fifth of all the meat you shoot—a kind of "squeeze." Meat is never yours until you have got it home hung up on the back of the house, and even then, don't be too sure you've got it!

Confidently I approached the area where I knew the bear should lie buried—without my rifle. Intuition seemed to warn me, but too late. There was no use going home for my rifle now, but I slowed my approaching steps. Yes, only a few yards away, I heard the snapping of bones and realized that the ghoulish feast was even now in progress! Thieves! One by one they rose up from my meat cache. I caught my breath as I counted three of them. Unconsciously my lips moved as I whispered once, and swallowed, and one of the feasters pricked up his ears then; he had heard this! Leisurely the others halted their eating and trotted up the ridge. One just turned around, sat down, and looked at me. Round as barrels from having eaten a hundred pounds of meat, they almost seemed to know I didn't have a rifle with me. Their coats were of burnished yellow and black; their furry faces Oriental in cast, with slanted eyes; their tails like plumes. I had never seen prettier sled dogs. It didn't seem right that they didn't belong to somebody.

I thought they were wolves, but their tracks discounted this. Bud and a trapping partner had taken dozens of coyotes in Arizona when he was working his way through high school and early college; he was not to be misled by old friends. These were actually immense coyotes in their arctic dress, quite a valuable fur here.

Coyotes arrive, it is said, when the white man comes into a new land. This means that the coyote thrives better on conditions of cultivation and settlement than he does in the actual wilds. He is a small, crafty fellow, as clever as a wolf, but not so easily starved out, for he can manage on odds and ends when he has to. In Arizona Bud had seen a coyote boldly trotting down the main street of a mining town in full light of day, passing himself off as a dog! The toll of game and songbirds taken by coyotes must run into thousands yearly now in the United States. Realizing the menace of the coyote, with its numerous litters and rapid increase, the Alaska Game Commission has put as high a bounty on the coyote as upon the wolf. One might anticipate millions of dollars' worth of havoc—assuming the destruction could be measured in mere dollars—if the coyote ever got well started among the arctic nesting grounds of the continent's migratory wildfowl! Presumably by winter he would have to live on lemmings and on ptarmigan, in this case; we know that he can live successfully all year, as far as the rabbits go, along the Alatna.

Originally no coyotes were recognized in the North, but reports seem to indicate that they may be coming in from southerly Canada and the United States, although how they have managed to cross over or avoid the vast glaciers and precipitous coastal ranges which successfully barricade interior Alaska is not known. The route must be intercontinental.

The coyotes came to our valley during the early part of the winter and we could hear them running rabbits; where they moved after that, we do not know. We were never able to trap them. They refused to visit again the bear cache where they had been alarmed.

4

The place in which I hid my meat pack was the best trapping site we ever had. Bud caught one female wolf and most of his ferocious Halloween wolverines at the old bear shoulder. The frozen shoulder blade torn away from scattered ribs, with no meat left on it, proved most attractive to these roving predators, whose curiosity caused them to investigate the tracks and smells of each preceding visitor, to their undoing.

"Bud, let's spring all the traps and take a trip for a few days! It's only about sixty miles over the Divide, and we could see the headwaters of the Noatak River! We could make it a ski trip!"

Most of us today think of skis just for coasting downhill, but ours awaited us as a conveyance by means of which we might tramp long distances across country. Our style was poor, of grace we had none, we were a queer but a hardy pair. The skis might help us plot our route to the Colville River head which at this time we still had hopes of attaining. For the ski trip we would take only one rifle, the sleeping bag, and some trail rations of dried meat and bear fat. We'd only be gone a week or so and then must hurry home before really cold weather struck.

Alas, it was never possible for us to find a route to the Colville River through the Endicott Mountains as we had planned. The project would have taken much more than one year, and much more equipment than we had. There is no room in this book to tell of every route we know which might be taken by a more enterprising person. Everyone in

Alaska has his own excursion which he hopes to make some day, and the routes are endless, and the dreams are endless. Perhaps this is why we are Alaskans.

Now for this trip Bud froze our bottles of film developer into blocks of ice and stacked them outside the door; their glass bottles would have burst. Tarpaulins covered the meat racks behind the house. That was about all we had to worry about.

Bud wrote in his diary: "Cut fifteen trees today. Connie is really lazy. Today she just ate and dragged slowly up and down the trail carrying wood. [The trees!] It is a luxury to be lazy and a complement to our way of life. All we have, we have made with a very few tools and just the materials of the country."

Yes indeed, we needed some exercise and a change, and we would take a ski trip sixty miles over to the western watershed and back, we thought.

"You go spring the Arrigetch traps," Bud told me, "and we'll leave right away in an hour or two." He himself headed to spring those traps which lay in the opposite direction.

I was still within sight of the house, going down the river. This was the arctic night. The world was all delicate pastels—silver snow, turquoise, flooded-over river ice, pink sky, and every tiniest sound carrying a long, long way as the temperature dropped. The twilight of the hours of daylight which come during the arctic night is very deceptive.

Suddenly I saw six big white wolves trot across the river ice below me, one after the other in a line. They must truly be wolves, I thought, because they stood so tall; you could see much daylight under their bellies. I had dropped down upon my stomach and lay watching them. I tried a shot with the .22 rifle which I carried, but the range was too far; they merely jumped up in the air and came down again in one spot, having no idea what a .22 rifle was all about. I couldn't see what I was shooting at, and, with a foolish feeling, I desisted. When they disappeared behind a river island, I got up from the ice and went to look for their tracks. Certainly, seeing six big bold wolves like this must be a rare occurrence anywhere.

The tracks of the wolves on hard-crusted snow and ice crystals were not clear; they led me, at any rate, to something I really couldn't figure out. An area of ground by the side of the river below was mutilated. Moss had been pawed out of the snow and lay scattered about as though by some animals digging. I had never seen anything quite like it. *As though great herds had but recently been here!*

There was no telling in the twilight how great an area the pawed-over ground comprised. I hurried on, with the mounting excitement of a momentous discovery. What was it? What could it be?

The unreality of the early twilight and the endlessness and confusion of the pawing tracks leading every which way offered no reasonable answer. Here was something we ought to know about, some movement, some occurrence in our environment of radical import.

I had just decided to bolt for home and Bud, when I found myself listening. From up on the side of partially timbered Red Mountain there came to my ear in that silence a faint crackling sound. I climbed up the hill, irresistibly drawn to this noise.

The crackling sound called me through the woods. Now I heard it, now I didn't. I was not prepared for the animated spectacle I did find. It was one of the most wonderful experiences I ever expect to have in my life. Peering through trees and bushes, I realized that before me was a herd of what I guessed to be around four hundred of my first wild caribou. I had never seen caribou before, but a five-year-old child would have known them well. The tossing alert heads, carrying antlers up to four feet tall, which had dozens of spirals, knobs, and curlycues, catching in the branches of the trees and knocking against each other—here were Santa Claus's real wild reindeer, walking, playing, fighting, and jostling each other before me!

The sound which had guided me to them was the rattling of their hoofs and horns! Knees were being lifted, sharp-cutting round little hoofs were striking the snow, and antler was cracking against antler amid a general rustle of moving deer bodies. Accompanying this was a kind of creaking, caused by the snapping of tendons on the legs near the hoofs, which punctuated the stillness. Except for these slight sounds, the big herd gave no warning of its presence and otherwise might not have been there, dwarfed into nothingness as it was by Red Mountain rising bleak above.

My .22 rifle gripped tensely, I backed out of the thicket with my eyes popping out and ran for home.

"Don't say a word!" I told Bud first of all, where I found him on the river ice by the house. "Don't make any noise!" I was so afraid that the nearby herd would hear a voice.

"What's up?" he said out loud. I could have choked him.

"Bud, we're never going to take that ski trip or see the Noatak River," I told him with certainty. "The caribou have come. Not one animal," I said. "Hundreds. Hundreds. They're all around us. It's the most wonderful thing. The valley below here, you know the valley, Bud—it's torn up. Trampled down! Not one inch of ground not pulverized, for miles maybe. I can't guess the extent of it yet. The bushes and the sides of trees are absolutely riddled. Hundreds of hoofs, coming right towards our house now, only a quarter of a mile away. First, I saw six big caribou wolves that guided me to them. . . ."

We stood there on the river ice. Bud's expression had changed to a look of serious wonder combined with marvelous joy, if that is possible. The words, "The caribou have come!" or "The caribou are coming!" are enough to fill any far northerner with that feeling. We had heard tales of this phenomenon occurring in the old days, even early in this century, but did it actually happen in our generation? Automobiles filled with people sometimes went out of Fairbanks on the highways to see the caribou migration there, but this was different. This was the primitive setting as experienced by two lone human beings living on nothing but meat and forcibly thrown into the primitive environment.

"I never dreamed we'd see caribou here this year in the middle of these rough mountains," said Bud. "It's the last thing you would have thought of. Why, this is way off their route."

"Maybe they're lost." But no one really knew the route of the caribou through the Brooks Range. Did this happen every year here, or was it an unusual event? We never did find out the answer to this question.

It is a peculiar thing about caribou. Some years they come, and other years they are not to be found. They are a very mobile animal. Known to make migrations on grand scales, they may be met yearly along their known migration routes by the waiting hunters, but on the other hand they may at any time change their range unexpectedly and not appear at all. Nobody knows where they come from or where tomorrow they may go. This year caribou poured out of the arctic into the Koyukuk in many thousands. Airplanes on the Fairbanks-Barrow run reported immense herds coming from the "other side" and along the Arctic Divide, covering wide areas. We probably got in on the edge of this somewhere. Few of these caribou were seen by man.

Did I say four hundred caribou? Reconnaissance of the next few hours brought us to believe we saw *four thousand* the first day, and they kept on passing intermittently for a *month*, during which time we saw at least some caribou almost every day.

This does not mean that there are endless caribou in Alaska, however. If all the deer in Pennsylvania were herded together and driven through one valley or mountain pass, they also would make a considerable spectacle. These caribou, probably less than a hundred thousand in all, represented the drainage of an area of country certainly as large as Pennsylvania, or larger.

What of the size of the caribou herds of the American arctic, Canada and Alaska, past and present? Dr. R. M. Anderson, who was second-in-command of the Canadian Arctic Expedition which Stefansson headed, has said:

> Owing to the remoteness of the range of caribou, the comparatively few people who have had experience with them, and the impossibility up to the present time of obtaining reliable contemporaneous reports from different districts in the real heart of the caribou country, there are in circulation more conflicting estimates as to the numbers of caribou than any other animal on earth, varying from a comparatively small number by the alarmists up to 20 or 30 million by the professional optimists . . .
>
> The range of the species extends from Labrador to northwest Alaska, and from Northern Alberta and Saskatchewan to the most northerly arctic islands. Caribou perform a sort of seasonal movement or migration, which seems to be a shifting of groups, for a limited distance . . . The great masses of caribou are confined apparently to an area in the heart of the "Barren Grounds," measuring . . . roughly about 210,000 square miles. Estimating a carrying capacity of five caribou to the square mile, we get 1,050,000 animals in this area of maximum density, and the scattered herds outside this area probably do not exceed half that number at the present time, although

of course the whole area is capable of carrying much more than that number . . . probably the total number of caribou in Canada is not now over 3,000,000.[1]

Dr. Anderson made these statements early in the twentieth century.

It may have been the famous naturalist, Ernest Thompson Seton, to whom Dr. Anderson was referring as one of the "professional optimists." He estimated 30,000,000 caribou in 1907 in Canada as preyed upon by a combined total of but 4521 Indians and Eskimos living in the caribou country. Thus, there has been wide disagreement even among the authorities as to the prevalence of this animal on our continent. There was never any estimate of the numbers of caribou in Alaska at all because a Game Commission and game laws for Alaska were not founded until 1924, when the Alaska Railroad was completed.

All of this is ancient history, but it is well to review it to get some understanding of the present. Stefansson's view of the arctic game situation as he saw it in the 1920's is still widely held by many people today. "The arctic grasslands have caribou in herds of tens of thousands and sometimes hundreds of thousands to a single band . . . Wolves that feed on the caribou go singly and in packs of ten or less, and their aggregate numbers on the arctic prairies of the two hemispheres must be well in the tens of thousands." [2] The great explorer has said that if it were not for the wolves which are their greatest destroyers, the caribou in their arctic grazing lands would possess almost unlimited capacities of increase.

The Stefansson view of the wolf and caribou cycle as the main control over caribou increase in the arctic implies that probably some of the earlier estimates of the caribou herds were exaggerated in the first place. Because of wolves, then, which are found wherever caribou exist, the total caribou at any time may not have been very different from what they are today. For a while in some areas the caribou were slaughtered in terrific numbers by natives and primitive white men

---

1   Quotation from "Conserving Canada's Musk Oxen" by W. H. B. Hoare, in *An Investigation for the Department of the Interior*, pp. 52 and 53, by Dr. R. M. Anderson, Chief of the Division of Biology, National Museum of Canada.
2   *The Friendly Arctic*, by Vilhjalmur Stefansson, p. 17. The Macmillan Co., New York, 1943.

after the repeating rifle was introduced into the North. Whaling crews used to be supplied with fresh caribou meat by hired Eskimo hunters along the arctic coasts, and we ourselves had talked to men who could tell tales of seeing dead frozen caribou stacked like cordwood. But this was more true of the past than it is today. Whaling vessels have not visited the Arctic Ocean since the early part of the century, and the Eskimo population in general has halved its numbers since then, so that the caribou are not being hunted by man today as much as they were forty years ago. This becomes especially significant when you realize that the native population living off the caribou in these areas has perhaps been diminished by as much as four fifths during the last three centuries.

The airplane will make possible a more accurate assay of the caribou migrations than could ever be made before. In the future the whereabouts of the arctic herds will be known, and facts only guessed at formerly can be proved scientifically.

Bud holds up a wolverine from our trapline

We walk the trapline regularly

5

Not knowing at first the extent of the migration which had come into our country, Bud and I set off to shoot a few of the caribou before they should be gone.

To secure food which had fallen into our laps was again the first consideration. "Do you know how much we are eating?" Bud had asked me a few days previously with dry candor. He hadn't wished to alarm me before. But he had made the interesting discovery that, including the bones, we were each eating approximately *our own weight in meat each month*. It was Bud who carried the quarters off the meat rack into the house and he knew. We now had twenty pounds of flour and twenty pounds of sugar left us and resolved to save it at least until Christmas. We seemed due to run out of salt, too, around February or soon thereafter, according to the present rate of consumption. Even now, the civilized food that we had left didn't count; you might say it was just to look at. Therefore, it was like an act of Providence when the caribou appeared to help us out.

Yes, we were due to learn about the primitive life in the American arctic at first hand, and more than we had imagined when we first started out. We had come into these arctic mountains with too little food, and although we didn't think of it in that way, our life doubtless would have been described as a starvation situation, were it known, or even by some people as a miraculous escape from death. We weren't alarmists, but we did thank our luck that a fat grizzly bear came along when it did, and we knew that we were in luck again now when the caribou arrived. We thought we had better lay in plenty of those caribou, just in case. If the jaws of death weren't openly drooling at our heels, as the novelist would put it, one might say that we would have to hunt ourselves up other supplies of meat one way or another.

The trap line might have prevented actual starvation of course. We had thought of eating wolf or wolverine, but naturally preferred caribou. Bud had cooked up a fox once; some of the Eskimos seem to enjoy those fat white arctic foxes that come in from the northern sea ice. But you can take it from us that those animals are no rose blossoms. We did not intend to let our meat pile get down to the last piece.

Bud stationed me at the edge of a stretch of forest on the slope of Red Mountain while he went around on the other side of the herd I had found, with the intention of shooting first and stampeding the herd right by me where I also would have my chance. Against Bud's stern judgment I had taken the camera loaded with colored film. It was high noon. The sun did not rise, but because of the large amount of light refraction on the white snow, colored pictures might be taken. At this point I would have given an arm for pictures, even at the price of future beefsteak. But to handle both a camera and a gun at the same time with any proficiency is a feat. We were hunting food. I had my camera opened up and was getting ready to focus it upon one of the pawing caribou surrounding me. "If Bud will only hold his fire a moment longer!" I thought.

Of course, my luck didn't last. Just then came the sound of Bud's shot, catching me unaware, and before I could close my camera lens, jump to my feet and grab my rifle, which was stuck butt first into the snow, my animals were off, and I secured nothing at all. Instantly the nearby caribou got out of range for a good shot between the intervening trees and the undulations of the ground. They joined the main herd of easily a thousand deer which had been hidden from us in the gullies of the mountainside. The whole herd sprang out of the timber and the gullies before our eyes, and we were aghast at the sight. Their bobbing white tails disappearing into the distance as they climbed the vast mountainside reminded us of the wonderful moving pictures we had seen of fleeing game herds in Africa. But it had not been really proved to us before that such game herds exist in America, too. The deer had seen the hunters, unfortunately, but otherwise did not know what

Winter Hunting

the sound of shooting meant. They halted a mile away, and there the thousand stood watching us, standing in a mighty group, looking back with all heads turned in the same direction, to see what had caused the disturbance.

Bud and I had been brought face to face with the dilemma which meets the sportsman who hunts his animals in herds—the veritable impossibility of shooting into a herd of this size! Of all the hunting techniques discussed in this book, the problem of dealing with the large herd is the least likely to come to the attention of today's average sportsman, but in case it does, we shall relate what we learned.

What we wanted was a few, well-chosen caribou. Yet it was impossible to pick out any animal to shoot at without running the risk of crippling a half-dozen others. Because an animal shot right through the heart may possibly bolt two hundred yards before dropping, one cannot hope even to tell the result of his shots in such a melee. There is no chance, furthermore, to trail your cripple to be sure of getting him, for a moment later he is lost in the center of the herd among all the others which look exactly like him!

This is what happened to Bud. Selecting an animal at the edge of the herd, he fired, wounded it, and it bolted away with a thousand others which miraculously appeared from all quarters. Bud had his binoculars with him and he spent much of the rest of the remaining daylight hours chasing the wounded old bull with its thousand companions almost to the top of the mountain. Up and up climbed Bud, driving the long-legged deer before him, until all were dots dissolved into nothingness. I had a pretty good idea of what had happened and sighed for Bud. I went home. There I was surprised to notice that the thermometer said 30 ° below zero.

Bud got home, very cold, after dark; he had killed his cripple up on the mountaintop. He had started skinning as fast as he could but completed only half of the job before darkness fell. His hands were freezing; skinning must be performed barehanded. The only way he could keep his grip on the knife was to thrust his hands into the deer's body at short intervals and bury them there to get the body warmth. His knife dulled before he was half through, and he had no whetstone with him.

From his general knowledge of the cattle ranges, Bud estimated that he saw from six to ten thousand caribou from the mountain-top, fanned out in all directions. It was only after he had killed the caribou which he had chased far up on the mountain that it struck him that had we waited or not bungled things, we could have killed our animals closer to home. He had been too afraid they would pass us by.

All of the animals Bud had seen closely were bulls, which, because of their breeding habits, were so lean that Bud wearily could only describe them, as well as the meat he brought back, by saying that a person could count their ribs from fifty feet. Never in his life had he seen skinnier animals. He had got onto the technique of herd shooting, which is to pick your animal from a small group at the fringe, and don't ever let the herd see you, but he felt dismal about the meat outlook.

Winter caribou which are traveling are all of them walking racks of bones—cows, calves, and bulls alike—but worst of all and almost impossible to live on, if you have nothing else to enrich the diet, are old bulls which have rutted. Most uninformed people imagine that forage and feeding conditions account for a herbivore's condition of fat, but an intimate knowledge reveals that their breeding habits have the greatest influence and that cow and bull caribou, for instance, are at their fattest at exactly opposite seasons of the year. With caribou, both sexes have antlers which are shed at opposite times, so that it takes some discrimination for the inexperienced hunter to tell them apart. Both sexes and the calves as well are the sportsman's legal game at the present time.

For food purposes, only the cows should be killed in the late fall, after the calves are large. Occasionally calves are good too, but usually they are of a skeleton leanness. Bulls are best in July, August, and September before rutting, for which purpose they have been putting on weight and gathering their strength for the entire year. In the late summer the old bulls have layers of thick back fat which is an article highly prized by arctic caribou eaters, and the older the bull the better the eating because of more fat. Caribou on migration should not, strictly speaking, be shot for food at all, except that the civilized persons for whom the laws are made would otherwise not secure any.

Because the caribou which the Indians get are shot on migration in the Koyukuk, the Yukon, and southward, the Indians come out poorly as compared with their more northerly brothers, the Eskimos, living in the caribou's true home where most of the caribou remain all the year around. The Indians have to eat lean, devitalized caribou meat when they get it and they have never been able to devise, even in their best days, the kind of fur clothing that the Eskimos know, because the caribou they see by winter are not suitable for it. The land of the northern Eskimo beyond the timber is a richer land for human food by far than the timbered regions!

Our caribou were almost pure white in their long winter hair; we did not know at this time that in summer the same animal, perhaps found hundreds of miles from here, is nearly black. A great attraction in getting caribou for us, in addition to the meat, was the chance of getting a parka. "Now we can make ourselves the Eskimo clothing that we lack!" we planned anxiously when we saw the herd. If we could only master the tanning of the hides we could cut and sew them. This we had already tried to do with rabbit skins, with no success because they tore. Bud had returned from his first hunt with one robe; it could be conveniently left rolled up and frozen outdoors until we had time to thaw and work it with the others we must get.

By the next morning the worst of our premonitions were realized when we awoke to find the thermometer saying -40°, while herds of caribou, visible from our window, poured over the mountaintop in a steady stream. Did the cold wave have something to do with bringing them? Zoologists say no. Our cold wave was but incidental. Caribou are arctic animals; they are quite as apt to migrate northward as southward in the winter, and those chilly mountain slopes rising above our chimney and our hidden valley held no dread for them. The binoculars showed a tangle of trails, beaten over the peaks, and one whole mountainside was laid bare for acres with their digging and pawing for moss and for the grass and vetch they ate as well. Later we would dream sometimes of those great, dimly lit, arctic-winter snowfields, black with traveling animals. Our dreams of the arctic night would be of these caribou, of a land where wolf trails leading up the face of the mountain to the kill would fairly spring at you when you lifted powerful binoculars to the eye.

AT FORTY BELOW ZERO WE started out hunting for caribou in the vicinity of the little home which of necessity becomes the boundary line for those who venture into the arctic with only ordinary fabric clothing and no furs or special arctic apparel. How lucky for us that we had been prevented from making that ski trip! But to let the thousands of caribou pass us by without securing some for supplies would have been madness. Somehow, we must accomplish this even if we almost froze in the process. We had fuel cut and a glorious, roaring-hot home to come back to if we could stand the cold a little while. It was a cold, cold job, upon which rested ultimate comfort and survival.

Bud had tanned some marmot skins of the previous summer and was engaged in sewing mittens, but at the present time they were not complete, and we had only the light wool and leather ones of conventional climes. We bound our feet in the skins of rabbits, fur in, and pulled over them four pairs of woolen socks. But even this did not suffice, because the slight perspiration soon condensed to frost on the outer socks in such a temperature, showing how the cold was coming through nonetheless; the stiffness of our rubber shoepacs, too, allowed little toe movement and noticeably cut off circulation in this degree of cold. Very loose, floppy boots of the Eskimo principle are, of course, the only thing, and all clothing should be loose, which ours was not. The more pairs of rabbit skins and socks we put on, the tighter our boots fitted, although they had been bought extra-large in the first place.

Hunting in the cold weather is severe at any time because its very nature entails endless watching and waiting in a motionless state which is difficult to maintain with any patience. Bud wouldn't hear of my staying home. "What!" he ejaculated, as though surprised at the suggestion. "I'll need you to do the shooting. I've got to try to get pictures." Pictures were my great weakness and his great drawing card for me. I would do anything for them.

During the hunt our hands and feet got so cold that it was necessary to pause and build a fire step by step; we literally progressed by fires. It was one of several excruciating adventures with cold which I have had myself in the course of learning to know different parts of Alaska, the hard way, while Bud has had a great many more of such times, all told. It was the most miserable and yet the most memorable day I had ever spent. Bud built the fires, took the responsibility of caring for both of us, and I merely did as he said. Hands could quickly be warmed by the swift twig fires, but there was no way of warming the feet without burning the boots. Up on the top of Old Rip Mound where we could look down at the roof of our house, we built a fire and paused to gaze around that cool blue land. It was from here that we saw a band of around fifty of the deer trooping over the beaten trails and into our view. They would pass below, through a narrow ravine which boxed them in along the base of Red Mountain proper, behind our house.

Our job was to slip around the rocks to where they would pass our stand at firing distance. Oh, miserable day! The swift deer stopped to paw and feed, while we waited.

"My feet are really going to freeze," I told Bud, and still we waited for the deer to pass. At last Bud built me another fire in the rocks; he did this regretfully, fearing it would ruin our hunting. "See," I demonstrated, "the wind will blow the smoke away from them"—and it did! The whole herd of caribou could have seen both me and my fire if they had looked to that stand of dead birches there, but perhaps they thought the rising smoke was fog rising over some body of water, a phenomenon to which they are used in their arctic waterings. Bud kept me posted on their doings from a few feet away at his lookout in the rocks, while I hurriedly pulled off boots and socks and, sitting on a rock which might as well have been ice as stone, stuck my agonized feet into the flames in an effort to warm them as quickly as possible. But the general icebox atmosphere in which the little fire blazed up was so all-pervading that one could not warm the bare fingers by it without freezing the wrist at the same time or warm the toes without freezing the extended foot itself. There comes a time, then, when an outdoor fire in the lower temperatures becomes quite useless for warmth. We did not know then that it was only the white man, during the last hundred years or so, who taught the Eskimos in the far North to burn wood and coal for fuel, and that originally, in fact, some of the Eskimos did not know how to build a fire at all, as we know fires for our bodily warmth, nor did they dream of it. People in an arctic land depend upon their fur clothing to keep warm, not upon open fires. Fires in this sense are useful only in comparatively warm weather. Presently I smelled burning flesh and looked around in time to jerk my foot out of the fire. It being numb, I had burned it so badly before I knew it that I was to have a tender toe for a year afterwards.

Now I scrambled to get on my stiff frozen socks and found that I had knocked some of them off the ledge into a deep fissure in the rocks. It was only by digging my burned and frosted feet into the snow and reaching down into the fissure to my shoulder that I was able to get my socks and boot back. I would have a certain skepticism about taking off my boots and socks in the winter arctic after that!

While I was still sockless and bootless Bud hissed at me that the caribou were approaching. "Get out of it!" he warned. "Do you want to be buried sitting up?" He meant, did I intend to sit there until I froze solid?

Blinding smoke rose in circles about me so that I could hardly see what I was doing as I fought frantically at the socks. Yes, here I was again in my typical situation, quite helpless and a useless burden—the winter scene! Forty degrees below zero and I had my socks off while the caribou were coming by!

"Go ahead and shoot," I hissed back at Bud, who warned me that the herd standing before him was getting restless. But his gun wouldn't go off! It had been given more careful attention than had my rifle and the oil had solidified in its firing pin! At the same time the whole herd abruptly lay down in the little pass right before us and waited for me! This gave me time to get on my socks and boots and limp to the lookout spot. "Golly," I said to myself as I thought of Bud and what must come after, "if he can skin them, I guess I can shoot them."

"How many do you want?" I asked.

Rifle and camera peered from behind the rocks. The camera had frozen solid and no pictures were to be had. We concentrated now on the hunting. The cold temperatures had distorted distances and we thought the caribou herd was closer than it actually was. Actually, the shots would be long ones. Some of the herd were lying down, some feeding, some rutting, the calves frolicking, and all of them, even if they had never seen a man before, were on the alert for their natural enemies at all times. People who imagine a wildlife paradise where the animals originally trusted men are mistaken, at least when it comes to the arctic; those caribou were born to be killed, and in their natural state not one of them would live to be more than four or five years old at the most before being dragged down by the cruel teeth; caribou have never been known to exist without wolves.

It was now or never for us. You don't miss your chance when the caribou come through. There was no buck fever—only cold feet. And as for missing under those circumstances, well, you just don't miss.

I was to select cows. Picking out one standing broadside nearby, I downed it, and then killed some others in five shots all together, while Bud dashed out with the pistol and got my cripples. The shooting left me doubled up and entirely incapable of reloading for several minutes thereafter; had we wanted more then I think it would have been impossible for me, since shooting was done barehanded. I could only let my rifle fall and thrust my hands, burned by the steel, into my coat. Blisters raised on my trigger finger which remained for some days.

The reaction of the herd at being fired upon was that those animals which were lying down merely got up and stood nervously. They did not know that anything had happened until we came out of our hiding place to dispatch the cripples dying on the field, and to get at the skinning. Then they filed reluctantly up the mountain and over the pink snowfields, not seeming to realize that they had left comrades behind.

How Bud skinned I would never know. Each job must be finished on the spot, and he had all he could handle in his race against time. Later in arctic life we would have Eskimo clothing and would become used to it. Many an Eskimo can kill fourteen caribou from a herd, without showing himself, and then can come out upon the field and skin them all in temperatures as low as fifty degrees below zero, but you have to know how. Even the Eskimos try to kill most of their animals when the temperature is a little warmer.

With packsack carrying our skinning equipment, including the vital whetstone, we ran to the first animal, and before it had more than ceased breathing, Bud had begun skinning up one hind leg to the "break joint" and was starting on a second leg. Fortunately, deer skin easily.

I hung over a little fire built at each carcass, just at timber line on Red Mountain, and thawed the frozen blood from Bud's skinning knife and hatchet by thrusting them alternately into the fire as they became too thick. I also stamped my feet and from sheer misery wept icicles which dripped off the end of my nose; it seemed to make us both feel better. But we had got our meat and skins and the day was saved.

We visit the caribou cache as winter sun departs

6

At the caribou pass we had a meat cache in the rocks convenient to the house, only a half mile away. Each day revealed lines of caribou crawling on Red Mountain above, while the temperature held steadily around 40° and 50° below zero. We killed them occasionally at the cache as they filed through the pass, but from now on we expected to have life a little easier compared to those first eight hours of anxious desperate exposure, with little to do but pack meat out from the cache as we needed it. We were becoming, of necessity, experts in our techniques. Day by day one of us would go up to the cache at the pass in the rocks, kick some leg bones out of the snow for "butter" and jello, bring home a sack of hearts or livers, or, skillfully avoiding the deadly hidden toothed traps which awaited intruders there, roll a frozen shoulder of about sixty pounds in weight squeaking along the snow and onto the pack board, tie it and hoist it up, and get along home.

Bud had been running his trap line at fifty below zero along the valley four miles from the house by making sprints on skis, carrying just his .22 pistol as trap-line weapon. At fifty below the automatic pistol was useful only as a single shot. One day I heard a whistle from the river and went out of the house. The air had that heavy smoky taste which one comes to know in estimating the degree of cold. Yes, Bud had something. What was it now? He was dragging it up the river ice on a rope. Reaching our path, he slung the burden over his shoulder and climbed the hill to the house. It was a caribou calf of about ninety pounds. Bud had brought it home with him much as one might have handled a white-tailed deer of the same size under the circumstances.

"Poor little fellow," he said as he handed the lifeless form in the door to me, "he got into one of the little No. 3 traps." Bud described how his trap and toggle were missing and how he had followed the calf through the wandering tracks of other caribou to where at last the calf waited, alone and deserted, wound up in entanglements. Because its lower leg was frozen, Bud killed it with the pistol and brought it home. Now we hung it up on a beam at the foot of the bed and I spent an absorbed afternoon skinning and butchering the calf and learning the cuts of meat.

The hide of each animal we had inspected, of which this calf was an excellent example, was infested with big worms or grubs. Bud said he had seen their like on most of the beef and dairy cattle he had known; only medication helps to keep them off domestic animals.

In regard to these parasites, Sir Wilfred Grenfell's findings in Labrador will help extend the information the public should have of our own game herds in Alaska. He says:

> The incredible cruelty of some of these little-known winged contemporaries is well illustrated by the bot fly, which attacks our gentle caribou. The mother is a small fly, so rapid as to be almost invisible in flight. She hit upon the idea that the safest place for her young would be in a nursery which would not merely automatically look after its own safety but should have "brains behind" that desirable quality. She decided that the most advantageous spot would be inside the warm, moist nostril of the living deer. Her fiendish end is accomplished by two preliminary precautions. First, with maternal devotion, she became a member of the Puparidae family, which does not deposit the helpless eggs in a cold world to take their own chance. She hatches them out in tubes in her own body, somewhat like torpedoes, and provides each with a hook and spines. Taking advantage of warm lazy days, she

suddenly fires these torpedoes into the doomed target. Sheep have been so terrified of these bot flies as to huddle together and bury their noses in mud to escape them. Once in, the invaders work straight through the sinuses next the brain, where they reside for ten months. They then return to the nostril, where the miserable deer at last blows them out . . . But it only means that they in their turn will become bot flies and replenish the army of atrocious enemies. Of the many deer I have examined, every one has been affected. Nowadays, however, it is not so easy for the bot flies. The deer have become scarcer and possibly more wary, so some cousins of the bot fly have devised a much simpler method and one easier for the mother. They fasten the eggs in a soluble covering, exactly like our tabloids, on the deer's hairs, on the flank or knees, so long as they are within reach of the animal's tongue. On licking his skin, he carries the eggs to his mouth. The capsule dissolves. The larvae are swallowed or crawl through the gullet into the tissues, to the warm fat tissue under the skin.

There they grow to a large size. [The grubs.] Not till some months does one bore its way out, drop to the ground, become a chrysalis, and once more a recruit for hosts of demons. Among hundreds and hundreds of skins which I have inspected at the Hudson's Bay Company stores or the Moravians' Posts, I have not seen one skin free from the scars of these fiends; and in many skins there were so many scars that there was not a piece large enough to make a perfect pair of moccasins. What more worthy life achievement for a lover of animals could be conceived than to discover some means to drive out these devils from the earth?[3]

---

3   From *The Romance of Labrador* by Sir Wilfred Grenfell. By permission of The Macmillan Company, publishers. New York, 1934. Page 103.

We certainly think that last sentence could bear repeating, as we extend Sir Wilfred's challenge for help: here is an entirely different and modern problem allied to game management. How could it be done? There's one to ponder on.

~

IT WAS THE DAY FOLLOWING the domestic scene of caribou investigation in our house that Bud came home from his traps and mentioned in his calm way that he had frozen his left foot. At first, I didn't believe him. Then a few minutes later he said, "Well, I guess I had better take off my sock and see."

"What do you mean?" I said. "I never froze my feet. Why, how could you freeze your foot today? It's much warmer, only 38° below. You must be fooling me." How I hoped he was!

Gingerly we removed the boot by unlacing it all the way. Bud said he could feel nothing in his foot aside from a sensation that his sock was bunched together under his toes. The sock was not bunched up but was found to be frozen to the flesh in a shroud of ice. As we watched it, this ice dropped off at room temperature, and enabled us to remove the sock. All the toes of that foot were dead white and seemed as solid as rock. Bud could not wiggle his toes, nor did we try to bend them. Expectantly we waited, wondering what was going to happen next. We did not know what to do, so we did nothing.

Fortunately, we did have an idea about what not to do. Throughout all the North there is a malicious superstition which is a hangover from other days. It exists even now among some of the Eskimos near Nome and Point Hope who learned it from the whalers and other early white men of a generation ago. This is that the only way to save a frosted limb is to drag the victim into a snowdrift and rub snow on him as fast and as hard as you can. This belief is devoutly held today by the average resident of our northern states and we ourselves had vaguely accepted it as a statement of fact since childhood. I have found "rubbing with snow" to be an approved practice in a medical book issued as recently as 1925; this book of medical reference was in use on an Alaska bookshelf as "proof"! But rubbing with snow is no longer approved.

Probably no one knows by now just how the erroneous belief came to be universally accepted except that it is realized that the thawing out of frosted persons should be very slow, in order to prevent swelling of the capillaries and inflammation; this part of it is correct enough. We didn't know much about frostbite, but we had become exposed to enough modern first-aid concepts to know that the injury is classified along with burns and is treated similarly. It should not even be touched, let alone massaged, for such rubbing may bruise injured tissues beyond repair. Furthermore, rubbing snow on the place to "restore circulation," as it has been imagined to do, certainly would not make any warmer a person who was already so frozen that circulation in that part had stopped! We knew that the snow lying on the ground outside our house and all other objects outdoors at 38° below on that day retained in themselves a latent cold of exactly 38° below zero, no more, no less, and even if Bud's toes had seemingly frozen they were not that cold yet.

The principle of using snow or ice water to thaw frozen flesh might in essence be correct provided the temperature of the snow were warmer than the frozen part. But it is extremely doubtful if this is ever the case.

We allowed Bud's foot to thaw slowly on the icy floor of the house and did not touch it. After an hour he commenced to be in great pain, but I had only aspirin to give him. This pain continued for around five hours, after which he seemed to be thawed out but could not move two of his toes and had no feeling in them. We waited, tales of gangrene in our minds, wondering if the toes would turn black; they didn't. They regained normal coloration but remained lifeless.

For a couple of weeks Bud enjoyed the state of occasional invalidism. He would get bored staying at home and would go off for ten miles, although I expect he would do just the same on a wooden leg; his mileage was little indication of his real condition. Meanwhile I got some valuable experience popping the wood under the ax at the lower temperatures and sawing enough three-foot logs for the heater to withstand a siege. The end of the affair was that Bud's toes remained stiff and lifeless for several weeks, but eventually got all right again—and we ourselves, it was to be hoped, were a little wiser. Bud started at once on a plan for fur boots for us, to be made out of the caribou hides.

This is the only experience we ever had with the dangers of freezing or frostbite, which came before Christmas of our first year in the arctic.

The ordinary freezing is no more serious than this. It is really surprising how severely frozen an extremity can become and still be restored. But such incidents are extremely rare among northern residents, who in fact seldom get frostbitten. On cold days your nose often enough goes white with a sudden pain and a pop that is almost audible, or you warn your companion that his nose is frozen to the eyes when he doesn't realize it—but the remedy for this is not rubbing with snow but merely warming the nose in the hand for a moment, until it resumes normal coloration; the affliction is no worse than sunburn and is regarded as an annoyance rather than a danger. Neither has a "frosted lung" been known from breathing cold air. Children at Fairbanks play outside at 50° below.

STILL THE CARIBOU WERE PASSING. Many were so lame that they were hobbling on three legs, bobbing like rocking horses as they limped by our door. We wondered if some of them actually had broken legs from falling over some mountain cliffs. If so, it would seem merciful to shoot them. But this could be but a guess, and we presumed they were merely severely lame, a temporary phenomenon which was indicative of the kind of country over which they had come to reach us. Bud said these unfortunate deer were so emaciated as to be worthless for human food. We wished the cripples luck on their pitiful way, but there seemed little chance of survival for some of them who could barely hobble. Where were they going, and what was this terrible ancestral urge which prompted them ever on to their destiny?

We shall always remember one day about four o'clock in the afternoon when Bud stepped out of the house in the dark and sensed a vague stirring. The sound was like the rustling of wind in the trees, but there was no wind.

"Come out, Connie," Bud called in the door, "and see a caribou crusade." I was at his side at once. We could see against the white of the frozen river below us a moving mass of weary trudging caribou as they creaked along. The few hours of daylight the following noon indicated that many hundreds of caribou must have passed by our door during the hours of darkness, using the river as a highway route.

Thanksgiving and Christmas passed during the caribou migration. Those were fat and happy times for us, with many a rush for stove and cupboard. What's on the menu today? Calves' tongue, fried brains, breaded veal cutlets, creamed sweetbreads, a half cup of rice with gravy, and some sweet potato mounds made from one quarter of a can of pumpkin baked in the oven; tea, of course, and a lemon ice made out of lemon powder, sugar, and snow, for dessert.

agutuk (akotok) was our greatest discovery in the arctic. Next to sourdough, this preparation, more often known as "Eskimo ice cream," is one of the best far northern tricks we learned. We had first got acquainted with it over on the Kuskokwim River beside the Bering Sea, although we never dreamed then that a time would come when it would be a food of our own. *agutuk* can be made in a variety of ways, according to one's location and circumstances. It is made by the natives differently all over Alaska. In the interior it is often made by mixing blueberries, snow, and chopped raw frozen whitefish; berries, snow, and commercialized lard or the big buckets marked on the traders' shelves as "Edible Tallow" make another popular mixture; near the coasts the berries and snow are usually dressed with rancid seal oil.

Well, we had more grizzly bear fat now than we had flour to use with it in baking, yet we needed the fat for food and must find a way to consume it enjoyably. What better solution than to invent an agreeable *agutuk* of our own for trail rations made with the bear fat and our own cranberries?

I wasn't too surprised to find Bud engaged soon after the killing of the bear at working out different mixtures of *agutuk*s. Soon he emerged with the perfect brew for us: pure warm, rendered bear fat poured over frozen whole cranberries in a bowl, to which were added a few tablespoons of beaten cooked rice and a few tablespoons of sugar to make a five-pound brick. It was not very good warm, in the liquid form, even Bud agreed. But after this concoction was frozen outdoors for a day and turned out of the bowl on a piece of wax paper to grace the middle of our dinner table, along with grizzly bear pork chops and a biscuit or two, the transformation in its attraction was amazing. The round brick was a creamy pink, and with the whole red cranberries glistening in it looked like a mosaic. No matter how cold the temperature in which it had been kept frozen on top of the roof, it sliced much like solidified cream—and tasted like it when eaten frozen!

Bud cut some dainty thin slices. I put mine on a hot biscuit, where it began to melt, and bit in. From that moment on, I am ashamed to relate the rest of the tale because Bud said he would hate to have it known how uncontrollable his wife became in eating straight bear fat in the *agutuk* form. The truth of it was that we could neither one keep out of it. I would sneak in and devour pounds of it when Bud was out, much as in another situation I might have sneaked into a box of chocolates. The only way the bear fat was kept safe from me, in order to save a little of it for the rest of the winter, was to leave it on the carcass out at the meat rack.

THANKSGIVING DAY HAD BEEN USHERED in by a restless night of insomnia in anticipation of the special feast we had planned. For a month ahead, we had discussed what we were going to eat on this day, and amusing as it may sound, the day itself found us nervously exhausted from the terrific strain of the excitement. Bud was up all night with his bread. He put it to raise at bedtime; then he had to get up to punch down the dough and loaf it out for the second raising at 1:00 A.M. After that, he kept getting up to see how it was doing. At eight o'clock our Thanksgiving was to begin, and we planned to start eating.

By six o'clock in the morning in the dark arctic night, hours before dawn, we were laboring and cooking. By nine o'clock we were maniacs to get at our food, being accustomed to eat earlier. The table set before us held hoarded caribou tongues; the usual fifteen-pound rare roast, sliced thin; a set of fried brains each, a most coveted food here; hamburger sandwiches with mustard and real canned tomatoes—Bud ate four of these; two kinds of *agutuk*s, and a bucket of tea.

This was just the Thanksgiving breakfast on display. The main holiday noon dinner was built around our Dutch oven full of chili beans; we had no chili, but we did have half that can of tomatoes which made hamburgers for breakfast, and we did have cayenne pepper which Bud had brought into the arctic in anticipation of making his favorite type of Mexican jerky or dried meat. This, with two loaves of bread, was consumed with the usual tea, and an ice cream flavored with molasses. Mincemeat for the pie had been prepared days ahead from chopped caribou meat, suet of grizzly bear, sugar, and the last six prunes; on top of the hot mince pie was hard sauce made from sugar and marrow, whipped up and frozen. It's odd, we once tried the same thing later amid more opulent circumstance in an effort to recapture the lost joys of those delightful mince pies but were never able to do so.

Were we sick? Yes, within two hours after eating mixed civilized food intestinal cramps can be pretty well expected by the simple native who is not used it; it is too rich for the system to assimilate after the more simple meat diet. But it was all in good fun and we kept right on eating. The only thing that was irksome was that we had gone beyond the stage where our small remaining supply of civilized food, taken on state occasions only, could be of use to us anymore. We wouldn't be able to assimilate it until we had had a chance for a few days to get back into practice again gradually.

We both lay down from three until six on the afternoon of our Thanksgiving Day, arose to work skins for a while in the evening, and then went to bed quite supperless, empty and content. The party was over.

Winter sun . . . going, going. November 1944

7

Now the kerosene lantern which was our only illumination in the cabin was on all day if we remained at home, and it came as a surprise to realize that the shortest day of the year was actually upon us. Here we sat gorging on meats of all kinds and combinations, having one party after another, drinking ice water and eating snow ice creams beside our stove while perspiration poured off, eating ourselves to death! "Lean times will come again. Better eat now while you can," some inner voice kept saying. As our joking and laughter rang out upon the arctic night we would often wonder if the folks at home in the civilized world were as carefree as we. On the shortest day of the year, Bud's diary recounts:

> Today Connie and I ran our trap line together, she on skis and I on snowshoes. The day was beautiful. The sky showed clear, while some very high clouds were pink at high noon. They were all colors, like a beautiful sunrise. We left the house at 10:00 and returned at 3:00. One of the happiest days of our lives. There were fully five hours of very good light. I took some pictures that developed well. All this talk about the dreaded arctic night was concocted by men who never spent a winter north of Dawson or Nome and perpetuated by those who were never north of Seattle.

Midwinter here is about as depressing to us as it is to a New Yorker, perhaps not as much so.

The temperature on this darkest day was 4° to 9° above zero.

Of course, we had our moments of discomfort or apprehension for the future, but even these seemed to make those comforts of home which we possessed more cozy and dear. There was the December day I fell into the river at 40° below zero. We were getting water in cans. I stepped on thin ice which Bud had detoured, and it broke with me. Fortunately, the thin ice was over the shallows where riffles ran. I fell on my stomach, chin on a level with the ice, and Bud pulled me out. My water bucket was mashed beneath me, held by the hand which was under the ice, and I didn't want to let go of it or the swift current would have carried it away, our only real bucket. I ran for the house rattling like a knight in armor.

Then there was the December day of -52° when both stoves ran out of wood at once and at the same time we were faced with the necessity of letting the fire go out in the monster so that he might be emptied of ashes. I was cross with Bud for having been so improvident about the fuel situation here in the arctic, but he said he had been waiting for the weather to get warmer before he cut any more wood. Now for fuel I had to get out and trim timber while Bud felled it, by the side of brush fires built to sustain us. We worked outside three hours all together, including the dragging of the trees from the forest down to the sawhorse on the hill. This supplied enough fuel inside the house, so we wouldn't have to worry about it for another week. It is true that the experience gave us a certain confidence that no recital by anyone else could have instilled, because we knew now beyond a doubt that it is possible to cut wood even at 70° below zero if it is necessary, and that actually no temperatures staged by mere nature need alarm anyone. So long as there was fuel to get, we could get it. Only when one goes beyond the timber line does he really learn the native point of view, however. Our life was the very epitome of providence here, although we thought it marginal. We would see the time when if we had but one or two sticks ahead to burn we were lucky, and timber like this would be an unimaginable fortune.

Bud had the painful experience about this time of squeezing his thumb in the jaws of one of those fearsome big toothed traps, but by his strength he was fortunately able to untrap himself from it.

Shortly before Christmas came the heavy snows we had waited so many months for in vain. Heavy snow is not typical in the truly arctic parts of the world at all, but this snow was typical of southerly Alaska inland from the continental divide. Fluffy, pillowy snow came at last to cover our world so that we learned for a truth that those chewing on bushes at the height of a moose's shoulder were not made by moose at all but by rabbits the winter before whose world during that season had been raised up to that level.

Floundering through to the woodpile just to locate the buried sawhorse was a chore. Why, we were prisoners! We couldn't move a step! If we had to hunt for meat now, how could we get it? The snow had fallen softly into the twigs and grass stems, leaving an air space between this debris and the ground, so that when a person stepped through this—"Whoosh!" the whole thing would say, as it settled for forty feet around. Beneath this snow dome traveled the whole world of small creatures which might not be seen aboveboard the long winter through from now on—the broad-backed fat little field mice—voles—in their heavy brown parkas, the shark-faced shrews, the sneaking weasels, and the tree-communicating squirrels, living under roots. Even the ptarmigan and rabbits buried themselves in it. Many of these creatures might starve with weather reverses in the spring. Should an unseasonal thaw come (which sometimes happens even in the arctic), and be followed by a hard freeze, the little creatures would find themselves trapped beneath ironlike domes of ice, unable to get out of their beds. Such a thaw would be serious for human beings, too, for it might spoil our meat. A thaw was one thing arctic people pray won't happen in the arctic.

Coming in warmer temperatures above zero, the heavy snow caused the roof to leak. For a few days a swinging canopy above us caught water as we slept in our bed; it drained off into cans and pans with a *ping!* and a *bong!* while the mosses in the chinks came alive and festooned themselves into hanging gardens. Bud shoveled off the roof, the temperature dropped, and everything froze up tight; we were warm and dry again. A day or two of winds followed, which was perfect. They drifted the soft snow into hard ridges which enabled us to cut large square snow blocks with our long-bladed snow knife, the machete of tropic lands, for which the Eskimos have a common name in their own language as a familiar tool in northern snow masonry. With these blocks, weighing around fifty pounds each, we built outside walls for our house, which went up to the roof on the three sides of the house overlooking the hill; these walls gave a total insulation of four feet in all between us and the outside world. This cut down the fuel consumption for the remainder of the winter by at least 25 per cent.

White Christmas Eve came with a silvery moon so large and bright that it lighted the surrounding sentinel peaks for miles about in splendor. While aurora flickered faintly in streamers in the northern zenith, wood smoke from our chimney wreathed the moon, which, shining through it, cast the shadow of the smoke upon the ground as it trailed over the snow. Bud said, "Look, I'll show you. I can read a page from this book by the moonlight."

The moon in arctic regions is not acronical, as astronomers say; it does not rise at sunset or set at sunrise at the full but floats around with seemingly no relationship to anything we had formerly been accustomed to. It never set at all from three to five days at a time at its full, except to dodge briefly behind a peak and pop out again. It was the fastest-traveling moon we had ever imagined. All winter long we chased that moon, trying to get what we thought would be particularly effective colored pictures of it during the daylight hours as it rose immense and yellow, rolling along the far plateau of the thousand-foot cliffs of Pingaluk; it silhouetted that tiny forest on the cliff miles distant like some illustration of those enormous moons frequently shown in children's books of fairy tales. Or again, appearing at some unexpected vista on the trap trail, among pink clouds, the dead planet in our low temperatures seemed so close that one could almost imagine walking to it. More beautiful, we believed, than the much-praised moon of tropic regions, our swift-moving arctic moon fairly whizzed around the horizon, laying its swath across forest and mountain, speeding visibly, slipping behind a mountain cliff, and gone.

Christmas Eve we skied downhill by the side of the house beneath such a moon and cut our Christmas tree. Coming into the warm house with the little tree under an arm, we commenced our celebration. The tree soon graced our table with pieces of red string and rabbits' fur tassels; silver and red ornaments cut into stars, hearts, diamonds, and bells were made from those left-over pieces of the Standard Oil can out of which Bud had cut and formed a lamp shade for our "study" table. Bud baked for us on Christmas Eve a rare Yuletide raised sweet bread with the essence of old wine to it, or so we thought. His recipe:

To 1 pint Alaskan lowbush cranberries, add
½ pint finely chopped grizzily bear cracklings
½ cup sugar
½ teaspoon salt
½ cup melted moose shortening
Mix thoroughly.
Then add
½ gallon well-ripened sourdough
½ teaspoon soda
Mix this well until it forms a mixture that will just pour.
Let raise two hours.
Bake slowly one hour in a Yukon stove.
Serves two hungry people if they are first nearly full of the last moose meat they have.

Two presents waited on the table Christmas morning. Santa Claus had come in the night to find deserving characters even here. One gift was a caribou hide portfolio of large dimension trimmed with yellow chamois along the seams, with a zipper running three quarters of the way around it. Inside it were several compartments for maps, papers, and the diaries of travelers. What work that simple lovely article represented in the way of tanning, scraping, and sewing there is not room in this book to convey fully. The other gift was a pair of Eskimo-type skin boots, popularly called "mukluks," just my size, also made entirely of caribou. This first experimental pair of boots was perfect. Bud thereafter made himself a similar pair in half the time. Quite a trick to master, he had "invented" out of our dire necessity a seam which he believed was waterproof after some Eskimo work he had observed casually before, and he had been able to tan the tough old bull hides soft enough so that the boots could be turned inside out at any time. These boots were knee length, were to be worn fur in, and had a handsome gray ruff of hair turned over the tops for trim. It had been necessary to shear the hairs of the caribou to a shorter length with scissors. Such complicated garments as parkas and fur pants we did not try to make, for we had come to realize that if we did so we would do nothing else all winter. The hides of winter-killed caribou are not regarded as suitable for anything but bedding, we later learned of Eskimo life, because the hair during the winter season is of the wrong length. All Eskimo-made clothing comes from summer-killed caribou, except footwear, for which old bulls are excellent, except that the boots are made entirely of the legs, one pair of boots from two animals, and thinking we could not use the legs of the hides, and not imagining their value, this year we threw all our legs away!

One very valuable object which materialized from the skins for ourselves was a large bed robe from which we were never thereafter separated. After you leave the spruce belt and can no longer cut spruce boughs for your bed in summer camping, it becomes imperative to have the robes of animals in your camp to live in comfort. The luxurious fur robe as an addition to camp life even here brought much comfort. It shed hairs all over everything—we had hairs in our hair when we slept and hairs in the soup—but that goes with living with caribou. It would have taken no detective to have found evidence of caribou with us wherever we went thereafter in the North, as we were never separated from our bed robe.

By Christmas our wonderful long marmot-hide mittens were completed at last, trimmed on the cuffs with ermine. All of this gave us a new outlook altogether on the North and northern ways; never more would cold hands or cold feet be a menace.

But something had happened to our sense of taste between Thanksgiving and Christmas. The Christmas party was to start with a light breakfast of baked pumpkin pudding and milk only. I passed Bud the powdered-milk solution which had haunted our dreams, being our favorite of all imported arctic foods, next to sugar and flour, and he tasted it with a mere, "Humph!"

"What are we drinking, anyway?" he queried. "So, you thought you'd fool me by mixing up flour and water?"

"Huh?" I ejaculated in surprise. I had a hard time reassuring Bud that it was real milk and that nothing whatever was the matter with it. We looked at each other as we tasted the pumpkin pudding. A dawning horror of disappointment must have shown on both our faces.

It didn't taste like real food somehow—this soft stuff! And sugar—

sugar had an underlying taste of bitterness on the tongue that we had never noticed before. It must have tasted to us somewhat as it did to the first Eskimos, who used to plunder abandoned arctic vessels for the wood and the iron, and who, not recognizing sugar and flour—such queer powdered stuff—to be edible food, threw all of it into the sea. There must be an actual change in the taste buds of anyone habituated to a certain diet, so that the sense of taste is affronted by unfamiliar flavors and cannot at once adjust to them.

"I wonder," said Bud sneakingly. "You didn't happen to have any left-over cold meat around here to sort of go with it, did you?"

"Why, we said we wouldn't have to eat any meat on Christmas morning. Maybe I can find something." I resurrected some rare roast beef about three days old from a corner, Bud sliced it into thin slices, and we ate that for our Christmas breakfast, leaving the civilized food untouched.

We weren't going to do any "work" on Christmas, but oh! the fluffy snow outside the window looked inviting, and what would we do with ourselves indoors if we just waited for dinner? After a pistol match driving nails inside the house (a shell case falling into the cooking mincemeat when we were firing over the stove), we felt restless for something to do. I wanted to try out my new Eskimo boots on my snowshoes. We had been unable to use snowshoes before together because we had only one extra pair of very cheap store moccasins between us; snowshoes require a soft boot of the moccasin type so that the strings of the racket will not be abused. Besides, there had not been enough snow for snowshoes until practically this very day. Bud had been doing his first practicing on snowshoes recently; I had never been on them before in my life. Christmas morning was the perfect time to start.

Putting the roast into the oven and banking the stoves, we lugged our new Eskimo-made snowshoes out of the door and gazed upon a glistening fairyland. The snow had leveled the country off; gone were the sharp snags, the tussocks, the ups and downs. A call resounded from the forested ridge—probably an owl, and who can find an owl? But we could try. We went chasing owls.

"Might as well take the pack along since we're going up that way," said Bud. "I ought to have the hatchet and dig out some of the traps, and I guess we might as well bring home a load of meat on the way while we're there. I've been wanting to get the head of your biggest bull caribou for some head meat, and I've an idea I might chop out a spruce frame for a sled and it might be handy to use your bull horns for turned-up runners in front."

When we got home the roast was done to a turn. Today's menu was to approximate the conventional Christmas dinner: old-fashioned chicken with hot biscuits and cream gravy, followed by ice cream and cakes, and nuts saved from cracked prune pits—just a taste. The "chicken" was the hind leg of a big lynx cat. It had fallen into the traps and we had saved it for this day, for as white meat it could not have been told from a genuine chicken dinner aside from differences in construction, we both said. All cats are white meat. The lynx and the great arctic owl are the chicken dinner of the North, and when fat they are excellent eating for human beings.

As the Yuletide passed into the New Year a new star appeared on our horizon, burning brightly in the sky. When a star is seen through a ground temperature of 50° below zero, and when a human being is furthermore assisted by binoculars, it looks like a sun. In the future it is possible much astronomical observation may take place in the arctic regions.

We thought of the star as a portent of the future. At this moment, while the New Year noisily broke in one great city of the world after another, we two were quiet, thinking of the brightness to the world we hoped the New Year would give.

PART SIX

Spring Hunting

Connie sets a trap

1

It is hard to set a day definitely as to when we ran out of all civilized food. It was so gradual all the way along. Our nibbles of civilized food became more and more scanty until finally, sometime in January, the last handful of cranberries was boiled up with the last handful of sugar, and the last thin sourdough pancakes were fried in the skillet, which was greased with a wax candle because we were out of fat. I offered to donate my cold cream for shortening and for frying grease, but we were skeptical about the preservatives in it and afraid they would kill us. For several months a handful of beans was kept. We had hoped to sprout them in a jar of water by the side of the windowpane for greens after the sun came back. They wouldn't sprout, possibly because they had been killed by freezing and age. We knew the beans didn't possess many life-giving properties and hardly considered them as food, but we could always go to the cupboard and run our fingers through them and know they were there. Their chief value was therefore probably a kind of moral support. They were eaten around the last of February, I think.

Our real support of course lay in our sacks of accumulating dried meat, called "jerky," and in our ever-present stock of traps and ammunition. We had always some last resource even after the other last resources had been spent—well, rabbits, if it came to that again. But boiled rabbits without grease to fry them in—ug!

THE WINTER WEEKS FOLLOWING CHRISTMAS went in packing our meat from the caribou cache and cutting much of it up into small strips for the drying racks. Not having dogs or dog sled of course we had to haul every ounce that we ate over that rough country on our backs, which runs into work, but had we possessed dogs we would have been hard put to feed them. Primitive man with his dogs runs an indescribably vicious cycle.

In back-packing meat, on the other hand, the more you carry home the greater your appetite to consume it speedily because it takes strength to support such loads.

Breaking trail through soft snow on snowshoes is like walking uphill steadily all day. Once a good trail is beaten, snowshoe travel along the timbered ridges and across valleys and even up over steep mountain peaks becomes amazingly rapid; you can rough-lock your snowshoes with rope to keep them from slipping on the precipitous inclines. No happier hours have I ever spent than those on my swift little running snowshoes, clinging like a squirrel to the mountainsides in the Brooks Range, coming home creaking along our trail under a big load from the meat cache. It's quite a trick to get a pack of meat up on your back when you have on snowshoes, to shoot snarling wolverines and not fall over your feet at the wrong moment, to handle a rifle, reset traps, chop out traps from flooded-over river ice. For six months we were never off snowshoes when out-of-doors and did practically everything but sleep in them.

People have since asked how one can live day by day in moccasins or Eskimo skin mukluks which give no arch support to the feet. Do not the feet get very tired? No, for you see everything in nature is on springs! By summer this springiness comes to the arches of your feet and hence to your body from the moss and the pliant earth which your toes grip through moccasins to keep your balance over uneven surfaces; this is why Indians in moccasins in our stories have always walked on the ball of the foot naturally rather than on the heel or coming down hard on an unresisting surface as city-bred folk in stiff shoes do. A person who hasn't lived in moccasins hasn't really known the North! In shoes the feet are confined and encased so that the average walker has no more feel of the live earth beneath him than if his feet were unconscious wooden clogs not a part of him at all. A good farmer will not even stand his cows or his chickens on cement. On the hard level floors of our houses and on the cement sidewalks of our cities we live our lives with crippled feet and a heavy tread. No wonder we need arch supporters! But in northern wilderness, or in any life close to nature, the senses in the feet become as sharp as a cat's. In summer you go bouncing over yellow-white reindeer moss or stepping into a canoe that is like a part of one's body and fragile as an eggshell; in winter you go striding over a five-foot layer of snow on springy snowshoe rackets for half a year.

Our snowshoes were made by Peter, a Kobuk Eskimo of the Alatna village down on the Koyukuk. The frames were of light birch, stained with a brew of alder bark, and the webs were of caribou hide. This type of snowshoe has been used for countless thousands of years, yet it is more than twice as light in weight as the best factory-made snowshoes we have yet seen, so when used along with the Eskimo skin boots, the joy of it is that one can travel on this gear feeling almost as light as though he were barefooted. The "native hitch" for binding the snowshoe to the foot is operated by merely stepping onto the snowshoe and twisting one's foot in a certain way. There are no straps or buckles with which icy fingers need fumble, only a moosehide thong hanging loose, just so. The tricky apparatus took me months to master, during which I stepped right out of my snowshoes on many a trail to plunge into many a snowbank. But the native hitch is a contrivance which might save your life sometime. If you should ever fall down in a deep snow tangled up in a willow thicket or around the base of a tree where the snow first gets soft in spring, you could lie there helpless and not able to get up again, quite like a turtle on its back, if you could not kick out of your snowshoes. The native hitch provides for just this emergency for those who travel much alone. Again, if you fell through ice with the white man's heavy snowshoes on you would drown or freeze in all likelihood because you could not get your snowshoes off to extricate yourself.

Bud had constructed a sled to help out on the meat transportation, according to his diary:

> Temp. -24°. Clear. I made a final trip to the meat cache today and returned with six quarters

of caribou, four traps, a tent, one ptarmigan, and a set of antlers on the sled, some 300 pounds or more in all. My nose was darned near on the snow, as pulling a sled so heavily loaded while you are on snowshoes is a job. Coming downhill toward home the sled ran up on my snowshoes and together we plowed up the snow . . . Tried ice fishing, but I was the only fish, a sucker.

In February we took a trip to get beavers, which were legal furs but whose great attraction now to us was the fact that they might be fat meat to eat:

> By daylight the sled was loaded—stove, tent, traps, bedding, some meat, rifles, ax, saw, the ice chisel, shovel, spare clothing. To say loaded is misleading. It was overloaded. On snowshoes we started, Connie breaking trail and I pulling the sled. Pulling is also misleading. Dragging is much better. The runners (narrow steel shoeing burned out of old trash found at the Kutuk Cabin) broke through, while the bottom of the sled dragged, acting like a brake. First one runner would break through while the other held up, thus upsetting the sled on its side. Then the other would break through and upset the sled the other way. Righting the sled again when you have on snowshoes is a real chore because it is hard to walk up close to it. Soon the load became loose and I had to repack. After some six miles of this the snow grew so soft that we were forced to trample it down several times. We repeated this twice, then tried to drag the sled over. In this manner we had to cover the same ground five times. After another two miles of this we decided to double-trip our things. Therefore, we unloaded the traps, the meat, and the sleeping bag, and left them in the middle of the river bed, intending to go back and get them on the next trip. Now the sled rode on top of our snowshoe trail and only upset every

hundred yards instead of every twenty. We made fair speed for perhaps four more miles when, upon nearing a spruce-covered bend in the river, Connie broke through the snow into two inches of overflow water running underneath the snow on top of the river ice. The sled, following right behind her, also broke through, getting big gobs of snow frozen to its steel shoeing. Connie's snowshoes were two masses of slush ice which quickly froze solid. It was all I could do to get the sled up on the shore while Connie was almost helpless to lift her heavy feet. As the snow was about five feet deep, progress without snowshoes was unthinkable. We had to make camp here, to thaw the ice off the snowshoes in the tent.

Making camp in the snow was a new experience to both of us. I cut six poles and made two tripods consisting of three poles each to support the ridgepole of the tent while Connie got off her useless snowshoes and started digging with our shovel to clear a place.

Connie dug and dug, while I cut all the poles. She dug a trench down to the ground five feet wide and fifteen feet long for our 8' x 10' tent. When I finally got the tent pitched over her snow crater I had to fill it in again. I banked snow against the tent and cut two big logs 8" x 2' to set the camp stove up on so that it would not melt into the snow. We carried in our belongings and started the fire. Soon it was warm and snug inside. I cut what I thought was enough firewood for the night and we decided to get the rest of the load we had cached in the morning. Here we had only our caribou blanket and one loose skin for bedding. Now the wind moaned among the trees, while snow flew in blinding clouds. Nothing to eat, and so to bed. The blankets proved a little inadequate because they were so lightweight that they kept slipping off with nothing to hold them down, while we were cramped for space. I slept fitfully while Connie sat up and fed the fire. The temperature on the surface of the snow inside the tent stayed at sixty degrees, warm enough if we had just had our good old sleeping bag!

My day began by crawling out into the wind at 4:00 o'clock in the morning to cut wood when our fuel gave out. I had to cut down a tree first and then trim it. Then carry it to camp and saw and split it. All work had to be done in the dark on snowshoes in the deep snow. I didn't mind, however, only wished we had some breakfast. Connie had had enough snow camping and wanted to return home. I had grown tired of being a sled dog, so for home we started. After a score of upsets, we arrived at the cabin tired, happy, and thankful—wiser in snow camping, though.

Yes, in February we made the above attempt to make a fifty- or sixty-mile trek to those beaver ponds discovered the previous summer, since we needed our beavers badly in every way. Other trappers got their beavers in February. But we did not.

The beaver season had rather recently been set in February, and that was a hardship. Usually a trapper must put up a cabin the previous summer, right at the pond he hopes to trap, in order that he may have shelter there; he must also have located his beavers during the summer season because it is hard even to find the same pond by winter sometimes, let alone recognize that beavers might live there. Beaver trapping, the backbone of the trapper's yearly income, is the main reason for retaining the dog teams—those chained dogs of summertime we saw along the timbered rivers of the interior—for then the dog teams may partially pay for their rations the rest of the year. Trappers not having a dog team are greatly restricted in their trapping range, as were we, who could trap only those animals right near home.

Trapping beavers under ice in February is one of the most disagreeable jobs in all the far North. Many feet of snow must be shoveled off the surface once you have arrived at your beaver pond, before you can even get at the ice. You take off your snowshoes then and stand them on end in the snow. Now you are down in a pit, looking up, as you begin to chip ice. You have lashed an ice chisel to the end of a long pole and there are three, four, or five feet of solid ice to go through before you can expect to strike water where the beavers are living underneath. It is more like mining or excavation than trapping. The pressure of the water held under the ice of arctic ponds often causes it to spout like a geyser when water is struck. Your hole in the ice turns into a veritable watermain; it floods the surface of the entire pond now underneath the snow.

You stand on your snowshoes far above on the snow and try to set your trap. You have tied it to a long pole which you have packed on snowshoes from the sidehill; you push the pole under the ice. Much of this work must be done barehanded. Birch or cottonwood shoots are tied in a bouquet beside the trap for bait. The unsuspicious beavers swimming along underneath the ice nibble the shoots and in this way reputedly are easily trapped and drowned. The hole in the ice which the trapper has chopped is frozen over almost during the time taken to write these lines, and another excavation must be made to get the trapped beaver out or to inspect the trap upon your next visit.

Some people must have success, considering the numbers of beaver skins tagged by the traders in Alaska at the close of each February. But to get the twenty beavers the two of us were allowed as our limit, think of cutting twenty or more such holes in the ice, and twenty poles equipped with traps and bouquets of bait hauled on snowshoes! After Bud had geysers of water shoot over him a few times experimenting with those supposed beaver ponds adjacent to home, and several times had hacked through the ice only to strike earth below and find he was on land rather than on sea, he said he thought that if he had to make a living on beavers, it would be better to farm them back in Illinois and feed them like hogs on corn and carrots than to excavate these arctic ponds in the ancient way of the trapper.

In this fast-changing world it will possibly come as a surprise to many people to learn that these primitive methods of trapping wild fur animals are still the life occupation of a considerable number of human beings in America. But for all practical purposes, so far as the great bulk of furs received on the market is concerned, trapping is on the way out. All future trends are pointing towards fur farming as fur bearers of the wild grow scarce and the wilderness shrinks. Although not all wild fur bearers can be domesticated enough to be farmed, and while some few types may possibly always have to be trapped to be obtained at all, experiments with many desirable standard furs have already shown during the last few years that man can raise more fur in these types than wild nature can supply, and, what is more, can control its very ingredients and makeup just as he can grow and control his breeds of dogs and horses and his garden vegetables.

One of the most thrilling prospects of future development in Alaska seems to us to be the fur industry. If people want more furs, and want them cheaply, there seems to be no reason why practically every woman in America living in the northern states could not have a mink or a sheared beaver coat or a silver, blue, or red fox neck piece, and so on. There are problems to be solved in fur production—how to produce and market it more cheaply—but with lower prices in living as Alaska becomes more settled and more accessible, these problems can certainly be solved, as they have been solved in other businesses elsewhere. Fur ranching to date has been the most risky of enterprises which no one should embark upon unless he has plenty of money to sink into it with his eyes open. Fur ranchers are brave individuals who have thus far played a hazardous game. This has been particularly true of the fox ranchers, not because they can't raise foxes, but because when they do raise a great many foxes at great expense nobody may buy them.

It is expensive and particularly hazardous to the individual rancher to experiment with raising any unfamiliar and not already proved fur bearer for the market because of the uncertainties of fashion and public taste.

We do not pretend to predict the future of the fur market for the North, but it would seem that the North has at least the right climate for it, which would seem to point to fur raising as one of its rightful, natural industries.

Take beavers, for instance. The limitations on the increase of beavers in their natural state along this particular arctic river were stringent. They had no good food supply. Only a certain number of birches grew, and these very slowly. For this reason, only a limited number of beavers could ever be supported here, yet there is reason to believe that beavers, otter, mink, muskrat, and probably all other northern fur bearers could go north indefinitely in their range were it not for food limitation. All of these do, in fact, range far north of timber line in some isolated instances, their tracks being found by Eskimos in unexpected places.

On the other hand, man could raise as many beavers as exist on the whole Alatna River on a small acreage of land, safe from their enemies, perhaps without even a pond, provided he supplied them with food artificially. The beaver meat could be marketed at pelting time, if you really wanted to get scientific about it, and the musk glands of beavers are of value in perfumery. We do not know of a beaver ranch yet established in Alaska, but beavers might be one of the most placid and easily ranched animals of all the fur bearers. To answer any query put to us about development of any industry in Alaska—the reply is the same one: "It's not so much a matter of conquering physical obstacles as it is a matter of economics."

The fact that all these animals could live as far north as we found them here was the wonder to us. The swimming fur bearers do not experience the cold of the outside world above the ice in most cases all winter long. Where they live enclosed it is never below the freezing point. The very ice, against which the beavers and muskrats have to store their food for a hibernation period of eight or nine months out of the year, is their protector against intense arctic cold. How their fur protects them against the wetness of the icy water in which they live was to us the greatest miracle of all, for the fur of *dead* trapped water animals is found to be wet. Only the magic property of life enables the animal to so control his fur that water does not get in to the skin.

We were convinced, in short, that none of our arctic animal friends know what cold is. The birds we saw had a higher bodily temperature all the time than that of the human being, in order to exist. Bird lice on the ptarmigan and arctic spruce chickens must keep continually thermos-heated upon the warm skin of the bird beneath the feathers, for they will die almost instantly if exposed to the chilling air. Ptarmigan, the grouse that flies high, seem to love nothing better than the coldest possible temperatures and the strongest winds. On such days ptarmigan are sheer clouds of joy. Walking along the flats before our house on their feathered snowshoe feet, they would dig with their long sharp toenails down to the most nearly exposed gravel bar, and there, what a wallowing! What raucous gaiety in the midst of the arctic night! They had hoarse but hauntingly lovable voices, those ever-loud, rusty-hinged, white leghorn chickens of the North.

Birds sit facing the wind. This is not only to make the approved aeronautical take-offs and landings, but because their feathers all grow downward so that no wind can penetrate to the body when the bird flies. Birds and animals control their bodily ventilation by molting and shedding for the hot season, but also by remarkable contractions of the muscles lying underneath the skin which enable feathers and hairs to puff out or lie flat on different days and according to how they feel. They raise and lower their coats to admit as much ventilation as they want, just as we may unbutton our overcoats, only more effectively.

In the wintertime, after the rutting of the herbivores, comes what civilized man has long believed to be the season of great arctic rigors, as the cold intensifies. But the caribou and the moose, after rutting season, now begin to fatten up. They are enjoying it and prospering! By midwinter, say late January, they will be in good shape again, both males and females. Why do animals in a northern climate put on thick layers of fat? Is it to keep warm when the weather is bitter cold? Many people have thought so, but what about fat tapirs in the tropics? Is this nature's way of providing against starvation in lean seasons? No, these are merely arctic animals; cold days do not mean lean days to the animal which is adapted to arctic life, and aside from the rutting cycle, there are usually no lean seasons here at all. Contrary to the notions of the romantic novelist who writes of the dreaded arctic winter as portending starvation, full winter is usually a fat time for both herbivores and their human hunters. In early winter the fluffy great snowy owl wrapped in his parka may be so fat that if you shoot him in the air he will sometimes burst open when he hits the ground.

The sun fairly vaulted into the sky as it commenced to return to us early in February. I remember we ran up a hill to stand in its orange glow; then the very next day it touched our house and peeked into the window. It was fortunate that we had not gone sixty miles from home on that wild beaver jaunt. A few days after our return we had the coldest temperature of the entire winter, coming not in the "darkness" but with the return of the sun. This was 62° below zero, not quite as cold as that registered down below on the Koyukuk at Allakaket, where it usually gets around 68° below once each winter and which found this winter to be no exception to the rule.

When the temperature gets down into the sixties you can run out of your hot house bare to the waist, like Bud, who was scraping hides again on the table, and be in perfect comfort for a moment, if you like, but the cold dishwater you fling rattles when it hits the ground, and your trailing breath freezes instantly with the rustle of silk as it is exhaled upon the air. Everything is perfectly still during the low temperatures. Storms with these conditions are mostly mythical, another of our superstitions. It is nearly unheard-of for there to be any wind when the temperature begins to drop below -40° because of the fact that as long as the air is in motion the friction warms it, so that the temperature doesn't drop lower. Many old-timers of Alaska agree that past 50° below zero it is a good idea to stick around close to home, for they argue that an inconsequential accident then could spell disaster. It must be remembered that such extremely low temperatures are rare in almost any part of the world and cannot last for long; ours broke in two days. But if we had been forty miles or so from home by now trying to pull our sleds or to pitch our little thin tent, it might have broken us, I thought. Bud didn't think so.

As a matter of fact, the dread of low temperatures, provided one is properly equipped with Eskimo clothing, may be just legend among us whites. No temperature is too low to prevent Eskimos from starting on a journey with all their children, including babes at the breast, simply because they don't have a weather thermometer and have little conception of what low temperatures are.

The chickadee on the feed tray outside the window, dining on the fatty tissue of hide scrapings, his little face covered with hoarfrost near the nostrils from the exhalations of his tiny breath, burst into his spring song on our coldest day of 62° below zero! We had never heard this song before and received it in startled wonder. February is the month when the camp robbers in the arctic nest and lay their eggs, high up in the dense spruce trees!

It seemed probable to us that the migration of the majority of our birds southward in the fall depends not on cold or a failing of the sun, as some have tried to demonstrate, but entirely on feed conditions, and that feed again calls them north in the spring. If you have ever been in the North in spring to see the birds come, you would understand this, for the very day of their arrival coincides exactly with the first crop of spring flies; such exact timing has never before been seen! Naturally the insect feeders have nothing to eat when winter comes, and they must go elsewhere, the water feeders likewise. The old birds teach the youngsters where to go for food, and if there are no old ones to teach a young bird, he will very likely become lost; some years thousands perish, according to Eskimos, who find the bird bodies lost in the far North for one reason or another.

We Live in the Arctic

BIRDS OBSERVED, ALATNA RIVER, BROOKS RANGE

January

1. Hairy Woodpecker
2. Willow Ptarmigan
3. Gyrfalcon
4. Peregrine Falcon
5. Northern Raven
6. Canada Jay (Camp Robber)
7. Siberian or Alaskan Chickadee
8. Redpoll
9. Spruce Chicken (a small northern grouse)
10. White-winged Crossbill
11. Hawk Owl
12. Rock Ptarmigan
13. Snowy Owl

April

14. Golden Eagle
15. Snow Bunting (?)
16. Horned Owl

May

17. Downy Woodpecker
18. Gambel's Whitecapped Sparrow
19. Western Robin
20. Yellow-shafted (?) Flicker
21. Bank Swallow
22. Tipup Snipe
23. Junco
24. Myrtle Warbler
25. Wilson's Snipe
26. Mallard Duck
27. Pintail Duck
28. Greater Scaup
29. Rusty Blackbird
30. Lesser Yellowlegs
31. Phalarope
32. Yellow-billed Loon
33. American Merganser
34. Common Tern
35. Belted Kingfisher
36. Hooded Merganser
37. Old Squaw Duck
38. Black-headed Gull
39. Small Yellow Warbler (?)
40. Varied Thrush
41. Wren (?)
42. Nelson's Gull (?)
43. Harlequin Duck
44. Canada Goose

On the Alatna River twelve different kinds of birds that we were able to identify stayed with us over the winter around our cabin this particular year. A sea gull was seen floating on open water here on a day of—40° in December, so that, returning in May by the first open water, the gulls were gone altogether for only four months, as were the eagles. The falcons and their food birds, the native ptarmigan and spruce chickens, remained the year around, as did a goodly percentage of the ravens and some kinds of woodpeckers and owls. At least half the ptarmigan of the world remain permanently north of the Arctic Circle. Some of these birds go to the most northerly islands known, their range depending upon the kind of food they eat and whether it is available.

The crossbills, flipping open spruce cones with their peculiar crossed bills, showered about us along the twilight trails of winter, making merry the grayest day. The ptarmigan walked on feathered feet in flocks of three hundred spread out before our house, or hopped onto bushes to peck at buds, loading the willows with their weight. One might defy anyone to estimate their numbers. Altogether they exist in unknown millions, feeding throughout the arctic wherever the willows go, with their raucous voices, or flying up all at once in swift alarm like whistling torpedoes as an arctic owl appears in his white sheets, or a falcon dives among them. Blood in the snow and a small pile of feathers tell the end of that story, the fate of the willow ptarmigan, one of the sportiest birds in America as well as one of the best eating. At present it is enjoyed almost exclusively by the foxes, lynx cats, ermines, and uncounted thousands of birds of prey which exist upon it in this part of the world.

None of these arctic friends are cold.

Connie catches a red fox

A gyrfalcon was caught in one of our traps

2

Perhaps it was the chickadee's spring song that made us restless to go someplace, but as soon as the sun came back in February we got spring fever. Our audacity in actually laying plans to leave our cabin for several weeks, with the thermometer plunging to 60° below zero, seems unfathomable until the small events which precipitated this departure are pointed out.

In February Bud built a muskrat canoe in the cabin. We did not know whether many muskrats inhabited this mountainous section, but the preceding summer Bud had observed a few marks on the bottoms of little puddles and ditches where a muskrat had dragged his tail.

Alaska muskrat furs were only worth $1.75 each, but we needed the $1.75 and wanted fresh meat in any form. Muskrats are a lucrative source of profit to the trapper where they are abundant enough. This widely distributed and common little rodent is as well known in Florida as in Canada's Mackenzie River delta. Some Indian villages in the vicinity of known muskrat lakes make their living largely from them; the meat of the muskrat, known as "marsh rabbit" on some hotel menus in the United States, is of course fine eating, too, or good dog food at least. To get fifteen hundred "rats" during the early spring season is not impossible for an Indian family in a good locality.

Rats in Alaska are not trapped for the most part but are almost all shot in the head with the .22 rifle, so that "ratting" is a sporting vocation, even though unknown to sportsmen. Formerly, a trapper's beavers were also taken in this way, while ratting in the spring. The hunter glides out upon the endless strings of ponds in a frail, one-man kayak, the muskrat or Indian canoe, with merely his .22 rifle laid across his knees and a toylike paddle, often double-bladed, which he whirls with his wrists. The smaller and lighter the person, the better for him; this is really a game for young children. Silence is imperative. You canoe and watch for swimming rats by night, and sleep in your tent by day, while the ice pans may still be floating in the lakes and the ground is still partially covered with snow. The sun has risen high in the sky and there is now no real night. From out of the great thawing swamps in that world of water which is breakup in the North comes the scent of flowers, but earlier than the flowers come. It is the courting perfume of the muskrats.

"A canoe is the only way to get around for a while after the breakup," argued Bud, in February. "We must make a little muskrat canoe to see us through that period. Our other one is too heavy. What we'll want to do is to leave the cabin about three weeks before we think the breakup will come. We'll put the little muskrat canoe on your skis and you can pull it along like a basket sled, filled with our stuff, and I'll pull the other sled. I think I'll take the steel shoeing off that and put it on the other pair of skis. Then we'll go and camp beside the muskrat lakes down below and wait there for the breakup, to get muskrats and maybe fresh fish to eat before the river itself breaks. Now, let me see, we'll need to take with us . . ."

The canoe was a perfect and complete little toy within a week. Bud sawed the pieces for the frame out of an actual plank with good grain that the old Kutuk Cabin again yielded up. He bent these pieces by steam heat, and lashed them together with twisted wet rawhide, made from moose, just as he had made the sled. The rawhide for both articles was an ideal material, as it allowed a certain "give" which is necessary for things intended to bear the strains of locomotion; nails would have been impossible even had we possessed many of them. Our old tarpaulin, used to cover the frame of the toy canoe, was made tight and waterproof by some linseed oil we had on hand. The canoe was nine feet long, twenty-four inches amidships, and nine inches deep.

"If we leave about the last of March or the first of April that ought to be about right," I readily agreed. "It's hard even waiting that long to get some new meat. We've eaten all our best, and I guess if we can stick it out here until then we'll be safe in leaving for a spring hunt. It shouldn't get very cold after April first."

"The muskrats ought to be fatter than what we're eating anyway. And you know, by that time the meat we have on hand, if we have any left, is going to be six months old."

We had long recognized that spring in the arctic was going to impose special problems as to food. It was unfortunate that Bud and I had missed a trick, too, when it came to keeping the caribou meat. We had done well to preserve it for half a year, but as the months ticked away, and we continued eating our meat pile, each piece gradually became more dried out and leathery than the last. The color of our meat, once a fine red, was now almost black. It did not occur to us how to prevent this aging, but we know now that some of it could have been prevented by painting each piece of meat with two or three coats of water on a cold day, which would seal it from the air by forming a protective casement of ice. We would certainly do this if there were ever a next time of this sort.

Therefore, after Christmas we prepared for drying all our remaining meat that would not be eaten by late March; we would be gone from home several weeks and could not return to the cabin until after the thaws set in, which would spoil any frozen meat that remained. Moreover, in anticipation of the lean weeks of spring to come, it seemed extremely desirable to have much dried meat in the meat sacks for early travel, in case mobility was necessary. Our real object was food; it would be necessary to do some spring hunting for fresh meat.

We ate the bony parts of the caribou and all along had been drying much of the meat itself for the spring, as it was too lean to get down. We had saved all the caribou heads in the cache by the pass, and before February head meat had become one of our hoarded luxuries. To prepare the head of an animal for civilized consumption we chop off the lower jaw with the teeth while it is frozen; then we thaw the remainder a day indoors, skin it, and clean out the nasal and ear passages as best we can; they are often filled with intestinal stuff which has been coughed up by a paunch-shot animal. Although Eskimos we have known do not mind this, we liked our head meat reasonably clean. It is difficult to clean a head properly, but it is well worth it, for there is a good deal of fatty meat to be dug from head bones, delicious to one with an arctic appetite. Before now we had eaten brains and tongue from the heads; the Eskimos value the eyes highly, but we did not try them this year. The head of any animal, no matter how lean, will contain some fat when it is boiled. The heads, therefore, along with the leg bones containing marrow, were our greatest treasure. Wild predators such as the fox or the mink will often eat only the head of an animal or fish or will eat the head first; I had observed this in my nature ramblings before now and had pondered the reasons. Now I knew. The craving for fat leads all animals and primitive hunters to prize head meat. This craving may also be behind the wolfs "love of killing" when he kills more animals than he needs and usually eats only the preferred part of each. We had plenty of meat, but most of it was so lean that it was not at once edible, unless preserved for the future, and therefore we must soon find something else.

By March 16, Bud, who was keeping our mutual diary, began to show a discontent not apparent before as a severe lack of fats began to be experienced along the last lap of the winter road. We watched the weather avidly, as each day dragged:

> March 16. Temp. -11° to 2° above. Clear, calm.
>
> The sun is extremely brilliant upon this world of white. The windows in the cabin fairly blaze. Sun glasses are a necessity if you travel far. I made knife sheaths for both our knives. We broke over today and dug up the last caribou leg bones and head and had a delicious meal.
>
> March1 17. Temp. -21° to -11°. Clear, calm.
>
> Yesterday I scraped off some fat from the bear leg and together with our lean meat we had a fairly good diet. We are really hard-pressed for meat. Our caribou that is left is so poor that a big pot of it boiled shows not a single globule or speck of fat. This is unfortunate as caribou is all we have left. The first bear of spring will look mighty good to us. However, we are quite happy, if sailing close to the wind. There is at least no danger of getting fat. Sunrise now 7:30

A.M. and sunset at 5:20, twilight until 9:00 at night. Soon it will be light all the time.

March 18. Temp. -28° to -3°. Clear, calm.

A beautiful day. Not one single cloud in the sky. In the shelter of the cabin and on dark objects snow melted while the temperature never rose above zero in the shade. Our meat supply is now nearly gone, and of course the food we brought with us has been gone for several months. The diet of lean meat has us on the verge of starvation. I have not hunted moose for fear they would be extremely poor, but we must have fat and food, or we may find ourselves in a serious plight. I am starting a hunt for moose tomorrow.

On this day a note says, "Bud ate half a caribou." This means he ate the bony parts boiled, but even the marrow in the bones of a very lean animal is only blood, so that Bud apparently derived little nourishment from half a caribou, according to his complaints.

March 19. Temp. -36° to -2°. Clear, calm.

Little sleep last night. Although we were stuffed with lean meat we felt hungry. Dysentery for two days now, due (we believe) to no fat in our diet. We have hopes of finding a moose. I hate to kill a moose now, but bears cannot be counted upon for food until May 1 while other small game is too poor and too small to count. My sides are gaunt and lean again. Later: Trailed a moose all day. Snowshoes make so much noise now upon the crusted snow that a moose can easily hear you 500 yards away. In the heavy spruce timber, it is hard to see 100 yards, and a moose has no trouble keeping hidden. Will try later . . . I am too tired to drag about, and so to bed.

March 22. -30° to -10° Clear, calm.

The diet of absolutely lean meat is beginning to tell on us. Although we eat all we can hold we are always hungry. I have given up moose hunting, and we are hurrying up our work in preparation for a forty-mile walk down to Takahula Lake to hunt for muskrats. We hate to kill a spring moose. Perhaps we won't have to if we can get there and can live on fat muskrats, but if one has to be killed we may as well do it where we intend to do our spring hunting. Then there is always hope we may be able to kill an early bear if we get out of the cabin. This would suit us much better.

March 25. Temp. -10° to 21° above. Overcast, calm.

Spring seemed close today as our warmest day in a long time broke. We talked of farming, gardens, and growing things, and of our more immediate next summer's explorations . . . We need fat badly but otherwise are fine. The cabin is warm and snug, and we sewed with the door wide open. We ate much dried meat today and a lot of old rabbit meat . . .

March 24. Temp. 10° to 15 above. Overcast. Windy.

With each passing day our hunger for fat increases while our sides shrink. Today the end of our woodpile also came. We have reached the end of our toy mukluks. They used over 60 squirrels and 21 ermine, to say nothing of some 600 old little tassels of snowshoe rabbit fur, so tedious to make. But we enjoyed fur work this year and kept busy without any trouble. Tonight, we arrived at an important decision to move into spring hunting. No use staying here growing weaker every day on our lean old meat. Might as well be traveling, and perhaps a bear or something will turn up.

It seems necessary to say something more about primitive nutrition in order to justify this decision. Nephritis, or derangement of the kidneys, which become overburdened with excess proteins, may occur in time if normal persons under peculiar circumstances eat only lean meat. Cases which have been diagnosed as nephritis occurred years ago among certain Athabascan Indian groups near Great Slave

Spring Hunting

Lake, Canada, when the Indians could sometimes find nothing to eat but rabbits. The other name for nephritis in the Northwoods areas has therefore come to be "rabbit starvation." The disease really is a starvation, and the victim starves to death on a full stomach. The Indians who died were stuffed on rabbits, but without the necessary fats and carbohydrates to go with this lean meat they were constitutionally unable to assimilate the food.

There was also the case of several scientists and sailors in 1914 who abandoned the vessel *Karluk* when it was crushed in the ice of the Arctic Ocean and took refuge on Wrangell Island off the Siberian coast. Supposedly they became afflicted with nephritis there, though it may have been Oriental beriberi with any of these cases. Several members of this stranded party became separated from their companions and died of exposure, but some, in the end, were rescued. A few victims are believed to have died of nephritis from existing for three months or more on ship's biscuits, tea, and a commercially packed explorer's pemmican which proved in emergency to lack sufficient fats. A swelling of the legs and bloating of the stomach resulted within a few weeks of living on this miserable fare, but the cause at that time was not guessed to be nutritional, as the disease seemed to have the symptoms of poisoning. It probably was protein poisoning, but only from a lack of fats; the body poisons itself. An Eskimo seamstress on this arctic expedition, and her husband and two small children, were found to be in good health when the survivors were picked up, because they had secured some of their own native foods, seals and polar bear, to eat along with the ship's rations.

Hence our general restlessness to leave home in hopes of trying something else after our fare became poor. There was no longer any reason to stay at the cabin, once warm weather permitted departure. We would take an empty five-gallon can for the collection of rendered bear fat, hoping we could secure bear during the spring hunting. How fat the bears would certainly be when they came from their hibernation shortly! What fun we would have taking shifts, one hunting bears by day and the other hunting muskrats by night!

But he who waits for the first bears to come from hibernation in the spring may have to wait a long day before he eats, and he who expects to float upon the waters in a canoe shooting fat muskrats may find that transition period a long ordeal.

No. 1

Date	TEMP. 6 a.m.	4 p.m.	Weather	Wind	Date	TEMP. 6 a.m.	4 .m.	Weather	Wind
1944									
Oct. 1	32°	30°	clear	slight	Nov. 3	10°	14°	clear	none
Oct. 2	24°	27°	snow	slight	Nov. 4	3°	8°	clear	none
Oct. 3	24°	32°	snow	none	Nov. 5[2]	2°	8°	clear	none
Oct. 4	28°	32°	cloudy	none	Nov. 6	10°	3°	clear	none
Oct. 5	24°	32°	cloudy	none	Nov. 7	-11°	2°	clear	none
Oct. 6	28°	32°	cloudy	none	Nov. 8	-10°	-14°	clear	none
Oct. 7	22°	28°	cloudy	none	Nov. 9	-18°	-24°	clear	none
Oct. 8	18°	22°	cloudy	windy	Nov. 10	-24°	-26°	clear	none
Oct. 9	24°	30°	cloudy	none	Nov. 11	-18°	-24°	clear	none
Oct. 10	28°	33°	overcast	none	Nov. 12	-30°	-32°	clear	none
Oct. 11	30°	26°	cloudy	none	Nov. 13	-32°	-24°	clear	none
Oct. 12	24°	30°	snow	slight	Nov. 14	-32°	-30°	clear	none
Oct. 13	25°	32°	snow	slight	Nov. 15	-13°	0°	cloudy	none
Oct. 14	30°	32°	snow	none	Nov. 16	-10°	-6°	cloudy	windy
Oct. 15	30°	32°	snow	none	Nov. 17	2°	-4°	snow	windy
Oct. 16	24°	28°	overcast	none	Nov. 18	10°	6°	cloudy	none
Oct. 17	26°	24°	overcast	none	Nov. 19	20°	10°	cloudy	slight
Oct. 18	24°	26°	snowing	slight	Nov. 20	5°	0°	overcast	slight
Oct. 19	30°	34°	overcast	none	Nov. 21	-2°	-2°	clear	none
Oct. 20	18°	24°	overcast	none	Nov. 22	-9°	-12°	clear	none
Oct. 21	20°	24°	overcast	none	Nov. 23	-10°	-21°	clear	none
Oct. 22	21°	24°	overcast	slight	Nov. 24	-26°	-20°	clear	none
Oct. 23	20°	10°	clear	none	Nov. 25	-26°	-26°	clear	none
Oct. 24[1]	8°	10°	clear	none	Nov. 26	-26°	-24°	clear	none
Oct. 25	1°	8°	clear	none	Nov. 27	-22°	-20°	clear	none
Oct. 26	-10°	2°	clear	none	Nov. 28	-24°	-26°	clear	none
Oct. 27	-11°	4°	clear	none	Nov. 29	-15°	-6°	snow	none
Oct. 28	-6°	4°	clear	none	Nov. 30	-20°	-24°	clear	none
Oct. 29	-8°	-12°	cloudy	none					
Oct. 30	10°	14°	clear	none	Dec. 1	-20°	-22°	clear	none
Oct. 31	11°	12°	clear	none	Dec. 2	-30°	-28°	clear	none
					Dec. 3	-30°	-28°	clear	none
Nov. 1	15°	20°	overcast	slight	Dec. 4	-28°	-48°	clear	none
Nov. 2	15°	18°	overcast	slight	Dec. 5	-48°	-50°	clear	none

[1] Freeze-up. [2] Nov. 5. Sun goes away.

Spring Hunting

No. 2

Date	TEMP. 6 a.m.	TEMP. 4 p.m.	Weather	Wind	Date	TEMP. 6 a.m.	TEMP. 4 .m.	Weather	Wind
1944 (cont.)					1945 (cont.)				
Dec. 6	-51°	-48°	clear	none	Jan. 9	-15°	-18°	clear	none
Dec. 7	-50°	-48°	clear	none	Jan. 10	-20°	-26°	clear	none
Dec. 8	-44°	-38°	clear	none	Jan. 11	-24°	-20°	clear	none
Dec. 10	-18°	-14°	clear	none	Jan. 12	-18°	-10°	clear	none
Dec. 11	-10°	-2°	snow	slight	Jan. 13	0°	4°	snow	none
Dec. 12	-2°	-2°	snow	none	Jan. 14	4°	2°	snow	none
Dec. 13	0°	0°	snow	none	Jan. 15	8°	5°	snow	none
Dec. 14	10°	6°	snow	none	Jan. 16	6°	4°	snow	none
Dec. 15	10°	12°	snow	none	Jan. 17	-6°	-24°	clear	none
Dec. 16	12°	16°	cloudy	windy	Jan. 18	-31°	-36°	clear	none
Dec. 17	30°	31°	snow	slight	Jan. 19	-38°	-36°	clear	none
Dec. 18	10°	16°	cloudy	none	Jan. 20	-12°	-10°	overcast	windy
Dec. 19	8°	10°	snow	slight	Jan. 21	-5°	-8°	clear	none
Dec. 20	6°	8°	snow	slight	Jan. 22	-2°	-10°	snow	windy
Dec. 21	4°	9°	overcast	none	Jan. 23	-3°	-5°	snow	windy
Dec. 22	2°	6°	snow	windy	Jan. 24	-6°	-6°	snow	slight
Dec. 23	0°	-5°	clear	none	Jan. 25	-7°	-4°	snow	slight
Dec. 24	-10°	-15°	clear	none	Jan. 26	-9°	-7°	snow	none
Dec. 25	-12°	-15°	clear	none	Jan. 27	-6°	-2°	snow	none
Dec. 26	-17°	-19°	clear	none	Jan. 28	-2°	4°	overcast	none
Dec. 27	-21°	-25°	clear	none	Jan. 29	4°	8°	snow	none
Dec. 28	-28°	-30°	clear	none	Jan. 30	9°	13°	cloudy	none
Dec. 29	-34°	-40°	clear	none	Jan. 31	8°	12°	cloudy	none
Dec. 30	-40°	-40°	clear	none					
Dec. 31	-28°	-24°	clear	none	Feb. 1	12°	14°	cloudy	none
1945					Feb. 2	24°	16°	cloudy	none
Jan. 1	-24°	-28°	clear	none	Feb. 3	1°	-1°	clear	none
Jan. 2	-28°	-30°	clear	none	Feb. 4	-4°	-8°	clear	none
Jan. 3	-3°	0°	clear	none	Feb. 5[3]	-8°	-6°	clear	none
Jan. 4	-12°	-16°	clear	none	Feb. 6	0°	8°	clear	windy
Jan. 5	-16°	-22°	clear	none	Feb. 7	-11°	-17°	clear	windy
Jan. 6	-29°	-27°	clear	none	Feb. 8	-19°	-12°	clear	windy
Jan. 7	-29°	-23°	clear	none	Feb. 9	-16°	-12°	snow	none
Jan. 8	-16°	-32°	clear	none					

[3] Feb. 5. Sun returns..

No. 3

Date	TEMP. 6 a.m.	TEMP. 4 p.m.	Weather	Wind	Date	TEMP. 6 a.m.	TEMP. 4 .m.	Weather	Wind
1945 (cont.)					1945 (cont.)				
Feb. 10	-30°	-24°	clear	none	Mar. 15	-8°	-3°	snow	windy
Feb. 11	-34°	-16°	clear	none	Mar. 16	-11°	-2°	clear	none
Feb. 12	-30°	-22°	clear	none	Mar. 17	21°	-11°	clear	none
Feb. 13	-34°	-40°	clear	none	Mar. 18	-28°	-30°	clear	none
Feb. 14	-58°	-51°	clear	none	Mar. 19	-36°	-2°	clear	none
Feb. 15	-62°	-49°	clear	none	Mar. 20	-32°	-7°	clear	none
Feb. 16	-54°	-30°	clear	none	Mar. 21	-26°	7°	clear	none
Feb. 17	-20°	-11°	snow	none	Mar. 22	-38°	10°	clear	none
Feb. 18	-21°	-10°	clear	none	Mar. 23	10°	21°	cloudy	none
Feb. 19	-8°	2°	clear	none	Mar. 24	10°	15°	cloudy	windy
Feb. 20	-8°	12°	clear	none	Mar. 25	0°	0°	cloudy	none
Feb. 21	10°	12°	snow	none	Mar. 26	-22°	2°	clear	none
Feb. 22	-2°	-10°	clear	none	Mar. 27	-26°	8°	clear	none
Feb. 23	-18°	-8°	clear	none	Mar. 28	-19°	23°	clear	none
Feb. 24	-28°	-3°	overcast	none	Mar. 29	-5°	23°	clear	none
Feb. 25	8°	12°	snow	none	Mar. 30	5°	28°	snow	none
Feb. 26	16°	20°	snow	none	Mar. 31	5°	12°	clear	windy
Feb. 27	22°	29°	overcast	none					
Feb. 28	16°	24°	snow	none	Apr. 1	0°	-18°	clear	windy
					Apr. 2	-20°	-8°	snow	none
Mar. 1	12°	25°	overcast	none	Apr. 3	-36°	-38°	snow	windy
Mar. 2	0°	9°	clear	none	Apr. 4	-40°	-19°	clear	windy
Mar. 3	-1°	19°	clear	none	Apr. 5	-12°	0°	clear	windy
Mar. 4	5°	11°	clear	none	Apr. 6	-2°	32°	clear	none
Mar. 5	-5°	9°	clear	none	Apr. 7	8°	34°	clear	none
Mar. 6	-8°	-2°	clear	none	Apr. 8	-4°	35°	clear	none
Mar. 7	-12°	-2°	clear	none	Apr. 9	11°	31°	clear	none
Mar. 8	-18°	-9°	clear	none	Apr. 10	16°	34°	clear	none
Mar. 9	-17°	-6°	clear	windy	Apr. 11	24°	30°	clear	none
Mar. 10	-18°	-5°	clear	windy	Apr. 12	12°	38°	clear	none
Mar. 11	-25°	-7°	clear	none	Apr. 13	10°	34°	clear	none
Mar. 12	-31°	-12°	clear	none	Apr. 14	20°	36°	snow	none
Mar. 13	-29°	-6°	clear	none	Apr. 15	28°	39°	cloudy	windy
Mar. 14	-25°	-10°	snow	windy	Apr. 16	24°	39°	clear	none

No. 4

Date	TEMP. 6 a.m.	TEMP. 4 p.m.	Weather	Wind	Date	TEMP. 6 a.m.	TEMP. 4 .m.	Weather	Wind
1945 (cont.)					1945 (cont.)				
Apr. 17	8°	34°	clear	none	May 20	25°	46°	clear	none
Apr. 18	12°	41°	clear	none	May 21	28°	56°	clear	none
Apr. 19[4]	26°	43°	clear	windy	May 22	32°	58°	clear	none
Apr. 20	42°	15°	clear	none	May 23	33°	56°	overcast	none
Apr. 21	16°	29°	clear	windy	May 24	34°	59°	overcast	none
Apr. 22	9°	29°	clear	none	May 25	38°	52°	clear	none
Apr. 23	3°	33°	overcast	none	May 26	32°	59°	clear	slight
Apr. 24	21°	39°	overcast	none	May 27	36°	45°	rain	slight
Apr. 25	32°	44°	overcast	none	May 28[5]	34°	45°	overcast	windy
Apr. 26	24°	44°	clear	none	May 29	28°	56°	clear	none
Apr. 27	-12°	34°	clear	windy	May 30	30°	55°	overcast	none
Apr. 28	-2°	36°	clear	slight	May 31	33°	46°	cloudy	windy
Apr. 29	-6°	38°	clear	slight					
Apr. 30	6°	34°	clear	none	June 1	30°	51°	cloudy	windy
					June 2	34°	59°	clear	none
May 1	3°	30°	clear	none	June 3	32°	48°	cloudy	windy
May 2	9°	33°	overcast	none	June 4	34°	49°	overcast	windy
May 3	12°	28°	snow	none	June 5	21°	46°	snow	windy
May 4	10°	28°	snow	none	June 6	30°	59°	cloudy	none
May 5	12°	16°	snow	none	June 7	34°	64°	clear	none
May 6	-8°	32°	clear	none	June 8	36°	76°	clear	none
May 7	3°	38°	clear	none	June 9	42°	68°	clear	none
May 8	0°	44°	clear	none	June 10	46°	73°	clear	none
May 9	27°	50°	clear	none					
May 10	30°	45°	overcast	none					
May 11	16°	38°	clear	windy					
May 12	18°	46°	clear	none					
May 13	20°	31°	snow	none					
May 14	15°	40°	clear	none					
May 15	12°	45°	clear	none					
May 16	28°	46°	cloudy	none					
May 17	26°	48°	clear	none					
May 18	30°	46°	overcast	none					
May 19	31°	49°	overcast	none					

[4] Warmest temperature in 6 months. [5] Breakup.

"You know, Bud," I voiced the presentiment just once, "the calendar we made up for this year can't be too far wrong, but just the same, it doesn't look like spring to me yet by the weather thermometer. Supposing breakup doesn't come three weeks from now? Maybe it won't come at all."

"Oh, it's bound to come sometime," he said. "Look at the date. April is upon us."

I looked out at the frozen land from our window. Yes, indeed, we were going to hurry the spring and the breakup! We had had experience only with southerly lands before, and we had never had to wait for spring to bring something to eat. What we did not realize fully is that there is a great deal of latent cold in the ground of the far North which hangs on for a long, long time. March is not the end of the winter, but just the middle of it.

In midwinter in the arctic interior of this continent, cold snaps of between 30 and 50 below may hold pretty steadily for several days at a time. During these cold snaps the advent of day or night seems to make little difference. If the temperature starts to swing cold, it may take two or three days to gather momentum, and then it becomes steadily colder with each passing hour, until it has gone its limit and exhausted its powers. Then slowly, as a rule, it will break again, relinquishing its grasp. Perhaps the thermometer will climb above zero but never to the thawing point in these mountains. As spring approaches—gradually, oh very gradually—the arc of the pendulum slows to lesser extremes of cold. But the longest day of the year will actually have passed before the cold earth begins to thaw out. Here a five-foot layer of porous snow protects the earth from thawing action far into the summer in such mountain valleys. Day after day the bright but feeble sun must pour its warmth upon this snow, first to shrink and compress it, before it can hope to sweep it away.

In the spring the degree to which the cold periods may swing is noticeably mitigated by the action of the sun at noonday, but the thermometer will yet fall low each night. Night becomes the time for travel rather than daytime and is, in fact, the favorite of all periods in the year for the dog sleds along the northern coasts. A crust is formed, even inland as in our valley, by the melting midday and the freezing nights, which makes snowshoe and sled travel a swift joy and far countryside more accessible to exploration than at any other

Spring Hunting

time of the year. When we planned our spring hunting we thought of conventional spring as we had previously known it, and we did not guess that all of our spring hunting would be done on snowshoes!

In this land, remember, the accumulated cold of centuries must be dispelled before summer can come. By the time this has begun in one season the sun has passed its longest day and has started away again. Out of the 365 days in the year we had 121 days on which the thermometer hit below zero temperatures; roughly, but one third of the year here is below-zero! A brief glance at the temperature chart will show how the cold waves gathered momentum slowly as winter progressed, by succeeding plateaus, and then declined in the same way, until finally the days that were above zero outnumbered the subzero days, and the last cold wave, 8° below zero on May 6, came all by itself among warm days which halted winter for a little while.

> March 31, 1945
> 12 Midnight
> TO WHOM IT MAY CONCERN:
> We are leaving today with two small ski sleds loaded with camp gear and a little dried meat. We also have a kayak on one sled. We have gone down river to prepare for muskrat hunting and look for bear as we need meat badly. No concern need be felt for us, however. We are well and happy. We expect to return after breakup and proceed to Alatna.
> There is some dried meat in a sack back of the stove but no other food. Help yourself. Ax and saw back of door.
> BUD AND CONNIE

The increasing light rekindles our spirit of adventure

With food gone, we leave our cabin March 31, 1945

3

It was downright amazing how much junk we could pile onto the sleds we had to drag, even when we had stripped to what we believed were the very essentials of primitive existence. Our food itself wasn't much: one day's hoarded rations of a lean grizzly bear roast, ready sliced so that we could get it easily after it froze on the sled, and a gunnysack of dried caribou meat which by itself almost obliterated the little sled from sight but which would actually last us less than a week if we ate nothing else. There would have to be something else. We were destined not to see our cabin again for close to two months, as it happened.

The venture ultimately would prove to be a wise one for us. But meanwhile we would have what is sometimes known as tough sledding, literally. And now there was the rather ridiculous picture of two uninformed persons pulling sleds loaded with such articles as raincoats and fishing poles through low temperatures and deep snow.

My own toy canoe sled held little beside the sleeping bag and our $3.98 pup tent; but Bud's sled was heavy, for he had the snow shovel, the ax, photographic equipment, the ammunition, and the traps. It doesn't take many traps to weigh fifty pounds. We had to have them because as a last resort we could always set them, even if we got too weak or too badly off to do anything else and fall back on our old friends the rabbits once more.

This time we were not taking the big eight-by-ten tent, because experience had taught us to cut down on the load somehow, and it seemed the tent must make the sacrifice. This time we had only the sleeping bag and the old pup tent to cover the bag for emergency shelter, and we would have to live entirely out-of-doors. "We must travel light and fast," we had said. After all, the big tent weighed twenty-five pounds, along with its pegs, and it took some time to pitch it when you had to cut the poles each evening. We would soon reach Takahula Lake. It was only a matter of a few days. There we could live in the old Takahula Cabin. We took no stove with us, for without the large tent to erect it in, there was no provision for using a stove. We had nothing to cook. All our spring cooking, when we got something to cook, would be done outdoors around an open fire or some kind of improvised fireplace, we supposed. Was this a mistake? It would soon be summer, wouldn't it?

It might have been summer theoretically, but the very day we left home, dragging our sleds, all of the elements began to gather their forces as though to pit themselves against human beings out of sheer malice. Because the temperature had been above zero of late, it was now time for a real cold spell to sweep the land again during the first week in April. The nastiest weather of the winter, especially winds and what are popularly called blizzards, may come in early spring like this. What is a blizzard? We had looked up this word in the dictionary once in the cabin. The definition was vague. There was no measurement given for it. We believed we had never yet seen one in the arctic. We were to formulate our own definition on this sled trip: "It is a blizzard if you are out in it."

Having taken our weather thermometer along on the sled in its case, that our record might be uninterrupted, we discovered on the second day that a cold wave was coming on. It was 18° below zero, which is a chilly temperature when you must dress out-of-doors. We had not used the pup tent; the skies were clear as a bell's tone.

Bud had tinder ready for a fire. The sleeping bag lay on a pier of spruce boughs; our snowshoes stuck on end beside. The night before, Bud had cut green logs, four feet in length, to build the fire on and keep it from sinking into the snow. It had sunk a bit, but its charred remnants were still there. As Bud reached under the head of the bag for his precious tinder I lay peacefully thinking how fortunate it was for me that I had agreed to build the fire during the summer if he would build it all winter—a good bargain in the arctic!

Now in the wild spruce forest Bud had to dress himself first and then start the fire for me. The fire was close to the head of the bed; its roaring flames enabled me to pull on frozen trousers, socks, and boots, over the long-handled underwear in which I had slept. Being unable to comb my hair without freezing my hands, with no more ado I pulled on my fabric parka and tied its hood under my chin, and with my belt tight over an empty stomach I stepped from the bedroll on to my snowshoes and began to roll the bed in preparation for travel. The last of the frozen bear meat was thawing in the light skillet. It was bolted down with little ceremony; frozen hands were thrust hastily back into mittens again. Snow, melted greasily in the same utensil, became tepid water in which ashes and small sticks floated; we drank it from the skillet's brim, burning our lips and spilling some of it into the snow. We had a few other utensils but in such temperatures all metal objects are so "hot" to touch that it becomes far easier to forgo using them when on the trail. Mittens are too big and clumsy to hold a cup, and then, too, we had only hot water to drink. One way you can drink from a cup with these big mittens on is to prop it against your chest with your palms and lift it up carefully, but this is at great risk of spilling the contents or especially of getting the mittens wet. Subsequently in the North we would usually hold a cup barehanded, but not for long. Eating and drinking are tasks to be completed as quickly as possible under these circumstances if you wish to avoid grief.

But hurry as we might to start traveling and exercising, we were not to travel far on this day. No sooner had we left the shelter of the spruce bend where we had camped than we were met by a head wind which turned our noses and chins white in an instant, so that it was impossible to buck it even if we bowed our heads as we pulled the sleds. To say that this wind blew right through our inadequate clothing is not half of it. We had discovered, too, that hands chill and soon become numb in mittens if they must support any pressure such as pulling a rope. To permit our hands to hang loosely at our sides we were pulling the sleds with our bodies.

Back into the spruce forest we were forced again, to stand on snowshoes around our breakfast fire, not daring to go too close to it, and wait for the slow hours to pass in hopes that the wind would die down on the river where our sleds might travel. I can't tell the hours that went by, or even the days, before we finally got under way once more. Down past the frowning rocky Arrigetch Peaks lay our way, past the cliffs at Pingaluk, the old familiar landmarks of our arctic home.

I was half a mile ahead of Bud, breaking trail, and the thousand-foot wall of Pingaluk reared up behind me. A caribou carcass, killed by wolves, lay in the river bed. It would be washed away when breakup came. Since the big snows, not a sign remained that the caribou had ever been in the country. The first wolverine I had ever seen free in the wild bounded out across the white expanse from the caribou carcass. I turned, grabbed for my rifle in its case on the sled, tripped on my snowshoes, and fell.

"We might as well camp a half mile below here," said Bud presently, admitting that he was pretty tired, "and set a couple of traps, and maybe that wolverine will be back tonight."

I didn't see how he could do it, but Bud was always that way. The fool wolverine never came back, but I worried all night, while we slept inside the bag among the spruces, for fear he might get into the dried meat left on our sled sitting in the river fifty yards away. Will wolverines eat dried meat? When a sack of dried meat is all you have, and so much depends upon small things going just right, you wonder about such things as a wolverine's diet. Among other things we considered was the possibility of the matches igniting in the glass bottle which was their container, or of losing our boots or part of our clothing in some snowstorm while we slept or setting our spruce bed ablaze by building the fire too near. None of these apprehensions materialized. We slept, exhausted.

The following morning at 20 below we crawled out of the frost-covered bag to find that the usual meal of dried meat and hot water was beginning to lack savor and that our stomachs felt decidedly fuzzy. Getting into the snowshoes I went at once for our traps before breakfast, and by the time I returned Bud had everything packed to proceed. Getting into the pulling harness was an effort, although after we got started we plowed along at a good rate. Our way led down a riffle covered with rotten ice concealed by snowdrifts running in diagonal walls several feet high. This tongue of ice led down the middle of the river with open water on either side along the shores. I was afraid of it and chose a route along the narrow edge of the cut bank beneath the entanglements of many overhanging boughs. Here my canoe-sled slipped sidewise down the bank and rolled the sleeping bag out on a little ice pan where it looked as though it might be difficult to get. I just waited there and watched it. When Bud came along he was able to climb down and retrieve it with a long arm. Together, we then got both sleds past the bad spot.

That evening we saw a flock of ptarmigan nearby, feeding on willow buds. So wary were they that an approach was not possible, but Bud secured one bird on a long shot with the .22 rifle. It had a broken neck—a lucky shot. He picked it of feathers and quickly peeling out heart, gizzard, and liver had it in a pot with snow in no time.

"I'll settle for the liver and one leg," I said. "It looks to me as if we'd better go back on our old rations again. Just like old times, huh? You need a lot more food than I do."

But Bud wouldn't hear of this; he insisted on half and half, so, after waiting for it to come to a boil, we soon fished the pieces out, and dividing them equally devoured them in our hands minus salt, and then drank the warm broth. In the North we retain memories of feasts more delicious than any we have ever known; it's odd how after so long the remembrance of that single ptarmigan, eaten standing up on snowshoes, comes back to haunt me. It was gone in a gulp and a snap, a mere morsel, when we could have done with twenty like it.

Snow was falling softly, and the evening had clouded in and turned black. "Guess it might be a good idea to erect the pup tent over the sleeping bag tonight," mentioned Bud, "else we might get buried."

We were very nearly buried this time, at that! All night long the snow kept falling; the wind rose, and the trees moaned and cracked until we thought they might come down, as a few of them may have. There was only a coarse cheap mosquito bar across the front of the pup tent, against which our heads lay, and the snow drifted through this nicely. By morning the driving wind had so chilled us that we were ready to get up with the first light and travel on in order to warm up by exercise. It was extremely crowded and cramped for two people inside the one-man bag, and this cramping tended to cut off circulation in a way which would quickly promote freezing in low temperatures. This was the only occasion that the sleeping bag did not seem entirely adequate, for it was guaranteed against an 80° below zero temperature. That the cold came through we blame upon crowding and cramping conditions, combined with the fact that the edges of the bag touched the tent and so conducted the cold through to us during the extremely high wind.

The first light of dawn, for which we waited, came suddenly as bright morning when we looked out at last; it was enough to fulfill our worst suspicions. I opened just one eye and then didn't look again. Later, in midday, we awoke for good and knew for a certainty that we were not to get out of the bag that day at all.

Getting out of the bag to dress, in that cyclone which swept through the little tent, was not possible. We never could have started a fire. Our woodpile and all kindling except that upon which we wisely lay, everything was buried from sight and made unrecognizable. We thought we knew where all our equipment was, but who wanted to get out there and commence digging? Our hands would freeze just getting our clothes on.

It took no investigation to realize that our hair had become frozen down on the ends where we lay, and we did not try to move except to turn over once in a while. The condensation of our breaths had formed an icy sheath which penetrated hourly ever deeper into the collar of the bag where our necks stuck out for air. We were complete prisoners, you might say, or much like chickens in a sack. Slowly the day dragged itself out and night came again. We were extremely thirsty, in fact almost dehydrated from five days on the trail with no shelter and no chance to sit down to eat and drink with any ease. The wind would soon blow itself out, of course, but it was hard waiting.

By the time we got out of the bag a day later we had rolled ourselves into such a wad by turning over and over that all movement other than breathing was at last impossible. We ached from head to foot from lying so long in this tomb. When Bud made the plunge, he was a cripple!

The morning was calm. It had run 36° to 38° below zero during the blizzard and it was now -40°. Shaking uncontrollably, Bud dug his outer clothes out of the drift and desperately struggled with them. His hands were freezing when it came to belt buckle and buttons. Imprisoned in the bag I lay watching each movement with some anxiety, as may well be imagined. Once dressed Bud soon had a high roaring fire blazing against the log reflector so providentially built near the opening of the tent when we had paused here two days before.

At 40° below two or three matches must be struck to warm up the driest tinder sometimes, for things will hardly burn at all until they get started. Bud saw his little finger go white while he held the first match. But the fire took.

He could hardly stand. Just the effort to keep warm in the sleeping bag during the storm had cost us more bodily energy than we knew; when one doesn't have plenty of the right food, cold quickly brings on weakness. There is simply no energy left.

I got dressed by the fire and we started on our way. I do not remember whether we ate, but we got a drink, at least. Our stomachs had shrunk, and we couldn't even drink much. The river bed led straight down the valley here, while snow whirled about our feet and the sleds sometimes slid sidewise on the hard-packed glare of what was apparently a permanently windy area. We experienced a mutual urge to hurry now. Takahula Cabin could not be more than fifteen miles away at most. Every day of exposure seemed to be taking more out of us. I realized Bud looked badly this morning, and with a feeling of some consternation quickly led the way ahead with my lighter sled. I was then stronger than Bud because he never spared himself; in his position, he couldn't. Furthermore, when you try to run a large machine on the same amount of fuel you allow for a small one, it is obvious that the larger machine under these conditions will give out first. I give these possible reasons, at any rate, for the fact that Bud abruptly, and quite to our mutual amazement, ceased to function.

Bud had caught up to me—by a supreme effort, and without his sled. "Got to get someplace and lie down," he said. He was wobbling on his legs, and his wind-burned face with its new growth of sharp stubbly whiskers looked just what it was—sore. His eyes were bloodshot. Looking at him, I could see myself, minus the whiskers. "I'm going down on my back," he explained with a wry smile through cracked lips, and with one look at his face I believed him. We had spoken only a few words to each other this day, and I noticed that he seemed almost incoherent. A pain in his chest, he said. Good heavens!

Pneumonia was my immediate diagnosis.

"And I shouldn't wonder," I thought, perfectly clearly, as though viewing us from afar. "Well, we'll make out. If I can get him into the sleeping bag and rested!" But I knew that the sleeping bag was wet with frost inside, and that it must be dried out in some shelter before it could be used again. "What do you suggest, old boy?" I tried to ask him casually.

"I'm going ahead," Bud said. He had the ax in his hand, I noticed. "The Nahtuk River can't be far away. I remember now, there's an old cabin in the forest there, pretty good one. I happened to run across it last summer, didn't I tell you about it? If I can remember where it is! With so much snow on the ground, everything looks different . . . You know, I never forget a place. Might have known that would come in handy sometime." With a drunken leer he wobbled off like one half-delirious.

I went back up the straight river bed and hitched myself to Bud's sled. It had our food on it. We couldn't leave it here. No wonder Bud had given out; the wonder was that he had stayed with this sled so many days, dragging it like a plow through soft snow. The sled had frozen down as soon as it stopped, and with snowshoes on the slick glare I thought at first that I couldn't budge it, yet I was too tired and sick at my stomach to stoop over and take off my snowshoes. "Oh, hell," I thought disgustedly, for I must admit that I would swear sometimes with weariness. However, after I got the sled started it went right along and I got it down the river bed beside my own sled probably within an hour. Here I became anxious over Bud. Should I have stayed with him? Suddenly becoming panicky with worry, I dropped both sleds where they lay; they were a pitiful and very temporary landmark of the story of two human beings without succor in the arctic, I thought, as snow already commenced to drift over them. With one hasty backward glance at their position I left the sleds and followed Bud's trail as fast as I could.

At any moment I expected to see ahead of me his unconscious form dropped along the way with snow drifting over it. The whole episode reminded me of the worst of what we had always joked about. At home in the United States, when we had talked about going to Alaska, we had called it "Mother's séance"—this clairvoyant vision of a worried mother: the arctic cold with a blizzard raging, Mother's children struggling on and on through it, dragging, in all likelihood, a pitiful little sled, and then all is blotted out in whirling clouds of snow, which is all a mother sees first and last of Alaska. It looked as though Mother's séance was really coming true. For once I was glad she couldn't see us now.

Bud meantime had lost his way. That is, he was trying to find the Nahtuk Cabin by investigating a river channel which he hoped was the frozen Nahtuk River coming in, but it turned out to be just a big island of our own river once more, and the Nahtuk itself was still further on. His trail wandered through soft snow, and I knew that the ordeal was sadly wasting his last remaining energy. Yet it is surprising how a person's strength holds out days and days even after he thinks that it is surely gone.

 At last I saw it, the cabin to which Bud's trail brought me. Just below the entrance of the Nahtuk River, on a slough off the main river channel, it was new to me. It lay almost buried in snow, with a white roof five feet thick dwarfing the structure itself, while each cut stump had a similar cap. It was not easy to approach, being separated from the snow-covered river ice on which we traveled by a small stream of open water running over gravel, and then by a steep bank overgrown with a thicket of willows and alder of the densest type. This thicket had grown up and the river had moved over into the other channel in all likelihood since the cabin was originally built. Detouring the open water and stepping across a part of it on rocks with my snowshoes, I attacked the bank. Pulling myself up this bank with the aid of branches took the last of my own strength, until I wondered how Bud had made it, with his own tracks as straight as a die and true. No smoke was coming from the chimney hole; at the moment there was no sound from the old cabin. Was Bud all right?

 I got into the cabin through a broken-out window. Here, following the tracks, I parked my snowshoes beside Bud's and stepped inside and onto a table and down onto the ax-hewn floor. What a relief to get off snowshoes for a few minutes and be able to stand on a solid foundation again!

 That the place had no stove was at once apparent. Bud had built a stove out of two empty five-gallon gas cans he had chopped out and joined together, and he was just now erecting a stovepipe made out of a conglomeration of cans of various sizes which lay about the room. As the heavy door had jammed with the years, it would take considerable ax work and shoveling of snow to get it open. In the meantime, some dry wood had been left ready on the floor of the room these many years for the rescue of the stranger, after immemorial custom in the North. This time that I know of may well have justified all those other times that people have left wood in cabins. It came near to saving a stranger's life indeed, because we were so weak that getting other fuel around and into the window on snowshoes would have been a well-nigh final obstacle for us. The half cord of wood which had been neatly stacked just outside the entrance beneath the overhanging roof was buried and not accessible at once, but the wood inside the cabin was safe.

The evidence of newspapers, magazines, and general trash ultimately proved that the cabin itself, a dandy, was nearly fifty years old, but had been inhabited by a succession of people since its beginning. The original owners were extremely skilled woodsmen and utterly resourceful. We had admiration for these early ones. One of my fondest souvenirs is from this cabin, an old recipe booklet from somebody's erstwhile flour sack, giving recipes for pudding cakes which call for eighteen eggs, family size, showing the large way in which America generally lived and thought in former days.

"That eighteen eggs sound like good eating to me. Now isn't that a little better than these recipes you see today which say to take two egg whites, beat them up with one half cup of something slenderizing, add a tablespoon of sugar, and it serves eight?" I asked, as one connoisseur to another.

Bud had got the fire to roaring. The house, while open at two sides from its broken windows, was a palace. And suddenly, gone were the fears and forgotten our cares. We had magazines spread out before us and were satisfying our hunger for the first new reading matter we had laid eyes on in three quarters of a year, turning the squirrel-chewed pages with our mittens still on. Aloud I read the old recipes to Bud, and we smacked our lips and nodded with the approval of true food experts as each ingredient was carefully balanced and added in imagination.

"Heck, I used to eat eighteen eggs just for breakfast," said Bud. "Remember?"

"No," I said. "You've forgotten. But sometimes you used to have eight or ten, with pancakes or waffles and fried ham and a quart or so of fruit juice, and left-over steak or ice cream in the icebox if you could find it. That's the trouble with you. You're not sick, it's just a very plain and simple case of starvation."

"Yes, and you know I've had a hard time to get that lean meat down all the last month," Bud agreed, when he thought it over. "I haven't been hungry, either. We just haven't had the right kind of feed for a long time before we started this trip. But I feel a lot better already just to sit down for a few minutes after all these days and get warmed up. I think the pain in my chest is just muscular, from pulling the sled. Some good grub will fix your old hunter up again, just like new."

Unfortunately, some recent visitors to the Nahtuk Cabin, about ten years gone, four prospectors for the summer who had apparently been flown in by chartered airplane, had used all of the available empty cans about the place for targets; they had managed to put at least one .22 slug in each one so that we were not able to melt snow to slake our thirst. Their lack of consideration in this regard almost prevented us from getting our sleds. But we made it, and, leaving them on the river ice across from the house, I was able to pack up all our necessities one by one, and with many a trip and fall in the entangling bushes got them at last indoors through the window. Bud plugged up one of the windows successfully with snow blocks, which kept the house quite warm; over our entrance window he hung the little pup tent. Then he crawled shaking into the sleeping bag laid out on the bunk and stayed there.

"You better start hunting for moose tomorrow," he said and dropped off to sleep.

Finding the old Nahtuk River cabin saves our lives

Fresh food at last! Starvation is over when Bud shoots a moose

4

In the dense spruce forest of the broad Nahtuk Valley I hunted moose. I always did love to hunt moose better than any other animal, but it didn't seem possible that I could find one now right off because I hadn't seen one in months. I hunted moose three days, while the cold snap wore off to 30° below zero and then to -20°, and finally to above-zero temperatures.

That Nahtuk Valley was a pretty place. There had been moose there; they had left relics which reminded you of a small boy who has gone through the bushes whittling and ripping off sticks at random. Some were stripped of bark, showing white wood; others were broken and left dangling. On the third day I found a moose trail and using all the skill I possessed got down on my hands and knees to decipher it. Taking off my mittens and reaching my bare hand into the snow, I scooped out the track in an effort to clear it, as I had seen Bud do, but it was no use. The trail had been made before the blizzard, and in all likelihood I followed it backwards until, emerging from the heavy spruce to more open pasture on the slope of the mountain, it circled and was obliterated completely by drifts as though wiped from the earth.

Returning home, I saw three grouse in the trees right by the house. Sneaking the .22 from the porch, I secured them in a thrice with one shot each. I gasped as I thought I lost the third bird, which flew off into a thicket, but a puff of feathers led me to the spot where it had plummeted into the snow stone dead. That was the only time I ever saved our lives or fortunes. From his bunk Bud managed to limp out with some traps and take more rabbits than I could have found in several days' exertions had I been hunting them. Once again, the small game kept us going for the time being so that hunting could proceed.

"Even if moose aren't here right now," I repeated Bud's confident words of last fall, "it can't be many days until one will be passing by, and then I'll be in the woods and catch him."

To my surprise Bud shook his head at this. "I wish you were right, but I'm afraid you're wrong."

"But you said they always do that."

"Conditions change, dear. I believe the moose have yarded up, wherever they are, and we'll have to find them. Because of the deep snow," he added, "I don't think they're traveling much at this season. You know, a moose doesn't like to plow through that sharp crust any better than we would. They break right through and it probably cuts their legs."

Just what to do was a matter for nice judgment. Muskrats and bears, we now knew for a certainty without delusion, were out of the question for indeterminate weeks. This was mid-April, but these were conditions of winter, not of summer. We both agreed it would be foolhardy to attempt to go back upriver to our own cabin. It goes without saying that there would have been no point in going back there since we had only a few pounds of dried meat half a year-old waiting for us at home—the same thing we had right here in more limited amount. Here we must stay and hunt. Already we loved our new home and needed only food to fill its larder to be perfectly content. We must get a moose in this vicinity immediately or, as Bud suggested, travel until we did, and after killing it build a lean-to and camp by the carcass for the next few weeks to tide us over. I could see the former possibility but not the latter. For myself, I had learned what happens to people from exposure, and I knew the value of keeping a roof overhead.

But getting moose last fall and getting moose in the early spring might be two utterly different propositions, we were beginning to suspect. We had never hunted moose in spring before, naturally, and now that we had to we knew nothing of their habits. Certainly, a moose was going to be very hard to get. The snow had begun to settle and to form a crust on its surface, and it would enable a moose to hear us coming on our snowshoes through the forest as the bird can hear the belled cat. *Crunch! Squeak! Crunch!* We knew at the outset that it would be next to a miracle if we found a fresh track, or, having found it, could ever follow it into the dense thickets where the moose presumably was. The crustiness of the snow and the realization that each passing day from now on would make this condition worse prompted Bud in his bunk to summon his resources and lay a plan.

We would be wise, I thought, to stay here at this cabin where we at least had shelter from exposure and conserve our energy. "Oh, heck, we can live on rabbits and starve it out for just a few weeks, I suppose," I said. "Summer can't hold off long. I'm really not worried."

"Yes, I know. I'm not worried either. Why worry? But today I just kind of got mad. Why should we sit here like a couple of idiots and starve when there's perfectly wonderful eating all around? I've just about made up my mind I want some fresh red meat, that's all." Bud's reaction was a kind of anger at the whole silly situation. Perhaps, like a lot of credulous folk, we had taken too seriously those stories of the American pioneers who filled their larder with a "haunch of venison" (which made exactly one meal for *those* eaters) or the tales of present-day people who have "lived off the country"—so they say. Haunch of venison, my eye. We could eat a moose apiece if we let ourselves go, right now.

"We'll start tomorrow with the idea that we're going to do some eating for a change. We'll each make a slow and systematic canvass of the country. The bad breaks can't last forever, and cabin or no cabin, we're going where the food is, and if I had pneumonia once, I'm over it now."

Bud decided from my observations to start by working over the country which lay below the Nahtuk River entrance. I had a great deal of confidence in Bud's hunting instincts. For myself, try as I would, I couldn't even conjure up the vision of a moose in these bleak April woods, locked so tight and still; I had forgotten what a moose looked like. But for Bud, a moose, or something, would materialize, with no "if's" about it. Nature had special provision for such as he, and I would eat, too, if I hung along with him.

IT WAS HARD TO THINK OF BUD so sick that he could barely manage his snowshoes on such a beautiful day. We wore sun glasses and perspired freely under a sky so blue it hurt your eyes. I had the country on the left hand, whose breathing forests resounded today for the first time in winter months with the drumming of the grouse and the feuding of the squirrels, which were sassy and full of barks. Abruptly above reared the gorgeous, desolate crags of solid rock; down their shoots snow slides were beginning to show their muddy scars.

I wasn't hungry. My stomach had in it a few scraps of lean dried meat and, after all, I felt pretty well for a "starving" person. If we could only find fat big game, or anything fresh, what more could we want? But it was hard to concentrate on hunting moose. Distant strange views of the Arrigetch Peaks rose up in unexpected vistas, like black iron spikes on a war mace.

One has much equipment to manage when navigating on snowshoes in full winter regalia. In the deep shade of spruce forest entanglements Bud was finding it hard to keep his feet and was concentrating carefully to make each step. He had found a week-old moose trail which led him to fresh trails. Then, up jumped a large dim form with a crash in the thickets. Automatically, as though from some old memory, Bud's rifle was up. He fell into a crouch down low on his snowshoes so that he might see underneath the timber.

From where I lay in the snow far away on an uptilted mountain plane, having the moment before stuck one snowshoe under a root in the drift, I thought I heard a sound. It wasn't really a sound; it was a disturbance of the atmosphere which penetrated my consciousness. I wouldn't have heard it at all except that I was in repose at the moment, digging snow out of my gloves and out of the muzzle of my rifle with a stick. Bud and I had hunted for a long time together. I had no idea how many hours had passed, and this whole day, out of an old superstition, I had purposely put him and his affairs out of mind for good luck. But now the thought occurred to me just as though someone had spoken it aloud, "I'll go find Bud now. The hunt's over for today."

Getting to my feet, I started immediately in search of him and found him by no prearrangement within the hour as he strode rapidly along the highway of the glaring white river bottom. His snowshoe stride over hard snow patches, crystal ice, and wind-swept eroded bare brown earth told me that, whatever had happened, he was done with the hunt for the time being.

Bud had done something out of necessity that he would never have done in a civilized land. He had shot his moose by sound as it ran. He had never got a look at it but heard it. That it was hit at least once was a certainty, for the trail showed that one bullet had knocked it down. But it had got to its feet and fled.

Together we followed the blood trail for what seemed an endless uncertainty. Following it at all in the first place was against Bud's better judgment, but because of our pressing need for a meal he was falsely encouraged onward by me. But it was a hopeless job. Not only had we already driven the moose miles from home, but in spite of the frequent bloody beds we finally despaired of ever getting it at all, for it was stronger than we. The end of the cruel hunt that day for us was hot water and dried meat again, when we had dragged ourselves home to the Nahtuk Cabin. The rabbit traps were empty. Our legs were tough, but our heads were giddy.

A hard trail awaited us on the morrow, the test of a lifetime of hunting, upon which everything depended. "Do you think we'll get him?" I asked Bud over and over, incredulous.

"We'll get him. We've got to."

To retrieve that particular moose was one assignment neither of us would like to repeat again. Bud chased down the crippled animal on sheer nerve. Because it could hear him coming on his squeaking, crunching snowshoes long before he could arrive, the only hope of getting the moose was to wear it out. That this is possible for a human being to do, given deep snow and the right conditions, we know now, but it is not an enjoyable pastime.

"You don't even know if it's a bull or a cow," I conjectured. "Are you sure we've got a moose? Which do you think it is by the tracks?" We were both hoping against hope, even in our extremity, that it was a bull, because we believed a bull might be in good fat condition and fat we needed above all things.

"I think it's a bull," replied the optimist. "The tracks are big enough and the shape of the hoof is broad. There's not a deer hunter in the States won't tell you the exact differences between the track of a buck and the track of a doe. Nor an Alaskan that won't claim he can tell between moose the same way. Looks as if we'd be having a chance to find out what there is to that theory, anyway. I've seen many a bull-moose track and it looks like a bull to me."

I myself could never have kept up on the trail that day. Fortunately, my job was geared to my strength and required none of the vigilance and alertness necessary to the hunter. I didn't even have to think. All I had to do was plod along slowly on Bud's trail, lagging a quarter or a half mile behind, and bring up the pack board carrying traps, the whetstone and ax, and a few other necessaries.

Perhaps Bud never would have got the moose but that the second day's trail led out of the thickets and into a more open kind of country where Bud's telescope sight could really shine at last in those long shots which even with a telescope is stretching a .30-30 carbine a bit.

It must have been well on into the afternoon of that day that the shots for which my ear waited rang out across the valley. But what a bombardment! What had happened to Bud? He was having some trouble and it didn't sound good to me. A magazine was emptied and then another, twelve shots all told. That wasn't like Bud. Six shots, I later learned, were direct hits through the chest cavity at six hundred yards distance and done by aiming several feet over the animal's back. This had never happened before to us, that a moose could take so many direct hits. Are not moose the easiest big gentle creatures in the world to kill? Yes, but at this range there is no expansion and the game can take much, much more punishment—another reason for not shooting from great distances. Once arouse any creature to rage or flight and you will see such resistance as you may never have dreamed of. Even the smallest deer can put on an amazing display of endurance, as many a deer hunter can tell, but this is not hunting as we like it or prefer it. This was an example of what we would call bad hunting at any time, and lots of trouble.

Bud was winded. Many of his shots went wide. He had sprinted the last mile in a lather and in the end ran the moose down in the deep snow on his snowshoes. It was only at close range that this pitiful drama of primitive existence was made complete by Bud's realization for a certainty that the staggering quarry before him at the end of our two-day chase was a pregnant cow. Big with young, she would have had a little calf in about six weeks had she lived.

But there was no time for regrets or delays. When I arrived, Bud had recovered his breathing and had two legs already skinned and the business at hand well underway. I had the light skillet with me. I at once began building a fire to cook.

There are many Alaskan citizens who will tell you in confidence that cow moose is very good eating. Almost all of the older men of the Territory have tried it at some time, for many another has been in a position like ours; that is a part of the point of this story. The untold stories of the North are the real ones.

Our crime against nature was ignorance; we didn't know what we were getting into. We had had no conception before now of exactly what it means to live entirely off the country. Modern people dealing with primitives and legislating to allow 35,000 natives, as in Alaska, to "take what they need" fail to realize what this amounts to. But with a few of the older men and the native populations, we knew now. We knew what it meant, by learning their life and living it.

When we thought it over we could not be entirely sorry about that one moose because we knew this had to be. This moose could never be of greater value here to anybody than to us who had to have it for food, unless the value of its death lies in the example, and in a warning. We killed moose in order to live in a country that is as yet not mapped, in order to penetrate it at all so that people might someday call that country good.

We move to the old Takahula cabin, April 1945

We feast on roasted moose

5

The moose proved in more ways than one to be a remarkable find. No meat was spoiled, for all the shooting. Three shots had entered the lungs, one the heart, and two the liver, missing all the good shoulder meat in every case. It was the fattest wild herbivore we had ever seen. Yes, arctic moose just enjoy their meals in the wintertime, during the arctic night, wandering, as they do, north and north, wherever the willows go. She must have weighed a thousand pounds; her coming motherhood had fattened her enormously.

In the background a quarter of a mile distant from our dead moose there poured from a mountain valley the falls of a broad frozen river. The beautiful river was not real; it was a vision, visible only at this season and under certain circumstances. Caused by the drainage of some sort of overflow, which had built up and up upon itself by uncounted successive freezings as the months passed, the whole marvelous column would soon decay beneath the sun, and summer would reveal nothing. So, it was with our moose, at first a large solitary wandering animal, now just a hide rolled up into a package and four quarters of meat looking rather small against the rivers and snows of a vast country. The changeability and transmutation of all things is the first law of nature.

Burying the quarters of meat and several precious piles of fat beneath the snow in this spot, and laying our traps, we took back to the Nahtuk Cabin a supply of about forty pounds of meat to last us a few days until we could get back upon our feet again. The parts we took with us in the packsack were the tongue, the heart encased in fat, and one side of the fat brisket. I carried the pack of meat home, Bud being so wobbly that he had difficulty in making it on his two legs. At home we nibbled pieces of fresh fat boiled meat, and it tasted strange; to our surprise we could not get much of it down. Our stomachs had shrunk so that it would be days before our appetites came back to normal, and the securing of the moose was therefore celebrated with none of the abandonment that we had anticipated.

"You know, I believe we chased that moose more than halfway from here to Takahula Lake," I mentioned later. "Instead of trying to haul it back here to this cabin, do you know what we ought to do? We ought to move ourselves down to the Takahula Cabin as we first planned and transport the moose there for the spring muskrat hunting."

"Just what I had in mind," agreed Bud. "We'll take our moose there to eat, and then when Takahula Lake breaks up, we'll have our little canoe there and can probably live on grayling and big lake trout anyway. There are supposed to be some tremendous fish in that lake, almost too big, in fact, to handle in a muskrat canoe and not get tipped over. Then there's Takahula Creek leading out through the swamps along the valley, and it seems to me there might be some nice bears you could get right from the canoe. If we could fill a couple of five-gallon cans this spring with rendered bear fat—well, we'd have something to take beyond the timber in our explorations this next year that would be worth a lot; we might smoke some bear hams, too. I've always wanted to try it. When we get to the trader a few weeks from now we'll buy some raisins and flour and a box of cinnamon and we can have cinnamon rolls with our tea to eat along the banks of the rivers this summer from now on. I've been thinking we'll have to live better after this. Next summer when we get to the trader's I plan all sorts of things for you and me."

"Why, I feel fine," I said. "This present life's not so bad. I've just about got used to it now."

"It's surprising how quickly a person recovers from an ordeal such as we had just come through and then how unusually well he begins to feel and how perfectly amazingly glorious the whole world looks! Maybe it was the spring in the arctic—what was it? We must have been tough in those days, tough, filthy, unwashed, and in rags, but how minor, how unnoticeable, are the humiliations of the body, if you wish to call them that, when the soul is gazing at sublime views! Suddenly we were so happy that it seemed as though we would burst. The prospect of new travel, new adventures, was all we ever wanted, given a new home down at Takahula Lake in the continuance of this spring hunting before us.

"Good-by, little Nahtuk Cabin." On snowshoes I turned to give it a farewell glance of affection. "You were kind to us once," I said.

Already the past had claimed its own. I was hitched to the big sled, which was reloaded. There was work ahead. It was ten miles in a beeline to Takahula Cabin, cutting across the curves of the wandering Alatna River—a white land in spring, softly misted-in today. Bud had gone on ahead to make a reconnaissance of the situation down there and in all probability build another stove out of what cans he could find. He would come back to the Nahtuk to sleep and take a load tomorrow. I was to pull this sled as far as I could and leave it on the river at the day's end. But I had made up my mind to surprise Bud at Takahula Lake by greeting him there with the transported load.

"Hello, Bud," I said. "Surprised?" I walked twenty miles just to say that.

In another day we were moved to our new home. Within a week we had freighted our moose, already fast diminishing, to the old cabin standing under the shadow of Takahula Mountain, and placed it in the cache there, where the first day the squirrels succeeded in stealing ten pounds of fat off it before they were discovered.

The Takahula Cabin leaned badly with the years; it seemed a wonder that the old wreck didn't fall down on our heads as we slept. Certainly, it would not survive many more seasons, but who can tell with such a cabin, already so old? With a low roof under which even I could stand upright only in the middle, it was yet built so broad that there was a waste of many cubic feet of air space which no stove could ever have been expected to heat thoroughly in an arctic climate.

"I'll bet those guys bumped their heads and shivered all winter long," we deduced of those men of fifty years ago, as we bumped our own. After a few days we learned to crack our heads somewhat less smartly by ducking about like moles in our open-air home.

It was much like living outdoors, but any temperature above zero by day was by now nothing to us after the winter temperatures we had known. Our tent and the raincoat covered the gaping windows, broken out by bears these many years. Squirrels, camp robbers, and chickadees flitted in and out through the cracks and played at our feet.

During the winter our cooking pots had shrunk in size. We had with us now a vessel Bud had made from an empty five-gallon gasoline can squared off, with a fitted lid of the same material supplied with handles of snare wire and caribou antler. This can full of boiled meat supplied our food for one day. Once we had recovered our appetites, we were ravenous as never before. Such delicacies as the gigantic boiled hocks rolled down our throats again, with quantities of boiled fat and T-bone steaks as a side course. We had only one lump of salt the size of a walnut to eat with that whole moose. I let Bud have it as he was always strongly addicted to salt while the lack of it was no more privation to me than the lack of sugar. It is miserable to subsist on lean meat without salt, but it seemed to me that the fat itself tasted salty enough, especially if it was fried, which brought out a salty flavor. Altogether we could only groan our appreciation of such eating. It seemed to us the taste of the fresh meat could be compared with the sensation one gets when biting into fresh ripe plums or sweet oxheart cherries. Having had no fresh meat for half a year, we had gradually become so used to eating old meat that only now was the vast difference in flavor appreciated.

In this way, sleeping on the soft thick moose rug spread out on the floor of Takahula Cabin at night and boiling our meat in a five-gallon can by day, we welcomed spring in the North. Overshadowed by the rock pinnacle of Takahula Mountain, living in the snow-burdened old wreck of a cabin with the river before and the deep precipitous mountain lake behind, we knew as we gazed: "Life springs eternal." We had seen hundreds of thousands of our squirrel and camp robber and spruce chicken friends, with their archness and their feuding, come and go, but hello! a brood is hatched this spring and there he is again, that one I know so well, the manifestation of an immortal spirit.

"Here is food and help yourself," says Bud to the fluffy villain perched on the handle of the ax. Last week that bird pecked all the fat off those two rabbits which we hung on a bush when we were almost starving to death. He seemed cruel then. Now we know he is just impersonal.

As for me, I'm content to stretch my length on the dirty floor by a tin-can stove and catch up with the magazines of 1925. Quite a commentary on human life to be able to look back! "Bud, I forgot to bring a comb for us on this trip, did you know it? Why don't you make us one?"

Bud carved me a fine comb. It had three teeth, made of nails from his pocket—sharp, but it served the purpose.

Counting our riches, we pawed into a chilly sack on the floor and pulled out great ropes of moose intestines with fat still clinging to them. We had been too weak to clean them in the snow. One of the happiest days I ever spent in my life passed in going over these and securing every tiny morsel of the white tallow. Cutting the tallow into cubes, we got it into the skillet for several successive batches, where it slowly rendered out into a rich pure fluid to be poured into buckets and cans to last us if we ever got back to dried meat again and to go with us the next summer in the canoe, wherever that might be. A caldron of boiling fat requires constant vigilance but watching it when you have nothing else to do is primitive delight; it is one of the most intrinsically vital of human occupations, which has come down to us as the very symbol of plenty and well-being, or the symbol of catastrophic upset when we announce, "The fat's in the fire." But people really meant it as the original invitation to hospitality when they first coined the phrase, "Come on over and chew the fat for a while this evening!"

During the spring weeks by Takahula Lake we chewed fat and dug remarkably creamy plugs of raw frozen marrow out of leg bones and consumed them from the blade of a skinning knife. From the sighing spruces a stirring fragrance pervaded the atmosphere, while the snow settled and became granular. We dug a pit by a large boulder near the house, and, selecting a sixty-pound roast for English-style rare roast beef, spitted it, and held our own private barbecue, and ate and ate.

We arrive back at our cabin at spring breakup, May 1945

6

It just didn't seem possible that Bud and I had been alone together in the wilderness without seeing another human being for a whole year. It couldn't be! Surely this had only been a week-end camping trip, or perhaps a day!

Was it true that we had got accustomed to living altogether on meat, and enjoyed such items as raw bone marrow and fat? Bud's uncut hair hung to his shoulders almost as long as mine, which assured us that some time had passed. Yet our experiences had come step by step and there was nothing amazing about our situation to us. Time had ceased to exist for us for a while, and the rest of the world also.

Had the dreaded "arctic night" made us queer, or had we quarreled from living alone, or suffered mentally from that strange malady sometimes recorded in novels as cabin fever?

Truly, modern life is fraught with superstition. We had not quarreled, we had been utterly content, and because we had come to the arctic with open minds, we had had all in all, a very good time—an unforgettable one.

I had a hole in the sole of one mukluk about the size of a fifty-cent piece and had to do my snowshoeing with a piece of cardboard or canvas in the hole, since we had no caribou skin to patch it. Regularly, I got used to stopping at intervals and putting the cardboard back in place, just as though this habit of life had always been and was a part of normal existence. Our snowshoe thongs needed replacements which we made by cutting off a chunk of our moose sleeping rug and scraping off hair; Bud then restrung our rackets. I had one needle and I sewed our socks and underwear with pieces of thread unraveled from old canvas.

The first eagles had appeared. We had tried ice fishing through a hole chiseled into the black crystal glass of Takahula Lake but met with no response from the fish. Matches were getting scarce. We cut down to one a day. Bud had found a little tube from some discarded kerosene stove primer in the cabin which he had discovered we might utilize as a blowpipe to fan sleeping embers into flame. When our little stove died down, as it did quickly, having no damper, a fire could be started up again by using scraps of birch-bark and spruce twigs set against a coal the size of a pea and blown upon through the little pipe.

We spent a great deal of time out-of-doors because the attractions of sitting humped over a little stove within a dark house which was probably never as warm as 50° could not compete with the attractions of the bright out-of-doors amid which we lived. A sprint of fifteen miles on snowshoes down Takahula Lake and across its frozen swamps at the lower end might reveal a pair of wolves, one black and one yellow, trotting with jaunty ease down the bend, or a rare silver fox at his hunting. You can call the fox to you by using an old Eskimo trick. Just inhale through tight lips to make a small sound that resembles the squeak of a mouse. A half mile away, given arctic temperatures, the fox will hear and come, if you remain perfectly still, for he thinks he has heard field mice underneath the snow, and he is very fond of them. Some of the vixens had dens thereabouts, in the banks, no doubt, but it would be a rarity indeed if a human being should find the vixen's nest. We were gone for three days at a time on prolonged trips of exploration, each one having a personal encounter of some sort. These trips took us sixty-five or seventy miles from our own cabin at the farthest; our rations were of course our wonderful moose.

April passed into May and May almost into June and with this our fourth wedding anniversary, which was celebrated by eating the last of the moose, the boiled head, on that day.

Then the moose gave out. It was eaten up, gone. The dried meat wasn't so bad now with tallow to go with it. Once in a while we got a ptarmigan. They were so wary you could not approach them for a shot. Eskimo women and children often keep the family going in spring by catching the ptarmigan in braided sinew snares which they hang in the willows, but I didn't know how. Presently the ptarmigan began to change their plumage and leave the valley for the high mountains above; they had picked every surrounding willow of its last single bud. As for rabbits, they left no tracks on the crust and our traps were useless.

Would summer never come? Why, we had killed and eaten a whole moose in the interim, and still the snow looked just about the same as it always had, with no perceptible thaw and not a trickle of running water to be seen anywhere.

A quotation from Bud's diary seems to sum up well the views on eating we had as the result of this year. We were versatile. In our kind of health, we could eat anything, and even starve to a certain extent when necessary. Says Bud's diary:

> I have known many men who must have their coffee before breakfast, then breakfast right on time, or else they were sick the rest of the day. From my own experience I have found that when we eat and how often we eat is mainly a matter of habit, and custom. As a boy living farm life I ate five meals a day. As a young man much of my life was baching it, and I grew less accustomed to regular meals. For the past years I have eaten whenever it was convenient. I have hunted all day without any breakfast and no supper the night before. Yesterday I hunted 18 hours on only a light breakfast and experienced no particular hardship. In fact, I prefer to eat in this irregular manner when leading this life. Nor is it strange to me, because I realize native people all live in much this way and are quite healthy in their native state.

About six miles' snowshoe distance from Takahula Lake there was a narrow winding canyon opening up into side canyons in the very bowels of the mountains. Closed in by thousand-foot walls of rock down which icicles wove cathedral designs, the subterranean passageways were like retreats from an *Arabian Nights* tale in ice. But no dream—dangerous.

Down these steep canyon floors poured undulating frozen tongues of turquoise rivers, often effectively barring the way. They weren't glaciers. Summer would remove them all with no trace but some tiny harmless brook.

It was from here that our binoculars spied out a band of sheep on the crag above and beyond. Even through strong glasses they were mere dots—pearls studding bare brown earth on the very top of a sharp crag of the Brooks Range, against a sky of arctic blue.

From where we were, the sheep were six or eight miles distant by air. If it was possible to reach them on foot, the hunter would have to climb up and around this mountain from its back because its face was unscalable.

On snowshoes in deep snow, at the season when hanging snow slides were ready to fall at the slightest disturbance, Bud was drawn to the haunts of the sheep by his appetite for fresh meat. One day he actually got to the top of the crag where the band had been, only to find them gone. In the hot sun of that midday I entered the labyrinths of the canyon below, thinking with each step forward that I was entering a death trap, listening to the distant rumbles of snow slides, wondering if Bud would ever come off that mountain alive. We found each other in the canyon the following midnight when his hunt was done. Bud had seen snow slides come down on two sides of him, but wisely sticking to a hogback ridge he was all right—just put-out and hungry as a bear.

We had brought no jerky to Takahula and were just in the process of drying a small supply from the recent moose when an unexpected accident occurred. An ermine came into the house in the night. We listened but could not see him in the darker hours within the dark cabin, since we had no light. Daylight disclosed a perfectly barren jerky rack. The angel-white villain, with a black tip to his tail, fell at the crack of the pistol as Bud shot him from bed that morning, but his skin could not atone for our serious loss. We had a little meat left from the barbecue and that was all.

"There's about eight pounds of caribou jerky hanging on a string from the ceiling of the Nahtuk Cabin," I offered. "I'll run up to the Nahtuk Valley and get it this evening. You must not go sheep hunting again. It's too dangerous."

"Better stay off the river as much as possible now," Bud cautioned me. "Stick to the banks or go overland." That was, in fact, why I was making the trip during the night when it was cool, that the ice might be more safe. I would have to cross the bends of the river several times at best.

This was also in essence why Bud had mentioned that he would commence his next sheep hunt by night, for the snow slides were more stable during the cool hours. But he simply must not be allowed to go again. All night I thought of this as I made my run over the rotting river ice to the Nahtuk Cabin and secured the precious sack of jerky, plus some new reading matter, during the twilight hours. A deeply imprinted wolf track was seen following a part of my trail on my return at dawn. Bud was sleeping now. Would he be gone again for sheep before I could return to stop him?

I made that twenty miles so fast that, to my relief, I found him still safely asleep in bed in the early morning. Taking authority for once, I absolutely forbade any more sheep hunts, and meant it. Bud agreed. We had not wanted to molest the sheep in the first place.

I was wrong when I said that no persons, white or native, visit the origin of the Colville River and the neighboring rivers of the Brooks Range along the Arctic Divide. There are Eskimos now hunting the headwaters of many of these rivers, unknown to the rest of the world generally. It is true that many of these rivers have never had a boat on them, for they may be entirely unnavigable by summer. But in the winter white men have traveled some of them in the past, and today Eskimos travel them with their dog teams, our own Alatna River being in fact a part of Eskimo hunting grounds. The basic economy of these inland Eskimos rests on the caribou and the Dall sheep.

These people leave little sign of camps where they have been, for they have no permanent dwelling place. Their camps are sticks and modern canvas tents which are taken up when they leave, and snow walls which melt in the spring. By summer the headquarters of some of them during the past few years has been Chandalar Lake, one of the sources of the Colville River in the heart of mountain sheep country. Great numbers of large lake trout are taken in their nets in this lake by summer and large bands of caribou are speared from canoes as the animals swim the lake, according to Eskimos with whom we talked.

Because of the migratory habits of these people, we had lived all year on the Alatna River without seeing sign of them, but this was no reason to believe that they had not been here or that they would not come back again within two or three years during their winter forays. We believe from our observations and from the tales of local informers on the Koyukuk that in recent years the arctic Eskimos have cleaned the Alatna country of sheep as one would mow a lawn, and that this very largely accounted for the sheep's absence. However, there is also some indication, from a recent study made at Mount McKinley National Park, that a disease of the mountain sheep causes them to lose their teeth; it may be that more sheep are disappearing from this cause than we know. This disease should be eradicated, and the natives restrained from their forays or there will soon be no sheep in their last stronghold, the mighty Brooks Range of the arctic. The Alatna village Indians and Eskimos down at the mouth of the river who, ironically, express a great fondness for "fat [pregnant] female sheep" in spring as the best of all meats have been unable to secure any during their early spring sheep hunts during the last few years. As it is inconceivable to them that they could have killed off most of the sheep themselves, they blame their absence on the hunters from the "other side."

Although there seem to be not more than 150 people in this particular group of sheep eaters, that is a lot of people for mountain sheep. That they are a healthy and fine-appearing Eskimo group, everyone who has ever seen them admits. They are also expert trappers of wolves in their life along the arctic divide.

But if one can visualize the numbers of sheep, moose, and caribou that it takes to keep a crowd of that size and their dog teams going in terms of what we have defined in this book he will see what feeding them does to the country. It runs into several hundred tons of animals yearly, dead weight. These Eskimos are armed with modern rifles and blue flame kerosene burners and buy some hundreds of dollars' worth of store food annually, which lasts them, native-like, but a few days out of the year. These supplies are paid for from their considerable joint fur catch and are dropped by pilots with them at Chandler Lake. The twentieth-century Eskimos of this group lead a life which many of us could well envy—if we would like to live entirely on meat! All other food they consume must be flown in by plane unless it is brought several hundred miles by dog sled from the nearest trading post on the arctic coast, in which case it might all be eaten up just on the hauling trip.

Primitive people armed with modern rifles, if they have no restraint, will consistently destroy their own food supply as fast as they can. If game vanishes they simply say that it has moved away: that is the primitive reasoning. Game has always supplied their ancestors for as far back as they can remember, and to them it is eternal and endless. Possession of the modern rifle enables the Eskimo to get a great deal more game to feed larger dog teams than he ever before could afford to own. The whole thing becomes a vicious circle: larger dog teams permit more extensive hunting to kill more animals to feed the dog teams.

There is even a movement afoot to award this whole great area to such groups permanently—*an area the size of England and Scotland put together!*—for their own private hunting reservation, just as Canada has closed down her Northwest Territories to all business and all individual enterprise for the sake of protecting native groups! We call that downright unprogressive!

The reservation principle for special groups in America has become in recent years more and more subject to doubt as a working proposition. If you want to see a backward, poverty-ridden place, just visit the average Indian reservation in the United States today, where Indians are given the "privilege" of making much of their living by "hunting" and by their ancestral ways! A good living can't be made out of it. Each human being needs a hundred square miles to live by hunting in almost any land. Originally the whole continent only supported a million or so primitives, remember, and even some of these died of starvation during lean years. In the case of the arctic people, 150 individuals are using about 100,000 square miles. Each of them will eat at least two or three tons of meat or fish a year.

The main thing which has kept Alaska Indians and Eskimos roaming free today rather than set aside on reservations is that thus far there haven't been enough white people in Alaska to care. Alaska still belongs to the natives in this sense. But what will happen to the natives if Alaska ever becomes sufficiently of importance to make for a large white population?

There may be a hue and cry then to place these natives on reservations and make them live there unless they have developed enough by that time to take their place in the mixed society which is now flourishing in the Territory. Why should "race" control our concepts of what to do with northern lands? We don't want a stupid policy repeated in Alaska, when the white man, now beginning to wonder about the value of these arctic lands, finally covets them, and wants to ascribe them to general world use.

Is it fair, either, to give to 150 people the whole Arctic Divide of Alaska when many whole villages are living on the very margin of existence in Alaska southward? How about the rest of Alaska natives generally? How about the future of the game herds in northern Alaska if natives with rifles continue to live off them?

The public thought that problem was solved years ago in 1902 with the introduction of domestic reindeer herds. The reindeer is a blood brother to the caribou and is just as wild and mobile when left untended; reindeer have to be guarded by herders constantly. The original reindeer imported to Alaska from Lapland increased to thousands, that is true. In the early part of this century it looked as if the reindeer business might become a great one for Alaskan entrepreneurs. Not only did the animals thrive on the wild grass and reindeer moss of their natural habitat, but the public in the United States, when the Department of Agriculture certified the excellence of Alaskan reindeer meat, began to become enthusiastic about it.

But it is believed that Western cattlemen fought the Alaskan reindeer menace before it could gain headway; they did not want competition with American beef. Certain cities managed to pass local ordinances making it impossible to sell the meat or to use it in restaurants; a silent warfare took place and, in general, the costs of advertising a new meat in the United States were prohibitive. The companies in Alaska which had tried to commercialize reindeer meat on a limited scale were small compared to the gigantic cliques of the opposition. The owners of Alaska reindeer herds could have little hope of a future market in the United States under existing conditions; their herds ran wild and joined their brothers, the native caribou.

Having gone wild, the reindeer became subject to the inevitable wolf cycle and were annihilated entirely in some areas, or at least swallowed up in the wilderness, never to be found. By 1940 nobody knew how many reindeer were in Alaska.

Meanwhile many of the missions had got reindeer herds started for the natives. The commercial companies, too, gave the natives opportunity to purchase animals for themselves while they were herding for the company. This worked well, and under competent direction the natives prospered, and their herds increased.

It was in 1935 that the last privately-owned herd of 3000 reindeer was rounded up, sold to the Canadian Government, and driven over to the Mackenzie Delta; native employees of Alaska's reindeer company were discharged when the company at last went out of business. In 1940 the United States Government took over Alaska's reindeer industry entirely and gave it to the natives so that they should become free from the stress of hunger and might develop their own industry without competition. Reindeer men under the Indian Service at present have the task of directing this project where native herds exist. Now there is no competition, an industry has been ruined, and no white man may own a reindeer in Alaska. The reindeer herds over which there was such a to-do to help the starving Eskimos have all but vanished, because it seems to be an uphill fight all the way to get these people to be constant herders and not kill their own animals for human and dog feed. They do not understand that a considerable public and world sacrifice was made to give them the entire reindeer industry, which might have been developing today in the hands of a more enterprising people. Indians and Eskimos in Alaska must turn to agriculture wherever agriculture is possible—it should be possible actually in much of the Arctic Zone, on the continental side of the Arctic Divide, for instance, if properly directed, and it is. They must turn to herding, already given over entirely to them for their living; to the harvests of the sea, whales, seals, and walrus, which no white man may hunt without permit; to fishing in the rivers; to their own native crafts, for the manufacture of trinkets and novelties of the North opens a great new field of opportunity, with proper guidance, in anticipation of the coming tourist trade. But so far, the natives are making almost nothing for sale, and cannot begin to keep pace even now with the demand; the reindeer parka and boot business offers a completely undeveloped and unexplored native resource. Eventually, to some extent, the natives must turn to industry as Alaska develops. That is, Alaskan natives should in the future begin to participate in American life like everyone else. How to find steady employment for thousands of unskilled laborers—how to make them even like it at once—is a big order, considering the employment problems which already face the rest of the world. Yet if it is not done somehow it may cost Alaska billions of dollars in the future to replace the wildlife now being slaughtered.

We prepare the canoe to continue our journey, May 1945

7

Still we waited, thinking that the ice of Takahula Lake was going to melt and that we could use our muskrat canoe and eat fresh fish and muskrats soon. We lived on dried meat dipped in liquid tallow melted in the skillet or ate the tallow in hard crumbs the size of a pea.

During this time, I began making out menus of the things we hoped to eat when we reached Hughes, where I would be cook in that kitchen for a few days again. With pencil and paper, I revised the menus over and over and each time thought: "No, I will never be able to crowd it all in." We would have to eat those things we missed, not only for this past year, but for the year to come after. My diary makes moan, "How can one politely reconcile long Italian spaghetti and candied apples and popcorn balls with hosts who may have false teeth—and will they think luncheons consisting of frankfurters and ginger ale and chocolate-marshmallow green mint sundaes incompatible with digestion?"

It snowed five inches of new snow over the old on the day these summertime hopes were voiced in late May. I wrote:

> Yes, it's back to the old rations of last fall when times were lean. Bud is starving and must be fed. We stretched out that long-ago moose for a whole extra week by tightening the belt, yet still ate it easily in a

month, while Bud teases me now by saying I ate most of it and more than my half. This month we have been living mostly on air, and for myself, I'm just about the same. About half a cup of tallow a day suits my full requirements nicely for a time, with a little lean to go with it. But poor Bud rapidly becomes a skeleton.

We spent much time with the binoculars. With a small fire between our knees for warmth, we would loaf above the valley on the sunny sides of promontories whose bare brown spots we reached by snowshoe. There was only dried meat and water to stay at home for, and besides, if we stayed in the cabin, we tended to eat it up too fast. Any active hunting, to our alarm, was becoming impossible because our snowshoes wouldn't hold us up any more.

Pretty close to June I was taken with a sudden and very positive urge to pack up and go back to our own cabin on the Alatna, and our canoe, the *Little Willow*. At least more dried meat awaited us there, and we had to go back sometime. Why not give up this idea of spring hunting as we had imagined it and face it as it was? The first numb, shivering blowfly had appeared, the first spider, and a small hopping insect similar to a grasshopper but only as large as the head of a pin. Breakup was only holding off from one day to the next. We had planned originally to walk back home after breakup by following the bank of the river and hunting each pond for rats with our light canoe along the way. In our vision of breakup somehow, we had not imagined snow on the ground, or at least not deep snow. We had not counted on miles of wet floundering through five-foot snowbanks which sank beneath us, nor the difficulties of crossing flooded-over country with its endless bogs and mires, with little food to eat. Getting home after the breakup came I began to think would be a hard trip—perhaps eighty miles instead of just forty, double the distance because of detours. Already snowshoes sank out of sight in the softer places. Could we make it home now? But if we couldn't, was it not possible that we might find ourselves stuck here, unable to reach our own cabin and our canoe, only to be held up in our coming summer's travel for added weeks? I think it was this last argument which convinced Bud. He was always such a stubborn person, set upon muskrat hunting or some other thing, whether or no.

Spring Hunting

I put my argument to him near the sunset hour, which was around eleven o'clock one evening after a rather full day, and we came to one of those characteristic decisions of wilderness life. As the primitive hunter does, so had we wandered from one camp to another, following the seasons, until there came a day quite out of the blue when we knew in our bones that the time had come to move on.

Preparations were simple. Our little kayak, which Bud had fashioned for me and which was destined never to be used on water but only to be pulled through deep snow, was suspended from the ridgepole inside the cabin. A few things were packed in it, including two pairs of skis, which we would pick up later on our way out to the Koyukuk by water. For the present we would carry with us only the sleeping bag, the cameras, the binoculars, the ax in its sheath, and of course each would carry his own rifle on his back. Before we got through with the list the pack must have weighed fifty pounds, however, for that's the way it goes. "With my rifle and my clothes and all, that gives me a total weight on the crust of 250 pounds," Bud estimated doubtfully. "Well, let's grab a wink for a couple of hours until it gets cooler," and throwing himself down upon the moose rug, with the down sleeping robe pulled over as a blanket, he was instantly asleep.

Neither of us will ever forget that last hike on snowshoes along our valley to our Alatna River home in a race against the breakup. To us it seemed the most beautiful of all our trips because it was the final one in this unbelievable land of the Brooks Range. Across the familiar loops of the river we strode, through silent stands of dwarfed arctic spruce, swinging down frozen lakes. Transfixed emerald-green waterfalls, gleaming from afar, flashed by one by one. A sleeping ptarmigan awoke from his bed, gave a single harsh cackle, and waddled off, watching us. We would have eaten him earlier in the day; we couldn't take him now. In the strange twilight of summer night in the arctic—for it was summer—the dim crags bending down over all were less white and more brown on the ledges than they had been the day before. A fox barked. In the darkest part of the night we saw a golden eagle searching the mountain peaks. Perhaps it could see the sun from on high where it circled. "Maybe that's Janet," I said as I always did when we saw an eagle.

"I shouldn't doubt it," Bud agreed.

It was a spring midnight again, at the Nahtuk Cabin. "I can't sleep," I said. "I'm thinking about the breakup. We're on the wrong side of the river if she breaks. I don't think we could ever cross it. We'd better get out of here."

"Wait another hour yet." It was hard to wait.

Thirty miles to go. Bud hoisted his pack onto his back and all the world was hushed as we stepped out. It was sultry warm. The temperature had not fallen below 30° all night. And suddenly, in the hush, the woods about us were alive with bird song! Birds warbling! Did we really hear it? Where did they come from? How did they get here? Summer—the miracle of it! —had come in this one night as we tried to sleep and something stirring in the air made sleep impossible.

Ptarmigan called from everywhere incessantly. The first robin warbled in the gathering dawn, song sparrows entranced the ear with their musical distant notes, the flickers had arrived. On the rotting snow the full hot daylight disclosed spiders and crawling caterpillars which seemed all to be going someplace. A kind of snow flea speckled our snowshoes with minute hopping forms.

It all said "Hurry!" to us. At first, we kept to the river for more solid walking where the wind had drifted the hardest snow, but when this grew soft under the sun and the river began to wind, we headed through the timber and straight overland. If we broke through the crust, we might as well make every step count. The day grew warmer and the going grew worse. We could expect to plunge in from a foot to four feet at any step. Sometimes the crust would hold for a few steps; then it would sink a snowshoe to the very bottom and the other racket would pack watery slush over the first as it joined it below. Sometimes we were stuck so solidly that we had to feel down under the granular heavy snow barehanded and dig out a trench to find the snowshoes and loosen them from our feet; then we must tug and pull to recover them. A thousand times we must have had our snowshoes off and on, that last thirty miles. To keep from falling was impossible, until at last, quite sopping wet, we fell every few yards.

After eighteen hours of this, we had paused panting in a thicket when Bud said: "Listen, what do you hear?"

An apprehension set our ears prickling as a familiar clear scream, not heard during these ice-locked months, was carried to us. "I hear sea gulls up ahead," I replied. "That means . . ."

"One thing. Open water."

Wheeling and screaming, over our heads the loud gulls swung, making the wilderness ring from the rocky cliffs and back again. Now we saw mallard ducks come in quietly with soft quackings and skid to a landing between the floating ice cakes of this piece of open water which comprised one river bend. All this happening in one day! How did they know? "There must be open water below," we thought, catching the spirit of the excitement. "Surely the Koyukuk has broken out!"

Above, the river was frozen solid, and we plowed onward in feverish haste. The thought of open water and the voices of the birds had increased our forebodings that there was not a moment to lose. Where the Kutuk River comes into the Alatna just opposite and below our house the ice had always been weak and reluctant to freeze, even in midwinter. Doubtless it would be one of the first places of the entire river to break out. Since the steepness of Red Mountain and its deep, overhanging snowbanks made progress virtually unthinkable on the side where our cabin lay, we would naturally come up the flats the last four or five miles on the opposite side of the river. Would we be able to cross to our house when we got there?

Offering scant explanation, Bud dived off ahead, walking on the solid but watery green river ice and leaving me to tag behind as best I could. Surrounded by pools and pockets of open water lying on the surface of the ice on every side, I followed Bud's route. He had taken off his snowshoes and was in the rubber shoepacs we wore now, having discarded our skin mukluks for more water-resistant apparel the week before. With his snowshoes in hand Bud probed for the bottoms of the murky pools he could not see and splashed forward through them. I didn't have enough energy to take my own snowshoes off and reasoned that my footing felt more secure wading the bottoms of these pools with them on. After all, I had worn snowshoes continuously for half a year, and scarce trusted myself to walk otherwise. Farther and farther behind Bud I fell in the slow caution of my own progress until I lost his trail.

Just as I had feared, by the time I caught sight of our house a mile distant upon its hill, the main stream bed, cutting close in to the base of the mountain, had developed into a swirling, ever-widening channel of angry yellow water flowing on top of the ice. How had Bud crossed it? He was probably already happily starting a fire now at home in the old drum monster for me.

I snowshoed along a peninsula of ice with running water on either side; it made me rather dizzy, I noticed, to look at such a movement of water when I hadn't seen it for so long.

How to cross that water to home? Was there solid ice on the bottom all the way or were there holes in it? Where was Bud? In weariness I was alone for a minute, surrounded in the floodgates of boiling seas.

Then Bud was coming down the trail from the house. "Just wade across in my steps. It's safe here," he directed from the opposite bank. My snowshoes unsteadily found bottom and the water rushed about my knees. "You'll soon be over, and I'll hand you the end of this oar," Bud shouted. "Are you glad to be home? She's going out."

"You're telling me!" I screeched back.

In the dim twilight I got out of my ruined snowshoes for the last time and we clambered up the muddy path together to our home. After seven weeks of absence, when we had to hunt to exist amid uncertain circumstances, we probably looked as healthy as any other young persons in the world and were probably as full of plans for future explorations as any of them, despite our tiredness on that particular day. We had no sprains or strains and were not even extremely exhausted, but were muscular, and our hair was long, and our cheeks were glowing red.

The cabin looked queer, with patches of muddy raw earth becoming exposed around it and that unfamiliar roaring of the river below in our ears. The snow walls of winter were gone as though someone had taken them down. The roaring continued during the night and grew louder.

We had always wondered how a river breaks up. Now we saw. In the canyons and from the mountain cliffs above, the incessant drip of icicles had become the flowing of brooks from every hill. Thawing begins above, close to the sun. Gathering momentum, and bearing its drift upon its crest, the water poured down the valley. The thick river ice was not melted by the sun. It was worn away by the new river of melted snow which flowed on top of it and which lifted this ice at last loose from the banks it gripped and carried it away.

Much of the ice in front of our house must have been frozen solid to the bottom because we saw layer after layer of it, even days later, pop loose and rise. We didn't know that northern explorers have a word for this: they call it anchor ice. We saw it come up and, emerging slowly to the surface like a submarine, turn over leisurely with grinding force or with screeches and hisses as one cake a hundred or so feet long slid across another, let fly with a shower of spray, and set sail down the river. For several days there was a big ice jam down below in the bend, visible from our door, where the mighty warriors battled it out with one another.

> In the breakup... when the volume of water running under the ice increases, the ice is bulged up and put under strain until it ruptures. Then a wild, crashing torrent of ice blocks and water sweeps down the stream, overriding low banks, twisting and plucking out bushes . . . Ice as much as five feet thick forms during the winter on the streams of northern Alaska, so that the noise, confusion, and appalling power of the streams when they break can be imagined, though they cannot be entirely realized by anyone who has not actually seen the breakup.[4]

Secure and safe, we sat upon our hill, watching the panorama of the breakup below. I spread out the brown bear rug and took sun baths in front of the door where the sun struck a sheltered place and birds hopped amid swarms of bluebottle flies. I wanted to get a good tan for the arctic coast.

Dried meat, tallow, and water were our fare. We actually ate two muskrats, too, at last.

Climbing to the top of Old Rip Mound one day I watched with the binoculars, always hunting. Hunting, why? Just to hunt, I guess. A long-legged monster of a bull moose wound along the base of Red Mountain below me, and not far away. He was the best moose we had seen in this country yet. Several hours the noon before Bud and I had watched a cow moose browsing the flats across from the cabin. And what do you know! High up on the bar by a newly stranded ice cake

---

4 *Geology and Mineral Resources of Northwestern Alaska*, p. 67. United States Department of the Interior, Bulletin No. 815, Geological Survey.

was a fresh grizzly track that might have been a twin brother to the one we got right there from the front door last year.

Watching this big bull moose with one eye, I dug a large blue hairy flower from between the snows in a little patch of mountain soil on my lookout. The flower had a strong thick woody root, wedged against solid rock. Carrying it home in muddy bare hands, clambering through the last spring snowdrifts in hip boots, I stood my rifle beside Bud's against the cabin, and planted the flower by the side of the door.

To see that flower a person would have had to spend the winter at this spot. He would watch the freeze-up and the breakup come and go, as once, in our twenties, so had we. For visible only now in its brief hour upon the lovely river was that unknown hardy bloom. Hidden from worldly eyes, illusive and beckoning, it lives only in a land that is free, where the spirit wanders as it may.

Acknowledgments

The author wishes to acknowledge her appreciation and indebtedness to Mrs. Fred Bennett of Englewood, New Jersey, who was President of the Women's Board of Home Missions of the Presbyterian Church of America; to Miss Amelia Hill, mission nurse of Allakaket, Alaska, whose rare volumes of Alaskan history have contributed background knowledge in this narrative; to Jack O'Connor, who heads the Alaska Game Commission; and to the Honorable Ernest Gruening, Governor of Alaska as this book goes to press.

Connie Helmericks with her grandson, Lucas Irons, 1986

About the Author

In 1942, at the age of twenty-four, Constance Helmericks and her husband, Bud Helmericks, paddled into the Alaskan wilds to live off the land. Over the next decade, Connie wrote five bestselling books on their adventures, and co-filmed and produced three documentaries with Bud. Their work was shown on national lecture tours, and was twice featured in LIFE magazine, including the cover. In her later books, Connie wrote of her wilderness journeys across Canada and around Australia with her young daughters, Jean and Ann Helmericks. She became an early environmental activist, walking much of the Pacific Crest trail alone while in her sixties. Connie was writing her ninth book about paddling Central American rivers when she died on Earth Day in 1987.

www.ingramcontent.com/pod-product-compliance
Lightning Source LLC
Chambersburg PA
CBHW050310120526
44592CB00014B/1853